Law's Virtues

Law's Virtues

*Fostering Autonomy and Solidarity
in American Society*

CATHLEEN KAVENY

Georgetown University Press / Washington, D.C.

Library of Congress Cataloging-in-Publication Data

Kaveny, Cathleen.
  Law's virtues : fostering autonomy and solidarity in American society / by Cathleen Kaveny.
      p. cm. -- (Moral traditions)   .
  Includes bibliographical references and index.
  ISBN 978-1-58901-932-4 (pbk. : alk. paper)
 1.   Law--Moral and ethical aspects--United States. 2.   Law and ethics.   I. Title.
  KF380.K38 2012
  174'.30973--dc23

                                                                    2012003150

♾ This book is printed on acid-free paper meeting the requirements of the American National Standard for Permanence in Paper for Printed Library Materials.

20   19   18   17   16   15   14   13   12   9   8   7   6   5   4   3   2

First printing

Additional Praise for *Law's Virtues*

"Through an impressive analysis that draws on her scholarly training in law and theology, Kaveny argues for a more nuanced view of how law can function as a moral teacher in a pluralistic society, reminding us that good lawmaking is practical, not merely theoretical, and the laws we make must teach lessons to ordinary people, not saints."

—**Vincent Rougeau**, dean, Boston College Law School

"Cathleen Kaveny, a moral theologian and law professor, writes this book from the perspectives of a pro-life commitment and acceptance of some moral teaching function for law, and a deep respect for our pluralistic representative democracy with its recognition of individual freedom. Her scholarly, thoughtful, well-written, balanced exposition of the complex issue of the role of law and its application to the burning issues of abortion, euthanasia, and genetics is must reading for all those interested in this contemporary discussion."

—**Charles Curran**, Elizabeth Scurlock University Professor of Human Values, Southern Methodist University

"*Law's Virtues* is an important and timely book. As the United States faces another presidential election, the fundamental questions Kaveny addresses about the relationship among law, moral theology, and political action will loom large before the public. In lucid prose she explicates a convincing, broadly Thomistic theory of "the law as teacher" and applies that theory to such vexing questions as abortion, euthanasia, and genetic testing. Moreover, she provides a truly traditional understanding of such misunderstood and frequently abused terms as "intrinsic evil" and "immoral cooperation." Kaveny helps us to understand what it means for voting to be a moral act, and how to navigate our way through the culture wars using sound theology as a compass. This will be an important book to read during this election season and in the years to come."

—**Daniel Sulmasy, MD, PhD**, University of Chicago

"True to the title of the book, the author aims to model ways to think of law as a teacher of virtue in a pluralistic society, thereby melding Aquinas's classical reflection on virtue with the rich way legal theorist Joseph Raz assesses autonomy, enriched by John Paul II on solidarity. A tall order executed elegantly in prose accessible to all while deftly clarifying distinctions, expressly to counter the way ethical tools (like "intrinsically evil") have been harnessed to misleading rhetorical use in "culture wars" rather than used to illuminate taxing ethical issues. This painstaking study of the ways ethics and law intersect invites an illuminating exchange between theory and practice to guide citizens in voting as well as ethicists in assessing."

—**David Burrell, C.S.C.**, Hesburgh Professor Emeritus in Philosophy and Theology, University of Notre Dame

To my parents,
Gerald Kaveny and Valerie Goulet Kaveny,
who taught all their children the importance of both autonomy and solidarity.

CONTENTS

∽

ACKNOWLEDGMENTS

❧

T HE PUBLICATION OF ANY BOOK is the fruit not only of the author's
autonomy but also of the solidarity and support extended to her by stu-
dents, colleagues, friends, and family. The University of Notre Dame has
offered me an unparalleled environment in which to consider questions at
the intersection of religion, morality, and law. Many thanks to Harrison St.
Germain, Esther Terry, and Craig Iffland, my research assistants; and Lu Ann
Nate, my administrative assistant. I am particularly grateful to Patti Ogden,
research librarian at Notre Dame Law School, who read through the entire
manuscript and made many valuable editorial suggestions.

I consider it an honor for this book to appear in the distinguished Moral
Traditions series published by Georgetown University Press. I am grateful
to Bill Werpehowski for suggesting to me that this would be an ideal home
for my manuscript. Anyone who knows Jim Keenan, the series editor, will
immediately grasp how helpful his energy and enthusiasm can be to an author
struggling to bring a manuscript to completion. Richard Brown, the director
of the press, has been extremely kind, patient, and helpful throughout the
process of publication.

The topics considered in this book have engrossed my attention for many
years, and have benefited tremendously from conversations in the hall and
over the lunch table with my law school colleagues, especially John Coughlin,
John Finnis, and John Robinson. Talking about our disagreements has been as
fruitful for me as considering the convergences in our thought.

I am profoundly grateful for the longstanding personal and professional
encouragement of four distinguished scholars and loyal friends: Gerhard
Böwering, Margaret Farley, Vincent Rougeau, and Robin Darling Young.

They have taught me a great deal about faith, hope, and charity by word and by example. Finally, let me extend my deep appreciation to my family, who never let me forget that the most important thing is how we actually treat each other, not how we talk about treating each other.

PREFACE

Law shall be virtuous, just, possible to nature, according to the custom of the country, suitable to place and time, necessary, useful; clearly expressed, lest by its obscurity it lead to misunderstanding; framed for no private benefit, but for the common good.

ISIDORE OF SEVILLE (D. 636)

T HE TITLE OF THIS BOOK is *Law's Virtues*. It has a dual reference. On the one hand, I contend that law functions as a moral teacher, as a teacher of virtue, even in pluralistic Western democracies like the United States. In such societies, I think it is particularly important that the law strive to support autonomy and solidarity, which can be understood as aspects of the virtues of prudence and justice, respectively. Autonomy and solidarity, then, are law's virtues in the sense of the virtues that human law should try to promote in our political and social context. On the other hand, I also maintain that good law must possess attributes—virtues—in addition to encouraging the citizenry to act virtuously. Many of those qualities are identified in the passage from Isidore of Seville's *Etymologies* quoted above. In his treatise on law, Thomas Aquinas endorses Isidore's list of the characteristics that sound human law ought to exhibit. While Isidore and Aquinas lived many centuries ago, in political and social contexts very different from our own, this list of the attributes of good law is still useful today.

Lawmakers are required to balance various factors in formulating sound legal norms for their particular communities. Human law cannot require all virtuous acts or suppress all vicious ones, in part because it must also be "possible to nature" and "according to the custom of the country." The challenges facing wise lawmakers striving to take into account *all* the virtues of sound legal norms have always been considerable. Those challenges, however, are particularly formidable in Western liberal democracies, which are characterized by significant disagreement about what actually constitutes virtuous action.

The overarching aim of this book is to explore the relationship, and even the tension, between these two meanings of law's virtues in the American legal and political context and, in so doing, to shed some indirect light on the situation in other Western liberal democracies.

Introduction

I N THIS BOOK I SKETCH A NEW FRAMEWORK through which to view the relationship between troubling "life issues" and the realm of law in pluralistic liberal democracies such as the United States. At present, many people who oppose practices such as abortion and euthanasia, including many Catholics, seem to assume the relationship between law and morality is limited to two antipodal options. On the one hand is the firewall model: personal opposition to such practices aside, the law should be morally neutral in order to avoid imposing one particular set of values upon the entire society. On the other hand is the enforcement model: abortion and euthanasia are immoral and should therefore be completely banned, and even subject to criminal penalties.

This book proposes a third way. Let me state at the outset that I think that the practices commonly described as abortion and euthanasia generally involve the wrongful killing of human beings. At the same time, I recognize that my judgment does not settle the question about how the law should treat these issues in our pluralistic society, where not only the moral status but even the proper definition of both abortion and euthanasia are deeply contested on a number of grounds. In my view, neither model described earlier does an adequate job of addressing the numerous factors involved in wise lawmaking. The first model gives too little weight to the socially important moral message of law while the second model mistakenly views the moral message as the only relevant factor.

Against those who would contend that the law must always be morally neutral in a pluralistic society, I argue that legal frameworks are never value-neutral; in fact, they invariably carry strong normative messages about how the denizens of a particular society ought to go about living their lives. By its nature, lawmaking privileges some activities as admirable and worth pursuing while discounting others as socially deleterious, less valuable, and even harmful to the persons who engage in them. The law *does* inculcate morality, and for that reason it is essential for lawmakers—and for those citizens who elect them to office—to take responsibility for the values the law communicates and conveys as well as for the habits of living that the law promotes.

Against those who would move directly from a moral condemnation to a legal (often criminal) prohibition, I propose that sound lawmaking has to take into account far more than the moral status of the acts it purports to regulate, particularly if the legislative process views those acts in the abstract and in isolation from the circumstances in which they are generally performed. If it is to be pedagogically effective, law must key its moral message to the actual culture and customs of the people it purports to govern. Moreover, lawmakers must be realistic about the goals they expect the law to achieve. No law can turn a band of brigands into a band of saints overnight. Finally, the most effective means of conveying a moral message may not be the most obvious and powerful. Criminal prohibitions are not the only tools the law has to communicate its moral judgments. In fact, other arrows in the legal quiver are likely to be more nuanced and effective instruments of moral pedagogy, particularly in situations of social conflict. For example, noncriminal regulations, tax breaks, and other regulatory incentives can effectively encourage morally acceptable behavior and discourage unacceptable behavior without incurring either the risks (e.g., rebellion and backlash) or costs (e.g., expenses of law enforcement and incarceration) associated with the enactment of criminal strictures.

In short, the overall purpose of this volume is to propose a nuanced view about how law can function as a moral teacher in a pluralistic society such as the United States, a view that is at once optimistic about the effectiveness of moral pedagogy without being utopian, and realistic about moral disagreement without being relativistic. Sketching generalities, however, is not the sum total of my efforts. I also attempt to work out the details of how the vision of law I endorse would deal with specific and neuralgic moral and social questions such as abortion, genetic testing and euthanasia. After considering what the substantive law on these issues should be (and, by implication, what legal frameworks the legislature should attempt to put into place), I then examine how voters should grapple with hot-button legal and moral issues in deciding how to cast their ballots for lawmakers and other government officials.

Someone might object that most of those who work to instantiate pro-life values in the law are realistic about their chances of success. Many, if not all, activists opposed to abortion and euthanasia are very clear-eyed about the dim prospects of fully instantiating their legal ideals in the United States or other Western liberal democracies. They know, for example, that the chances of passing amendments to the US Constitution banning abortion or euthanasia are very slim. They realize that there is no momentum to recriminalize all abortions, especially abortions in the first three months of pregnancy. In other words, these activists "take what they can get" legislatively, although they never stop pushing for their legislative ideals.

My approach is somewhat different. In my view, attending to the practical limits of the law in inculcating a moral message is not merely a matter of pragmatic resignation. Instead, it is an essential part of sound jurisprudence. Even if it were politically manageable to do so, there are principled reasons why lawmakers should not attempt to legally impose a moral vision that is too far out of step with community values, particularly if that vision relies heavily on the tools of the criminal code for its implementation. Making a good law is not reducible to legally enforcing sound morality, particularly in a society that disagrees about what counts as sound morality.

What, then, are the criteria of good law? I have found no better compact summary of those criteria than the description proposed in the seventh century by Isidore of Seville and endorsed in the thirteenth century by Thomas Aquinas: "Law shall be virtuous, just, possible to nature, according to the custom of the country, suitable to place and time, necessary, useful; clearly expressed, lest by its obscurity it lead to misunderstanding; framed for no private benefit, but for the common good."[1] Virtuousness and justice are necessary but not sufficient attributes of good law; according to Isidore, law must also be "possible to nature" and "according to the custom" of the particular country. Moreover, in my view, these latter attributes are not mere pragmatic concessions to human intransigence but instead are integrally related to the Thomistic idea that law should function as a teacher of virtue. After all, no lesson plan can be effective if it outstrips the knowledge, abilities, and commitments of those it purports to instruct.

ASSUMPTIONS, PRESUPPOSITIONS, AND AUDIENCE

A central purpose of this book is to articulate and illustrate how a normative and nuanced commitment to the pedagogical function of law can be applied in a representative constitutional democracy, centrally the United States. By this rather unwieldy description of the legal context I mean a nation that systematically values individual liberty and is structured such that its citizens elect political leaders who make and enforce laws—laws that are interpreted by an independent judiciary that, at least at the federal level, is appointed and confirmed by elected political leaders. I also assume that this nation is significantly pluralistic, by which I mean that its citizens have significantly diverging views not only about religion but also about the nature and purpose of human life and the morality of certain controversial acts, including but not limited to abortion and euthanasia. Moreover, I take it for granted that disagreements on moral questions can be found not only between and among different religious communities but also between and among individual adherents of each community.

Nonetheless, I do not believe the moral, religious, and cultural pluralism that characterizes American society precludes the possibility for our law to function as an effective moral teacher. In fact, I think we can find several models of federal legislation that have effectively communicated a clear vision about how Americans ought to regard one another as fellow citizens and fellow human beings. The archetypal examples, of course, are the Civil Rights Acts, which are aimed to secure equal political and social rights for African Americans; I discuss less prominent but equally instructive examples in the first part of the book.

Can we use law's function as a moral teacher to calibrate legislative approaches on highly controversial topics such as abortion, genetics, and euthanasia? I believe we can. One of the tasks of the book is to explore how we might prudently go about doing so. In this sense, the book is an exercise of applied jurisprudence, working in the conceptual region between fundamental moral arguments, on the one hand, and comprehensive frameworks of law and policy, on the other. To keep the reader's focus on this middle area of the discussion, and to hold the book to a reasonable length, I must make certain assumptions about fundamental morality and leave unaddressed certain crucial matters of practical implementation, such as the relationship between state and federal regulation.

More specifically, as I noted earlier, I assume without arguing that each individual human being is a person of equal fundamental dignity who merits respect and the protection of the law. I assume that it is morally wrong to intentionally kill a human being who is not in the process of causing serious harm to another human being. In my judgment, most of the acts that we call abortion or assisted suicide or euthanasia involve the intentional killing of human beings who are not engaged in causing harm to someone else. For that reason, I do not think such acts are morally justified. But I also recognize and emphasize that not every act to which these labels are commonly attached fits this general pattern. We need to give careful consideration to the precise definitions of wrongful acts, particularly when they are as contested and neuralgic as abortion and euthanasia. Moreover, in evaluating the acts committed by others, we must begin by putting ourselves in their shoes. We must attend to the immediate and more remote purposes for which they acted, as well as the circumstances they believed to bear upon their decision to act in the way that they did. We cannot morally judge the purposes of another's action simply by evaluating the foreseeable consequences of that action, particularly in hard or complicated cases. In some instances, sorting through the agent's purposes in acting in light of the facts of the situation can be difficult. For example, a doctor may order a dose of morphine to quell the patient's pain, not shorten the patient's life, although the doctor foresees that the drug will depress respiration and hasten death. That act does not, in my view, count as an impermissible attempt at euthanasia. Hard or borderline cases must be given due and careful consideration. But the fact that justifiable exceptions exist does not undermine the fact that there are many clear cases that deserve the lion's share of legislative attention.

Concentrating primarily on these more ordinary cases, I want to work out what my view of respect for human dignity entails for making law in a society in which many people either do not share that same view of dignity or have reservations about what respecting it requires. To put my question another way: How should pro-life Americans envision embedding their values in the legal system when it is clear that fellow citizens disagree on any number of fronts?

This question, of course, presses us to reflect on the phenomenon of moral disagreement. How should we respond to other citizens who do not accept our premises about when human life merits equal dignity and demands equal respect, a demand that is sometimes phrased as the respect due to "person-hood"? How should we interact with those who do not share our conviction that respecting human dignity always precludes intentionally killing those who are not engaged in causing serious harm to others? Let me state up front that I do not dismiss such people or their concerns. I think the questions raised by abortion and euthanasia are difficult, not easy. For example, pinpointing exactly when an individual, equally protectable human life begins has long been a topic of fierce debate among different religious and philosophical frameworks. Moreover, pregnancy not only sustains the life of the unborn, it also imposes significant physical and emotional burdens on women. Whether and when a society committed to the equal dignity of women can legitimately require them to endure these burdens is another troubling and difficult problem. While I have come to my own conclusions on these moral matters, I am acutely aware of the cogency and good faith of those who disagree. One point of this book, in fact, is to frame a pro-life jurisprudence that does not depend upon painting all the millions of Americans who adopt a pro-choice position as unreasonable or morally corrupt.

While some readers of this book will agree with its broadly pro-life moral presuppositions, certainly not all will agree. Consequently, the latter readers will reject some or all of the moral substance incorporated into my proposals regarding the pedagogical function of American law. I trust, however, that all readers will see in the book my efforts to take seriously both the existence and good faith of fellow citizens who disagree with me on these important questions. I know that I would be very interested to read a normative juris-prudential proposal by a pro-choice thinker who takes seriously the existence and good faith of people with my views. I hope those who disagree with me feel the same way.

This work is an interdisciplinary effort. I am by training and long experi-ence both a religious ethicist working primarily out of the Roman Catholic tradition and an American law professor. In making my arguments I draw upon—and draw together—sources from Catholic moral theology as well as Anglo-American law and legal theory. My understanding of the role of law as a teacher of virtue, for example, is drawn from Thomas Aquinas's treatise on law. My illustrations of how law can operate effectively as a teacher of virtue in a pluralistic Western society are drawn from sections of the federal statutory code. In the course of my discussion, I engage, adopt, criticize, and revise a number of normative frameworks and positions from both moral theology and secular law. Let me emphasize that I am asking my readers to consider the proposals I make on their own terms and for the reasons I advance, not because they are endorsed by any particular religious or secular authority. I no more expect readers to accept any moral proposition I advance because it is endorsed by the pope than I expect them to assent to a legal position because it is accepted by the Supreme Court.

I hope this book will be helpful to those who are interested in the tangled relationship of religion, morality, and law in the United States and, by exten-sion, in other pluralistic representative democracies in the West. Like all inter-disciplinary work, this project has its hazards. While I draw on occasion upon the technical vocabularies of both Catholic moral theology and American law, I have tried to make the meaning clear enough to be interesting and useful to those who do not come from those backgrounds. Again, I want to stress that it is the meaning of these terms and their use in the contemporary discussion of legal and moral issues that concern me—not simply their sources. I hope readers who do not share my academic background will find the discussion fruitful because it illuminates broader discussions of importance in American political life.

THE CONTENTS OF THIS BOOK

The first part, "Law as a Moral Teacher," sketches the jurisprudential framework of the book. In chapter 1 I make the case that the law plays a significant role in inculcating a model of the virtuous life, even in pluralistic societies such as our own. What virtues should the law teach? Obviously, a comprehensive answer to this question is beyond the scope of this project, which broadly aims to move successively from theoretical background, to applied issues, and to the ethics of voting—all in a single monograph. I do maintain, however, that the American legal system as a whole should aspire to encompass the overarching virtues of autonomy and solidarity.

These terms are susceptible to multiple definitions. Drawing upon the writings of the legal philosopher Joseph Raz, I argue that autonomy should not be understood simply as negative freedom—that is, as individual freedom *from* as many legal and social constraints as possible. Rather, the point of negative freedom is positive freedom—freedom *for* the opportunity to become the "part-author" of one's own life. But it is important to realize that the exercise of positive freedom is socially conditioned; it requires mixing one's own initiative and plans with the opportunities to flourish made available by a particular society. Moreover, promoting the exercise of autonomy as understood by Raz is a multifaceted social task. In my view, Raz's conception of autonomy, particularly its emphasis on the key role played by society in making available to its citizens a sufficient array of morally valuable options, dovetails nicely with the account of the social virtue of solidarity developed by Pope John Paul II. Solidarity, in my view, takes seriously the fact that enabling people on the margins of society to become "part-authors" of their lives requires a firm and steady social commitment.

Together, the virtues of autonomy and solidarity acknowledge the dignity of each human being as uniquely responsible for his or her own life and choices while underscoring the essentially social nature of human beings. The goal of any legal system is to promote the common good; the virtues of autonomy and solidarity remind us that the good of the community and the good of the individuals that comprise it are intricately intertwined. I use the Americans with Disabilities Act as a specific example of how this understanding of the relationship between individual flourishing and the common good can operate in the contemporary United States.

Whereas chapter 1 outlines the positive role that law can play in inculcating moral values, chapter 2 emphasizes the limits that lawmakers ought to recognize in pursuing this objective. The more coercive elements of the law must be restricted to teaching only the most basic moral lessons. Moreover, if the law's requirements and prohibitions attempt to move too far beyond the current moral consensus, there is a risk of provoking a backlash that could undermine not only the moral lesson but also the stability of the legal framework itself. Another limitation to keep in mind is that the law teaches moral lessons to ordinary people, not saints. In pluralistic societies, moreover, due regard has to be given to the fact that not everyone agrees about the nature, qualifications, or even the existence of sainthood. Finally, good lawmaking is a practical, not merely theoretical, endeavor. Questions of effectiveness and enforceability are central to the crafting of a wise legal framework. In addition, the concrete methods we use to detect and prosecute lawbreakers must be evaluated with respect to their monetary and nonmonetary costs.

The second part of the book, "Life Issues and the Law," extends the framework of the first part to contemporary questions about abortion, genetics, and euthanasia. Chapter 3 considers the jurisprudence of the pro-life movement and how it could be framed more broadly to include the law's positive support for the value of unborn life, rather than to simply concentrate on outlawing abortion. In evaluating the law on abortion and childbirth, for example, we need to consider a broad array of interlocking prohibitions, requirements, incentives, and disincentives that affect women's choices to continue a pregnancy. It is not sufficient to simply examine whether the criminal law bans abortion. A broader understanding of what it means to be pro-life, moreover, can yield legal strategies for inculcating respect for unborn life even in a society, such as our own, that currently has no strong consensus to ban or significantly restrict abortion.

The pedagogical function of the law is important. The effective exercise of that function, however, does not depend only on the moral content of the law in question. In fact, the pedagogical function of a given piece of legislation cannot be separated from more pragmatic considerations identified by Aquinas as essential to good law. I explore the connection between a law's moral message and its operational functionality in chapter 4, taking as my case study the controversy that developed over the Freedom of Choice Act (FOCA) during the context of the 2008 presidential election. Many Americans deeply objected to the moral message of FOCA, which aims to protect abortion rights against state and federal encroachments. The utter lack of clarity in the bill's operational provisions only exacerbated the existing moral and social divisions over abortion. That lack of clarity allowed pro-life Americans to read the bill as an expansive threat to the dignity of unborn life rather than as a mere protection of the status quo, as many of those in the pro-choice movement believed it to be. From this controversy I draw a general jurisprudential lesson: a law cannot be effective as a moral teacher unless the manner in which it will operate is clearly understood. Otherwise, the law merely sows confusion, mistrust, and doubt. When the moral message of a particular piece of legislation is controversial, operational details must be clearly defined, lest existing divisions in the community be enflamed by misunderstandings over ambiguities.

Chapter 5 moves from established to emerging controversies, looking at the changes to medical testing that have resulted from the Human Genome Project, an international ten-year effort to map the DNA sequence of the human genome that was completed at the dawn of the new millennium. For the foreseeable future, it appears that our medical knowledge will outrun our healing capabilities. Genetic medicine is increasingly able to inform patients of the probabilities that they will suffer one or more debilitating diseases for which there is no effective means of prevention or treatment on the immediate horizon. I ask how this emerging era of ominous probabilities is likely to affect persons trying to exercise Razian autonomy as part-authors of their own lives and how the law should treat the prospect of direct-to-consumer genetic testing. In my view, the unreliability of these tests coupled with the striking inability of most people to deal with the probabilistic information that the tests generate provides sufficient reason to limit their commercial availability.

Chapters 6 and 7 grapple with questions of end-of-life decision making. Chapter 6 explores questions of what it means to die well, drawing upon the late Joseph Cardinal Bernardin's reflections on his own terminal illness in *The Gift of Peace*. Bernardin's experience provides a vehicle to explore a key question: What can the virtue of autonomy—the commitment to being part-author of one's own life—possibly mean in a situation where one's strength is ebbing and one's days are numbered? The cardinal's journey also provides a further example of the interrelationship between Razian autonomy and solidarity. Communal support and commitment is important in enabling young and healthy persons to be part-authors of their own lives; this solidarity is even more essential for persons experiencing profound physical and mental diminishment and dependence. At the same time, as Bernardin's life shows, enabling and allowing others to care for us in our suffering can also be an autonomous act, which testifies to both the vulnerability and the dignity of all human beings, no matter what their state of dependence.

Building upon the reflections in chapter 6 on the role of autonomy and solidarity at the end of life, chapter 7 moves on to discuss American law on assisted suicide and euthanasia. While the underlying questions about human dignity are found in both instances, the jurisprudential beginning-of-life questions are very different from those that arise at the end of life. In stark contrast to its approach to abortion, the Supreme Court of the United States consigned the difficult questions about assisted dying to the "laboratory of the states."

Most states prohibit assisted suicide and euthanasia while making explicit provision for patients to refuse life-prolonging treatments either directly or through a surrogate decision maker if they are incompetent to make their own decisions. In my view, this general legal framework appropriately balances the concerns for both autonomy and solidarity while still offering legal protection to those vulnerable persons who might be pressured to hasten their deaths for the convenience of third parties. As the reader will see, I do not believe that endorsing such a framework means denying either the existence or the significance of hard cases.

The final part of the book is titled "Voting, Morality, and the Law." It attempts to connect the jurisprudential issues discussed in the first two parts with the moral obligations of voters. In a representative democracy such as the United States, the people are at once the sovereigns and the subjects of the law. By casting their ballots, citizens choose their representatives and leaders to make law on their behalf and in their collective name. Chapter 8 examines the morality of voting by considering what voters actually do when they vote. The chapter's central argument is that a moral analysis of voting must begin with the recognition that voters select among candidates, not among issues. In my view, a serious flaw of many election guides, including the recent guides issued by the US Catholic bishops, is that they can easily be read to suggest that voters ought to evaluate and prioritize issues in an abstract way. These election guides do not help voters think about the likely impact that various candidates would have on those issues if elected to the particular office in question. If we treat issues properly as action items, we see that they are not all commensurable in a way that permits a unified ranking. Some issues, such as abortion and euthanasia, are important because they go to fundamental questions about who counts as an equally protectable member of the society. Other issues, such as the economic crisis of 2008, are urgent because they threaten the ability of people to provide basic needs for themselves and their families and because they further impair the lives of the vulnerable, including children and the elderly. In deliberating about how to cast their ballots, therefore, voters need to be mindful of the different ways in which issues can be important to the common good.

Chapters 9 and 10 consider two objections to the theory of voting developed in chapter 8 that appeared in the 2004 and 2008 elections, and that will doubtless appear in the 2012 and 2016 elections as well. These objections were originally formulated in the technical terms of Catholic moral theology in order to influence American Catholic voters, but it is not difficult to recast them in ways that have broader intelligibility and appeal. Chapter 9 engages the objection that voters should never cast their ballots in favor of pro-choice candidates because abortion is an "intrinsic evil" deserving paramount consideration in selecting political leaders. I argue that this objection is unpersuasive because, in the vocabulary of Catholic of moral theology, the term "intrinsic evil" points to the reason why an act is wrong, not to the gravity of the wrong. The gravity of the wrong, not the ground of its wrongfulness, is most relevant to voters. At the same time, I acknowledge that the discussion reveals an emerging use of "intrinsic evil" as a term of prophetic indictment. Unfortunately, like most prophetic indictments, this use of the term does not help us with the practical analysis so essential to good lawmaking. In particular, to denounce a practice as intrinsically evil does not advance our judgment about whether the most effective way to combat that practice is by the enactment of legal strictures. This limitation, of course, applies not only to prophetic condemnations of abortion but also to similar denunciations of other deeply embedded forms of social injustice.

Chapter 10 addresses a related objection that charges that voters who cast their ballots for candidates favoring abortion rights "cooperate with evil" in a morally troublesome way. The Catholic moral tradition developed the category of "cooperation with evil" to consider questions involving one agent's complicity in the wrongdoing of another. The point of the category is to distinguish situations in which it is objectively wrongful to act in a way that facilitates the wrongdoing of another party from those situations in which it is merely regrettable to do so. In my view, however, this category does not translate well to the special challenges presented by voting in pluralistic liberal democracies such as the United States. In most cases, a citizen's vote is very remote in terms of time, space, and causality from a political official's legislative wrongdoing. In fact, a vote is likely too remote to qualify as wrongful, provided that the voter does not actually intend to further the unjust policies in question. The category of cooperation with evil does not help us address the real question here, which is not "How do voters avoid committing wrongful acts?" but rather "How do voters mobilize and organize to address wrongful structures that can be ameliorated only by coordinated action?"

In the concluding reflections, I make explicit what is an implicit theme running throughout all the chapters. In the past fifteen years many of the discussions surrounding issues such as abortion, euthanasia, and genetics have been framed in terms of the "culture wars," a political image that depicts one group of Americans pitted against another group in an inexorable battle for the moral soul of the country: conservatives versus liberals, Republicans versus Democrats, and churchgoers versus secularists. In my mind, this way of framing the debate is unhelpful and even obstructive. Nor, as the reader will see, do I judge this divisive approach to best instantiate in the political realm a commitment to the equal dignity of each human being as made in the image and likeness of God. Thinking of law as a moral teacher does not require reimagining citizens and lawmakers as moral warriors. In fact, I believe the opposite is the case After all, the education of the young is often among the first casualties of physical warfare—and I suspect the same is true of ideological warfare as well.

NOTE

1. Thomas Aquinas, *Summa theologica*, 3 vols., trans. Fathers of the English Dominican Province (New York: Benziger Bros., 1948), II-II, q. 95, art. 3 (citing Isidore of Seville).

PART I

Law as a Moral Teacher

⌒

CHAPTER 1

Autonomy, Solidarity, and Law's Pedagogy

A WOMAN WITH AN OBVIOUS DISABILITY making her way along Chicago's Michigan Avenue in December 1970 would not have been simply enjoying the spectacle of one of the nation's busiest commercial venues at the height of the Christmas shopping season. Whether she knew it or not, she also would have been engaged in an illegal act, for on the books of the Chicago Municipal Code at that time was an ordinance colloquially known as "the ugly law," which provided that "no person who is diseased, maimed, mutilated or in any way deformed so as to be an unsightly or disgusting object or improper person to be allowed in or on the public ways or other public places in this city, or shall therein or thereon expose himself to public view, under a penalty of not less than one dollar nor more than fifty dollars for each offense."[1] Cities such as Columbus, Ohio, and Omaha, Nebraska, had similar laws—and they were not repealed until the mid-1970s.[2]

Most of us today recoil at the ugly law's view of persons with disabilities; to contemporary ears, the law's title is an accurate, if ironic, reflection of the moral quality of the law's expressed sentiments. But what, precisely, is objectionable about it? In my view, the salient objections can be grouped into three categories.

First, the ugly law places significant practical barriers in the way of persons with disabilities. It prevents them from going about their business; it dissuades them from living their day-to-day lives. If they nonetheless decide to attempt to do so, they risk being arrested, penalized, and publicly shamed for engaging in activities that most of us take for granted, such as going shopping, visiting friends, and attending worship services.

A second problem has to do with the normative presuppositions behind the ugly law—the concrete prohibitions and penalties are infused with a morally freighted vision of how human beings should live their lives together. The ugly law adopts a particular view of the value of an individual, conveying the message that it is important to be "normal"—to be aesthetically pleasing (or at least not disgusting) to others. In addition, it communicates a clear vision of the respective obligations of different groups of persons within the broader society. Those with disabilities have an obligation to stay out of the way—and out of the line of sight—of those who are "normal." By contrast, "normal" persons have very few, if any, obligations to extend themselves in any way toward the mentally and physically challenged individuals who come across their paths. In the vision of reality inculcated by the ugly law, chance and accident can create a moral and social chasm between people. The random circumstances of one's conception or birth (e.g., I was born with Down syndrome, you were not) or of one's life (e.g., the drunken driver hit her but missed him) can determine whether one is deemed worthy to participate in the public life of the community.

Third, the broad ramifications of the message conveyed by the ugly law are also very troubling. Assume that the citizens of Chicago internalize the normative vision of the worth of persons with disabilities that is tacitly presupposed by the law. Does it not seem likely that those citizens will also apply the law's norms even in contexts where the law does not explicitly govern? For example, how will so-called normal people relate to persons with disabilities in private settings? And how will persons with disabilities view themselves? If they do not have the right to walk the city streets in peace, will they ever be able to see themselves as anything but second-class citizens in other areas of their lives? Will they not be forced to confront internal and external pressures, sometimes subtle, sometimes overt, to make themselves invisible and to refrain from making any claims on the attention or concern of "normal" members of the community?

Thus the problem extends far beyond the fact that the ugly law tightly restricts the ability of persons with disabilities to go about their day-to-day lives; the deeper difficulty is the intrinsic messages that the law conveys about the relative worth of persons with disabilities. The effects of these messages are not limited to the streets of Chicago but can also influence interactions between people in many other contexts. Consequently, any adequate moral analysis of the ugly law must move beyond its concrete requirements and prohibitions to consider these wider ripple effects.

More generally, the example of the ugly law suggests that a crucial challenge facing those of us concerned about the relationship between law and morality is to find a way to grapple with the issue of law's underlying normative vision in a manner that is both straightforward and sophisticated (incongruous as those qualities might seem). Always and everywhere, law teaches a moral lesson—it imbues a vision of how the members of a particular society should live their lives together. Political communities need to acknowledge the fact that law teaches and to take responsibility for what it teaches. Needless to say, in highly complex and pluralistic societies, deciding what values and virtues various bodies of law should embody and foster is a daunting task. I do not claim otherwise. But if citizens deliberately leave these questions about law unarticulated and unaddressed, we will only heighten the challenge of forging just political and civic communities.

In the remainder of this chapter I begin to grapple with the issue of how to take responsibility for law's pedagogical function in the context of Western liberal democracies. My central case is the United States, although my argument could be extended by analogy to other developed countries marked by increased pluralism, complexity, and a commitment to the value of individual liberty. I set out in some detail the theoretical view of the relationship of law and morality that animates the more topically oriented chapters that compose the rest of the book. In a nutshell, I argue that the civil law can, should, and does function as a moral teacher, even in pluralistic societies such as the United States.

Let me begin by critically examining the components of a contrasting understanding of law that I will call "law as police officer," which has become highly influential among Anglo-American legal theorists and in American society. This metaphor describes a strand of liberal legal theory that has its roots in the thought of John Stuart Mill.[3] By "liberal legal theory" I mean any legal theory that holds individual liberty to be an overriding moral and social value. Consequently, in framing law, legislatures ought to exercise a "presumption in favor of liberty," understood as the absence of coercion. Any infringement upon individual liberty requires a good reason. In the view of liberal legal theorists, then, "liberty should be the norm, coercion always needs justification."[4] This statement, of course, could be adopted by a wide range of legal theorists, including those who are not liberal. It needs to be supplemented by the recognition that liberal legal theorists not only place the bar of justification very high but also do not consider certain reasons for passing coercive laws to be legitimate in the first place.

Many advocates of the "law as police officer" approach contend that the law (particularly the criminal law) should generally be restricted to prohibiting actions that wrongfully harm other persons; in their view, it is morally inappropriate to use the tools of the criminal law to proscribe so-called harmless immoralities or to enforce community values. Taking as my conversation partner Joel Feinberg, whom I believe to be the most rigorous and interesting contemporary representative of this strand of liberal legal philosophy, I argue that the "law as police officer" approach is deeply inadequate.[5] Drawing in part upon Thomas Aquinas's understanding of the nature, purpose, and limits of positive law, I then sketch my own alternative understanding of "law as teacher."

Before proceeding, let me emphasize that I mean the two labels of "law as police officer" and "law as teacher" to function as heuristic devices, not as comprehensive and exhaustive analytical categories. They are designed to focus the reader's attention on the question of the fundamental purpose of human law. I do not mean to deny that roughly similar answers to that fundamental question exhibit great variety among themselves. For example, I do not suggest that liberal legal theory is homogenous; indeed, it is far from it. With its touchstone in the writings of the great twentieth-century Oxford legal scholar H. L. A. Hart, contemporary analytic jurisprudence has deeply probed interrelated issues such as (1) the differences between natural law theory and positivism; (2) the effects of subjectivist or constructivist accounts of moral values, on the one hand, and objective or intrinsic account of such values (whether based on rights or natural law), on the other; and (3) the relationship of law, morality, and liberty in a pluralistic society.[6] Different positions on the first two issues can lead legal theorists to have different views on the third issue.

Moreover, as complicated as the discussion in Anglo-American jurisprudence may be, it is rivaled by the intricacies of the debate over what counts as a sufficiently "Thomistic" moral or legal theory. In this realm, significant topics include (1) whether and in what respect Aquinas's moral theory has to be understood as a virtue ethic as well as an ethic of natural law; (2) the relationship of rights language to both the language of virtue and natural law;[7] and (3) the manner and degree to which natural law ought to exert its influence on the human law.[8]

My purpose in this chapter is not to engage or even to survey these extensive bodies of literature but to develop my own constructive approach in dialogue with a few key conversation partners. My approach is broadly Thomistic in that I take my central theme from Aquinas's view that the major purpose of law is to lead human beings to virtue.[9] At the same time, I build upon and adapt Aquinas's reflections on the purpose of human law in order to deal with the challenges of lawmaking in a political society such as the United States, which is very different from the political context in which he wrote. To take but one example, I argue that autonomy and solidarity are key virtues for American law to foster, precisely because they enable both individual and communal flourishing in pluralistic liberal democracies. I do not claim, of course, that my account is the only way to update Aquinas's views on the purpose and limits of human law to deal with contemporary challenges.

LAW AS POLICE OFFICER

I believe that the metaphor of "law as police officer" best evokes the basic approach of much (but, as we will see, not all) contemporary liberal legal theory. In essence, this approach to the relationship between law and morality suggests that the role of the law as a teacher of virtue is extremely limited because law operates negatively rather than positively. Many liberal theorists would claim that law, properly understood, centrally functions like a police officer guarding the boundaries of a piece of property. The fundamental purpose of law, under this view, is to keep people from acting in ways that wrongfully harm others (or their property); in operating as a negative constraint, law is not concerned with inculcating a positive vision of the way that people should live and flourish together. According to liberal legal theorists of this sort, it would be no more appropriate for law to tell a member of the community which view of flourishing to adopt than it would be for the security guard protecting a property's boundary to dictate to the adjoining landowner what type of lawn grass to grow.

Advocates of the "law as police officer" approach rely upon a key theoretical tool known as the harm principle, which posits that the coercive function of the law, particularly the sanctions of the criminal law, should be invoked only to prohibit behavior that constitutes a wrongful harm to someone else. Some liberal legal theorists, such as Feinberg himself, narrowly supplement the harm principle with an offense principle that permits lighter criminal sanctions to be used against seriously offensive public behavior.[10] Nonetheless, the bulk of Feinberg's interest and attention is devoted to a defense of the harm principle. According to Feinberg, a wrongful harm to another has two key characteristics: it is a setback to that person's interests, and it is a violation of that person's rights.[11] The way he develops each of these characteristics merits both attention and criticism.

As his choice of the word "interests" suggests, Feinberg adopts a subjectivist account of value. That is, in his view, human beings do not seek to promote or protect goods, goals, or states of affairs because they are objectively valuable; rather, the inverse holds: these goods, goals, and states of affairs are valuable because they are sought after and valued by human subjects. In other words, they are valuable because they have become the focus of a particular human being's interest.[12] Because human beings adopt innumerable, diverse goals as their ultimate interests, the law cannot possibly commit itself to protecting the ultimate interests of each and every person. Instead, the legal system must focus on safeguarding what Feinberg calls "welfare interests"—the various aspects of life that people need to have in place as necessary means for their attempts to realize their own particular ultimate interests. In contrast to wide-ranging ultimate interests, welfare interests are generally the same for the vast majority of persons; they include a predictable span of life, health, absence of pain and disfigurement, financial security, and freedom.[13]

To trigger the possibility of a legal prohibition, however, it is not sufficient that an action harm a person's welfare interests; the action also must violate his rights. In other words, the law should concern itself only with a setback to a person's interest that is also wrongful.[14] The assumption here is that people frequently suffer from a variety of setbacks to their interests that are not wrongful. For example, if I harm you in self-defense, your interest in a predictable span of healthy life may be set back substantially; nonetheless, you have not been wronged. If one professional tennis player beats another in a tournament, the loser's interest in victory is obviously compromised. Nonetheless, the loser is not wronged, provided the contest was not rigged.

To be fair, virtually no legal theorist of any theoretical stripe would argue that the harm suffered either by an unjust aggressor or by the loser in a fair contest constituted a wrong against that person. For Feinberg, however, there is a crucial way in which actions that are both arguably morally wrong in themselves and harmful to another person can have their character as a legal wrong erased: if the victim consents to the behavior that caused the harm. Under the *volenti* maxim, if an individual consented to an action (his own action or the action of another) and is harmed as a consequence of that action, there is no violation of the individual's rights. The action may be morally wrong, as in, for example, a sadist beating a masochist; if, however, the masochist consents, he is not "wronged" in a way that justifies criminal punishment of the sadist's action—even if the action seriously impedes the masochist's welfare interests in health or absence of pain.[15]

What, then, are the practical implications of the "law as police officer" approach? First and most important, it implies that law, especially criminal law, should not prohibit the vast majority of activities that do not count as wrongful harms to welfare interests. Why? A conjunction of two reasons supports this conclusion. To all liberal legal theorists, liberty has a fundamental value that overrides nearly every other value. Moreover, to liberal legal theorists such as Feinberg, the coercive power of the government, particularly when exercised through the arm of the criminal justice system, constitutes the most severe threat to individual liberty. Feinberg writes: "The threat of legal punishment enforces public opinion by putting the nonconformist in a terror of apprehension, rendering his privacy precarious, and his prospects in life uncertain. The punishments themselves brand him with society's most powerful stigma and undermine his life projects, in career or family, disastrously."[16] Consequently, with few exceptions for deeply offensive public behavior, the sole legitimate target of the awful power of the criminal law is the constellation of actions that wrongfully harm others.[17]

On this basis, Feinberg argues that a number of behavioral categories do not justify criminal prohibition. As I noted earlier, these categories include harmful behavior to which the person harmed has consented as well as arguably immoral behavior that is not harmful to another person.[18] For Feinberg, this latter category includes any and all sexual activity between or among consenting adults. To combat the obvious objection that moral corruption—sexual or otherwise—constitutes a real harm to the person corrupted, Feinberg draws upon his subjectivist conception of value to argue that corruption is a harm only to those who have developed a prior ultimate interest in being a good person. Moreover, if such persons engage in corrupting behavior, the ensuing harm to their character does not count as wrongful because they consented to the actions that produced it.

Feinberg furthermore argues that it is wrong to criminally prohibit what he calls "free-floating evils"—moral evils that do not constitute "a personal harm, offense, or exploitative injustice" to an identifiable person or group of persons. The category of free-floating evils includes the violation of social and religious taboos, evil and impure thoughts, wanton squishing of bugs or other small wiggling creatures in the wild, and the extinction of a species.[19] Feinberg also identifies a number of free-floating evils connected with social change, such as the extinction of a national or cultural group, drastic shifts in moral or aesthetic climate, and general environmental ugliness or drabness.[20]

In the four-volume treatise in which he lays out his theory, Feinberg carefully confines his discussion to the moral limits of criminal law. He does not explicitly treat other branches of the legal system, such as contract law, administrative law, corporate law, tax law, or the law of property. Nonetheless, the normative import of his work seeps beyond the specific realm of the criminal law to affect the action-guiding function of all spheres of the legal system. More specifically, the fundamental presuppositions of his theory suggest that the strictures developed by all areas of the law should leave the greatest possible scope for individual choice. Moreover, in adopting a subjectivist account of value, Feinberg's approach implies that the law—in all its branches—should avoid, to the greatest possible extent, adopting or imposing any external theory of value.

Under Feinberg's theory, apart from deterring wrongful harms with criminal law, the state has no obvious theoretical justification for using less extreme means of coercion in other situations. Feinberg rightly notes that the criminal law poses the harshest threat to personal liberty. But the civil law poses a more likely threat given that the burden of proof in a criminal trial is so much higher than in a civil one. For example, an accused drug dealer might avoid criminal conviction but suffer the government confiscating his home and property in a civil forfeiture case.[21] Moreover, nearly all citizens are subject to the pervasive and constant pressure to conform to the incentives built into the income tax code, which promotes some ways of living (such as marriage) at the expense of other ways (such as cohabitation).

The view of law adopted by the "law as police officer" approach is compelling in a number of respects. It recognizes that the tools of the government can be a dangerous and destructive force if they are used incorrectly. It also places at the center of our attention the disparity in power between the individual and the government. Finally, it honors the fact that many socially beneficial insights began as highly controversial propositions advanced by individuals or small groups under conditions that led them to fear for their personal safety and freedom at the hands of a majority. But Feinberg's strategy is also associated with substantial costs. More specifically, it can be critiqued both with respect to its underlying political values and with regard to the coherence and power of the theory of law that he develops around those values.[22]

A main difficulty with Feinberg's approach stems not so much from the weight it places on human freedom as from the impoverished definition it provides for that term. Feinberg depicts freedom as comprising three primary characteristics. First, freedom is primarily negative in nature; that is, agents can be called free if no other agent, particularly the state, impedes them from acting in the manner in which they wish. Second, freedom is almost exclusively oriented toward the future. According to Feinberg, it is more important for the state to refrain from interfering with agents who are doing what they want to do in order to bring into existence the future they have imagined for themselves than it is for the state to protect the fruits of other agents' past exercises of freedom. Third, as Feinberg understands it, freedom is primarily individualistic. The entities around whom freedom revolves are almost exclusively individuals; broader groups, such as families, churches, and nations, are largely presented as threats to individual freedom rather than as constitutive safeguards and expressions of it.

AUTONOMY, SOLIDARITY, AND THE COMMON GOOD

In my view, each of the foregoing three features of Feinberg's view of freedom merits criticism, not from a perspective opposed to freedom but from one committed to a more adequate understanding of its nature. The necessary appraisal at this point is internal rather than external to liberalism. More specifically, I think the work of the contemporary Oxford legal philosopher Joseph Raz can be used to develop a powerful critique and corrective of Feinberg's liberal legal theory. Along with Ronald Dworkin and John Finnis, Raz has carried forward the Oxford analytical jurisprudential tradition so indebted to H. L. A. Hart.[23]

Raz shares Feinberg's commitment to liberty's preeminent value but defines and justifies it in ways significantly different from Feinberg. Most significantly, Raz is often referred to as a "perfectionist liberal" because he thinks that human freedom is not value-free but is oriented toward enabling and supporting human beings in living morally valuable ways of life.[24] As Raz points out, the ultimate point of negative freedom is positive freedom; the agents' freedom from the restrictions and requirements of others bears fruit only when the agents grab hold of that opportunity in a positive way to help shape their own identities and place their imprints upon the circumstances under which they will live. In Raz's terms, the purpose of negative freedom is positively to allow agents to become "part-authors" of their own lives.[25] Positive freedom, for Raz, is autonomy.

Raz's argument also suggests that it is possible—indeed, preferable—to justify the protection of liberty without adopting Feinberg's subjectivist account of value or interest. In other words, one does not have to ground the protection of a wide range of freedom in Feinberg's twin claims that (1) there is no value, nor any way of life that can be said to have value, apart from the fact that someone exists who values it; and (2) any activity, item, or way of life is to be treated as valuable if someone does indeed value it. Raz contends that the reason for protecting freedom stems not from a dearth of objective value but rather from a surfeit of such value. More specifically, he holds that the rationale for protecting freedom stems from the recognition that there are a number of mutually incompatible but objectively morally worthwhile ways of living one's life, all of which deserve protection precisely because they are objectively morally worthwhile.[26] Moreover, for Raz, protecting autonomy does not require making morally unacceptable forms of life available to persons merely so that they can reject them. In fact, he maintains that "autonomy requires a choice between goods. A choice between good and evil is not enough."[27] In addition, he goes further, claiming that "autonomy is valuable only if exercised in pursuit of the good. The ideal of autonomy requires only the availability of morally acceptable options."[28]

Feinberg is also wrong to suggest that freedom is relentlessly forward-looking and individualistic. In fact, positive freedom—autonomy—also includes a backward-looking component as well as a communal dimension. People exercise their autonomy in part by working together to found institutions, create communities, and implement their vision of the good life together. Consequently, these collective social constructions should not be construed solely as a threat to freedom in the manner that Feinberg frequently seems to suggest.[29] They also constitute freedom's fruits, and they consequently merit protection as the tangible manifestations of the exercise of autonomy. Raz captures these aspects of freedom in his insight that autonomous persons must be loyal to their commitments, which, he recognizes, are socially embodied. He writes: "Our projects and relationships depend on the form they acquire through social conventions. This means, as we saw, that they depend on complex patterns of expectations, on the symbolic significance of various actions, and in general on remaining loyal, within the recognized limits set for improvisation and change, to their basic shape. Failure to do so is failure to succeed, or even to engage, in the pursuits one has set oneself to make the content of one's life."[30]

I do not mean to suggest, of course, that there can never be any tension between freedom and the accumulated weight of custom, tradition, and institutional values. My only point is that to present the relationship between freedom and these other values as an absolute dichotomy is to go too far. Both those who defend the institutions to which they have dedicated their lives and those who wish to modify or even demolish the same institutions to create room for new projects can justify their claims by invoking the importance of freedom. The defenders focus on freedom's backward-looking elements while the demolishers/modifiers emphasize the forward-looking aspects of freedom.

To make this abstract distinction more concrete, consider Feinberg's engaging example of the conflict between Terrence Truview and Farley Fairjoy. Truview devotes twenty years of his life to building and sustaining a community of fundamentalists, only to discover that young Mr. Fairjoy, a member of the community's second generation, has been discreetly reading romantic novels, sneaking an occasional can of beer, and listening to popular music at low volume on his mini radio.[31] Needless to say, Truview wants Fairjoy to cease these heretical activities, whereas Fairjoy points out that his private pursuits are not disturbing anyone's peace. In assessing the conflict, Feinberg frames it as one between Fairjoy's personal freedom and Truview's desire to preserve a way of life. Not surprisingly, then, freedom wins: "When two persons each have an interest in how one of them lives his life, the interests of the one whose life it is are the more important."[32]

In my view, however, the conflict is actually between different aspects of freedom—its forward-looking aspect, as embodied in Fairjoy's aim to do what he pleases now and in the future, and its backward-looking aspect, as embodied in Truview's desire to protect the fruits of his past labors in order to continue realizing his own goals. Positive freedom—autonomy—is not merely the capacity to choose, willy-nilly, what one wants to do here and now. It is also and more fundamentally the capacity to commit oneself to an overarching project that will take years to realize, with each new step building upon the last. In such cases, constructing the future requires protecting the foundational achievements of the past.

A further problem with Feinberg's approach is that it fails to acknowledge a social component to both the exercise and protection of autonomy, even with respect to the forward-looking aspect outlined earlier. More specifically, it is a mistake to construe autonomy only in a way that places it in opposition to tradition, community, and culture. It is impossible to preserve a political community committed to autonomy unless that commitment is collectively passed down from generation to generation. Transmitting that commitment requires constant efforts in order to articulate the moral value of autonomy in new contexts and to communicate the rationale for giving autonomy political protection even in situations where restrictions on freedom seem to be the most practical and efficient way of organizing civil life.[33]

Finally, it should be clear by now that the individual's exercise of freedom—particularly positive freedom—cannot exist without significant social commitment. Raz helps us to see why. He argues that individual autonomy has three fundamental requirements: (1) the raw mental capacity to make and carry out choices; (2) freedom from attempts at manipulation as well as from coercion on the part of other people; and (3) a range of morally worthwhile choices from which to choose.[34]

Feinberg's individualistic theory can certainly account for some aspects of Raz's second requirement. Raz, like Feinberg, does not believe that coercion ought to be used to discourage nonharmful opportunities, even if they are not morally worthwhile. He thinks that coercion "violates the condition of independence and expresses a relation of domination and an attitude of disrespect for the coerced individual."[35] Moreover, coercion by means of criminal penalties is a "global and indiscriminate invasion of authority" since imprisonment is inconsistent with almost all autonomous pursuits.[36] At the same time, Raz emphasizes that the harm principle is not an end in itself but a limitation on the means used by the state in promoting its ends. Consequently, in his hands, it does not function as an absolute barrier but as the fulcrum of a balancing test. The greater the invasion of autonomy involved, the greater the state's justification must be. Raz writes: "This vindication of the [harm] principle goes hand in hand with its demotion. It is not to be seen as the whole but merely as a part of a doctrine of freedom, the core of which is the promotion of the conditions of autonomy."[37]

The state, in Raz's view, "has the duty not merely to prevent denial of freedom, but also to promote it by creating the conditions of autonomy."[38] Unlike Feinberg, Raz frames the harm principle in a way that can help us assess and appreciate the various ways that the noncriminal law infringes upon individual choice. Because it is ultimately in service of positive liberty, the harm principle, in his view, allows "full scope to autonomy-based duties," such as the duty of the state to promote the autonomy of its citizens. Taxes are permissible because "the government has an obligation to create an environment providing individuals with an adequate range of options and the opportunities to choose them."[39] Moreover, tax policy legitimately incentivizes morally worthwhile and socially beneficial options because perfectionist considerations dominate when we are trying to decide which options should be encouraged.[40]

For Raz, then, unlike for Feinberg, the "primary concern is the promotion and protection of positive freedom which is understood as the capacity for autonomy, consisting of the availability of an adequate range of options, and of the mental abilities necessary for an autonomous life."[41] Consequently, Feinberg cannot account as well for Raz's first and third requirements for enabling individuals to exercise autonomy, which I briefly identified earlier. Most basically, Raz's requirements suggest that a society committed to raising children to become autonomous members of community will have to ensure that the children have a secure and nurturing environment so that they are physically and psychologically equipped to assume responsibility for their adult lives. That forward-looking society will need to provide high-quality education that not only refrains from manipulating the children but also gives them the tools to recognize manipulation on the part of others. Raz does not see the necessary formation as value neutral; children must acquire the "character traits essential or helpful for a life of autonomy," including "stability, loyalty, and the ability to form personal attachments and to maintain intimate relationships."[42]

In addition, a society that values autonomy must foster the development of a sufficient range of morally worthwhile options from which persons may choose as substrates to shape their own identities. Raz observes that coercion and manipulation are not the only threats to the exercise autonomy; a lack of a sufficient array of positive options also undermines it, as his two imaginary cases make clear. "The Man in the Pit" has fallen into a small, deep hole in the ground, where he must remain for the rest of his life. He has enough food and water. But "his choices are confined to whether to eat now or a little later, whether to sleep now or a little later, whether to scratch his left ear or not."[43] "The Hounded Woman," in contrast, is trapped on a small island with a carnivorous beast; she must use all of her mental and physical energies to evade its deadly bite. Raz observes that neither person has sufficient options to count as autonomous, although their problems are quite different. The Man in the Pit only has trivial choices available to him, while the Hounded Woman's choices are all "potentially horrendous in their consequences."[44]

Raz recognizes that the vast majority of options possessing sufficient attractiveness to shape an individual life cannot exist outside the creative and constructive social context of a group; they are not otherwise open to isolated individuals. For example, there is no law that explicitly prohibits a young boy from aspiring to become a medieval knight.[45] Nonetheless, that option is not available to him because the broader social context undergirding that role, as well as the particular understanding of honor, virtue, and loyalty that animate knighthood, have long faded into the past. A young boy can wish he were a medieval knight, or even go to great lengths in pretending to be one. He cannot, however, actually become the genuine article. Many of the contemporary world's professions that shape an individual's identity also require the maintenance of elaborate social structures; for example, one cannot become an auto mechanic, a radiation oncologist, an astronaut, a race-car driver, or a nuclear power plant operator without the existence of a particular range of socially supported practices, institutions, and values. One cannot even become a wife or a husband without the social institution of marriage, which may or may not also be reflected and supported in legal institutions.[46]

Raz's three conditions for the exercise of autonomy—pointing beyond Feinberg's rather stark image of the individual constructing his own identity in isolation—lead to a richer vision of the person situated in and interacting with a community in order to develop an identity that draws equally upon his internal, unique talents and motivations as well as those opportunities provided by the broader society. Consequently, Raz's multifaceted approach encourages us to move beyond an artificial opposition between individual self-fulfillment and communal claims and commitments. In fact, he remarks that "the morally good person is he whose prosperity is so intertwined with the pursuit of goals which advance intrinsic values and the well-being of others that it is impossible to separate his personal well-being from his moral concerns."[47]

Here a bridge can be built between secular liberal legal theory and Catholic social teaching, in particular the notion of "solidarity" that gained prominence in the writing of Pope John Paul II. In his 1989 encyclical *Sollicitudo rei socialis*, he offers the following definition: "[Solidarity] then is not a feeling of vague compassion or shallow distress at the misfortunes of so many people, both near and far. On the contrary, it is a firm and persevering determination to commit oneself to the common good; that is to say to the good of all and of each individual, because we are all really responsible for all."[48]

The virtue of solidarity, as understood in contemporary Catholic thought, has three fundamental components that correspond to and supplement Raz's conditions for true human autonomy in ways that are very illuminating.[49] First, solidarity requires us to meet the basic needs of each person inasmuch as that person is not only an abstract chooser but also a being who is an integrated unity of body and soul. Second, solidarity requires us to recognize the nature of each person as essentially social. The role of society is to draw every individual out of isolation and into the community in a healthy way, thereby preparing each person to act and to respond in a manner that leads to the flourishing of both the individual and the community. Third, solidarity requires us to provide vehicles through which all persons can contribute to the community through the expression and development of their own talents and interests.[50] Needless to say, this third requirement must not be interpreted in a way that reduces the individual to a cog in the machine dominated by the collective; this "contribution to the community" must be understood in a fashion that takes full account of the often painful need to critique and reform the structures and norms of a community for its ultimate benefit and for the benefit of those living within it. Nonetheless, this requirement forces us to recognize that human flourishing generally requires the development of some ultimately positive, even if at times difficult and complex, relationship between individuals and the broader communities to which they belong.

LAW AS MORAL TEACHER

If Feinberg's "law as police officer" approach is inadequate, is there a way of understanding the nature and function of positive law that can better accommodate the complicated relationship between individual freedom and communal values and opportunities? I believe "law as moral teacher" provides a better model—a model that realizes law does far more than set up "fences" to protect each citizen's freedom from invasion by another. Instead, this model recognizes, emphasizes, and takes responsibility for the fact that human law communicates something to its subjects about the ways in which they should and should not go about living their lives. I believe that the jurisprudential challenge currently facing us is to take responsibility for the law's pedagogical function in contemporary societies in a realistic and nuanced way. Always and inevitably, the law teaches. What, then, should be its lessons?

St. Thomas Aquinas provides us with helpful tools to address this question in his treatise on law in the *Summa theologica*.[51] More specifically, in considering human law, he shows how it can lead men and women to virtue in order to promote the common good.[52] In proposing such a vision of law, Aquinas is no ivory-tower idealist. His theory is quite capable of accommodating the fact that legal systems are not designed for communities of the morally perfect, or even those with an average moral character. At the same time, however, Aquinas maintains that one of the functions of the positive law is to facilitate the moral growth of those subjected to its strictures.

The striking combination of moral realism and moral aspiration is the most compelling feature of Aquinas's legal theory, and it makes it a useful source of insight in addressing the contemporary situation. In addition, it is precisely this combination that allows us to highlight significant points of contact between Aquinas's work and that of contemporary legal theorists, even liberal legal theorists. More specifically, I suggest that bringing Aquinas's legal theory into critical conversation with the work of Joseph Raz yields a number of fruitful avenues for considering how law can function as a moral teacher even in societies that value individual autonomy.[53]

Aquinas describes the purpose of law in the following manner: "It is evident that the proper effect of law is to lead its subjects to their proper virtue: and since virtue is *that which makes its subject good*, it follows that the proper effect of law is to make those to whom it is given, good, either simply or in some particular respect."[54] He goes on to explain that the purpose of human law is to make its subjects "good" with respect to the values of a particular government—of a particular political community.[55] For example, he would argue that the legal systems of both Nazi Germany and the contemporary United Kingdom aim to make their subjects "good" in a formal sense, although the material content of "goodness" in the two regimes varies substantially. Indeed, what was "good" in Nazi Germany is now nearly universally condemned as deeply evil. In that sense, the "law as moral teacher" approach recognizes the intimate connection between legal theory and political theory. In many cases, the most urgent object of critique and reform is not the existence or lack of existence of particular laws but the fundamental values of the political system enacting those laws to further its own vision of both the polis and the individual good citizen living within the system.

The fact that Aquinas understands positive law as a teacher, and, more specifically, as a teacher of virtue, does not mean that he perceives the political community's coercive and regulatory aspects to operate in the same manner as a Sunday morning catechism class designed to produce pious and well-behaved citizens in a nice suburban community. Aquinas is far too realistic about the unwieldiness of human nature, as well as the inevitable clumsiness of the tools provided by positive law, to make such a mistake. He fully recognizes that there must be both practical and moral limitations on the power of positive law.

Both sorts of limitations are evident in a key passage that Aquinas quotes from Isidore of Seville, which articulates the range of qualities that good law must demonstrate: "Law shall be virtuous, just, possible to nature, according to the custom of the country, suitable to place and time, necessary, useful; clearly expressed, lest by its obscurity it lead to misunderstanding; framed for no private benefit but for the common good."[56]

The requirement that the law be "according to the custom of the country," for example, indicates that governmental officials should not use the law as a tool to implement their own vision of the perfect community, without any regard for the particular practices to which their subjects have become accustomed in living their respective lives. The stricture that law be "suitable to place and time" expresses sensitivity to the fact that, in some cases, different rules are appropriate to guide behavior in different circumstances. It also allows that different modes of enforcing the same rule may be called for in different times and places. The mandates that the law be "necessary" and "useful" focus our attention on both the practical nature of law and the costs of enacting and enforcing it. Law is not merely the window-dressing of power; it should not be enacted merely to serve as a verbal monument to the influence of the lawgiver. At best, an unnecessary or useless law will be left unenforced, thereby eroding the general respect for law present within the community. At worst, it will be duly enforced—creating resentment that the limited resources of the legal system are used in such a senseless manner. Finally, the demand that law be clearly expressed reminds lawmakers that the primary purpose is to guide the action of its subjects in a way that furthers the common good; a law whose requirements are delineated in only a vague manner may inadvertently encourage persons to engage in actions that impede rather than promote the worthy objectives of the lawgiver.

In addition to these practical limitations, Isidore's list of criteria also points to a number of important moral limitations with which sound law must comply. First, in saying that law must be "possible to nature," Isidore hints at a requirement that Aquinas then articulates far more explicitly: the strictures of the criminal law should be designed for ordinary persons, not for saints.

The law is a moral teacher, but the curriculum is not advanced; the law offers only the most elementary lessons in the ways of virtue. Aquinas states, for example, that a primary purpose of the criminal law is to provide those who are too obstinate to be trained by friends and family with a forceful introduction to the rudiments of virtue, which largely consist of refraining from the major vices.[57] In my view, a rich, Thomistic vision of "law as moral teacher" can account for many of the most persuasive aspects of Feinberg's vision of law, particularly his insight that the tools of the criminal law must be used sparingly. In fact, Aquinas and Feinberg might agree that it would be a mistake to invoke the strictures of the criminal law against most of the items on Feinberg's list of "free-floating evils." However, in Aquinas's framework, it would be a mistake not because, or not only because, the actions in question are not wrongful harms but because using criminal law in this context would violate Isidore's criteria for good law—regardless of whether the wrongs are harmful. Applying the Isidore–Aquinas criteria for the practical limitations of law to some of Feinberg's examples, consider how the government would detect and prosecute such actions as the wanton squishing of a small bug in the wild. Similarly, devoting the scarce resources of the criminal justice system to defining and prosecuting offenses such as general environmental ugliness or drabness seems unjustifiable.

More important, the Thomistic pedagogical concern of seeing law as a teacher of virtue presses us to ask what the enforcement of certain prohibitions would do not only to the alleged perpetrator but also to the police officers and governmental attorneys charged with detecting and prosecuting the actions in question. For example, Feinberg worries about the psychological and emotional damage done to those charged with having had "impure thoughts," or those who are arrested for performing certain consensual acts in private.[58] The "law as moral teacher" approach would share those worries. It would also, however, expand the sphere of concern to include an assessment of how the actual mechanics of detecting, arresting, and prosecuting such behavior would affect the character of the governmental actors charged with doing so. What kind of habits, what kind of relationships with other people, would these government officials develop in the course of doing their jobs?

Those who advocate a Thomistic view of "law as moral teacher" must of course be prepared to articulate and defend the range of virtues they believe the law should teach. If law is to function as a teacher of virtues, which ones should be considered within the scope of its pedagogy? To answer this question, we need to take a step back and reflect on the general purpose of a legal regime. According to Aquinas, an overarching aim of law is to promote the common good, not merely the flourishing of individuals considered in isolation from their broader social and familial context. Aquinas's detailed account of the common good is deeply imbued with the hierarchical presuppositions of his own social and political order; for that reason it is unsuitable as a blueprint for our own liberal democratic community. Nonetheless, we can make fruitful use of his more general insights about the relationship of law, virtue, and the common good.

The virtue most relevant to law is, of course, justice, which Aquinas defines as "a habit whereby a man renders to each one his due (*ius suum*) by a constant and perpetual will."[59] It is important to note that the virtue orients itself to a matter that is external to the agent—what is due to others. Justice directs our attention to the actual effects that our actions have upon the lives, property, and interests of other people. Aquinas notes that it is "in respect of external actions and external things by means of which men can communicate with one another, that the relation of one man to another is to be considered."[60] For this reason, I think it makes sense to call justice an external virtue.

As Aquinas also recognizes, there are two aspects to the virtue of justice because agents can relate to others through their external actions in two ways. First, particular justice concentrates on the ways our actions affect relationships with other private individuals.[61] Second, general justice, sometimes called legal justice, describes the relationship of our actions toward others with respect to the common good."[62] The two aspects of justice are enmeshed; individuals are part of the community, so acts that wrongly detract from their well-being affect the well-being of the whole community. Moreover, what actually counts as detracting from the well-being of another needs to be identified while keeping in mind the fact that the person's identity stems in part from their participation in community, including the political community.

Legal justice is a general virtue not because it constitutes part of each virtue by definition but because it directs the acts of all the virtues toward the common good.[63] Its focus is not the inner disposition of the acting agents but instead the manifest situation of right relations that ideally would be produced when such agents act virtuously. Accordingly, the law targets its strictures at externally directed actions that disturb the appropriate situation of right relations between and among various members of society, not on actions primarily affecting the internal realm of a person's character.[64] At the same time, in Aquinas's account, the law has a gravitational thrust that extends beyond enforcing the basic requirements of a network of rightly ordered relationships. Although the law's coercive energies are generally triggered only by violations of justice, its pedagogical message must emphasize the importance of the other cardinal virtues as well because people who lack those virtues even in the most rudimentary form are the most likely to violate the norms of justice. For example, in the first instance, excessively daring people lack the virtue of fortitude, which is a virtuous mean between cowardice and recklessness. While such a deficiency is bad for their character, it does not in itself fall within the sphere of the positive law. However, excessively daring persons are often prone to taking disproportionate risks, thereby unjustly inflicting harm upon others.[65]

In other words, legal justice calls for a network of right relationships mediated through external goods and actions. That network cannot be honored and protected by a citizenry utterly lacking fortitude and temperance, which regulate the passions that often propel persons to violate the rights of others. As Aquinas says, "temperance intends that man should not stray from reason for the sake of his concupiscences; fortitude, that he should not stray from the right judgment of reason through fear or daring."[66] But getting rid of the barriers imposed by desire, fear, or rashness is not enough. We still need to discern what right judgment actually does require in particular cases. Aquinas says that "it belongs to the ruling of prudence to decide in what manner and by what means man shall obtain the mean of reason in his deeds."[67] Even persons who are committed to rendering each other their due will fail if they do not possess the reliable habit of evaluating what they owe each other in concrete cases and assessing what course of action will best fulfill their obligations. Directing that evaluation is the job of prudence.

In short, while the strictures of law must be focused on violations of justice, the moral message animating and supporting the laws must encompass and promote the three other cardinal virtues as well. The web of right relationships mandated by justice cannot be promoted and protected by a citizenry that lacks prudence, fortitude, and temperance.[68]

The cardinal virtues, of course, mark the character of a virtuous person who lives in any time and place, although the precise shape they take (as well the particular vices opposed to them) can vary substantially across eras and cultures. In my view, however, in cultures such as that of the contemporary United States, the law also needs to teach and support two virtues particularly appropriate to our time and place: autonomy (understood in Joseph Raz's terms) and solidarity (understood in the terms of Catholic social teaching). Without denying the existence of significant tensions between these two realms of thought, I nonetheless believe that bringing Catholic social thought into conversation with the work of perfectionist liberal legal theorists such as Joseph Raz highlights ways in which both are mutually necessary.

THE INTERACTION OF AUTONOMY AND SOLIDARITY: THE AMERICANS WITH DISABILITIES ACT

The conception of "law as moral teacher," rather than that of "law as police officer," explains some of the most important pieces of legislation enacted in the United States in the second half of the twentieth century, including the Civil Rights Acts, the Family and Medical Leave Act, and the Americans with Disabilities Act.[69] These pieces of legislation share four important characteristics. First, they all adopt a normative and holistic attitude toward the function of law; in other words, each law gestures toward a vision of how the citizens of the United States should live their lives in common. None of the laws narrowly targets a disjointed set of wrongful harms in the manner contemplated by the "law as police officer" model. Second, the laws do not attempt to penalize the citizens for failing to exhibit the full range of relevant virtues. As Aquinas recommends, they instead generally limit requirements and proscriptions to specified external actions; they do not extend their coercive force to reach the full range of internal acts that a fully virtuous person would manifest. Third, each piece of legislation signals the hope that the subjects of the law will move beyond mere compliance with the external requirements of the law to appreciate the broader vision of community that it wishes to encourage. Fourth, that broader vision of community exemplifies the fruitful relationship between autonomy and solidarity.

To explain more fully how these four key features of the "law as moral teacher" approach play out in a concrete situation, I take as my example the Americans with Disabilities Act (ADA), which was enacted in 1990.[70] The ADA's purpose is encapsulated in the name of the law: the sponsors chose Americans with Disabilities Act rather than Disabled Americans Act. In so doing, the legislators emphasized the law's paramount goal of encouraging Americans—when they encounter fellow citizens unable to walk, unable to see or hear normally, or unable to perceive and process information in the way that most people do—to see the whole person before they see the disability.

As part of its pedagogy, the ADA begins by reflecting at length upon the status of persons with disabilities in the contemporary United States. In its section "Findings and Purposes," the ADA states that "some 43,000,000 Americans have one or more physical or mental disabilities, and this number is increasing as the population as a whole is growing older."[71] It also finds that "individuals with disabilities are a discrete and insular minority who have been faced with restrictions and limitations, subjected to a history of purposeful unequal treatment, and relegated to a position of political powerlessness in our society, based on characteristics that are beyond the control of such individuals and resulting from stereotypic assumptions not truly indicative of the individual ability of such individuals to participate in, and contribute to, society."[72]

The ADA goes on to state its fundamental purpose: "The Nation's proper goals regarding individuals with disabilities are to assure equality of opportunity, full participation, independent living, and economic self-sufficiency for such individuals."[73] Note how closely the ADA's goals correspond to Raz's requirements for autonomy, particularly his second and third requirements. Individuals with disabilities are not to be coerced or manipulated; ideally, they should achieve a level of independence with respect to their living and working arrangements that will prevent them from being utterly dependent upon the whims, wishes, and good will of others. Moreover, in calling for "equality of opportunity" and "full participation," the ADA clearly recognizes that persons with disabilities, if they are to exercise their autonomy in a fruitful manner, need a range of worthwhile options from which to choose.

Note, as well, the intimate connections between autonomy and solidarity with respect to the purposes of the ADA; it presupposes both that persons with disabilities need the assistance of the community in order for their autonomy to develop and flourish, and that the community will benefit from the exercise of their talents in turn. In contrast, the negative conception of freedom generally associated with the "law as police officer" approach is virtually absent from the ADA. It is not, of course, that the negative freedom is irrelevant for persons with disabilities. They too need protection against wrongful harms. It is simply that negative freedom is nowhere near sufficient to enable such persons to participate in and contribute to their communities. "Leaving them alone" is not enough to let them flourish; they need to be actively included so that their disabilities do not impede them from engaging in worthwhile activities. Moreover, once we see how autonomy and solidarity can be mutually supportive of persons with disabilities, we may reconsider how the two values interact in the lives of "normal" persons, newly appreciating the ways in which flourishing of their autonomy also requires the support and contribution of the community.

The specific mandates of the ADA must be understood in light of its general purposes. The provisions are not isolated prohibitions or requirements but are fundamental planks in an integrated program that articulates and partially implements a vision of the common good that precludes the marginalization of persons with disabilities. The ADA covers two basic aspects of social existence: employment and accommodation in public facilities. In the employment context, covered by subchapter 1, the general rule provides that no employer shall discriminate against "an otherwise qualified individual with a disability." This requirement, however, is not merely a negative prohibition against discrimination; it also encompasses a positive requirement that the employer "make reasonable accommodation to the known physical or mental limitations of an otherwise qualified individual with a disability who is an applicant or employee"—unless accommodation would cause undue hardship.[74]

It is necessary, but not sufficient, to enable persons with disabilities to take their place in the work world. It is also essential to allow them to participate more generally in the public sphere, to become active and visible parts of the common life of the community. Subchapter 2 of the ADA requires those operating public transportation to adopt plans to ensure they have equal access. Subchapter 3 imposes significant obligations on private entities that operate public accommodations and services. By "public accommodation" the ADA means to include all the business establishments most people patronize as part of their day-to-day lives: hotels, restaurants, movie theaters, Laundromats, hairdressers, museums, parks, and the offices of doctors and other professionals.[75] It prohibits such establishments from discriminating against persons with disabilities—including by providing them with less-than-equal services and by separating them from persons who have no disabilities. It also requires covered establishments to remove physical barriers that prevent persons with disabilities from having physical access, unless doing so would fundamentally alter the nature of the establishments, would result in an undue burden upon the business, or would not be readily achievable.

The enforcement mechanisms of the ADA are modeled on those included in the Civil Rights Acts; they include equitable relief, including injunctive relief, as well as monetary damages. Unlike the Civil Rights Acts, the ADA does not impose criminal penalties for the most egregious violations of the law; if such provisions were deemed necessary to deter the worst forms of discrimination against persons with disabilities, the legislature could amend the law later to incorporate the penalties.

While the ADA is animated by and communicates a normative vision about the place of persons with disabilities within the broader community, it does not attempt to immediately realize each and every element of that vision by using the coercive force of the law. The world the ADA regulates, unlike the world it aspires to create, is significantly flawed. For example, the ADA includes no requirement of affirmative action on behalf of persons with disabilities. It does nothing to change the fact that governmental employment services for adults with disabilities frequently focus on those who suffer from the least severe problems and who therefore are likely to count as "success stories" in the annual report of the relevant agencies without much effort on the agency's part.

Nonetheless, the ADA does teach by gesturing beyond its requirements to its aspirations. Taken together, the law's three prongs attempt to bring into existence a culture where "normal" persons, more accustomed to seeing persons with disabilities in public places, have overcome any sense of discomfort with respect to persons with disabilities. That, in turn, eventually may encourage everyone to begin looking beyond disabilities to see very real abilities, which could greatly benefit the broader community. Once this stage is reached, those who are legally bound by the ADA's strictures (and those who are not) may find themselves willing to go beyond the law's technical requirements in order to begin realizing its ultimate goals. In other words, the ADA points us toward and attempts to teach us to participate in an expansive vision of economic and social participation of persons with disabilities, a vision that the law itself only partially instantiates.

The ADA's normative vision is diametrically opposed to the vision animating the ugly law, with which I began this chapter. The ADA pursues autonomy, as generally understood in Joseph Raz's terms, and solidarity, as generally understood in the terms of Pope John Paul II. In the words of the latter: "Solidarity helps us to see the 'other'—whether a person, people or nation—not just as some kind of instrument, with a work capacity and physical strength to be exploited at low cost and then discarded when no longer useful, but as our 'neighbor,' a 'helper' (cf. Gen 2:18–20), to be made a sharer, on a par with ourselves, in the banquet of life to which all are equally invited by God."[76]

LAW'S MORAL PEDAGOGY: A BALANCE OF MORAL REALISM AND MORAL IDEALISM

This chapter lays the foundation for the consideration of more specific—and more controversial—questions of the relationship of law and morality to be considered more fully in later chapters. I show here that a theoretically and culturally dominant understanding of law's nature and purpose—"law as police officer"—is actually far too narrow to account for many important pieces of American federal legislation. The Civil Rights Acts, the Family and Medical Leave Act, and the Americans with Disabilities Act do much more than simply enforce boundaries protecting the rights of individual citizens against encroachment by one another. They also propose a positive moral vision of our communal life, a vision that emphasizes engagement with one another rather than isolation. The normative orientation of such laws, I argue, is better captured by an understanding of "law as moral teacher" than by "law as police officer."

To claim that it is appropriate to view law as a moral teacher immediately raises additional questions. Foremost among these questions is, in pluralistic liberal democracies such as our own, what virtues should law teach? I argue that two overarching virtues ought to guide lawmakers in societies such as the United States: autonomy, understood in Joseph Raz's terms, and solidarity, understood in the terms of Pope John Paul II. These special understandings exhibit fruitful convergences and powerfully illuminate the moral vision behind legislation such as the Americans with Disabilities Act.

How rigorously should the civil law propose its lessons? On this question, I suggest that the insights of Aquinas's treatise on law can be very helpful, even in our own era. Civil law can neither dictate all virtuous actions nor prohibit all vices; in the main, its lessons must be geared to persons of ordinary virtue. Its most severe sanctions, the sanctions of the criminal law, must be applied to reinforce its most basic, remedial lessons. Severe sanctions should be used to reinforce and maintain a moral consensus, not to establish a brand-new consensus. Less severe tools, such as the incentives of tort law, administrative law, and tax law, can be used to direct society in a more morally appropriate direction, without provoking a counterproductive backlash. As Aquinas recognized, sound law must be geared to the custom of the country; the very legitimacy of law itself is threatened if legal sanctions, particularly criminal sanctions, are ignored by large numbers of the citizenry. Consequently, effective governmental response to widespread social injustice such as racism or other forms of discrimination needs to encompass a broad array of legal tools, not merely criminal prohibitions. All these tools, however, ought to be deployed in order to move, albeit gradually, toward a society in which individuals help define and contribute to their own flourishing in community—toward a society more deeply committed to autonomy and solidarity.

What are the special challenges that face the understanding of law as a moral teacher in a society such as our own, in which there is significant disagreement about the requirements of morality in a wide range of cases? How should we deal with situations where legally enforcing the basic requirements of justice seems practically impossible in a particular time and place? I will turn to these questions in the next chapters.

NOTES

This chapter is based on M. Cathleen Kaveny, "Autonomy, Solidarity and Law's Pedagogy," *Louvain Studies* 27, no. 4 (Winter 2002) 339–58.

1. Chicago Municipal Code, § 36034 (repealed 1974).
2. Columbus, Ohio General Offense Code, § 2387.04 (1972); Unsightly Beggar Ordinance, Omaha, Nebraska Municipal Code of 1941, § 25 (1967). See also Marcia Pearce Burgdorf and Robert Burgdorf Jr., "A History of Unequal Treatment: The

Qualifications of Handicapped Persons as a 'Suspect Class' under the Equal Protection Clause," *Santa Clara Lawyer* 15 (1975): 855–910. A recent volume looks at the history of this type of legislation: Susan Schweik, *The Ugly Laws: Disability in Public* (New York: New York University Press, 2009).

3. As will become clear as this book progresses, liberal legal theorists have developed a number of very different ways of articulating the meaning, requirements, and limitations of "individual liberty." John Stuart Mill, *On Liberty* (1859; repr. ed. New York: Penguin, 1974). A key late-twentieth-century discussion was sparked by debates among Patrick Devlin, H. L. A. Hart, and Lon Fuller. See Patrick Devlin, *The Enforcement of Morals*, 2nd ed. (Oxford: Oxford University Press, 1968); H. L. A. Hart, *Law, Liberty, and Morality* (Stanford, CA: Stanford University Press, 1963); and Lon Fuller, *The Morality of Law*, rev. ed. (New Haven, CT: Yale University Press, 1969).

4. Joel Feinberg, *The Moral Limits of the Criminal Law*, vol. 1, *Harm to Others* (New York: Oxford University Press, 1987), 9.

5. Joel Feinberg, *The Moral Limits of the Criminal Law*, 4 vols. (New York: Oxford University Press, 1984–88).

6. For a helpful overview, see, e.g., Brian Bix, *Jurisprudence: Theory and Context*, 5th ed. (Durham, NC: Carolina Academic Press, 2009). For a comprehensive anthology, see M. D. A. Freeman, ed., *Lloyd's Introduction to Jurisprudence*, 8th ed. (London: Sweet & Maxwell 2008). A more technical treatment is Gerald J. Postema's *Legal Philosophy in the Twentieth Century: The Common Law World*, vol. 11, *A Treatise of Legal Philosophy and General Jurisprudence*, ed. Enrico Pattaro (Dordrecht: Springer, 2011). Particular topics are explored in depth in Jules Coleman and Scott Shapiro, eds., *The Oxford Handbook of Jurisprudence and Philosophy of Law* (Oxford: Oxford University Press, 2002). A magisterial overview from the perspective of the leading exponent of the "new natural law theory" is John Finnis, "A Grand Tour of Legal Theory (2002)," in *Philosophy of Law*, vol. 4 of his *Collected Essays* (Oxford: Oxford University Press, 2011), 91–156.

7. I have discussed the relationship of rights language and virtue language in M. Cathleen Kaveny, "Imagination, Virtue, and Human Rights: Lessons from Australian and American Law," *Theological Studies* 70, no. 1 (March 2009): 109–39.

8. See, e.g., John Finnis, *Natural Law and Natural Rights*; (Oxford: Oxford University Press, 1980), 267; and John Finnis, *Aquinas* (Oxford: Oxford University Press, 1998) Robert P. George, *Making Men Moral: Civil Liberties and Public Morality* (Oxford: Oxford University Press, 1995); Russell Hittinger, *A Critique of the New Natural Law Theory* (Notre Dame, IN: University of Notre Dame Press, 1989); Mark C. Murphy, *Natural Law and Practical Rationality* (Cambridge: Cambridge University Press, 2001); Mark C. Murphy, *Natural Law in Jurisprudence and Politics* (Cambridge: Cambridge University Press, 2006); Jean Porter, *The Recovery of Virtue: The Relevance of Aquinas for Christian Ethics* (Louisville, KY: Westminster/John Knox Press, 1990); Jean Porter, *Natural and Divine Law: Reclaiming the Tradition for Christian Ethics* (Grand Rapids, MI: Eerdmans, 1999); and Jean Porter, *Ministers of the Law: A Natural Law Theory of Legal Authority* (Grand Rapids, MI: Eerdmans, 2010).

9. How, exactly, does human law function to lead people to virtue? In my view, Anglo-American law functions much like a tradition as defined by Alasdair MacIntyre, in

which conceptions of virtue, character, action, and practice are intertwined. See, e.g., M. Cathleen Kaveny, "Listening for the Future in the Voices of the Past: John T. Noonan, Jr. on Love and Power in Human History." *Journal of Law and Religion* 11, no. 1 (1994–1995): 203–28.

10. See Feinberg, *Moral Limits of the Criminal Law*, vol. 2, *Offense to Others*. I discuss Feinberg's understanding of offense in M. Cathleen Kaveny, "Obscenity, Communal Values, and the Law: Joel Feinberg and the Failure of Liberalism," *Annual of the Society of Christian Ethics* (1989): 93–112.

11. Feinberg, *Moral Limits of the Criminal Law*, vol. 4, *Harmless Wrongdoing*, xxvii–xxix.

12. Feinberg, *Harm to Others*, chap. 1.

13. Ibid., 37.

14. Ibid., chap. 3.

15. Ibid., 115–18.

16. Ibid., 4.

17. For a summary of Feinberg's position, see Feinberg, *Harmless Wrongdoing*, ix–xx. The core of his position is found in the first three items in his list of liberty-limiting principles on page xix.

> 1. *The Harm Principle:* It is always a good reason in support of penal legislation that it would be effective in preventing (eliminating, reducing) harm to persons other than the actor (the one prohibited from acting) *and* there is no other means that is equally effective at no greater cost to other values.*
>
> 2. *The Offense Principle:* It is always a good reason in support of a proposed criminal prohibition that it is necessary to prevent serious offense to persons other than the actor and would be an effective means to that end if enacted.†
>
> 3. *The Liberal Position* (on the moral limits of the criminal law): The harm and offense principles, duly clarified and qualified, between them exhaust the class of good reasons for criminal prohibitions. ("The extreme liberal position" is that only the harm principle states a good reason . . .)
>
> * The clause following "and" is abbreviated in the subsequent definitions as "it is necessary for . . . ," or "the need to . . ." Note also that part of a conjunctive reason ("effective *and* necessary") is itself a "reason," that is, itself has some relevance in support of the legislation.
>
> † The clause following "and" goes without saying in the subsequent definitions, but it is understood. All the definitions have a common form: *X* is necessary to achieve *Y* (as spelled out in definition 1) and is an effective means for producing *Y* (as stated explicitly in definitions 1 and 2).

18. Feinberg, *Harm to Others*, 115–18.

19. Feinberg, *Harmless Wrongdoing*, 20–25.

20. Ibid., chap. 29.

21. See 18 USC § 981 (2006).

22. I develop my critique of Feinberg's theory in more detail in M. Cathleen Kaveny, "Ethics/Civil Law and the New Millennium," in *Ethical Dilemmas in the New*

Millennium (I), ed. Francis A. Eigo, OSA, 161–88 (Villanova, PA: Villanova University Press, 2000).

23. For representative and to a certain extent canonical works within this tradition, see H. L. A. Hart, *The Concept of Law*, 2nd ed. (Oxford: Oxford University Press, 1994); Ronald Dworkin, *Law's Empire* (Cambridge, MA: Harvard University Press, 1986); and Finnis, *Natural Law and Natural Rights*.

24. Raz's work on perfectionist liberalism, of course, is extensive and merits careful study. See also Raz, *Ethics in the Public Domain*; Raz, *Engaging Reason: On the Theory of Value and Action* (Oxford: Oxford University Press, 1999); and Raz, *Value, Respect, and Attachment* (Cambridge: Cambridge University Press, 2001). See also Raz, *The Practice of Value* (Oxford: Oxford University Press, 2005), which includes Raz's 2001 Berkeley Tanner Lectures on Human Values, published with comments by Christine M. Korsgaard, Robert Pippin, and Bernard Williams. For a broader scholarly discussion of perfectionistic liberalism, see Steven Wall and George Klosko, eds., *Perfectionism and Neutrality: Essays in Liberal Theory* (Lanham, MD: Rowman & Littlefield, 2003). For a discussion of Raz's work see, e.g., R. Jay Wallace, Philip Pettit, Samuel Scheffler, and Michael Smith, eds., *Reason and Value: Themes from Moral Philosophy of Joseph Raz* (Oxford: Oxford University Press, 2004); and Lukas H. Meyer, Stanley L. Paulson, and Thomas W. Pogge, eds., *Rights, Culture, and the Law: Themes from the Legal and Political Philosophy of Joseph Raz* (Oxford: Oxford University Press, 2003).

25. Joseph Raz, *The Morality of Freedom* (New York: Oxford University Press, 1986), 410.

26. Ibid., 396.

27. Ibid., 379.

28. Ibid., 381.

29. See, e.g., Feinberg, *Harmless Wrongdoing*, chap. 29.

30. Raz, *Morality of Freedom*, 383.

31. Feinberg, *Harmless Wrongdoing*, 57–64.

32. Ibid., 61.

33. It is far more difficult to be committed to autonomy and civil rights in wartime than in times of peace. For example, during World War II the US government decided to intern more than one hundred thousand Japanese Americans in detainment camps to prevent them from assisting the enemy. See *Korematsu v. United States*, 323 US 214 (1944). In the current era, there are those who believe it would be expedient and efficient to place restrictions on persons of Arab descent to combat the threat of terrorism. Only a robust moral commitment to the importance of individual dignity and autonomy will act as an effective counterweight against such beliefs.

34. Raz, *Morality of Freedom*, chap. 14.

35. Ibid., 418.

36. Ibid.

37. Ibid., 420.

38. Ibid., 425.

39. Ibid., 417, 418–19.

40. Ibid.

41. Ibid., 425.

42. Ibid., 408.

43. Ibid., 374.

44. Ibid.

45. The theorist who has most vividly made this point is Alasdair MacIntyre. See his *Whose Justice? Which Rationality?* (Notre Dame, IN: University of Notre Dame, 1988).

46. Raz's account of the relationship between autonomy, virtues, roles, practices, and institutions also dovetails nicely with Alasdair MacIntyre's account of the socially embodied nature of virtue in *After Virtue* (Notre Dame: University of Notre Dame Press, 1981).

47. Raz, *Morality of Freedom*, 320.

48. Pope John Paul II, *Sollicitudo rei socialis* (*On Social Concern*) (1987), para. 38.

49. For other general explorations of the concept of solidarity in Catholic social thought, see Kenneth R. Himes, Lisa Sowle Cahill, Charles E. Curran, David Hollenbach, and Thomas Shannon, eds., *Modern Catholic Social Teaching: Commentaries and Interpretations* (Washington, DC: Georgetown University Press, 2005); Charles E. Curran, *The Moral Theology of Pope John Paul II* (Washington DC: Georgetown University Press, 2005); Curran, *Catholic Social Teaching, 1891–Present: A Historical, Theological, and Ethical Analysis* (Washington, DC: Georgetown University Press, 2002); Paulinus Odozor, *Moral Theology in an Age of Renewal: A Study of the Catholic Moral Tradition Since Vatican II* (Notre Dame, IN: University of Notre Dame Press, 2003); and David Hollenbach, SJ, *The Common Good and Christian Ethics* (Cambridge: Cambridge University Press, 2002). For more specific exploration of the concept of solidarity's roots in broader philosophical and geographical context, see Uzochukwu Jude Njoku, *Examining the Foundations of Solidarity in the Social Encyclicals of John Paul II* (Pieterlen, Switzerland: Peter Lang, 2006); Steinar Stjernø, *Solidarity in Europe: The History of an Idea* (Cambridge: Cambridge University Press, 2004); Arista Maria Cirtautas, *The Polish Solidarity Movement: Revolution, Democracy and Natural Rights* (London: Routledge, 1997); and Kevin P. Doran, *Solidarity: A Synthesis of Personalism and Communism in the Thought of Karol Wojtyla/Pope John Paul II* (Pieterlen, Switzerland: Peter Lang, 1996). Attempts to connect solidarity to the global human community include Hauke Brunkhorst, *Solidarity: From Civic Friendship to a Global Legal Community*, trans. Jeffrey Flynn (Cambridge, MA: MIT Press, 2005); and Vincent D. Rougeau, *Christians in the American Empire: Faith and Citizenship in the New World Order* (Oxford: Oxford University Press, 2008).

50. On the importance of work, see Christine Firer Hinze, "Economic Recession, Work, and Solidarity," *Theological Studies* 72, no. 1 (March 2011): 150–69.

51. Thomas Aquinas, *Summa theologica*, 3 vols., trans. Fathers of the English Dominican Province (New York: Benziger Bros., 1948), I-II, qq. 90–108.

52. Ibid., I-II, q. 90, art. 2, and q. 92, art.1.

53. A recent work by Jean Porter has also brought Raz as well as many other prominent legal philosophers into conversation with the larger Scholastic legal tradition, and Aquinas in particular. For her treatment and evaluation of some of Raz's central claims see *Ministers of Law*, 34–40.

54. Aquinas, *Summa theologica*, I-II, q. 92, art. 1. Italics in original quote from Aristotle.

55. Ibid.

56. Ibid., I-II, q. 95, art. 3.

57. Ibid., I-II, q. 96, art. 2.

58. See, e.g., Feinberg, *Harmless Wrongdoing*, 155.

59. Aquinas, *Summa theologica*, II-II, q. 58, art. 1.

60. Ibid., II-II, q. 58, art. 8.

61. Ibid., II-II, q. 58, arts. 7–8.

62. Ibid., II-II, q. 58, art. 5.

63. Ibid., II-II, q. 58, art. 6.

64. Ibid., I-II, q. 96, arts. 2 and 3, and II-II, q. 58, arts. 8 and 9.

65. Aquinas explains how this works in general terms at ibid., II-II, q. 58, art. 9.

66. Ibid., II-II, q. 47, art. 7.

67. Ibid.

68. Ibid., II-II, q. 58, art. 9.

69. Civil Rights Act of 1964, Pub. L. No. 88-352, 78 Stat. 241 (codified as amended in scattered sections of 28 and 42 USC); Civil Rights Act of 1968, Pub. L. No. 90-284, 82 Stat. 73 (codified at 25 USC §§ 1301–1341 [1994] and in scattered sections of 18, 28, and 42 USC); Family and Medical Leave Act of 1993, Pub. L. No. 103-3, 107 Stat. 6 (codified as amended at 2 USC §§ 60m–on; 3 USC §§ 2601, 2631, 2651 [1994]); and Americans with Disabilities Act (ADA), Pub. L. No. 101-336, 104 Stat. 328 (1990) (as amended in scattered sections of 29, 42, and 47 USC).

70. Article 26 of the Charter of Fundamental Rights of the European Union calls for the integration of persons with disabilities, recognizing their right to "benefit from measures designed to ensure their independence, social and occupational integration and participation in the life of the community." Article 13 of the Treaty of Amsterdam has given priority to the battle against all kinds of discrimination, including discrimination on the basis of disability. European Council Directive 2000/78/EC (November 27, 2000) establishes a general framework to fight discrimination, and calls for the social and economic integration of elderly and disabled people. As European countries are also following the lead of the ADA, much of my analysis could also apply outside the United States.

71. ADA, § 12101(1).

72. ADA, § 1201(7).

73. ADA, § 1201(8).

74. Needless to say, what constitutes an "undue hardship" is a heavily litigated issue, as is who falls into the category of "an otherwise qualified individual with a disability."

75. ADA, § 12181(7).

76. John Paul II, *Sollicitudo rei socialis*, para. 39.

CHAPTER 2

❧

Law and Morality

Understanding the Relationship

I T SEEMS AS IF EVERY COMPLICATED MORAL issue sooner or later becomes a legal issue, at least in the United States. Consider, for example, the recent tobacco litigation in which persons harmed by smoking and the states responsible for paying their costs sued tobacco companies for monetary damages.[1] The underlying moral question was whether tobacco companies should profit by selling such a dangerous product. This moral question immediately generated numerous legal questions. For example, why should we allow those harmed by smoking to sue the cigarette manufacturer under tort law? Does it matter if a smoker knew about the risks when he or she took up the habit? Suppose he or she was a minor at that time? Should states be able to recover from the tobacco companies the Medicaid dollars spent on persons who died of lung cancer caused by smoking? Or should the states save money by refusing coverage to anyone whose illness is largely attributable to individual faulty choices, such as excessive eating, drinking, or smoking?

Or think about the controversies currently surrounding homosexuality.[2] How do moral positions map onto legal ones? Is someone who thinks homosexual activity is immoral thereby committed to believing it should also be prohibited by the criminal law? At the other end of the spectrum, does internal consistency require a person who believes that homosexual activity is not morally different from heterosexual activity to support gay marriage as well? What about people in the muddled middle? What should their legal stance be?

Law and morality intersect in many other matters of grave public concern, such as affirmative action, the death penalty, and school choice. Nowhere have they become more hopelessly intertwined than in the case of abortion. Moreover, the entanglement is not likely to sort itself out any more easily with respect to the fruits of the human genome project or euthanasia. But we must make the effort. Understanding the relationship between law and morality in our pluralistic society will require finding our way between two opposite and equally damaging extremes.

We should not make the mistake of assuming that law and morality are coextensive, on the one hand, or of maintaining that they should have as little as possible to do with each other, on the other. In very different ways, both mistakes can be traced to the same fundamental problem: ignoring the full range of ways in which moral considerations enter into wise lawmaking. The first mistake is made by some activists—at all points on the political spectrum— who believe that the legal system should accurately mirror their normative vision of society in every respect. They treat any divergence between the two as an unfortunate compromise, to be overcome as soon as politically feasible. This approach tends to reduce the moral analysis of lawmaking to scrutiny of the actual content of the legal norm at issue. It assumes that all morally good acts should be required and all morally bad acts should be prohibited. This analysis wrongly treats an act of law almost as if it were an act of magic. It mistakenly assumes that by passing a law we can bring about a desired state of affairs instantaneously, without any effort, cost, or abuses.[3]

But this is not the case. The legal system is both administered by flawed individuals and institutions and applied to flawed individuals and institutions. Moreover, the law is not a collection of discrete elements but a complicated and interlocking web of prohibitions, permissions, and requirements. Making and enforcing laws are themselves human actions subject to moral and practical evaluation. Moral analysis of the human activity of lawmaking must take into account far more than the moral content of the law in question, considered in the abstract. It must also consider how the law will actually function in the particular time, place, and community that it purports to govern.

The opposite mistake is made by those who say that law has no business imposing or even promoting one or more particular visions of morality, that the law's purpose is simply to function as a police officer by preventing people from being harmed without their consent. I describe this approach, which is heavily indebted to the nineteenth-century liberal philosopher John Stuart Mill, in some detail in the first chapter.[4] According to its modern proponents, such as Joel Feinberg, the law should ban neither "harmless immoralities" nor even harmful activities to which all participants have consented.[5] This approach fails to grapple straightforwardly with the considerable influence that moral considerations do have on our views of what law is and of what it should be.

First, the "law as police officer" approach does not contend with the fact that there is substantial disagreement about what constitutes a harm that justifies legal intervention. As I note in the first chapter, Joel Feinberg attempts to avoid this problem by adopting a subjectivist account of harm: if an agent does not believe that he or she is harmed by an activity, there is indeed no harm. But why are we as a society obliged to adopt a subjectivist account of harm for purposes of lawmaking? After all, we can and do use objective accounts of harm in other areas of social life. We do not hesitate to judge, for example, that individuals who spend most of the day drunk are in fact injuring themselves through the undeniable physical and social harms relating to alcohol abuse. Moreover, adopting a subjectivist account of harm makes it more difficult to account for the way self-harming activities frequently tend to lead to collateral harm of others.[6] People who drink excessively tend to ignore their responsibilities not only to themselves but also to other people. Feinberg would say, of course, that the law can punish with criminal sanctions an alcoholic who indirectly inflicts harm by neglecting a child. But surely society would prefer to address the excessive drinking at an earlier stage and thereby preempt harm to the child. Although we may agree with Feinberg that the law ought not to criminalize private drunkenness, we have other alternatives. Precisely out of concern for both the harm to self and the harm to others, the law has developed other tools with which to discourage alcohol addiction. For example, a family court judge might order that a parent attend Alcoholics Anonymous meetings as a condition of retaining custody of a child.

Second, as the foregoing example suggests, the legal theory of "law as police officer" may be an approach that has some plausibility with respect to criminal law, but it does not adequately explain how law operates in other areas that have a far greater impact on the lives of those subject to it. For even when law does not explicitly condemn or mandate a particular course of action, law routinely encourages some life choices while discouraging others. To take an everyday example, the tax system clearly prefers homeowners to more mobile apartment dwellers, although neither lifestyle actually "harms" anyone in the strict sense defined by Feinberg.[7] For example, the interest that a homeowner pays on a mortgage is usually fully deductible from federal taxable income, as are state and local real estate taxes.[8] From 2008 through 2010, the federal government attempted to reinvigorate the stagnant national housing market by offering both first-time and repeat home buyers substantial tax credits.[9] One basis for the policy favoring home ownership is the judgment that homeowners take more steps to preserve the good repair and good order of their property, which in turn leads to more stable and better-ordered communities with lower crime rates.[10]

Third, even in the context of criminal law, moral considerations enter into our common judgments in a way that some liberal legal theorists find difficult to explain. Murder-for-hire and murder as a hate crime do not tangibly "harm" their respective victims any more than garden-variety homicides do. All the victims are equally dead, and they may all have suffered equally in the course of dying. Nonetheless, we judge contract killers and murderous bigots more severely and punish them more harshly. We believe that the moral evaluation of the crime of homicide should take into account not only the harm to the victim but the motivations of the perpetrator as well.[11]

If we are to make progress in sorting out the complicated issues of law and morality, we need to begin by refusing to oversimplify their relationship. In this regard, the Roman Catholic jurisprudential tradition—anchored in St. Thomas Aquinas's theory of law—has a great deal to contribute to the contemporary public conversation.[12] Although formulated in the context of thirteenth-century life, Aquinas's theory continues to provide a remarkably sophisticated and powerful way of analyzing the interaction between legal and moral concerns, even with respect to contemporary American society. Drawing on the Thomistic tradition of the nature and purpose of law will help us consider several key points in our collective deliberations about controversial legal-moral issues. Of course, as I emphasized earlier, applying Thomas's insights to the challenges we face in a pluralistic liberal democracy will require extension and revision of his key principles, not merely automatic application.[13] What I am offering, therefore, is a constructive appropriation and application of Thomistic legal thought to the contemporary context.

PROMOTING THE COMMON GOOD

In the Catholic jurisprudential tradition, human law is not merely a police officer but also plays an ultimately positive role; its goal is to enable and direct human beings living in the same community to find their flourishing with one another in a coordinated social life. According to Aquinas, the ultimate function of law is to further the common good of the community whose members are subject to its precepts.[14] What is the common good of a political community? The Second Vatican Council describes it as encompassing "the sum of those conditions of the social life whereby men, families and associations more adequately and readily may attain their own perfection."[15]

A moment's reflection suggests that a wide range of activities and institutions are necessary to promote the common good. We need ways to facilitate the manufacture and exchange of goods and services, ways to assume responsibility for the procreation and education of children, ways to decide which projects should get priority when we cannot fund them all, and ways to ensure the orderly transfer of political power. The goal of the legal system, which makes possible and organizes all of these activities, is to foster and to channel human creativity, not merely to restrain people from committing wrongs. In the words of the contemporary natural law theorist John Finnis, human law "shapes, supports and furthers patterns of co-ordination" in ways that would be desirable even in a world entirely unmarred by human sin.[16] In short, the criminal sanctions of a political community constitute only a small sliver of the total corpus of its legal framework. Adequately addressing the relationship of law and morality requires broadening our scope far beyond the question, "if an action is immoral, should it also be criminally prohibited?"

LAW AS A TEACHER OF VIRTUE

As explained earlier, according to the positive focus of Catholic jurisprudence, human law enables human creativity and cooperation. In addition, as I describe in chapter 1, Aquinas maintains that the aim of law is to lead persons to virtue, to a state of flourishing.[17] How does this relate to his other claim that the purpose of law is to promote the common good? The relationship becomes clear when we remember that the Catholic moral and legal tradition has long recognized that the flourishing of a community is not separable from the flourishing of the individual human beings who belong to it. Accordingly, Aquinas recognized that lawmakers aim to lead persons to virtue—not virtue in the abstract but as it is understood in the particular community in question.[18]

Seeing law as a teacher of virtue is ultimately more respectful of the dignity of the law's subjects than the "law as police officer" approach. A police officer does not care why an individual conforms to the law; his interest does not extend beyond the fact of the conformity. But the "why" has to be important to those who appreciate the pedagogical function of law since it is not by happenstance but for appropriate reasons that a virtuous person does the right thing and refrains from doing the wrong thing. What are such reasons? Ideally, virtuous persons will obey just laws not because they fear the penalty that could be imposed if they disobey but instead because they grasp the fundamental purpose of the law and freely incorporate that purpose into their own process of practical reasoning. So a virtuous person will choose to stay within the speed limit in a school zone not because she fears the financial burden of the hefty fine but because she does not want to subject children to an unreasonable risk of bodily harm. People can, of course, grow in virtue. For most of us, this growth is a gradual process in which lines of development are apparent only in retrospect. Adults look back with chagrin at the risks that they took—and imposed on others—when they were teenage drivers. They remember with embarrassment that they were dissuaded from the worst forms of risk-taking by the threat of punishment, not by a clear recognition of the injustice of such actions. As Aquinas understood, one aspiration of a good legal system is to encourage just such slow-and-steady progress in moral development. Even the threat of harsh legal penalties has an ultimately positive purpose: "Since some are found to be depraved, and prone to vice, and not easily amenable to words, it was necessary for such to be restrained from evil by force and fear, in order that, at least, they might desist from evil-doing, and leave others in peace, and that they themselves, by being habituated in this way, might be brought to do willingly what hitherto they did from fear, and thus become virtuous."[19] If lawmakers respect the fact that law is a teacher of virtue, they will not simply impose legal obligations and prohibitions upon unwilling citizens but also will take pains to communicate a law's rationale in a way that the public can understand, accept, and endorse. Even in Aquinas's social context, where the lawmaker was a sovereign whose power did not derive from the consent of the people, this pedagogical dynamic existed. And the same process is found in our modern social context of a constitutional democracy, in which the people retain ultimate sovereignty. American citizens are not only subject to our laws; we are also ultimately responsible for those laws by virtue of our power to elect the members of the legislature, who legislate in our name. As citizens, we need to insist that the laws that are made in our name are morally intelligible in that their contribution to the flourishing of the community and of the individuals that comprise it is readily apparent, at least in its broad outlines.

JUSTICE: A NETWORK OF RIGHT RELATIONSHIPS

What virtues should the law try to inculcate? The primary concern of the legal system is the virtue of justice. As Aquinas recognizes, justice is centrally concerned with actions that have significant external effects upon the lives and well-being of other people.[20] It nurtures the common good by promoting right relationships among the members of a community as mediated by their exchanges of external things, such as actions, goods, and property.[21] For that reason I call justice an external virtue.

As I mention in chapter 1, following Aristotle's lead, Aquinas distinguishes between general or legal justice, which concerns external actions as they affect the common good, and particular justice, which concerns external actions as they affect the claims of other people.[22] It is important to recognize that this distinction does not rise to the level of an absolute difference. That is, one and the same action can be a violation of both general and particular justice. For example, an individual who deliberately kills another person may be the defendant in both a criminal case and a tort case. The criminal case, brought by the state, treats the homicide as a violation of the common good; the tort case, brought by the victim's family, treats the killing as a harm to the private well-being of the relatives who may have relied on the victim for their livelihood.

Seeing justice as an external virtue—as a virtue that focuses on the tangible effects of actions upon other people and upon the community as a whole—gives us a way to honor the truth in liberal legal theory while transcending its limitations. Aquinas would agree with Feinberg that criminal prohibitions ought to focus upon external acts that gravely harm the well-being of others, not upon those acts in which the main effect is internal, through the erosion of the agent's own character. Aquinas's own example is apt here: legal justice is concerned with an act of theft because the resultant loss is a violation of the victim's right to peaceful enjoyment of his property. The law's concern with such an act does not lie in the fact that the theft both demonstrates and reinforces the agent's immoderate desire for wealth; for Aquinas, the indisputably flawed character of the thief is not the province of the law.[23]

At the same time, Aquinas does not forget that human beings are integrated unities of body and soul. Promoting justice requires that we pay significant attention to other virtues as well. These other virtues shape a person's character, and a person's character both influences and is influenced by his or her actions. For example, many acts of violence are rooted in the vices of excessive ambition or anger, and those passions are countered by the personal character traits that fall under the cardinal virtues of fortitude and temperance. Other acts of negligence are rooted in a defect of the cardinal virtue of prudence. While legal justice may command us to perform the external acts of a courageous person or the external acts of a temperate person, the legal system can take note of the fact that those acts are more easily and regularly performed by those persons whose passions are regulated by the virtues of fortitude and temperance, and whose capacity for practical reason is not withered. Legal justice is thus appropriately concerned with the development of these virtues precisely because they help regulate actions that have tangible impact upon the lives of other people.

Aquinas's framework, then, gives us a way to situate the stark prohibitions of the criminal law within the broader framework of virtue. We can acknowledge that the strict sanctions of the criminal law should generally be targeted at serious violations of legal justice, at external acts that threaten the well-being of the community as a whole or its individual members. At the same time, we can forthrightly acknowledge that people tend to act in ways that violate legal justice when they lack other virtues. The cardinal virtues of temperance and fortitude regulate their passions while the cardinal virtue of prudence enables the application of "right reason to action" by integrating knowledge of general principles with accurate grasp of particular circumstances.[24] Consequently, there is no reason that the legal system as a whole should not encourage these virtues, perhaps through publicly funded programs of education and service, especially those targeted at young people.

PRUDENCE AND JUSTICE, AUTONOMY AND SOLIDARITY

In a pluralistic society, which virtues should the law adopt? This, of course, is the most difficult question; it is also a question that cannot be dodged, as some legal philosophers do, by attempting to devise a value-neutral legal system. Whether we like it or not, law always affirms certain visions of how we should live together while undermining other visions. We are far better off taking responsibility for what law teaches—and arguing about what it should teach—than in denying altogether either the law's inherent bias for specific values or its pedagogical effects. Moreover, if we address the question forthrightly, we may find that we share more broad-based (although by no means unanimous) agreement about core elements of some virtues and vices than the combatants in the contemporary "culture wars" admit.[25]

In *Whose Justice? Which Rationality?*, eminent philosopher Alasdair MacIntyre argues that different moral and political traditions operated with different conceptions of justice and prudence (practical reason).[26] His argument suggests that while prudence and justice are cardinal virtues that need to be fostered by any political community in its legal system, the precise conceptions of these virtues will differ significantly from one community to another. I proposed in chapter 1 that the overarching virtues the law should inculcate in our society are autonomy as understood by Joseph Raz and solidarity as framed by Pope John Paul II. I want now to submit that those same virtues serve as partial instantiations of the prudence and justice so urgently necessary in our social and political context.[27]

More specifically, autonomy as conceived by Raz can be seen as a configuration of the virtue of prudence that is particularly necessary for persons who live in pluralistic liberal democracies. Prudence is the habit of practical reason; it is the virtue that applies right reason to action.[28] Those who live in societies such as the United States have the task of constructing their lives among an array of options not conceivable in premodern societies. Raz writes, "The autonomous life depends not on the availability of one option of freedom of choice. It depends on the general character of one's environment and culture. For those who live in an autonomy-supporting environment there is no choice but to be autonomous: there is no other way to prosper in such a society."[29]

In Raz's framework, building the autonomy of individuals within a community includes three components: (1) promoting their physical, intellectual, and emotional capacity to exercise the capacity of reflective choice; (2) protecting a sphere of choice for them that is free of coercion and manipulation; and (3) offering them a sufficient (although not unlimited) array of morally valuable life plans from which to shape a plan for their own lives.[30] Autonomy, in his view, is the capacity to be the "part-author" of one's own life by making a successive series of choices that forge a more or less coherent narrative. Raz's view of autonomy overlaps significantly with Aquinas's understanding of prudence or practical reason as right reason about things to be done to achieve an end.[31] For Aquinas, the ultimate end of humanity is happiness or human flourishing; we all want to flourish, although many of us may have deeply mistaken views of what constitutes flourishing. Accordingly, we formulate and execute immediate, intermediate, and long-term plans that we believe will help contribute to our flourishing, either as instrumental steps to it (such as obtaining a license to work in a certain field) or component parts of it (such as building a family).

In Aquinas's social context, the vocational options available to most people were limited. Social mobility was extremely constrained; the vast majority of individuals worked toward their flourishing within the confines of well-defined political, social, familial, and economic roles. The social context of Western liberal democracies, however, is significantly different, at least for many people, and aspirationally different for all people. American society places a premium on social mobility and individual vocational choice. We are not fated to enter a particular guild or profession simply because our parents and grandparents did so. We can make our own choices about which vocations to pursue; indeed, our society understands the exercise of such choices on one's own behalf to be a key part of individual flourishing. We can therefore interpret Raz's account of what it takes to be autonomous, to be a part-author of one's life, as a specification of what practical reason requires for human flourishing in our own social and political context.

Autonomy, then, is related to human flourishing. What about solidarity? Pope John Paul II defines it as "a firm and persevering determination to commit oneself to the common good; that is to say to the good of all and of each individual, because we are all really responsible for all."[32] The virtue of justice, as defined by Aquinas, covers much the same ground; he writes that justice "directs man immediately to the common good," whereas particular justice directs a man "immediately to the good of another individual."[33]

How, then, does the virtue of solidarity provide necessary shape to the virtue of justice in our own social context? It seems to me that it does so in three ways. First, our political communities are large, unwieldy, and anonymous. The call to solidarity supports justice by pressing lawmakers and citizens to attend to the unseen members of their community whose lives will be affected by their actions. Second—and relatedly, given the scale of our society—the lives of most people are affected not only or primarily by the actions of individual persons or corporations, or even by individual pieces of legislation, but also by large social patterns of action and reaction far beyond the control of individual agents. The papal call to solidarity presses us to transcend consideration of the justice of our actions in isolation and to evaluate their larger effects and currents of influence.

Justice is not merely an external virtue; it is also an internal virtue—a particular individual's firm determination to render each person his or her due or right (*ius suum*).[34] The pluralism, mobility, and fissiparousness of American life impedes our capacity to recognize each other as fellow members of the same political community, and threatens our ability to perceive what each member needs to become a full and flourishing participant in that community. The habit of solidarity, the practice of seeing ourselves as actively responsible for all persons, particularly those on the margins of the community, is a way of making sure that everyone receives their due in a complicated, cacophonous, and fluid society.

No more vivid example of the necessity of such attention can be found than the financial crisis of 2007–11, which was caused by irresponsible lending practices in the American banking system. As a result, large financial institutions around the world collapsed, national governments were forced to subsidize bank bailouts, and global stock markets plummeted. Irresponsible mortgage-lending practices crashed the housing market, resulting in numerous evictions and foreclosures. The lives of countless families have been deeply and deleteriously affected by this financial crisis, second in severity only to the Great Depression.[35]

Third, by emphasizing how the common good and the good of individuals are intertwined, the virtue of solidarity presses us to attend to the social dimensions of individual flourishing. Assuming, for example, that the exercise of autonomy, understood in Raz's terms, is necessary for an individual to flourish, our society must adopt policies that provide all children with the food, shelter, education, and support that will nurture their capacity to make and carry out the series of choices that will shape their lives as adults. We must protect the children against third parties who, for their own ends, attempt to manipulate children's choices—a substantial problem in the era of increasingly ubiquitous advertising. Finally, it will be necessary to ensure that children do not assume that the circumstances of their birth mean that their lives are essentially dead ends, without hope of improvement. Individual autonomy is ultimately a social achievement.

THE LIMITS OF LAW

Are there any limits to the role of law in promoting virtue? Yes. In fact, there are both practical and moral limits upon the power of law to require good acts and prohibit bad ones. First, it costs money to enact laws as well as to publicize and enforce them. In some cases, that money may be better spent on other things. For example, the United States is currently waging a war on drugs; opponents of that war frequently cite its exorbitant price tag. Some studies estimate that legalizing drugs would save more than $40 billion dollars annually in governmental expenditures on law enforcement.[36] The cost of making and enforcing a law needs to be evaluated in terms of benefits as well as effectiveness. To be fair, those same cost-effectiveness standards need to be applied to social-benefit programs such as welfare and Head Start.[37]

Second, the actions required to deter and detect violations of the law are themselves subject to moral evaluation. In some instances, the concrete steps a state would need to take to enforce a particular law are themselves morally repugnant. For example, in *Griswold v. Connecticut*, the Supreme Court of the United States declared that a state law prohibiting the use of contraceptives by married couples was unconstitutional because identifying violations of that law might require police officers to invade the privacy of the marital bedroom.[38] Moreover, as Vatican II teaches, there are spheres of personal and social activity that lie entirely beyond the proper authority of the state. No government, for example, has the authority to compel religious belief or practice.[39]

Third, it is important to remember that while it teaches virtue, the law's most basic lessons are for ordinary persons, not for saints. As we learned from our experiment with Prohibition, it is disastrous to attempt to enforce laws, particularly criminal laws, if there is no voluntary compliance among the vast majority of persons. But not all law exerts its force with the same harshness as criminal law. Particularly in contemporary bureaucratic society, there are many tools that the law has at its disposal—tools that do not immediately spring to the minds of nonlawyers—to promote a vision of a good society. Moreover, precisely because law functions as a teacher, it can invite persons to rise to a standard of behavior that exceeds what the criminal law can realistically require in a particular time and place. There are many ways in which law can promote acts that lead to personal and communal flourishing without actually requiring them, and can discourage acts that are inconsistent with such flourishing without actually prohibiting them under the threat of penal sanctions.

In fact, criminal law is just a small sliver of the legal framework necessary to promote the common good. All the various components of that framework are infused with a normative vision. Constitutional law articulates a political society's basic framework and core values. Corporate law allows persons to form entities (corporations) that will continue to pursue worthwhile purposes long after the original visionaries have left the scene. The institution of marriage is supported not only by laws regulating divorce but also by laws governing inheritance. For example, probate laws in all states protect a surviving spouse against the deceased spouse's attempts to disinherit him or her.[40] Tax law also functions to promote the common good. By granting tax-exempt status to charitable corporations such as hospitals and schools, the community is in effect giving them a subsidy roughly equal to one-third of their gross income.[41]

Each of these bodies of law has its own way, with its own costs and benefits, of encouraging and discouraging behavior in order to advance the common good. Take, for instance, surrogate motherhood, which many people judge to be morally problematic. One clear way to express that judgment is to enact a criminal prohibition against the practice. But the very same people who are morally troubled by surrogacy might recoil at the prospect of penalizing emotionally desperate couples and financially desperate surrogates. They might also believe that the scarce resources of the criminal justice system could better be directed elsewhere.

Criminal law, however, is not the only way of tackling the surrogacy problem. We could also turn to contract law, which uses less severe but more flexible tools to discourage surrogate motherhood. In the celebrated Baby M case of 1985, for example, the New Jersey Supreme Court refused to enforce a surrogacy contract because the agreement violated public policy.[42] Unlike the criminal law, contract law does not interfere with surrogacy arrangements that are voluntarily brought to completion. However, contract law can at least ensure that no surrogate mother will be held to an agreement to terminate her parental rights until she has had the opportunity to see the face of the child she has borne.

SHOULD THE CRIMINAL LAW ALWAYS SECURE FUNDAMENTAL RIGHTS?

Thus far, I have argued that it is appropriate for the law to inculcate virtues, particularly the virtues of autonomy and solidarity, often and mainly by using legal tools that are more subtle and flexible than the criminal law. Some might object that my emphasis on the pedagogical function of the law is sorely inadequate, or at least incomplete. They might charge that I am failing to consider matters from the perspective of the victims. The deterrence provided by the criminal code may or may not serve to lead would-be malfeasants to virtue, but it does secure a definite advantage for those who would otherwise suffer at their hands. On this basis, they might argue that the criminal code of each and every polity must always protect fundamental rights, such as the right to life, liberty, and personal property, entirely apart from other concerns, including but not limited to the pedagogical function of the law.[43]

This objection cannot be ignored, for it has wide-ranging implications. It reveals, for example, a larger tension between virtue language and rights language. Virtue talk, after all, generally focuses on the character of acting agents, whereas rights talk frequently centers on how actions affect the just claims of persons other than the agent.[44] That distinction, in my view, is often overblown. Certainly, any adequate understanding of law as a teacher of virtue has to take into account the just claims of third parties. To the extent that the purpose of law is to promote the common good by protecting a network of objectively right relations among its subjects, lawmakers are directed to look carefully at the effects of an action upon third parties, not merely at the moral character of the agents who produced those effects. That is part of what Aquinas means when he stresses that justice is an external virtue that establishes the basic conditions of right relations among members of a society. Surely, one could argue, basic rights to life, liberty, and personal property are part of that framework of right relations in any society.

The objection also highlights a potential fault line between human law and moral norms. As many scholars have pointed out, Aquinas recognizes a close normative connection between human law and the natural moral law. He writes, for example, that "every human law has just so much of the nature of law, as it is derived from the law of nature. But if in any point it deflects from the law of nature, it is no longer a law but a perversion of law."[45] Certainly, one could say that failing to protect basic rights of life, liberty, and personal property against invasion by others counts as a "perversion of law."

Fully responding to these concerns would require a detailed exploration of Aquinas's theory of law, which is beyond the scope of this volume. Let me at least outline, however, the key elements. It is crucial to remember that for Aquinas, all law is directly oriented toward the practical realm; it does not consist merely in a theoretical statement of moral truths. Along with grace, law is one of the divinely ordained extrinsic principles shaping human actions.[46] The role of law, in other words, is to affect human action from the outside by changing the circumstances under which a person chooses to act or to refrain from acting. Moreover, law protects basic rights not directly but indirectly, by influencing the actions of those who might be tempted to interfere with them. More specifically, the law does not install a protective shield around people's objective claims. Nor is it an omnipresent security guard who will repel every attack on those claims. Instead, the law protects the situation of objectively right relations among persons indirectly, by affecting the practical deliberation of agents in a position either to respect it or to undermine it.

Making law, then, is a purposeful activity that strives to alter the purposeful activity of others; lawmakers attempt to exert influence, even pressure, on the way their subjects choose to act.[47] Their purpose in so doing is to benefit the entire community, as Aquinas's definition of law makes clear. He states that a law "is nothing else than an ordinance of reason for the common good, made by him who has care of the community, and promulgated."[48] In other words, in making law, a legitimate lawmaker combines the force of reason and will in promulgating norms to benefit the general good. Consequently, wise lawmakers must consider whether their prospective ordinances will actually achieve their purposes before enacting them.[49]

The prospects for success depend on a number of factors, including the identity, position, and power of the lawmaker, the type of law at issue, and the character of the subjects involved. Needless to say, if the lawmaker is God and the law in question is the eternal law, there can be no question of ultimate success. The eternal law is identical with God himself. It is unthinkable that God would not be able to ensure that the entire universe operates ultimately according to the perfect divine governing will.[50] The ability of human law to achieve the ends of the lawmaker is another matter entirely, in part because no human being, and therefore no human lawmaker, is omniscient, omnipotent, and comprehensive in authoritative action. Aquinas is extremely sensitive to the limitations of human law; indeed, he devotes an entire question to that very issue.[51] Virtuous lawmakers must take into account those limitations in formulating legal policy. If they do not do so, the law will not serve its ultimate purpose, which is to further the common good of the community.

Consider three general types of practical limitations restricting the reach of human lawmakers. The first limitation pertains to knowledge. A human lawmaker, Aquinas says, only "can make laws in those matters of which he is competent to judge." Consequently, human law cannot curb and direct interior acts, which are necessary for the perfection of virtue, because a human lawmaker is "not competent to judge of interior movements, that are hidden, but only of exterior acts which appear."[52] The second limitation pertains to targeting precision. Aquinas says that "human law cannot punish or forbid all evil deeds: since while aiming at doing away with all evils, it would do away with many good things, and would hinder the advancement of the common good."[53] A contemporary instance of this point is the American approach to free speech. We refuse to prohibit all sorts of malicious and useless speech because we are afraid that such measures will also impede the sort of vigorous political discussion so necessary in a representative democracy. The third limitation relates to scope. Human law must be framed for the majority of instances, not for every single conceivable case.[54] Consequently, there may be some occasions in which a subject may rightly act against the letter of the law to further its clear purpose. Aquinas gives the example of making an exception to a law prohibiting opening the city gates to allow the soldiers defending the city to come into safety.[55]

Aquinas understands, then, that wise lawmakers must take into account the limits of their own capacity to formulate and enforce rational commands as they go about their business of enacting precepts to further the common good. Significantly, however, he also appreciates that in addition to recognizing their own limitations, wise lawmakers also must grapple with the challenges their subjects will face in following the law. Human lawmakers do not have the same ability that the divine lawmaker has to work in, around, and through the frailty and recalcitrance of those subject to the laws in question. In a key passage, Aquinas reflects: "Now human law is framed for a number of human beings, the majority of whom are not perfect in virtue. Wherefore human laws do not forbid all vices, from which the virtuous abstain, but only the more grievous vices, from which it is possible for the majority to abstain; and chiefly those that are to the hurt of others, without the prohibition of which human society could not be maintained: thus human law prohibits murder, theft and such like."[56]

In this passage we see two key criteria for sound legal (particularly criminal) prohibitions: they prohibit vicious actions from which it is possible for the majority to abstain, and they prohibit those vicious actions that seriously harm others, the prohibition of which is necessary to maintain human society. While this guidance is helpful, it is also insufficient. The question we must ask is how to deal with situations in which the two criteria conflict. What should we do in cases where it is not possible, for some reason, for most people in a society to abstain from vicious actions that cause serious harm to others?

In my judgment, in cases of conflict, the "possibility" criterion trumps. A close reading of Aquinas suggests that it is never conducive to the common good to enact legal prohibitions, even criminal prohibitions, that are likely to be widely flouted. Why is this so? One reason is predictable backlash from the recalcitrant; he writes that attempts to impose prohibitions too stringent for the populace at large will likely end up by making the situation worse: subjects imperfect in virtue will despise the precepts in question and "from contempt, break into evils worse still."[57] In my view, there is a second, closely related reason: the likely erosion of the rule of law itself. Contempt for a particular law can easily expand into contempt for the law as such.

A third and more complicated reason has to do with the relationship between custom and statutory law. Aquinas is very aware of the influence that custom exerts in maintaining the legitimacy of the legal system as a whole. Consequently, he places a heavy burden of proof on any change in law, even a beneficial change: "Wherefore human law should never be changed, unless, in some way or other, the common weal be compensated according to the extent of the harm done in this respect."[58] Aquinas allows that a change might be justified by some "very great and very evident benefit," or by an urgent need to remedy a clearly unjust law or to remove a law whose observance is clearly harmful.[59]

Suppose an unjust law is changed for precisely such a grave reason. How does the new, presumably more just law fare against the older, unjust custom? Aquinas recognizes that to some degree and in some respects positive law must trump custom. One purpose of enacting a statute, after all, is to reshape a nation's customs so that they are more congenial to the common good. If the reason for the law continues to hold, "then it is not the custom that prevails against the law, but the law that overcomes the custom."[60] In the end, however, custom has the last word. "Custom has the force of a law, abolishes law, and is the interpreter of law."[61] Aquinas recognizes that even if the purpose of a law is sound, it cannot prevail if it "is not *possible according to the custom of the country*. . . . For it is not easy to set aside the custom of a whole people."[62]

Lawmakers, then, must take their subjects where they find them. They can revise and improve the legal system only gradually; moving too fast for the moral capacity of the citizenry can only be counterproductive. In short, the lawmaker must acknowledge that entrenched custom sets limits upon the types of law that can effectively and properly be enacted in a given time and place. But how can this acknowledgement be reconciled to the idea that sound human law must be consistent with the natural law? Aquinas would say that the natural law itself requires wise lawmakers to recognize the limits imposed by the social context in which they are operating. More specifically, he straightforwardly maintains that "the very fact that human law does not meddle with matters it cannot direct, comes under the ordination of the eternal law."[63]

Nonetheless, Aquinas also claims that human law ought to relate to the natural law in one of two ways.[64] Human law should reflect conclusions (*conclusiones*) derived from the premises of the natural laws, such as when one reasons to the specific prohibition "one must not kill" from the more general principle "one should do harm to no man." Alternatively, it should reflect determinations (*determinationes*), which apply general norms of the natural law to specific situations, such as when lawmakers affix particular penalties to particular wrongful acts. How can we reconcile this seemingly tight and rigid account of the relationship of human law to natural law with Aquinas's claim that custom, even morally problematic custom, places limits upon the efforts of human lawmakers to promote virtuous actions and prohibit vicious ones?

In my view, the key is to recognize that *conclusiones* and *determinationes* are meant to apply the norms of the natural moral law in the context of actual communities, which differ in many respects, including the degree of virtue in the population and the resources to expend in law enforcement.[65] Aquinas notes, for example, that "general principles of the natural law cannot be applied to all men in the same way on account of the great variety of human affairs: and hence arises the diversity of positive laws among various people."[66] Some communities may be blessed with a more virtuous population while others may have more resources available to dedicate to law enforcement. Both of those factors will affect the precise shape of the wise lawmaker's *conclusiones* and *determinationes*.

But Aquinas also says that a human legal norm that violates the natural law is not a law properly speaking, but "a perversion of law."[67] How can a criminal code that leaves certain basic rights unprotected be anything but such a perversion? The key element of the response to this question is to emphasize his distinction between requiring or encouraging actions that are against the natural law, on the one hand, and leaving certain actions unpunished, on the other. Aquinas observes:

> Human law is said to permit certain things, not as approving them, but as being unable to direct them. And many things are directed by the Divine law, which human law is unable to direct, because more things are subject

to a higher than to a lower cause. . . . It would be different, were human law to sanction what the eternal law condemns. Consequently it does not follow that human law is not derived from the eternal law, but that it is not on a perfect equality with it.[68]

Perhaps an example will help make the foregoing general reflections more concrete. Consider a hypothetical boomtown roughly modeled on Deadwood, South Dakota, in the second half of the nineteenth century.[69] Such a settlement is not planned; it develops gradually as explorers and fortune-seekers created a base camp from which to search for gold in the Black Hills. Entrepreneurs providing ancillary services to the miners slowly gravitate to the area, opening a general store, a saloon, and even a bordello. The population is far from genteel in either morals or manners; there are few women and even fewer children in the camp. Unfortunately, many settlers conform to Aquinas's observation that those who make a habit of vicious living suffer from greatly occluded insight into natural moral norms. The daily stagecoach brings violent opportunists as well as honest fortune seekers to the region. Each settler is wary, constantly on the lookout for ambushes and schemes. Finally, the miners face additional dangers from the native population whose land they are usurping. In this context, the settlers' motto is "shoot first, ask questions later."

Isolated in the middle of territory belonging to the Native Americans, the settlers are under the effective jurisdiction of no government they recognize. If a group of honest, upright citizens decides to institute some basic legal framework to govern their common existence, how should they proceed? Their only viable option is to move step by step, beginning by enacting prohibitions for which there is wide public support and that can be enforced effectively. For example, our little group—let's call them the Upright Citizens Brigade[70]—might begin by guarding the arrival of the stagecoach and escorting the passengers to the hotel in town. A plausible next step would be to patrol the boomtown's only street for several hours in broad daylight, ensuring that new settlers can get their supplies without being caught in the crossfire.

The brigade should not begin by attempting to outlaw private violence in all forms and contexts, for reasons Aquinas helps us see clearly. It would make a mockery of the law to prohibit criminally wrongful acts that cannot be effectively detected, deterred, and punished in that community, such as midnight muggings in town. Thugs will flout the law merely to show they can do so, eroding the respect and confidence of law-abiding citizens in the budding legal system. In the absence of a strong police force, the settlers will rightly assume they have the natural authority to secure their own establishments and to defend their own lives and property in private settings. Given the weakness of the political community, the law cannot effectively claim a monopoly on the use of force. If honest citizens are harmed with impunity in situations in which the law purports to protect them, any commitment to the rule of law will quickly fade. It is far better for lawmakers not to promise what they cannot deliver, and to build up both their power and credibility gradually.

At the same time, however, the law ought not to endorse morally questionable private uses of force by the settlers. It is one thing to say that the law will not punish a saloonkeeper who shoots a patron within the premises because the lawmakers recognize the saloonkeeper's right to maintain order in the saloon. It is another thing to say that this right is meant to legitimate not only neutralizing a drunken customer who is threatening to open fire on the bar but also eliminating one's romantic rival who is flirting with the barmaid. In cases such as this, Aquinas's distinction between leaving certain wrongs unpunished and sanctioning what the natural law condemns is particularly important.

Over time, the Upright Citizens Brigade ought to be able to extend its reach to prohibit actions that are widely perceived to involve the wrongful exercise of violence, provided they convince their fellow residents of their ability to impede and punish those actions. Yet brigade members will also face a different problem. In their wisdom and concern for the common good, they may rightly recognize that certain acts of violence generally perceived to be legitimate are not in fact so. For example, the settlers might think that it is morally permissible to shoot on sight anyone who is seen nosing around their claim sites or handling their mining equipment without permission. Addressing this issue will require long and careful discussions of the value of human life versus competing values of property and privacy. Perhaps that conversation will result in a consensus that, in an isolated mining community, it is morally permissible to shoot those who are attempting to steal one's livelihood but not those who inadvertently or innocently trespass on one's claim or who finger one's property. That consensus, of course, will quickly generate another set of questions, such as what sort of investigation or inquiry settlers are morally obliged to make of interlopers' intentions before cocking their guns.

Other conversations may be more difficult—on both sides. Suppose, for example, the wise members of the Upright Citizens Brigade recognize that dueling is morally wrong because it requires participants to deliberately kill or to seriously wound each other merely to avenge or defend their honor. The brigade members rightly reject the argument that defending one's honor justifies the intentional infliction of death or serious bodily harm on another person. Nonetheless, they know that many of their fellow citizens, including some well-respected members of the community, do not see the matter in the same way. Those other citizens believe that the public defense of honor is an important practice, one that preserves the peace by deterring gratuitous insults and challenges to established authority and dignity, especially on the part of young upstarts determined to make a name for themselves. Furthermore, they think that the ritual of dueling helps direct deep and unavoidable conflicts into situations and contexts that are less likely to harm bystanders. They maintain, in other words, that the choice to engage in the practice of dueling is both *a right* and, on occasion, *morally right.*

In this context, the Upright Citizens Brigade must focus its efforts on changing the honor-based custom as well as the judgments that support the custom before it can change the law. Simply enacting a prohibition against dueling will backfire. In all likelihood, the prohibition will be ignored. If it is given any regard, the result will be to drive duels into the woods and into the twilight, where they become more dangerous, not less so.[71] Dueling may be a dangerous and immoral practice, but at least it is subject to an elaborate code of rules that functions to contain the harm, at least to some degree.[72]

Ultimately, Aquinas holds, the power of custom trumps the power of legal enactments. In our hypothetical boomtown, dueling cannot be effectively legally prohibited merely by passing a statute. The inner purpose and rationale of the statute must first be accepted by a significant number of the population so that most citizens refrain from the practice of their own accord. Only then, once a comfortable majority rejects dueling, can a law be passed to deter the others from participating in it. Changing law requires changing custom, and changing this particular custom requires reconfiguring the moral commitments of the populace.

How should the Upright Citizens Brigade go about changing the custom of their community regarding dueling? In my view, they must advance their arguments simultaneously along several different lines. First, the brigade members must call into question the concept of "honor" that requires ritual bloodshed in order to defend it. Second, they must highlight the collateral damage done by the practice of dueling—not merely to the participants themselves but also to spouses and children of those wounded or killed in a duel. Third, they must promote alternative strategies to settle disputes involving pride and disrespect. Fourth, they must show how a legal prohibition of dueling is best considered a legitimate extension of the general prohibition against intentional killing, rather than an illegitimate suppression of the permission to kill (or to inflict great bodily harm) in order to defend oneself. The Upright Citizens Brigade, in other words, must convince the population that defending one's honor is not the moral equivalent of defending one's life.

Does this mean that the brigade must refrain from enacting any restrictions whatsoever on dueling, through which it expresses deep moral reservations about the practice? No. However, it should remember that law must be made for ordinary persons, not saints, and must not try to reform too much too fast. A good first step would be to enact a widely accepted dueling code into law, criminally prohibiting duels that do not conform to those strictures. Cautionary measures, such as "cooling off periods," could be instituted and extended. Participants in a duel could be required to assume responsibility for each other's family members in the event they caused death or grievous bodily harm. The immediate aim would be to use criminal prohibitions to reinforce the existing consensus, while invoking the law's pedagogical powers to encourage people to take the further step of rejecting dueling altogether. Those enacting the positive law must proceed incrementally in their efforts to inculcate virtue; otherwise, their efforts will backfire. Even in matters of life and death, human lawmakers can only impose burdens and restrictions that the population can bear, both practically and morally.

CONCLUSION

If we look closely at the American legal system, we will find ample evidence of how law can still function as a powerful moral teacher by holding up a compelling, integrated vision of our common life that inspires people to move beyond its strict requirements. As I argued in the first chapter, the Civil Rights Acts, the Americans with Disabilities Act, and the Family and Medical Leave Act do not simply impose isolated sets of mandates. They point holistically toward a society infused with the virtue of solidarity and move incrementally toward its realization. In this chapter, I delved more deeply into the challenges involved in seeing law as a teacher of virtue, particularly in a pluralistic society such as our own. I argued that wise lawmakers must balance moral realism and moral idealism in formulating law for the communities for which they are responsible. They are making law for ordinary men and women, not saints; consequently, the limits of the law must be the limits of ordinary virtue. Criminal law, in particular, cannot do more than protect basic rights, and it must be limited to prohibiting actions that the majority of persons are willing and able to refrain from performing. At the same time, the inability of the law to prohibit all vices, even serious vices, does not mean that it must take a positive or even a value-neutral stance toward actions that the lawmakers recognize to be morally wrong. As my hypothetical involving a "Deadwood"-like boomtown suggests, it is both necessary and possible to take a gradualist approach toward eliminating even serious moral wrongs. As my example of dueling shows, the challenges faced by lawmakers are particularly great when they wish to stand against a custom or action that is both widely supported and frequently practiced in their particular society.

Dueling, fortunately, is no longer a thorny legal-moral problem in the United States or other Western liberal democracies. I believe, however, the nuanced understanding of law's function as a moral teacher that I tried to develop with reference to that example is still relevant in the contemporary context. In the next section of the book, I will attempt to extend that understanding to illuminate three controversial issues in our time and place: abortion, genetic testing, and euthanasia.

NOTES

This chapter has its seeds in M. Cathleen Kaveny, "Law, Morality, and Common Ground," *America*, December 9, 2000, 7–10.

1. For a helpful overview, see Donald G. Gifford, *Suing the Tobacco and Lead Pigment Industries: Government Litigation as Public Health Prescription* (Ann Arbor: University of Michigan Press, 2010).
2. For an introduction to some of the key cases and issues, see the legal textbook, William Rubenstein, Jane S. Schacter, and Carlos A. Ball, *Cases and Materials on Sexual Orientation and the Law*, 3rd ed. (Eagan, MN: Thomson West, 2007). The discussion is highly polarized. For different approaches to the issues see, e.g., Robert George and Jean Bethke Elshtain, eds., *The Meaning of Marriage: Family, State, Market, & Morals* (Dallas: Spence Publishing, 2006); and Martha C. Nussbaum, *From Disgust to Humanity: Sexual Orientation & Constitutional Law* (New York: Oxford University Press, 2010).
3. A clear example is Prohibition. See Daniel Okrent, *Last Call: The Rise and Fall of Prohibition* (New York: Scribner, 2010); Edward Behr, *Prohibition: Thirteen Years That Changed America* (New York: Arcade, 1996); and David E. Kyvig, *Law, Alcohol, and Order: Perspectives on National Prohibition* (Santa Barbara, CA: Greenwood Press, 1985). For an analysis of the market aspects of prohibition of both alcohol and drugs, see Mark Thornton, *The Economics of Prohibition* (Salt Lake City: University of Utah Press, 1991).
4. John Stuart Mill, *On Liberty* (1859; repr. ed. New York: Penguin, 1974).
5. Joel Feinberg, *The Moral Limits of the Criminal Law*, 4 vols. (New York: Oxford University Press, 1984–88).
6. For a vigorous response to leading critics of "morals legislation," see Robert George, *Making Men Moral* (Oxford: Oxford University Press, 1995).
7. Feinberg, *Moral Limits of the Criminal Law*, vol. 4, *Harmless Wrongdoing*, xxvii–xxix.
8. See, e.g., Internal Revenue Service, "Publication 936: Home Mortgage Interest Deduction" (Washington, DC: Government Printing Office 2010); Internal Revenue Service, "Topic 503: Deductible Taxes," February 7, 2011, www.irs.gov/taxtopics/tc503.html.

9. Worker, Homeownership, and Business Assistance Act of 2009, Pub. L. 111-92, 123 Stat. 2984 (codified as amended in scattered sections of USC); American Recovery and Reinvestment Act of 2009, Pub. L. 111-5, 123 Stat. 115 (codified as amended in scattered sections of USC); Housing and Economic Recovery Act of 2008, Pub. L. 110-289, 122 Stat. 2654 (codified as amended in scattered sections of USC).

10. See, e.g., National Association of Realtors (Research Division), "Social Benefits of Home Ownership and Stable Housing," August 2010, www.realtor.org/Research .nsf/files/05%20Social%20Benefits%20of%20Stable%20Housing.pdf/$FILE/05%20 Social%20Benefits%20of%20Stable%20Housing.pdf. The policy favoring home ownership is indebted to a seminal, controversial article by George L. Kelling and James Q. Wilson, "Broken Windows: The Police and Neighborhood Safety," *Atlantic Monthly*, March 1982, 29–38. In recent years, however, the social benefits of home ownership have been questioned; see, e.g., "Home Ownership: Shelter, or Burden?," *Economist*, April 18, 2009, 76–78. www.economist.com/node/13491933.

11. See, e.g., US Sentencing Commission, *2010 Federal Sentencing Guidelines Manual* (Washington, DC: Government Printing Office), § 2A1.5 "Conspiracy or Solicitation to Commit Murder" and § 3A1.1 "Hate Crime Motivation or Vulnerable Victim."

12. Thomas Aquinas, *Summa theologica*, 3 vols., trans. Fathers of the English Dominican Province (New York: Benziger Bros., 1948), I-II, qq. 95–97.

13. As I note earlier, for example, Aquinas's own notion of the common good is too hierarchical to serve us well today.

14. Aquinas, *Summa theologica*, I-II, q. 90, art. 2.

15. Vatican II, *Gaudium et spes* (*Pastoral Constitution on the Church in the Modern World*), (1965), para. 74.

16. John Finnis, *Natural Law and Natural Rights* (Oxford: Oxford University Press, 1980), 267.

17. Aquinas, *Summa theologica*, I-II, q. 92, art. 1.

18. Ibid. Aquinas understood, of course, that some definitions of virtue are in fact vicious. We can recognize that the law of the Third Reich aimed to produce "good" Nazis, even as we criticize Nazism's entire scheme of "virtues" as being morally bankrupt.

19. Ibid., I-II, q. 95, art. 1.

20. Ibid., II-II, q. 58, art. 9.

21. Ibid., II-II, q. 58, art. 8.

22. Ibid., II-II, q. 58, arts. 5–8.

23. Ibid., II-II, q. 58, art. 9.

24. Ibid., II-II, q. 47, art. 4.

25. The term was popularized by James Davidson Hunter's *Culture Wars: The Struggle to Define America* (New York: Basic Books, 1992), which looked at how a number of controversial issues such as abortion, church-state separation, gun ownership, homosexuality, and censorship divided Americans, attributing controversies on specific questions to broader ideological conflicts. In the late 1990s and early 2000, the meaning of the term became influenced by Pope John Paul II's encyclical *Evangelium vitae* (*Gospel of Life*) (1995), which limned a sharp contrast between the "culture of life" and the "culture of death." While some Republican politicians and strategists attempted to merge the two frameworks, equating the "culture of life" with American

conservatism, it is clear that they are not entirely compatible, as I describe more fully in Concluding Reflections.

26. Alasdair MacIntyre, *Whose Justice? Which Rationality?* (Notre Dame, IN: University of Notre Dame Press, 1988).

27. For another effort to specify virtues necessary in our contemporary context, see James F. Keenan, SJ, *Virtues of Ordinary Christians* (Lanham, MD: Sheed & Ward, 1996). See also James F. Keenan, SJ, and Daniel Harrington, SJ, *Jesus and Virtue Ethics: Building Bridges between New Testament Studies and Moral Theology* (Lanham, MD: Sheed & Ward, 2005).

28. Aquinas, *Summa theologica*, II-II, q. 47, art. 4.

29. Joseph Raz, *The Morality of Freedom* (New York: Oxford University Press, 1986), 391.

30. Ibid., chap. 14.

31. Aquinas, *Summa theologica*, II-II, q. 47, art. 2.

32. Pope John Paul II, *Sollicitudo rei socialis* (*On Social Concern*) (1987), para. 38.

33. Aquinas, *Summa theologica*, II-II, q. 58, art. 7; and II-II, q.58, art. 7, rep. ob. 1.

34. Ibid., II-II, q. 58, art. 1.

35. For an account of the causes of the crisis accessible to the general reader, see Charles Morris, *The Trillion Dollar Meltdown: Easy Money, High Rollers, and the Great Credit Crash* (Philadelphia: Public Affairs, 2008).

36. Jeffrey A. Miron and Katherine Waldock, "The Budgetary Impact of Ending Drug Prohibition," white paper for the Cato Institute, September 27, 2010, www.cato.org/pub_display.php?pub_id=12169.

37. For an analysis of the welfare reform program of the mid-1990s, see Jeffrey Grogger and Lynn A. Karoly, *Welfare Reform: Effects of a Decade of Change* (Cambridge, MA: Harvard University Press, 2005). See the Coalition's website "Social Programs that Work," http://evidencebasedprograms.org/wordpress. The Coalition for Evidence-Based Policy uses findings from rigorous randomized controlled trials to identify worthwhile policy interventions in the area of early childhood education (K–12), youth development, crime and violence prevention, healthcare financing and delivery, substance abuse prevention and treatment, mental health, employment and welfare, and international development.

38. *Griswold v. Connecticut*, 381 US 479 (1965). In contrast, *Eisenstadt v. Baird*, 405 US 438 (1972) extended constitutional protection to the right of unmarried individuals not only to use contraception in the privacy of their own bedrooms but also to purchase and possess it in other contexts.

39. Vatican II, *Dignitatis humanae* (*Declaration on Religious Freedom*) (1965), para. 2.

40. Laura A. Rosenbury, "Two Ways to End Marriage: Divorce or Death," *Utah Law Review*, 2005, 1243; Washington U. School of Law Working Paper No. 05-09-02. http://ssrn.com/abstract=813285. The level of protection varies from state to state, with Georgia offering the least protection to the surviving spouse.

41. There is increasing and, in my view, justified pressure to ensure that tax-exempt hospitals provide sufficient benefit to the community to justify relieving them of the obligation to contribute to the public coffers by paying taxes. The Internal Revenue Service evaluated the community benefit provided by tax-exempt hospitals; its report, based on a survey completed by approximately 500 such hospitals, is available at "IRS

Nonprofit Hospital Project—Final Report" (2010), www.irs.gov/charities/charitable/article/0,,id=203109,00.html.

42. *In re Baby M*, 537 A.2d 1227 (NJ 1988). In December 2009, in *A.G.R. v. D.R.H. & S.H.*, a New Jersey Superior Court judge extended the precedent of Baby M to gestational surrogacy (in which the surrogate carries a baby created by the egg and sperm of others), deeming the gestational mother the legal mother of the babies in question. The ruling is available from the *New York Times* at http://graphics8.nytimes.com/packages/pdf/national/20091231_SURROGATE.pdf. The states are divided about how to treat gestational surrogacy.

43. The views of John Courtney Murray, SJ on this question, of course, have shaped the Catholic approach to this question, particularly in the United States. See, e.g., Gregory Kalscheur, SJ, "John Paul II, John Courtney Murray, and the Relationship between Civil Law and Moral Law: A Constructive Proposal for Contemporary American Pluralism," *Journal of Catholic Social Thought* 1 (Summer 2004): 231–75.

44. See M. Cathleen Kaveny, "Imagination, Virtue, and Human Rights: Lessons from Australian and American Law," *Theological Studies* 70, no. 1 (March 2009): 109–39.

45. Aquinas, *Summa theologica*, I-II, q. 95, art. 2.

46. Ibid., I-II, q. 90.

47. On this question, see also John Finnis, "Law and What I Truly Should Decide," *American Journal of Jurisprudence* 48 (2003): 107–30.

48. Aquinas, *Summa theologica*, I-II, q. 90, art. 4.

49. I have discussed the implications of recognizing that law is both an act of the will (an "ordinance") as well as a reasonable act in M. Cathleen Kaveny, "What Is Legalism? Engelhardt and Grisez on the Misuse of Law in Christian Ethics," *Thomist* 72, no. 3 (2008): 443–85.

50. Aquinas, *Summa theologica*, I-II, q. 93, "Of the Eternal Law."

51. Ibid., I-II, q. 96, "Of the Power of Human Law."

52. Ibid., I-II, q. 91, art. 4.

53. Ibid.

54. Ibid., I-II, q. 96, art. 6, rep. ob. 3.

55. Ibid., I-II, q. 96, art. 6.

56. Ibid., I-II, q. 96, art. 2.

57. Ibid., I-II, q. 96, art. 2. rep. ob. 2.

58. Ibid., I-II, q. 97, art. 2.

59. Ibid.

60. Ibid., I-II, q. 97, art. 3, rep. ob. 2.

61. Ibid., I-II, q. 97, art. 3.

62. Ibid., I-II, q. 97, art. 3, rep. ob. 2.

63. Ibid., I-II, q. 93, art. 3, rep. ob. 3.

64. Ibid., I-II, q. 95, art. 2.

65. For contemporary (and competing) readings of the relationship between the general conclusions of the natural law and the specifications of those conclusions in human legislation, see Robert George, *In Defense of Natural Law* (Oxford: Oxford University Press, 1999): 102–11; and Jean Porter, *Ministers of Law: A Natural Law Theory of Legal Authority* (Grand Rapids, MI: Eerdmans, 2010), 63–141.

66. Aquinas, *Summa theologica*, I-II, q. 95, art 2, rep. ob. 3.
67. Ibid., I-II, q. 95 art. 2.
68. Ibid., I-II, q. 93, art. 3, rep. ob. 3.
69. I draw some of my inspiration from the HBO series *Deadwood* (2004–6).
70. I borrow this name, of course, from the Chicago-based comedy improv group that first became popular in the 1990s.
71. For a general history, see Barbara Holland, *Gentleman's Blood: A History of Dueling from Swords at Dawn to Pistols at Dusk* (New York: Bloomsbury, 2003); and Richard Hopton, *Pistols at Dawn: A History of Duelling* (London: Piatkus, 2011). For an account of the practice of dueling in the American legal context, see Alison L. LaCroix, "To Gain the Whole World and Lose His Own Soul: Nineteenth-Century American Dueling as Public Law and Private Code," *Hofstra Law Review* 33 (2004): 501–70. The legal debate was not limited to the United States; see, e.g., David S. Parker, "Law, Honor, and Impunity in Spanish America: The Debate over Dueling, 1870–1920," *Law and History Review* 19, no. 2 (2001): 311–41.
72. See, e.g., Joseph Hamilton, *The Dueling Handbook (1829)* (Mineola, NY: Dover, 2007).

PART II

Life Issues and the Law

CHAPTER 3

❧

The Pro-Life Movement
and the Purpose of Law

*R*oe v. Wade has been the law of the land for about forty years, or about the average length of a woman's reproductive span.[1] For an individual, forty years is the age of mature adulthood, of continued vigor combined with good judgment. Perhaps that is true of political movements as well. Perhaps the pro-life movement is just now reaching mature adulthood, coming into its own, ready to take responsibility not only for itself but also for the broader community that it is trying to teach and trying to serve. To take responsibility for the future, however, we need to come to terms with the past. And for the pro-life movement that means coming to terms with *Roe*—both with the legal decision itself and with its broader meaning within American law and culture. When *Roe* was handed down in 1973, it hit many people like a bolt from the blue. Legal scholars focused on the radical nature of *Roe* as a matter of constitutional law. In *A Private Choice*, a powerful and eloquent examination of the decision's presuppositions and ramifications, John T. Noonan Jr. considered how a surprised Martian might evaluate *Roe*'s holding that the Constitution protects a woman's right to abortion. "Our Martian might reason: What the framers knew to be a crime at common law in the states when they made the Constitution, they did not intend to legalize."[2]

And many ordinary, previously apolitical citizens viewed *Roe* as simply incredible; in fact, the decision galvanized some into pro-life activism. In *Abortion and the Politics of Motherhood*, sociologist Kristin Luker captures the reaction of one such woman to the decision: "Well, I think just about like everyone else in the [Support Life] League, we felt as though the bottom had been pulled out from under us. It was an incredible thing, I couldn't believe it. In fact, I didn't. For a couple of months I kept thinking, 'It can't be right, I'm not hearing what I'm hearing.'"[3] Largely unaware of movements to liberalize abortion on the state level that had been operating in the late 1960s and early 1970s, these newly galvanized pro-life activists simply could not believe that any so-called responsible, right-thinking person (such as a Supreme Court justice) could hold that the unborn were not "persons" deserving equal protection under the law.

I do not mean to deny the truth in Noonan's comments about the extremeness of *Roe* as a matter of constitutional law. Nor do I mean to denigrate Luker's first-wave pro-life activist and her perceptions about the shocking nature of *Roe*'s denial of personhood to the unborn. But I think we need to probe a little deeper. In my view, the pro-life movement needs to look not only at the way in which *Roe* is a startling departure from long-standing values in American law but also at the ways it is a tragic reflection of them as well.

In this chapter I do three things. First, I suggest that *Roe* and most of its progeny embody a particular view of law that is well established within the Anglo-American legal tradition: law as a police officer. Unfortunately, most of the debate over *Roe* has been carried out—by pro-lifers as well as by pro-choicers—without serious examination of this view of law and its inadequacies. Second, I argue that as it comes more fully into its own, the pro-life movement might more helpfully draw upon a different (and older) view of law that has its roots in the thought of Plato, Aristotle, and Aquinas: a view of law as a teacher, particularly a teacher of virtue. Third, I submit that the main challenge facing the pro-life movement during (and after) the *Roe* regime is to begin discerning how the law can inculcate a different set of values from that commonly inculcated by the "law as police officer" approach. In particular, I argue that we need to think about how the law can begin teaching the virtue of solidarity.

LAW AS POLICE OFFICER

One view of the purpose of law is essentially to act like a police officer. To understand this perspective, picture a marshal in the Old West, policing the vast, open prairies populated by strong, tough, independent cowboys. Each cowboy controls his own piece of property; he can do what he likes within its confines but he cannot trespass upon the property of anyone else. Think of the law as akin to the fences that keep these cowboys from treading on each other's land. They are crude instruments of restraint that place protective barriers around persons and their properties to keep them from being impinged upon by others.

This way of understanding the law presupposes a certain idea about human persons, who are seen as fundamentally disconnected from each other, as atomistic individuals who above all prize the ability to pursue their own plans without interference from anyone else. It also presupposes a certain view of morality. According to this view, morality is sharply divided into two sets of obligations: what you owe to other people and what you owe to yourself.

What you owe to yourself is largely to figure out what it is that you owe to yourself. The fundamental task for each person in life is self-creation: to define one's identity as an individual, to come to one's own personal understanding of the meaning of life. By its very nature this task is something that must be worked out alone, free from the undue influence of others. Each cowboy has to make the best of his own ranch. (For those familiar with the relevant Supreme Court opinions, this position is expressed in the famous "mystery passage" of *Planned Parenthood v. Casey*: "At the heart of liberty is the right to define one's own concept of existence, of meaning, of the universe, and of the mystery of human life. Beliefs about these matters could not define the attributes of personhood were they formed under compulsion of the state."[4])

What you owe to other people is compliance with a list of negative prohibitions: "Do not murder." "Do not rape." "Do not assault." "Do not steal." On this view, the reason such actions are wrong is not that they radically disrupt the fundamental relationship of care and respect that one person owes another by reason of their common humanity. Instead, such actions are wrong because, by engaging in them, one person is grossly interfering with the ability of the other person to pursue an individual life plan. Metaphorically speaking, by engaging in such actions you break down the fence between your land and your neighbor's and trespass on his property.

Adherents to this notion of "fenced" relationships among individuals also subscribe to a constrained interpretation of law's rightful aims: the law and, in particular, the criminal code should not be used for any purpose other than preventing one person from harming another. If someone's private behavior is not harmful to another, it should not be interfered with, no matter how morally wrong it might be or how harmful it might be to the agent. Private behavior is "a private choice." In essence, this perspective sets the terms of the abortion debate that we see in *Roe v. Wade* and, more particularly, in the decisions that followed in *Roe*'s wake. Against this legal background, the sole question becomes whether the fetus is a person. Following the logic of *Roe*, pro-choice advocates see the abortion issue as involving only one such person: a woman who must decide whether to bear a child. Once pro-choice advocates have concluded that a fetus does not count as a person, they can then easily argue that abortion is a purely private matter of no concern to the state one way or the other. In contrast, pro-life advocates count the unborn child as a person—as a fully rights-bearing human being. Since the core purpose of the law is to harness the power of the state to protect one person against the harm another person might do, the pro-life advocate believes it is imperative to use the law to protect an unborn child against the assault of abortion.

The persistent intensity of this well-worn argument between some pro-life and some pro-choice activists blinds both groups to the fact that they have far more in common than they believe. Both groups believe that the law's role is essentially that of a police officer. Both groups believe that the main purpose of law is restraint; both think law is to be used to prevent one person from harming another person. From the vantage point of their shared understanding of the nature and purpose of law, many pro-lifers and pro-choicers see their disagreement as revolving around one largely factual question: does the act of abortion involve one person or two?

LAW AS A TEACHER OF VIRTUE

Instead of seeing law as a police officer, one can think of law as a teacher. More specifically, one can construe the fundamental purpose of law as helping people to become respected and flourishing members of the community in which they live. Seen in this light, law is not fundamentally a fence that separates persons from one another. The legal system is an integral part of the moral framework that binds society together. In articulating that framework, the law not only builds up the common good but also fosters the ability of individuals to participate in that common good.[5]

In contrast to the police officer model, which assumes that individuals are atomistic, the "law as a teacher" perspective takes as a given that persons are essentially social and that a key part of flourishing as persons is participation in a variety of shared, communal activities. In the same vein, while recognizing the importance of making one's own choices, proponents of the "law as a teacher" stance also note that those choices are made in response to and have an effect upon the broader community. No person is an island. According to this view, law's function is not essentially restraint of wrongdoers; rather, all good law must have a pedagogical component. The law cannot be satisfied with merely restraining a wrongdoer; it must also seek to educate the wrongdoer about why those restraints are necessary. Law certainly does include elements of coercion and restraint, but these functions are not ends in themselves. Rather, a primary function of law is to orient its subjects toward a life of virtue and a concern for the common good in all citizens. Taken as a whole, the law tells a story about what counts for—and against—a life of virtue in a particular society, a story whose elements extend far beyond the specific prohibitions and requirements that the law enacts. As I argue in the first chapter, the Americans with Disabilities Act gestures toward a society in which virtuous people, both normally abled and with disabilities, regularly move to include each other in both private and public life.

If law is always and inevitably a moral teacher, then the "law as police officer" paradigm fails to recognize and take responsibility for this fact. So what should those committed to a pro-life stance say that the law should teach? Let me first explain what I mean by a pro-life stance. I maintain that to be pro-life is to contend that the dignity of human beings does not depend upon any achievement on their part; it does not depend on physical independence, mental acuity, "normalcy," or any ability to contribute in a tangible way to our society.[6] To be pro-life means to hold that society is measured by its willingness to care for the most vulnerable in its midst: the elderly, the chronically ill, the disabled, the immigrant—and the unborn. To have a pro-life stance toward the law means to hold that the fundamental legal category of "person" should be interpreted to include human beings falling in all of these categories.

What of the unborn, in particular? In my view, if a society is committed to honoring the dignity of all human beings—all human beings, no matter what their degree of dependence—then honoring the dignity of the unborn should be the "easy case," for two reasons. First, and in general, unborn life is full of promise: a long life, untold possibilities, boundless potential. The unborn child, who has prospects of outgrowing dependency, should consequently be the easiest type of dependent life for a community to support. If our polity cannot nurture dependent life full of promise of independence, how can we find it within our hearts to care for dependent life that has no hope of one day becoming independent and making an active contribution to our economic and social life? Second, the bond of support at stake here—the bond between mother and child—is commonly understood to be the strongest of all bonds between human beings. If our society cannot promote and protect the shelter offered by this bond of blood and bone and flesh, how can we possibly hope to create and nurture bonds of commitment and protection that extend to vulnerable strangers and even to vulnerable enemies? I think here of the atrocities committed by American soldiers at Abu Ghraib prison.[7]

A PRO-LIFE VISION AND AMERICAN LAW

In my judgment, the center of a pro-life vision is a commitment to the equal dignity of all human beings, no matter how weak, dependent, or vulnerable they are. But a moment's reflection suggests how ineffectually the "law as police officer" values operate to protect the weak and the vulnerable. Those values work very well for some members of the community. If people are young, strong, and vibrant, the basic thing they need in order to flourish is for other people to leave them alone. If people in their prime are vigorous, the negative prohibitions can provide sufficient protection. They will be just fine, provided nobody robs, beats, rapes, or kills them. They are mobile, independent, and can provide for their own basic needs.

But that is not the case for other members of the community: the weak and the vulnerable. Consider first the very elderly or the severely handicapped. It is only a first step—an important first step, but only a first step—not to kill such people. How long are they going to survive if no one brings them food, bathes them, keeps them warm, or makes sure they get their medicine? They need positive assistance, not merely to be left alone. A baby or even a toddler will soon die if no one feeds it, keeps it warm, and actively protects it. What about the unborn? The fetus requires not merely to be left unharmed by the woman who carries it but also needs her bodily life support and care.[8] Where would the unborn child be if the woman were somehow able to clamp off the nutrition she provides to it? What if she said, "I'm not going to abort the baby but I'm not going to nourish it, either"?[9]

Unfortunately, the "law as police officer" conviction has long held sway in important aspects of American law. I touch briefly upon only a few examples of its influence here. Generally speaking, no obligation in tort or criminal law requires one person to help another unless the two of them have some well-defined personal or professional relationship.[10] So, in the great majority of American states, if a man hurries past a two-year-old tipped over in a puddle, thereby letting her drown rather than being five minutes late for his movie, he commits no legal wrong. Even in the few states where his failure to aid the child is against the law, it is penalized only lightly. What about the obligations of parents to their children? Yes, parents do have a legal obligation to fish their own toddler out of the puddle. But they are not legally required to give her a blood transfusion even if it is the only way to save her life, although doing so is likely to cause them only minimal inconvenience.

What about the elderly and infirm? Historically the common law did not recognize any duty to support one's elderly parents. Today most Americans have only limited legal obligations to their own parents; currently only about half the states impose upon children what is usually a weak financial duty to aid their mother or father.[11] The relationship between legal and moral obligations is always complicated; nonetheless, I think it is accurate to say that our law does a very bad job of inculcating the moral duty to care for one's parents—a duty that, in the parents' dire circumstances, Thomas Aquinas believed would supersede even the moral duty to care for one's children.[12] What about persons with disabilities? Until recently, they were understood as having an obligation not to offend "normal persons" with their presence. As I describe in chapter 1, for years the Chicago Municipal Code included an ordinance colloquially known as "the ugly law," which restricted the rights of persons with disabilities to appear in public places in the municipality. This law and similar ones were not repealed until the mid-1970s.[13]

Regarded in this light, *Roe* does not seem to be so much a legal anomaly as it is the logical end of an outlook in which there is no positive obligation to aid the weak and vulnerable. In addition to the contention that a fetus is not an equally protectable "person," a second major argument in favor of legalized abortion is that the woman does not have a positive legal duty to give a fetus bodily life support, even if the fetus is a person. Unfortunately, that argument resonates all too well with those strands of American law that content themselves with the negative prohibitions that suffice for those in the full vigor of life, rather than moving on to the positive assistance so essential to the flourishing of those who cannot take care of themselves.

What is the flaw in assuming that normal human persons are autonomous, independent, self-contained, and therefore protected sufficiently by negative prohibitions? Alasdair MacIntyre's book *Dependent Rational Animals* offers a powerful response to this question.[14] The basis of his argument is a key conviction of Western philosophical anthropology: the human being is body and soul, a rational animal. As animals, we all start out small and helpless. Throughout our lives we remain vulnerable to disease, injury, and disability. And if we are fortunate enough to live to old age, our lives will be marked by a return to relative helplessness. MacIntyre reminds us that it is only during a portion of our lives, and sometimes only during a small portion, that we are relatively independent—yet we remain the same people over the waxing and waning of function.[15] "Disability is a matter of more or less, both in respect of degree of disability and in respect of the time periods in which we are disabled. And at different periods of our lives we find ourselves, often unpredictably, at very different points on that scale. When we pass from one such point to another we need others to recognize that we remain the same individuals that we were before making this or that transition."[16]

For MacIntyre, what is "normal" for the species Homo sapiens is to be vulnerable and dependent. In my estimation, the entire fabric of the Anglo-American legal system needs to be adjusted to take account of this fact. We need to supplement the rich legal concept of the "reasonable person" with a fuller concept of the "vulnerable person."

More specifically, a foundational concept in the Anglo-American legal system is that of the "reasonable person," sometimes called the "reasonable man," who as a hypothetical person always acts in accordance with the basic virtues and in consonance with society's basic norms of behavior. The "reasonable person" standard appears in tort, criminal, and contract law as the normative standard against which a particular defendant's action is measured. Someone who acted negligently, for example, did not act with the care that a reasonable person would have exercised in the same situation. According to a vivid definition found in *Black's Law Dictionary*, "The reasonable man connotes a person whose notions and standards of behaviour and responsibility correspond with those generally obtained among ordinary people in our society at the present time, who seldom allows his emotions to overbear his reason and whose habits are moderate and whose disposition is equable. He is not necessarily the same as the average man—a term which implies an amalgamation of counter-balancing extremes."[17]

The hypothetical "reasonable person" provides a normative standard for acting in a wide range of circumstances. The law, however, does not provide a "vulnerable person" standard, which points to the burdens that it is reasonable to expect persons to suffer and to bear—whether those burdens are caused by biology, natural disaster, or the acts of others.[18] A legal framework that takes seriously the dependency of human beings would devote far more attention to the hypothetical norm of the "vulnerable person" in assessing the way solidarity should be legally instantiated in our society.[19] Drawing upon insights from the growing field of disability studies should make it possible to develop a richly textured account of the level of suffering it is reasonable to expect persons to endure without significant assistance from the community.[20]

The addition of a "vulnerable person" standard would enable us to address inequitable situations brought about by our legal system's almost exclusive focus on the agent of harm rather than on the sufferer. For example, a baby whose serious disability is due to the negligence of a health care provider may well receive the financial resources necessary to enable a good life through a tort settlement. A baby who suffers a similar disability that is attributable only to the vagaries of genetics or fate will not have the same resources, although she has the same needs. A society committed to the virtue of solidarity would think it important to remedy this disparity. Moreover, MacIntyre's analysis has a further implication for pro-life work that he does not spell out himself.[21] Life does not sort itself out so that weak persons are always matched up with strong persons who can take care of them. Often the most vulnerable members of the population are virtually entirely dependent upon people only slightly less vulnerable than they are.

For example, in her book *Last Rights* Barbara Logue describes the significant burdens that many caregivers of the elderly bear. Her statistics demonstrate that more than one-third of those caregivers are themselves elderly, almost one-third are poor, and one-third suffer from precarious health.[22] She notes that one study of caregivers for Alzheimer's victims showed that 42 percent of those under the age of sixty-five and more than half of those over sixty-five showed clinically significant depression.[23] Moreover, the vast majority of caregivers of the elderly are women, who are likely to forsake their jobs in order to provide eldercare.[24] As Logue observes, in our system early departure from the workforce often means sacrificing pension benefits, group health benefits, and wage benefits—and therefore one's own security into old age. Accordingly, she cites statistics showing that women constitute 58.7 percent of the elderly population but a full 72.4 percent of the elderly poor.[25]

What about the vulnerable who depend upon the vulnerable in crisis pregnancies? According to a fairly recent study, women with incomes below 200 percent of the poverty level constituted 30 percent of all women of reproductive age but accounted for 57 percent of the abortions in 2000–2001.[26] Abortion rates decreased as women's income increased, from forty-four per one thousand pregnancies among poor women to ten per one thousand among the highest-income women. Adjusting for different pregnancy rates, high-income women are still the least likely to abort their pregnancies (15 percent) while poor and low-income women are the most likely to do so (33 percent). Furthermore, only one in six women who had an abortion was married. Nearly one in five women who had an abortion was a teenager; about half of the women who had an abortion were younger than twenty-five.

What is the basic pedagogical challenge facing the law if we assume that (1) weakness, vulnerability, and dependency are in some sense "normal" for human beings; and that (2) the weak and vulnerable are frequently dependent upon those only slightly less weak and vulnerable than they are? As I argue in chapter 2, a key virtue that the law has to foster is solidarity. As a specification of justice appropriate for our era, it is both a personal and a social virtue. Psychologist Sidney Callahan, who is both a feminist and pro-life, has aptly summarized the necessary patterns of response in women who carry a crisis pregnancy to term, in a society that supports such women, and, by extension, in a society that supports all vulnerable persons. Her account of solidarity is in tension with an understanding of autonomy as independence. It can, however, be reconciled with Raz's account of autonomy, provided it is treated as a worthwhile form of life to which people can commit themselves.

Feelings of sacrificial love and gifts of self to others are called for. Empathy and nurturing feelings are focused on the fetus, which is fiercely identified with either as a family member or as a powerless, helpless being in need of protection. Communal memberships and the giving and receiving of love are seen as the highest emotional fulfillments and attractions to achievement and independent autonomy are secondary. Life is with people, and being a good person is the all-important good. Creative receptivity to unplanned events is admired as a display of basic trust in the goodness of life and the universe. One has a duty to meet new personal demands with love and sacrificial work, even if they entail suffering, for relief of suffering is not the most important human goal. To suffer is preferable to doing harm or choosing evil because trust in the order of the universe delivers the individual from the lonely exercise of control and from a final autonomous responsibility for the future.[27]

At the same time, we need to remember that solidarity is not primarily an emotion, although it shapes and makes use of human emotions. It is a habit of the reason and the will, exercised through our actions, not merely through our feelings. According to Pope John Paul II, solidarity is not "a feeling of vague compassion or shallow distress at the misfortunes of so many people, both near and far" but rather "a firm and persevering determination to commit oneself to the common good; that is to say the good of all and of each individual because we are all really responsible for all."[28] Moreover, precisely because it is a commitment to the common good, the virtue of solidarity cannot remain solely a personal virtue; it has to become a general virtue that is reflected in the social and legal structures of the entire society. Solidarity requires, says John Paul II, building a "culture of life." In *Evangelium vitae* he writes: "Where life is involved, the service of charity must be profoundly consistent: It cannot tolerate bias and discrimination, for human life is sacred and inviolable at every stage and in every situation; it is an indivisible good. We need then to 'show care' for all life and for the life of everyone. Indeed, at an even deeper level, we need to go to the very roots of life and love."[29]

TOWARD A LEGAL PEDAGOGY OF SOLIDARITY

The relationship of law and morality is undeniably complicated. To develop a comprehensive jurisprudence centered on Razian autonomy and solidarity is beyond the scope of this book. But we can at least ask whether there are positive models in American law of nurturing solidarity with the vulnerable. For example, the Americans with Disabilities Act, which I first discussed in chapter

1, requires public services, public accommodations, and private services that are open to the public, such as restaurants, to be accessible to those with disabilities.[30] It prohibits employers with fifteen or more employees from refusing to hire an otherwise qualified person who is disabled. It requires employers to make "reasonable accommodations" that would allow such a person to do the job despite a disability. But the act is about more than imposing a discrete set of requirements and prohibitions; by extending its objective to transforming the minds and hearts of Americans toward persons with disabilities, its pedagogical thrust reaches far beyond its mandates. In short, the Americans with Disabilities Act is the anti–"ugly law."

Similarly, we could consider the Family and Medical Leave Act of 1993.[31] The Act entitles eligible employees of covered employers to take twelve weeks of leave in a twelve-month period in order to care for a newborn, newly adopted child, or a child newly placed in foster care; to look after a seriously ill spouse, child, or parent; or to deal with the employee's own serious illness. In addition, special provisions apply to the needs of military families. The goal of the act is not only narrowly to confer a three-month unpaid leave of absence upon those with a needy family member but also more broadly to encourage us all to recognize that workers have legitimate obligations to family members that can at times conflict with and take precedence over obligations to be at the workplace. In fact, the law states that one of its purposes is "to balance the demands of the workplace with the needs of families, to promote the stability and economic security of families, and to promote national interests in preserving family integrity."[32]

A third example is the health care reform package enacted into federal law in March 2010.[33] The Patient Protection and Affordable Care Act attempts to expand the net of health care coverage to the approximately fifty million Americans who were without coverage at that time—about one-sixth of the US population. According to the US Census Bureau, the ranks of the uninsured swelled at the end of the first decade of the second millennium as the great recession reduced the relative availability of health coverage as an employment benefit. More specifically, although 64.1 percent of the population was protected by job-related coverage in 2000, that number shrank to 55.3 percent in 2010.[34]

Expanding access to health insurance promotes both autonomy and solidarity.[35] A recent study conducted by Harvard Medical School and Cambridge Health Alliance suggests that the lack of health coverage shortens life; approximately forty-five thousand deaths annually are linked to the lack of health insurance. Furthermore, Americans under the age of sixty-four who do not have insurance run a 40 percent higher risk of premature death than those with private insurance, even after adjusting for socioeconomic factors, baseline health, and behavior.[36] Not only are the uninsured at greater risk of premature death, they are also more likely to be in bad health overall.[37] People who die too soon or who languish due to bad health are impeded from making the contributions they otherwise would have made to our common life.

Like the Americans with Disabilities Act, the 2010 health care reform package is limited and realistic in its goals. It introduces its mandates in staggered fashion.[38] It does not function as a thoroughgoing overhaul of the American health care financing and delivery system, which is a Byzantine network of contracts and legal regulations structuring relationships between and among patients, employers, providers, third-party payers, and the government.[39] Furthermore, it will not be a panacea for all the financial challenges faced by those burdened with health problems. It is true that about 60 percent of personal bankruptcies filed are caused by expenses related to medical illness; it is also true that nearly 80 percent of those bankruptcies were filed by those who did have health insurance.[40]

I do not mean to suggest that the Americans with Disabilities Act, the Family and Medical Leave Act, and the Patient Protection and Affordable Care Act are completely adequate pieces of legislation.[41] As advocates for persons with disabilities, family rights activists, and health care policy analysts indicate, that is not the case. Nor am I implying that the three laws are immune from critique on either moral or policy grounds. Pro-life groups were not wrong, for example, to scrutinize health care reform legislation for its impact on abortion, in effect arguing that solidarity must encompass the unborn as well as the born.[42] At the same time, I do think all three pieces of legislation attempt both to teach and to instantiate the virtues of autonomy and solidarity, with particular attention given to the vulnerabilities that attend to human beings because we are embodied beings, not pure bundles of mental energy.

ABORTION, LAW'S PEDAGOGY, AND LAW'S LIMITS

The law, of course, plays an important role in inculcating solidarity with the unborn—or in failing to do so. *Roe* and most of the Supreme Court cases that followed did not merely legalize abortion in "hard cases"; they did not present abortion as a drastic option to be considered only "in necessity and sorrow."[43] Instead, by year after year striking down legislative effort after legislative effort to encourage women to choose childbirth over abortion, *Roe* and its progeny effectively denied that abortion was morally problematic. The high-water mark of this misguided pedagogy can be found in Justice William Brennan's claim that "abortion and childbirth, when stripped of the sensitive moral arguments surrounding the abortion controversy, are simply two alternative medical methods of dealing with pregnancy."[44]

The fundamental task facing the pro-life movement now is to demonstrate how deeply mistaken Justice Brennan's view is. The law cannot strip out "sensitive moral arguments" for either the woman or the unborn child. And we as a society cannot strip out consideration of moral virtues either. The challenge facing the pro-life movement is to help the American people expand beyond rights talk and move toward the virtue of solidarity—solidarity with the unborn, solidarity with others who are vulnerable, and solidarity with those upon whom these most vulnerable persons depend. We must also not forget that the most vulnerable—the unborn—are entirely dependent upon those only slightly less vulnerable than they themselves are: women facing crisis pregnancies.

The picture is not totally grim. In *Planned Parenthood v. Casey* (1992), the Supreme Court partially rectified some of the pedagogical harm done by *Roe*. By conceptualizing the right to abortion more modestly as a "liberty interest" rather than as a "fundamental right," the Court allowed more room for communal moral discussion of the nature, appropriate use, and limits of that interest. In addition, by explicitly acknowledging that the state's interest in unborn life is present from the beginning, the *Casey* Court helps undermine Brennan's implication that the choice between childbirth and abortion should be viewed in a morally neutral manner by the law. The question then becomes not whether the state can encourage childbirth but what means the state can permissibly use to do so. Finally, *Casey* abandoned *Roe*'s trimester framework, which allowed the state to regulate abortion with a view to promoting the well-being of the unborn only after viability. Instead, it substituted a more flexible test that allows states to enact regulations restricting abortion and promoting unborn life throughout pregnancy, provided they do not impose an "undue burden" upon a woman's right to choose abortion before viability. After *Casey*, many states enacted provisions designed to encourage childbirth over abortion, such as requirements for waiting periods, mandated counseling, and parental involvement in the case of minors seeking abortion.[45]

Casey continues to impose significant restrictions upon the ability of the states to restrict abortion, particularly in the first months of pregnancy. Nonetheless, it is important not to think that eliminating constitutional protection for abortion will be sufficient to eradicate the practice. Even if *Casey* and *Roe* are overturned (an event whose likelihood in the immediate future is highly debatable), abortion will not necessarily be declared unconstitutional. Nor will it automatically become even illegal. States would simply then be free to do as they did before *Roe*, namely, to make their own legislation about abortion. Abortion, in other words, would be in the same constitutional status as assisted suicide: not prohibited and not protected. The fifty states will be free to function as "laboratories" (to use Justice O'Connor's term[46]) experimenting with different ways of dealing with the issue. How might the states experiment? The Center for Reproductive Rights considers twenty-one states at "high risk" of banning abortion, and nine states at "medium risk" of so doing. The Center for Reproductive Rights believes abortion rights are secure in twenty states.[47]

If the opportunity for a freer hand in crafting law and regulations about abortion should somehow present itself in our society, how should lawmakers convinced of the equal dignity of unborn life think about their task? Wise lawmakers will take into account a number of considerations in addition to the moral status of the actions prohibited, permitted, or required by a prospective statute. They must give due consideration to a number of countervailing factors. On the one hand, human law must attempt to lead people to virtue; on the other, it can only do so gradually. On the one hand, human law ought to point toward and encourage virtuous action; on the other hand, it ought never to engage in coercion or manipulation to secure it. This criterion is particularly important in framing informed consent requirements for abortion, which ought not require women to review sensationalistic or emotionally manipulative materials in order to dissuade them from going through with the procedure. On the one hand, human law ought not to endorse or explicitly to encourage morally unacceptable actions; on the other, it cannot require all virtuous actions or prohibit all vicious actions. Legal prohibitions and requirements that impose burdens too heavy for a significant portion of the population are counterproductive and are likely to provoke a backlash.

These broad limitations upon the power of human law apply not only to matters of secondary importance, such as whether the state should prohibit intoxicating substances such as alcohol or drugs. They also apply to questions that centrally pertain to justice, such as violent assaults on human life. Wise lawmakers take into account the practical limits on the law's ability to reshape the mores of the community even in framing norms prohibiting acts that inflict harm on innocent persons—including abortion. What about the related objection that the right to life is fundamental and therefore must be secured against unjust encroachment, ideally by criminal prohibitions, before attempting to use the law to encourage positive action to nurture life and to promote human flourishing more generally? I have suggested in the foregoing pages that this key theme of the negative "law as police officer" approach does not account for many of the positive actions necessary to protect vulnerable human beings, including the unborn. Now I want to propose that it does not take into account practical exigencies in the manner necessary to good law.

To say that the right to life is "fundamental" does not mean that wise lawmakers must make it a practical priority to criminalize wrongful takings of human life in every context in which they occur. My hypothetical example of the nineteenth-century boomtown "Deadwood" is designed to make that point. The community leaders who attempt to bring law and order to that lawless land ought not to begin by outlawing all unjust private killing; they could not begin to enforce such an injunction. Instead, they need to tailor their prohibitions with sensitivity to the current customs and mores of the people as well as to their own enforcement abilities. Otherwise their efforts might prove counterproductive, generating widespread contempt for the law and greater disorder than ever. I suggest that they might begin, for example, by outlawing killing on the main street in daylight hours, and prohibiting robbery of new prospectors traveling between the stagecoach depot and the hotel. I also emphasize that the fact that the lawmakers cannot effectively prohibit other sorts of unjust private killing does not mean that they ought to endorse or promote it.

What light can my Deadwood hypothetical shed on the current legal situation of abortion in the United States? I think it helps us to focus on both the legal and operational practicalities involved in protecting the fundamental right to life in particular cultures and contexts. And the particularities matter. It is not possible, first, to isolate unborn children in order to protect them; the unborn can be protected only by influencing the situation and the actions of the women whose bodies shelter and nurture them. This simple fact sets abortion apart from most, if not all, cases of unjust killing. In most cases of homicide, a person tempted to kill another has the alternative of walking away from the victim and from the situation as a whole. In the case of abortion, however, this is not the case. The mother not only cannot walk away from the unborn child, she is positively obliged to nurture and protect it with her own body for the better part of a year. Not only must she endure the physical changes, significant discomfort, and sometimes the real health risks that come with pregnancy, she must also endure the excruciating pain of labor and delivery, which can be blunted but not eliminated by medical means.

Does this factual distinction make a legal difference?[48] American law is sorely deficient in solidarity in that most states do not impose even a minimal "duty to rescue" another person in distress, absent special circumstances. While a parent does have a legal duty to rescue his or her own child, that duty does not extend to risking his or her own life. Nor does it include providing bodily life support or sustenance to a child who will die without it. A parent who refuses to give a dying three-year-old child bone marrow or even a pint of blood may be morally guilty but commits no crime. Lawmakers who want to impose greater restrictions on abortion will need to consider whether, when, and why it is permissible to require pregnant women to endure the burdens of continuing a pregnancy in a legal context that places no analogous demands of providing bodily support on parents—mothers or fathers—after the child's birth.

In addition, any broad state prohibition of abortion is likely to be difficult to enforce. Abortion is not a difficult medical procedure to perform; not only doctors but also nurse practitioners and nurses can easily be taught to perform them. Furthermore, chemical abortion by means such as RU-486 is readily available. Women will be able to travel to states in which abortion is legal. Abortion-inducing drugs will easily be smuggled across state lines. It will be difficult for law enforcement officials to distinguish early chemical abortions from natural miscarriages. For these reasons, wise lawmakers would do well to consider the evidence that countries that have prohibited abortion manifest abortion rates that are similar to those in countries where the procedure is legal.[49] In all these respects, the idea of prohibiting abortion by criminal means ought to make legislators think carefully about the analogies to the prohibition of the use of alcohol in the early twentieth century. Women who want abortions will find a way to obtain them.

Moreover, many of these women will think, subjectively, that they have a right to obtain abortion, just like many of the men in my Deadwood hypothetical thought they had a right to engage in a duel. Assuming that some states do manage to ban abortion if *Roe* is overturned, they will not be doing so in a historical, cultural, or geographic vacuum. Abortion will have been protected as a constitutional right for at least a half century. Neighboring states will offer access. Pro-choice activists will be shaken out of their complacency and will be galvanized to make their case and activate their lobbying and voter base to repeal the new law. It is one thing to deprive women of a service they think they need; it is another thing entirely to deprive them of a service to which they think they have a right.

How, then, should virtuous lawmakers who oppose the exercise of violence against the unborn approach their task? I think they should do so in much the same way that I suggest the lawmakers in my hypothetical Deadwood should approach theirs. The strictures of the criminal law ought to be deployed in order to reinforce, and perhaps slightly extend, the commitments of the majority without taxing the abilities of persons of ordinary virtue. I think, for example, it is entirely appropriate for states to prosecute persons who kill infants born alive after an abortion, or who flout state laws and regulations pertaining to the safety of their patients. The horrendous case of Philadelphia abortion provider Kermit Gosnell furnishes a good example. Gosnell was charged in 2011 with eight counts of murder, encompassing one adult woman who died after a botched abortion and seven infants whose spinal cords he allegedly severed after they survived late-term abortions.[50] It would not be wise, however, for our lawmakers to enact criminal sanctions against first-trimester abortions in the current context, for the same reason it was not appropriate for Deadwood's lawmakers to target private killing in the saloons. It is not that the life of the unborn—or the inebriated prospector—is of lesser value. It is that the law is less able to act to protect them, given the practical limitations of their circumstances and the society.

What about the moral objection voiced by John Paul II, who proclaims in *Evangelium vitae* that "laws which legitimize the direct killing of innocent human beings through abortion or euthanasia are in complete opposition to the inviolable right to life proper to every individual" and therefore can never be legitimate?[51] Some people have interpreted this provision as requiring citizens of good will to press unceasingly for recriminalization of abortion to protect the fundamental right to life. I think, however, the text supports a more nuanced reading. Certainly, John Paul II would say that states in which abortion is illegal ought not to "legitimate" the practice—to declare it good or proper. At the same time, these particular words do not offer much specific guidance to citizens who live in countries such as the United States, where abortion has long been established as a woman's legal right.

It is one thing to refrain from implementing an unjust legal framework; it is another thing entirely to reform one that is already well entrenched. The pope, in my view, recognizes the difference between the two situations. Here are his key reflections on the second situation:

> The Church well knows that it is difficult to mount an effective legal defence of life in pluralistic democracies, because of the presence of strong cultural currents with differing outlooks. At the same time, certain that moral truth cannot fail to make its presence deeply felt in every conscience, the Church encourages political leaders, starting with those who are Christians, not to give in, but to make those choices which, taking into account what is realistically attainable, will lead to the re-establishment of a just order in the defence and promotion of the value of life. Here it must be noted that it is not enough to remove unjust laws. The underlying causes of attacks on life have to be eliminated, especially by ensuring proper support for families and motherhood. A family policy must be the basis and driving force of all social policies. For this reason there need to be set in place social and political

initiatives capable of guaranteeing conditions of true freedom of choice in matters of parenthood. It is also necessary to rethink labour, urban, residential and social service policies so as to harmonize working schedules with time available for the family, so that it becomes effectively possible to take care of children and the elderly.[52]

Three points strike me as important. First, John Paul II recognizes that lawmakers are not theoreticians; their activity is both practical and goal-oriented. It is only, in fact, by "taking into account what is realistically obtainable" that they can hope to reestablish a just political order—not all at once, but step by step.

Second, John Paul II clearly recognizes that the law and social policy as a whole must be pro-life, for both moral and practical reasons. He does not endorse a lexical order demanding that criminal prohibitions be enacted before supportive social service programs are implemented. Indeed, he seems to recognize that any attempt to prohibit abortion will not be successful unless such programs are already in place. Abortion is not a rare procedure; an estimated one in three American women obtains an abortion in her reproductive lifetime. It stands to reason that many voters will not significantly restrict access until other workable ways of dealing with crisis pregnancy emerge.[53] It is not enough to say that women facing crisis pregnancies ought to give their children up for adoption. The evidence supports the fact that very few women do so. Having nurtured their children in their wombs for nine months, many new mothers cannot bear to part with them. It may be heroic virtue for some women to relinquish their babies to be raised by others. The law, however, cannot require heroic virtue of its subjects.[54]

Third, we must not forget that the most vulnerable—the unborn—are entirely dependent upon those only slightly less vulnerable than they are: women facing crisis pregnancies. We must provide these women with substantial assistance in meeting the challenge of their pregnancies, including the assistance (if the mother so desires) of the baby's father. This too is both a moral and a practical imperative. In discussing *Roe*, pro-life advocates frequently quote the claim of Thomas Aquinas that an unjust law is not, properly speaking, an act of law but rather an act of violence.[55] We need to remember that Aquinas says precisely the same thing of laws in which "burdens are imposed unequally on the community, although with a view to the common good." He also labels them unjust and hence "acts of violence rather than laws."[56] To cite Aquinas here, of course, does not settle the question of what counts as a just distribution of communal burdens. In my view, however, the idea that justice must be interpreted through solidarity strongly suggests that our legal system cannot rightly allow family members to bear the entire burden of caring for the most vulnerable members of society.[57]

CONCLUSION

While the right to life may be "fundamental" in the order of logic, the order of practicality demands a multifaceted strategy to protect that right in Western liberal democracies where abortion has long been legal and widely used. Recognizing lawmaking's nature as a practical activity designed to further the common good leads to the insight that pro-life legislators must broaden their focus beyond the criminal law. Too narrow a strategy will backfire and end up harming rather than promoting the overall well-being of the entire community, including the elderly and the unborn. Thus efforts to use the law to inculcate the value of unborn life must widen their focus beyond the criminal code, which details only one of many types of legal norms in our complex, postindustrial society. As Mary Ann Glendon notes in her groundbreaking book *Abortion and Divorce in Western Law*, reducing the number of abortions requires taking a long, hard look at far more than criminal law. Describing the protection for unborn life mandated by the West German Basic Law, she noted that "what is important is that the *totality* of abortion regulations—that is, all criminal, public health and social welfare laws related to abortion—be in proportion to the importance of the legal value of life, and that, as a whole, they work for the continuation of the pregnancy."[58]

NOTES

This chapter has its seeds in M. Cathleen Kaveny, "How Views of Law Influence the Pro-Life Movement," *Origins*, no. 34/35 (February 17, 2005): 560–65.

1. *Roe v. Wade*, 410 US 113 (1973). Although *Planned Parenthood v. Casey*, 505 US 833, 846 (1992) significantly modified the framework that the Court used to assess abortion, it also reaffirmed *Roe*'s "essential holding":

    It must be stated at the outset and with clarity that *Roe*'s essential holding, the holding we reaffirm, has three parts. First is a recognition of the right of the woman to choose to have an abortion before viability and to obtain it without undue interference from the State. Before viability, the State's interests are not strong enough to support a prohibition of abortion or the imposition of a substantial obstacle to the woman's effective right to elect the procedure. Second is a confirmation of the State's power to restrict abortions after fetal viability, if the law contains exceptions for pregnancies which endanger the woman's life or health. And third is the principle that the State has legitimate interests from the outset of the pregnancy in protecting the health of the woman and the life of the fetus that may become a child. These principles do not contradict one another; and we adhere to each.

2. John T. Noonan Jr., *A Private Choice* (New York: The Free Press, 1979), 6.

3. Kristin Luker, *Abortion and the Politics of Motherhood* (Berkeley: University of California Press, 1985), 141.

4. *Planned Parenthood v. Casey*, 505 US at 851 (1992).

5. For elaboration of this idea, see M. Cathleen Kaveny, "The Limits of Ordinary Virtue: The Limits of the Criminal Law in Implementing *Evangelium Vitae*," in *Choosing Life: A Dialogue on Evangelium Vitae*, ed. Kevin Wm. Wildes, SJ, and Alan Mitchell (Washington, DC: Georgetown University Press, 1997), 132–49; and Kaveny, "Toward a Thomistic Perspective on Abortion in the Law in Contemporary America," *Thomist* 55, no. 3 (1991): 343–96.

6. For other representative arguments of this point regarding the abortion issue, see Robert P. George and Christopher Tollefsen, *Embryo: A Defense of Human Life* (New York: Doubleday, 2008); Francis J. Beckwith, *Defending Life: A Moral and Legal Case against Abortion Choice* (New York: Cambridge University Press, 2007); and Christopher Kaczor, *The Ethics of Abortion: Women's Rights, Human Life, and the Question of Justice* (New York: Routledge, 2011). For nuanced pro-choice perspectives, see Margaret Little, "Abortion and the Margins of Personhood," *Rutgers Law Journal* 39 (2008): 331–48; David Boonin, *A Defense of Abortion* (Cambridge: Cambridge University Press, 2003); Jeff McMahan, *The Ethics of Killing: Problems at the Margins of Life* (New York: Oxford University Press, 2002); and Naomi Wolf, "Our Bodies, Our Souls," *New Republic*, October 16, 1995, 26–35. See also Gene Outka, "The Ethics of Love and the Problem of Abortion," an occasional paper published by University of Iowa School of Religion (1999).

7. See Jane Mayer, *The Dark Side: The Inside Story of How the War on Terror Turned into a War on American Ideals* (New York: Doubleday, 2008); and Karen J. Greenberg and Joshua L. Dratel, eds., *The Torture Papers: The Road to Abu Ghraib* (Cambridge: Cambridge University Press, 2005). For perspectives on torture from the field of religious ethics, see the essays in the "Focus on the Ethics of Torture," section of the *Journal of Religious Ethics* 39, no. 4 (2011): 585–621.

8. See Margaret Little, "Abortion, Intimacy, and the Duty to Gestate," *Ethical Theory and Moral Practice* 2 (1999): 295–312; and Margaret Little, "Procreative Liberty, Biological Connections, and Motherhood," *Journal of the Kennedy Institute of Ethics* 6, no. 4 (1996): 392–96.

9. The classic philosophical articulation of this position is Judith Jarvis Thomson, "A Defense of Abortion," *Philosophy and Public Affairs* 1, no. 1 (1971): 47–66. For a related argument from a Christian religious ethicist, see Patricia Beattie Jung, "Abortion and Organ Donation: Christian Reflections on Bodily Life Support," *Journal of Religious Ethics* 16 (1988): 273–305.

10. See, e.g., Restatement (Second) of Torts §§ 314-314A (1965) (no duty of affirmative action to aid or protect unless special relations) and J. D. Lee and Barry Lindahl,

Modern Tort Law, 2nd ed. (St. Paul, Minn.: Thomson/West 2002), vol. 1, § 3.9 (discussing "no duty to rescue rule" and its exceptions).

11. See, e.g., Lara Queen Plaisance, "Will You Still . . . When I'm Sixty-Four: Adult Children's Legal Obligations to Aging Parents," *Journal of the American Academy of Matrimonial Lawyers* 21 (2008): 245–70; and Charlotte K. Goldberg, "The Normative Influence of the Fifth Commandment on Filial Responsibility," *Marquette Elder's Advisor* 10 (2009): 221–44.

12. Thomas Aquinas, *Summa theologica*, 3 vols., trans. Fathers of the English Dominican Province (New York: Benziger Bros., 1948), II-II, q. 31, art. 3, rep. ob. 4: "Nevertheless in a case of extreme urgency it would be lawful to abandon one's children rather than one's parents, to abandon whom it is by no means lawful on account of the obligation we lie under toward them for the benefits we have received from them, as the philosopher states (Ethic. iii, 14)."

13. Chicago Municipal Code, § 36034 (repealed 1974).

14. Alasdair MacIntyre, *Dependent Rational Animals* (Chicago: Open Court, 1999). The focus on embodiment has also been a major theme of various feminist retrievals of Aristotle. For a helpful feminist complement to MacIntyre's work, see Eva Feder Kittay, *Love's Labor: Essays on Women, Equality, and Dependency* (New York: Routledge, 1999).

15. See Lisa Sowle Cahill and Diethmar Meith, *Aging* (London: SCM Press, 1991).

16. MacIntyre, *Dependent Rational Animals*, 73–74. See also Margaret Farley and Lisa Sowle Cahill, eds., *Embodiment, Morality, and Medicine* (Dordrecht: Kluwer, 1995).

17. *Black's Law Dictionary*, 9th ed., s.v. "reasonable person."

18. For an interesting theoretical discussion of the reasonable level of risk citizens should bear in a morally legitimate political or legal society, see Ronald Dworkin, *Sovereign Virtue: The Theory and Practice of Equality* (Cambridge, MA: Harvard University Press, 2002), 65–119.

19. Emory University has launched a fascinating interdisciplinary initiative, "Vulnerability and the Human Condition," with the following mission statement on its website: "The concept of 'vulnerability' at the heart of the Initiative is anchored in the realization that fundamental to our shared humanity is our shared vulnerability, which is universal and constant—inherent in the human condition. Further, societal institutions are shaped by the recognition of, and need to respond to, this shared vulnerability." Key contributions from a legal perspective are Martha Albertson Fineman, "The Vulnerable Subject: Anchoring Equality in the Human Condition," *Yale Journal of Law & Feminism* 20, no. 1 (2008): 1–23; and Fineman, "The Vulnerable Subject and the Responsive State," *Emory Law Journal* 60, no. 2 (2010): 251–75. See also Margaret Farley, *Compassionate Respect: A Feminist Approach to Medical Ethics and Other Questions* (New York: Paulist Press, 2002).

20. Katherine M. Boydell, Brenda M. Gladstone, and Elaine Stasilius Crawford, "The Dialectic of Friendship for People with Psychiatric Disabilities," *Psychiatric Rehabilitation Journal* 26 (2002): 123–31; Michael Solomon, Nancy Pistrang, and Chris Barker, "The Benefits of Mutual Support Groups for Parents of Children with Disabilities," *American Journal of Community Psychology* 29 (2001): 113–32; and Tom Shakespeare, "Disability: Suffering, Social Oppression, or Complex Predicament?" in

The Contingent Nature of Life, ed. Marcus Düwell, Christoph Rehmann-Sutter, and Dietmar Mieth (Dordrecht, Netherlands: Springer, 2008), 235–46.

21. Robert George and Patrick Lee defend one particular implication of MacIntyre's work for abortion in *Body–Self Dualism in Contemporary Ethics and Politics* (New York: Cambridge University Press, 2008), 148–50.

22. Barbara J. Logue, *Last Rights: Death Control and the Elderly in America* (New York: Lexington Books, 1993), 141–42. Although Logue's statistics are now somewhat dated, the general picture remains accurate. For one possible approach to solidarity with elderly women, see M. Cathleen Kaveny, "The Order of Widows: What the Early Church Can Teach Us about Older Women and Health Care," *Christian Bioethics* 11, no. 1 (2004): 11–34.

23. Ibid., 197.

24. Ibid., 201.

25. Ibid., 205–6.

26. Rachel K. Jones, Jacqueline E. Darroch, and Stanley K. Henshaw, "Patterns in the Socioeconomic Characteristics of Women Obtaining Abortions in 2000–2001," *Perspectives on Sexual and Reproductive Health* 34 (2002): 226–35. The investigators are associated with the Alan Guttmacher Institute, a research center affiliated with Planned Parenthood Federation of America.

27. Sidney Callahan, "Value Choices in Abortion," in *Abortion: Understanding Differences*, ed. Sidney and Daniel Callahan (New York: Springer, 1984), 300. See also Lisa Sowle Cahill "Abortion, Autonomy, and Community," in *Abortion and Catholicism: The American Debate*, ed. Thomas Shannon and Patricia Beattie Jung (New York: Crossroad, 1988), 85–98.

28. Pope John Paul II, *Sollicitudo rei socialis* (*On Social Concern*) (1987), para 38.

29. Pope John Paul II, *Evangelium vitae* (*Gospel of Life*) (1995), para. 87.

30. Americans with Disabilities Act, Pub. L. No. 101-336, 104 Stat. 328 (1990) (as amended in scattered sections of 42, 47, and 29 USC). Several Supreme Court decisions have narrowed the protections offered by the ADA.

31. Family and Medical Leave Act of 1993, Pub. L. No. 103-3, 107 Stat. 6 (codified as amended in scattered sections of 3, 5, and 29 USC).

32. FMLA § 2(b)(1).

33. See Lawrence R. Jacobs and Theda Skocpol, *Health Care Reform and American Politics: What Everyone Needs to Know* (New York: Oxford University Press, 2010). For an account of the political machinations surrounding the controversial legislation, see Staff of the Washington Post, *Landmark: The Inside Story of America's New Health-Care Law and What It Means for Us All* (New York: Public Affairs, 2010). The Supreme Court upheld the constitutionality of most provisions of the Act (except for the Medicaid expansion program) in *National Federation of Independent Business v. Sebelius*, 132 S.Ct. 2566 (2012).

34. For a summary, see Les Christie, "Number of People without Health Insurance Climbs," *CNN Money*, September 13, 2011, http://money.cnn.com/2011/09/13/news/economy/census_bureau_health_insurance/index.htm. The data is available at the US Census Bureau's website in the section "Health Insurance."

35. See Maura Ryan, "Health and Human Rights," *Theological Studies* 69, no. 1 (2008): 144–63. On the dangers of seeing health care as a mere commodity, see M. Cathleen

Kaveny, "Commodifying the Polyvalent Good of Health Care," *Journal of Medicine and Philosophy* 24, no. 3 (1999): 207–23.

36. Andrew P. Wilper, Steffie Woolhandler, Karen E. Lasser, Danny McCormick, David H. Bor, and David U. Himmelstein, "Health Insurance and Mortality in US Adults," *American Journal of Public Heath* 99 (2009): 2289–95, doi:10.2105/AJPH.2008.157685.

37. Lisa Dubay, Allison Cook, and Bowen Garrett, "How Will the Uninsured be Affected by Health Reform," Urban Institute, August 27, 2009, www.urban.org/url.cfm?ID=411950. See also Kaiser Commission on Medicaid and the Uninsured, *The Uninsured: A Primer—Key Facts about Americans without Health Insurance*, October 13, 2011, Pub. No. 7451-07, www.kff.org/uninsured/7451.cfm.

38. For a balanced summary, see Hinda Chaikind, Curtis W. Copeland, C. Stephen Redhead, and Jennifer Staman, *PPACA: A Brief Overview of the Law, Implementation, and Legal Challenges* (Washington, DC: Congressional Research Service, 2011). Effective before 2014 are a number of coverage expansions (e.g., creating temporary high-risk pools to insure persons previously denied insurance because of preexisting conditions) and private health insurance market reforms (e.g., extending family coverage to adult children up to age twenty-six, and prohibiting major medical plans from imposing any lifetime dollar limits on essential benefits). The act's major provisions, however, take effect in 2014. With federal subsidies, state Medicaid programs will be required to expand programs to cover all eligible residents with incomes up to 133 percent of the federal poverty level. Each state will be expected to create a health insurance exchange through which individuals and small employers can purchase insurance; the premiums of those with incomes below 400 percent of the poverty level will be subsidized. When these structures are in place, the law will require most people to obtain insurance or to pay a penalty. Moreover, most employers with fifty or more employees will be required to provide insurance. In addition, other mandates will come into effect at this time, such as a blanket prohibition of exclusion based on preexisting conditions.

39. For an overview of the current system and its development, see Steven Jonas, Raymond Goldsteen, and Karen Goldsteen, eds., *An Introduction to the US Health Care System*, 6th ed. (New York: Springer, 2007); and Donald A. Barr, *Introduction to US Health Policy: The Organization, Financing, and Delivery of Health Care in America*, 3rd ed. (Baltimore: Johns Hopkins University Press, 2011).

40. David U. Himmelstein, Deborah Thorne, Elizabeth Warren, and Steffie Woolhandler, "Medical Bankruptcy in the United States, 2007: Results of a National Study," *American Journal of Medicine* 122, no. 8 (2009): 741–46.

41. Even the question of what is to be included in the benefit package is problematic. See M. Cathleen Kaveny, "Distributive Justice in the Era of the Benefit Package: The Dispute over the Oregon Basic Health Services Act," in *Critical Choices and Critical Care: Catholic Perspectives on Allocating Resources in Intensive Care Medicine*, ed. Kevin Wm. Wildes, SJ (Dordrecht, Netherlands: Kluwer, 1995).

42. The controversy was long, complicated, and intense. A good way into the debate is Annenberg Public Policy Center, FactCheck.org, "The Abortion Issue," April 1, 2010, www.factcheck.org/2010/04/the-abortion-issue/.

43. The phrase comes from Magda Denes, *In Necessity and Sorrow: Life and Death in an Abortion Hospital* (New York: Basic Books, 1976).

44. *Beal v. Doe*, 432 US 438, 449 (1977) (Brennan, J., dissenting) (quoting *Roe v. Norton*, 408 F. Supp. 660, 663 n.3 (Conn. 1975)).
45. For a fuller summary, see Guttmacher Institute, "State Policies in Brief: An Overview of Abortion Laws," www.guttmacher.org/statecenter/spibs/spib_OAL.pdf. See also Guttmacher Institute, "States Enact Record Number of Abortion Restrictions in First Half of 2011," July 13, 2011, www.guttmacher.org/media/inthenews/2011/07/13/index.html. One pro-life scholar argues that some of these restrictions correlate with abortion reduction. Michael J. New, "Analyzing the Effect of Anti-Abortion US State Legislation in the Post-Casey Era," *State Politics & Policy Quarterly* 11, no. 1 (2011): 28–47. See also Michael J. New, "Analyzing the Effect of State Legislation on the Incidence of Abortion among Minors," Heritage Foundation, February 5, 2007, www.heritage.org/research/reports/2007/02/analyzing-the-effect-of-state-legislation-on-the-incidence-of-abortion-among-minors.
46. See, e.g., Justice O'Connor's dissenting opinion in *Gonzales v. Raich*, 545 US 1, 42–43 (2005).
47. Center for Reproductive Rights, "What if *Roe* Fell?" (2007), http://reproductiverights.org/sites/crr.civicactions.net/files/documents/WIRF_FINAL_factsheet_with_LOGO.pdf.
48. For a helpful analysis of the limits of analogy in understanding the abortion situation, see Lisa Sowle Cahill, "Abortion and Argument by Analogy," *Horizons* 9, no. 2 (1982): 271–87.
49. Gilda Sedgh, Stanley Henshaw, Susheela Singh, Elizabeth Åhman, and Iqbal H. Shah, "Induced Abortion: Estimated Rates and Trends Worldwide," *Lancet* 370 (October 13, 2007): 1338–45.
50. See Office of the District Attorney, City of Philadelphia, Grand Jury Report, "Investigation of Women's Medical Society," January 19, 2011, www.phila.gov/districtattorney/grandjury_womensmedical.html.
51. John Paul II, *Evangelium vitae*, para. 72.
52. Ibid., para. 90.
53. Guttmacher Institute, "Facts on Induced Abortion in the United States (August 2011)," www.guttmacher.org/pubs/fb_induced_abortion.html.
54. Aquinas, *Summa theologica*, I-II, q. 96, art. 2.
55. Ibid., I-II, q. 96, art. 4.
56. Ibid.
57. See Todd Whitmore, "Moral Methodology and Pastoral Responsiveness: The Case of Abortion and the Care of Children." *Theological Studies* 54, no. 2 (1993): 316–38.
58. Mary Ann Glendon, *Abortion and Divorce in Western Law: American Failures, European Challenges* (Cambridge, MA: Harvard University Press, 1987), 28. Glendon was talking about Germany's treatment of abortion. See also Donald P. Kommers, "The Constitutional Law of Abortion in Germany: Should Americans Pay Attention?," *Journal of Contemporary Health Law & Policy* 10, no. 1 (1994): 1–32. For a more recent assessment, see Donald P. Kommers, "Looking to Germany," letter to the editor, *Commonweal*, November 4, 2011. See also Charles E. Curran, "The US Catholic Bishops and Abortion Legislation: A Critique from within the Church," an occasional paper (no. 28) published by the Cary M. Maguire Center for Ethics and Public Responsibility, Southern Methodist University (2011).

❦

CHAPTER 4

Bad Pedagogy, Bad Law
What FOCA Is—and Isn't

I N CHAPTER 3 I ARGUED THAT, even in a pluralistic liberal democracy such as ours, accounting for the function of law as a moral teacher is an important aspect of both theorizing about law and law-making itself. At the same time, the moral message of a law is not the only thing that matters. The law's pedagogical function cannot be separated from other aspects of good law, such as its capacity to coordinate the activities of various groups and individuals, in large part by providing clear direction to those it purports to bind.

Thomas Aquinas clearly recognizes that the pedagogical function of law, while important, is not exhaustive of the criteria that define good legislation. In fact, as I have emphasized, he approvingly cites the multifaceted summary of the characteristics of good law compiled by Isidore of Seville (d. 636): "Law shall be virtuous, just, possible to nature, according to the custom of the country, suitable to place and time, necessary, useful, clearly expressed, lest by its obscurity it lead to misunderstanding, framed for no private benefit but for the common good.[1]

While good law communicates a virtuous moral message, it is not reducible to its moral message. Law, says Aquinas, is fundamentally "a rule and measure of [human] acts";[2] its purpose is to coordinate or "direct" those actions to the common good.[3] Such coordination does not happen automatically. It is most realized when those bound by the law actively incorporate the law's lessons into their own practical reasoning about what to do and what not to do.

No matter how virtuous the legislative moral goal may be, law fails in its fundamental function if it is not promulgated (that is, communicated to those it binds), or not promulgated in a sufficiently clear manner to function as a reliable action guide.[4] No matter how sound the resultant law's moral message, if a piece of proposed legislation will operate in a manner that is not clear to those charged with implementation or obedience, the law will be inefficient and to that degree ineffective. In fact, one could say more strongly, to that degree it is a bad law because the uncertainty it precipitates will bring disorder rather than order to the community.

Moreover, if the normative goal of a law is not virtuous, if its moral message is not sound, lack of clarity about its operational effect will only compound its deleterious effects. A law with a vague scope provides opportunities for supporters to extend—and to entrench—its mistaken pedagogy. Opponents of the unjust law will be forced to deal not only with its immediate effects but also with its amorphous reach. Consequently, they will perceive such a law as doubly dangerous to the common good.

What about a situation in which a political community is deeply divided about whether the underlying moral message of a law is virtuous or vicious? This question is not hypothetical. We face such situations with some frequency in the United States, particularly with respect to "culture war" issues such as abortion, embryonic stem cell research, and gay marriage. If morally controversial laws are also operationally unclear, they can be significantly destabilizing to the community because their lack of clarity enhances the scope and intensity of the underlying moral and political battle. To those who support the governing moral vision of the proposed law, the vagueness seems like a fruitful opportunity to expand the law's reach, while to those who oppose that vision, the cloudiness prompts consideration of worst-case scenarios. The existence of this phenomenon is not lost on political activists. Provoking this very dynamic can be strategically useful to those on both sides of a controversy because the resulting uproar galvanizes attention. In some cases, the vagueness is so extreme as to raise questions about whether the authors actually drafted the bill with the intention of enactment or with some other purpose, such as attracting political attention and support.

FOCA: AN UNCLEAR BILL WITH A CLEAR PEDAGOGICAL MESSAGE

What would a piece of legislation look like if it were focused on sending a particular moral message with virtually no attention to its practical, operational details? What kind of a reaction would it provoke, not only from those who agreed with its moral message but also from those who vehemently disagreed with that message? We have, I think, a good case study with which to address these questions in the Freedom of Choice Act (FOCA) controversy, which reached a fever pitch during the 2008 presidential election.[5] FOCA, however, was not a newcomer to the political scene. It was first introduced by pro-choice activists in the 101st Congress in 1989 and has been reintroduced in several congressional sessions since that time. At no point did the bill ever make it out of committee to the floor of either house for a vote, even in 1993, when Democrats controlled both houses and President Clinton was in the White House.[6]

What, then, catapulted FOCA to national attention? Pro-life worries about FOCA and the 2008 election crystallized initially around a remark made by Barack Obama at a Planned Parenthood event in July 2007. At that event Obama promised that signing the act would be the "first thing I'd do as president."[7] Taking that statement as their rallying point, pro-life activists, including the Catholic bishops, mobilized to fight FOCA. At their annual conference, held just days after Obama's election, the bishops expressed resolute opposition to the bill, with Francis Cardinal George, president of the United States Conference of Catholic Bishops, warning that "FOCA would have lethal consequences for prenatal human life."[8]

Just how sweeping the potential effects of FOCA would be has been a matter of some dispute. While NARAL Pro-Choice America claimed that FOCA would merely "codify *Roe v. Wade*'s protections," it is clear that other pro-choice activists expected far more from the bill.[9] In April 2007 the National Organization of Women issued a press release forecasting that FOCA "would sweep away hundreds of antiabortion laws [and] policies."[10] In 2004 Planned Parenthood predicted the demise of "laws that prohibit the public funding of abortions for poor women or counseling and referrals for abortions." Additionally, the group said, FOCA would eliminate "onerous restrictions on a woman's right to choose, such as mandated delays and targeted and medically unnecessary regulations."[11]

Many pro-lifers agreed about FOCA's far-reaching effects, sometimes quoting their pro-choice opponents to support their own interpretations. In a September 2008 letter to Congress, Justin Cardinal Rigali warned that under the act "abortion on demand would be a national *entitlement* that government must condone and promote in all public programs affecting pregnant women."[12] One month later, in an essay titled "Obama's Abortion Extremism," Princeton's Robert George, an eminent pro-life legal scholar, predicted that "FOCA would abolish virtually every existing state and federal limitation on abortion," from parental consent and notification laws to conscience protections for pro-life workers in the health care industry. Such workers, he predicted, could be "forced to participate in the practice of abortion or else lose their jobs."[13]

FOCA: AN OVERVIEW

Is FOCA truly such a powerfully transformative piece of legislation? Not necessarily. Given the intense controversy, one might expect that the law contemplated a fully worked-out legal regime that aggressively protects abortion rights. Yet despite its bold rhetoric in favor of a "fundamental right" to choose abortion, FOCA does not entail a clear, detailed, and effective legal schema to protect that right. In fact, the act's operational details appear to be little more than an afterthought, as even a cursory examination of the 2007 bill makes clear.

FOCA describes itself as a bill "to protect, consistent with *Roe v. Wade*, a woman's freedom to choose to bear a child or terminate a pregnancy." It is a short bill, comprising six sections printable in three pages. Section 2, "Findings," offers an extended and passionate defense of a woman's right to choose abortion, grounding it in the recognition that "individuals are free to make the most intimate decisions without governmental interference and discrimination." Section 2(1) proclaims that "the United States was founded on core principles, such as liberty, personal privacy, and equality, which ensure that individuals are free to make their most intimate decisions without governmental interference and discrimination." In section 2(4), the bill goes on to laud *Roe v. Wade* (1973) because that opinion "carefully balances the rights of women to make important reproductive decisions with the State's interest in potential life." *Roe* is necessary, proclaims FOCA, to protect women's lives and economic interests. Section 2(5) raises the specter of illegal abortions and their "risk of unsanitary conditions, incompetent treatment, infection, hemorrhage, disfiguration, and death." After outlining the threats to legal abortion, the bill finally proclaims in section 2(10) that "legal and practical barriers to the full range of reproductive services endanger women's health and lives." Section 2(12) wraps up by stating that "to guarantee the protections of *Roe v. Wade*, Federal legislation is necessary."

Clearly, the drafters viewed section 2 not only as the pedagogical heart of the bill but also as the center of their interest and concern more broadly. From a pragmatic, operational point of view, however, the heart of FOCA is section 4, "Interference with Reproductive Health Prohibited." Compared to the "Findings" section, section 4 is noticeably skimpy. In fact, its three short paragraphs generate a word count that is not even one-fifth that of section 2's ringing proclamations of the importance of the right to choose abortion. Here is section 4 in its entirety:

(a) Statement of Policy—It is the policy of the United States that every woman has the fundamental right to choose to bear a child, to terminate a pregnancy prior to fetal viability, or to terminate a pregnancy after fetal viability when necessary to protect the life or health of the woman.

(b) Prohibition of Interference—A government may not—
   (1) deny or interfere with a woman's right to choose—
      (A) to bear a child;
      (B) to terminate a pregnancy prior to viability; or
      (C) to terminate a pregnancy after viability where termination is necessary to protect the life or health of the woman; or
   (2) discriminate against the exercise of the rights set forth in paragraph
      (1) in the regulation or provision of benefits, facilities, services, or information.

(c) Civil Action—An individual aggrieved by a violation of this section may obtain appropriate relief (including relief against a government) in a civil action.

RESTRICTIONS ON PREVIABILITY ABORTIONS

What would FOCA do? The key, obviously, is section 4(b), which forbids a government to "deny or interfere with" a woman's right to choose, and prevents "discrimination" against the exercise of this right. But what, concretely, does this language mean? To understand the prohibition, we need to assess the scope of the protected right, as defined by *Roe v. Wade* and as interpreted in subsequent cases.[14] Once we do, we find ourselves quickly fogged in by ambiguity. Some pro-life commentators have suggested that the "noninterference" provision in section 4(b)(1) would invalidate all restrictions on previability abortion, including those necessary to protect the health of the mother.[15] Yet section (4)(b)(1) closely tracks *Roe* itself, which, while prohibiting restrictions on abortion in the first trimester, allowed restrictions that are "reasonably related to maternal health" from that point until viability, and which permitted states to proscribe abortion entirely after viability unless the abortion is necessary to preserve maternal life or health.

True, in several post-*Roe* cases, a number of states' attempts to regulate around the edges of the abortion right (for example, spousal notification and informed-consent provisions) were declared unconstitutional. However, some restrictions on abortion were also upheld by later cases interpreting and apply-ing *Roe*. In *Webster v. Reproductive Health Services* (1989), the Court, reaffirm-ing that the right to abortion created by *Roe* did not establish an affirmative right to governmental aid, supported reasonable requirements for doctors who perform abortions to determine whether a fetus is viable before going ahead with abortion.[16] In *Planned Parenthood v. Casey* (1992), the Court upheld both "the essential holding of *Roe*" and several state restrictions, including requirements for a twenty-four-hour waiting period, informed consent, and parental notification (with judicial bypass).[17] The effect that this line of cases interpreting *Roe* would have on FOCA is extremely unclear. Both pro-life and pro-choice activists have contended that FOCA would sweep away the regulations allowed by these cases.[18] In fact, FOCA first emerged as a pro-choice legislative strategy that was partially a response to the Supreme Court's decisions in *Webster* and *Casey*.[19]

Yet the current language of the bill makes not a single disparaging remark about *Casey*; in fact, FOCA's sole mention of the case is positive.[20] Moreover, the most significant change brought about by *Casey* had to do not with the substance of the constitutional right affirmed in *Roe* but with the standard used to review laws that might conflict with that right. *Roe* demanded that any legal restriction touching upon a woman's right to choose be reviewed under the "strict scrutiny" standard, which requires that the regulation must protect a compelling state interest and be narrowly tailored to interfere as little as possible with the right in question. The controlling plurality opinion in *Casey* substituted a more lenient test, which prohibited legislation from imposing an "undue burden" upon a woman's choice. FOCA nowhere addresses *Casey*'s shift in standard of review; furthermore, if FOCA were to be passed, the courts might well be occupied with the tedious task of deciding whether laws that passed muster under *Casey*'s "undue burden" test would also pass muster under FOCA's "no interference" test. What, after all, is the difference between a law that "interferes" with a right to choose and a law that "places a substantial burden" in the path of a woman seeking an abortion?

PARTIAL-BIRTH ABORTION

The most recent combustible topic in the abortion wars was partial-birth abortion, which prompted renewed discussion of FOCA on the part of both pro-choice and pro-life activists. A close reading of the 2007 text reveals that FOCA's import is equally unclear in this sphere. Although the bill does make critical remarks about *Gonzales v. Carhart* (2007)—the Supreme Court case that upheld the federal law banning partial-birth abortion—FOCA's operative language is probably insufficient to undo that ban.[21] FOCA explicitly allows the prohibition of postviability abortions if they are not necessary to preserve the life or health of the mother. But in *Carhart*, the Court emphasized that Congress had found that the partial-birth abortion procedure is never necessary to preserve a woman's health. In addition, the majority opinion explicitly made room for an "as applied" challenge to the ban in the unlikely event that a physician believed that such a procedure was in fact necessary. So FOCA in its current form and *Carhart* do not clash directly. In the absence of clear congressional intent to repeal the Partial Birth Abortion Act, a court could reasonably decide to read FOCA in a way that preserves the former.

ABORTION FUNDING

What about the use of state or federal funds to pay for the abortions of indigent women? One can certainly read the nondiscrimination provision (4)(b)(2) as mandating abortion funding. But does this reading make the most sense of the text as a whole? The language prohibits discrimination against the exercise of the right to choose. Yet the abortion right as protected by *Roe* has repeatedly been held by the Supreme Court to be a negative right, not a positive right: no one has a constitutional right to have the government pay for an abortion, at least not an elective one.[22] Accordingly, the operative language of FOCA nowhere clearly demands funding.

Furthermore, a court interpreting FOCA could observe that if Congress wanted to fund abortion, the easiest mechanism would be through a provision in the annual catchall legislation, the Omnibus Budget Reconciliation Act. At the very least, Congress could simply repeal the Hyde Amendment, which since 1976 has prohibited federal funds from being used for most types of abortions.[23] Despite its portentous rhetoric, FOCA cannot simply "trump" the Hyde Amendment, which is also federal law—especially if the Hyde Amendment is passed again after FOCA is enacted. In the event of a conflict between two federal laws, the courts would have to reconcile the two pieces of legislation, and would most likely do so by reading the ambiguous FOCA in a less expansive manner. And what about requiring the states to fund abortion? Such unfunded mandates are politically controversial; again, if Congress desired the states to pay for abortions, it has a clear, practical, and legally less controversial way to achieve that end. Using a carrot rather than a stick, Congress could easily make a state's participation in the Medicaid program contingent upon covering elective abortions.

All in all, then, the text of FOCA would seem to yield regulatory effects less clear and far-reaching than its more ardent supporters—or its more alarmist interpreters—might claim. For instance, in section 4(b)(2) FOCA forbids the government to "discriminate against the exercise of the rights" the bill sets forth "in the regulation or provision of benefits, facilities, services, or information." Some commentators have read this provision broadly as requiring the law to ensure that abortion and childbirth receive equal support.

But such a broad reading is closer to an affirmative action requirement than a nondiscrimination requirement. In civil rights law, the prohibition against discrimination generally means that one cannot purposefully disfavor an individual on the basis of the protected category, but such a nondiscrimination provision does not mean that one has to ensure equal outcomes in every case.[24] So, for example, while a state would need to license both private abortion clinics and pro-life crisis-pregnancy centers, that state would not have to require either that the pro-life center perform abortions or, for that matter, that the abortion clinic provide prenatal care. Furthermore, state choices made on grounds other than disfavoring either abortion or childbirth would be acceptable. For example, a state hospital or program that offers medically necessary services but not elective procedures would have to offer medically necessary abortions but would not need to offer elective ones.

CONSTITUTIONAL ISSUES

Some pro-lifers have claimed that the "nondiscrimination" provision of FOCA will invalidate any state "conscience clause" provisions, which protect hospitals and health care providers from retaliation if they refuse to perform abortions. This outcome strikes me as unlikely.[25] FOCA says that the state may not "discriminate against" the exercise of the right to choose in the "regulation or provision of benefits, facilities, services, or information." But it says nothing about the regulation of individual providers. Moreover, religious citizens, as well as religious institutions, have a First Amendment interest in acting in accordance with their beliefs.[26] If Congress were to demand that the states override that interest, far more explicit language would be required.

Even if FOCA is eventually passed by Congress and signed by the president, it faces another significant hurdle. In my view the sweeping boldness of the bill's language generates significant constitutionality questions that could tie up the legislation in litigation for years. While FOCA denies that it is creating new constitutional rights, its proclamation that a woman has a "fundamental right" to choose whether to seek an abortion certainly sounds like a proclamation about a constitutional right. Moreover, some of the language suggests that this fundamental right is meant to function like a constitutional right, potentially altering every other federal, state, and local statute within its ambit. For example, FOCA purports to invalidate not only inconsistent federal laws enacted prior to its passage but also those subsequently enacted. In doing so, it operates more like a constitutional provision than a federal law.

Is it within the power of Congress to override the Supreme Court's interpretation of the rights protected by the Constitution, or to add constitutional rights to the Constitution in a manner that circumvents the amendment process? These are essential questions. Not surprisingly, the Supreme Court has not taken kindly to past congressional attempts to undercut its interpretation of the Constitution. For example, after the Court substantially restricted the right to religious freedom in *Employment Division v. Smith* (1990), Congress passed the Religious Freedom Restoration Act (RFRA).[27] In essence, that act attempted to overrule the Court by requiring states to adhere to the more expansive understanding of religious freedom in place before *Smith*. But in *Boerne v. Flores* (1997), the Supreme Court rejected this move, emphatically reaffirming its own power to interpret the rights guaranteed by the Constitution.[28] According to the Court, Congress is permitted under section 5 of the Fourteenth Amendment to enact measures that "remedy or prevent" unconstitutional actions on the part of states, but this constitutional provision does not empower Congress to "make a substantive change" in the constitutional rights recognized by the Court. Moreover, such legislative measures must exhibit "congruence and proportionality" between their remedial or preventative purpose and the means they deploy to achieve this purpose.

How would FOCA fare under the *Boerne* standard? In my view it would not fare very well, at least to the extent that the law is interpreted as creating a de facto constitutional right. If *Roe* were to be overruled by the Court, FOCA would arguably then be viewed as akin to RFRA: a congressional trump of the Supreme Court's interpretation of the Constitution. Even if *Roe* were left untouched, FOCA might still be considered an unconstitutional circumvention of later cases such as *Casey* or *Carhart* that interpreted the right to abortion. Moreover, even if FOCA's purpose is deemed to be a legitimate attempt to "remedy or prevent" unconstitutional violations of a woman's right to choose, as currently understood by the Supreme Court, there remains a serious question: does FOCA's broad-gauged approach exhibit sufficient "congruence and proportionality" between means and ends?

There is also a second reason why FOCA might be unconstitutional. The bill, asserting that the abortion business is a matter of interstate commerce, grounds its exercise of power over the states in the Commerce Clause of article

1, section 8. That contention, however, might not survive judicial scrutiny. After years of generous deference to congressional claims of lawmaking authority under the Commerce Clause, the Supreme Court began to set limits to that authority in *United States v. Lopez* (1995).[29] FOCA asserts a connection between abortion and interstate commerce, but that connection has not been supported by extensive congressional fact-finding. And under *Lopez*, Congress must make a showing that abortion "substantially affects interstate commerce." Moreover, FOCA arguably encroaches on "traditional state regulation" in the area of family law, which the Court expressed a concern to protect in *United States v. Morrison* (2000).[30] While the Court veered back toward congressional deference in *Gonzales v. Raich* (2005), that development may not help FOCA, which is not part of a "comprehensive regulatory scheme" like the vast web of federal antidrug law and regulation at issue in that case. Most recently, the Court again backed away from an expansive reading of the Commerce Clause in its consideration of the federal health care reform law. While most of the law was upheld on other grounds (the Taxing Clause), five of the nine justices expressed the view that it would be unconstitutional in its entirety under the Commerce Clause.[31]

Before moving to a more holistic evaluation of FOCA, I would like to address an objection to my analysis of its operational provisions. Both pro-life and pro-choice activists, ranging from the National Right to Life Committee to the National Abortion Rights Action League, seem to agree about its effects, which they portray as both clear and wide-ranging. Should this rare hermeneutical convergence between political actors with antithetical purposes be considered conclusive evidence of what FOCA would do if enacted? In my judgment it should not be viewed in this way for three reasons. First, political activists are not judges. Their vocation is to promote a particular political perspective, not to incorporate new legislation into an already existing web of state and federal legislative, regulatory, and judicial law.

Second, and relatedly, activists, particularly on such morally freighted issues as abortion, are not dispassionate. By definition, the abortion issue is of overriding importance to them; all other issues tend to pale in comparison. People who adopt a "culture war" mind-set often tend to presume that everyone else does as well; those who are not working for their cause with total dedication are assumed to be working against it. There is no reason to think, however, that the state and federal judiciary (or the American people) as a whole views the abortion issue in such stark terms—and it is the judiciary that will be interpreting and applying the law. In so doing, the judges' primary reference point will be the text of the law— not the statements of the political action groups that supported or opposed it.

Third, the fact that perennial antagonists such as pro-life and pro-choice groups interpreted FOCA's potential effect in similar ways suggests that their interests were not, in fact, divergent on this point. In other words, while FOCA remained prospective legislation, both groups had an interest in maximizing its impact. Obviously, this harmony would not have endured if FOCA had been passed; in such a situation, pro-lifers would have attempted to minimize the new law's impact. The fact that they did not do so while debating FOCA in the context of the 2008 presidential election and its immediate aftermath strongly suggests that they did not see FOCA as likely to become law. But then, as I will explain, I do not believe FOCA was ever viewed as a serious piece of proposed legislation.

BAD PEDAGOGY, BAD LAW

Sound law requires clarity so that those bound by it know what is required of them. If enacted, a statute as hopelessly vague as FOCA would tie up governmental resources at both the federal and state levels for years to come as lawyers battled over its interpretation and constitutionality. It would inflame the social divisions in this country rather than quell them. In short, one need not be pro-life to see that enacting FOCA is not a good idea. Its combination of rhetorical recklessness and operational vagueness makes for very bad law. This fact did not escape the notice of pro-choice lawmakers. A few months after his inauguration, President Obama stated that enacting FOCA was not his "highest legislative priority."[32] Speaker of the House Nancy Pelosi also indicated that she had no interest in pursuing the matter.[33]

The same combination of audacity and vagueness, however, makes FOCA a very good (that is, useful) weapon in the abortion battles that have divided this country for almost forty years now. In my view, the true purpose of the bill, which has been lurking around Congress in various versions for nearly two decades, is to sustain the rhetoric of the culture wars. Ultimately, FOCA should be seen less as a serious attempt at lawmaking than as abortion-war propaganda dressed up as prospective legislation. It is noteworthy that, from a purely political perspective, FOCA is useful to both pro-life and pro-choice activists. The bill helps pro-choicers ward off any perceived threat to the right to abortion—even as, in the gray shadows of the bill's text, pro-lifers see new threats to unborn life, and mobilize accordingly.[34] And a new battle begins.

Is it possible, then, to separate our evaluation of the pedagogical and practical aspects of FOCA and similarly structured laws? More specifically, can we say that the merit of FOCA's moral and political message, incorporated in its section 2, swings free of the merit of its operational program, described in section 4? I do not think we can defend such a separation. Obviously, pro-life citizens are going to find the moral message of section 2 extremely misguided and problematic. I do not dispute that finding. My point, however, is that even if one does not find that moral message deeply objectionable in itself, one ought to realize that the manner in which it is operationalized is extremely troubling as a jurisprudential matter. In other words, this objection is also applicable to pieces of proposed legislation in which the moral message is salutary. The moral problems with FOCA extend beyond its content to the manner in which it attempts to communicate with the subjects of the proposed law.

Fundamentally, FOCA is an act of political manipulation, not an act of pedagogy. Precisely because it does not carefully work out the ramifications of its operational provisions for the vast network of extant abortion-related laws and practices, it does not function as a reliable action guide. Rather than providing citizens with a clear directive to incorporate into their practical reasoning, it only sows confusion. Because it sows confusion, it engenders suspicion and fear among citizens, particularly among those who are not disposed to accept its moral message in the first place. At the very least, therefore, it is unlikely to be pedagogically effective. Pro-lifers, of course, will view that ineffectiveness as welcome. At the same time, however, they ought to take care that they do not make analogous mistakes with their own legislative initiatives. More broadly, all citizens should recognize that in sound lawmaking, pedagogical and practical effectiveness are inseparable.

NOTES

This chapter is based on M. Cathleen Kaveny, "Bad Law: What FOCA Is—and Isn't," *Commonweal*, January 30, 2009, 16–19.

1. Thomas Aquinas, *Summa theologica*, 3 vols., trans. Fathers of the English Dominican Province (New York: Benziger Bros., 1948), II-II, q. 95, art. 3, quoting Isidore, *Etymologies*, v, 21.
2. Ibid., q. 90, art. 1.
3. Ibid., art. 2.
4. Ibid., art. 4.
5. Freedom of Choice Act (FOCA), H.R. 1964, 110th Cong. (2007) (companion bill to S. 1173).
6. Prior versions of FOCA include H.R. 3700, 101st Cong. (1989); S. 1912, 101st Cong. (1989); S. 25, 102rd Cong. (1991); H.R. 25, 102rd Cong. (1991); H.R. 1068, 103rd Cong. (1993); H.R. 25, 103rd Cong. (1993); S. 25, 103rd Cong. (1993); H.R. 776, 104th Cong. (1995); H.R. 371, 108th Cong. (2004); S. 2020, 108th Cong. (2004); S. 2593, 109th Cong. (2006); and H.R. 5151, 109th Cong. (2006).
7. Annenberg Public Policy Center, FactCheck.org, "What Are the Facts on the Freedom of Choice Act?," February 11, 2009, www.factcheck.org/2009/02/freedom-of-choice-act/; "Barack Obama Promises to Sign FOCA," *YouTube*, July 9, 2008, www.youtube.com/watch?v=pfoXIRZSTt8.

8. United States Conference of Catholic Bishops, "Cardinal George Voices Hope for Obama Administration, Points to Possible Obstacles to Our Desired Unity," November 12, 2008, http://old.usccb.org/comm/archives/2008/08-174.shtml.

9. NARAL is the acronym for National Abortion Rights Action League.

10. National Organization for Women, "Freedom of Choice Act Would Guarantee *Roe* Protections in US Statutes," April 30, 2007, www.now.org/issues/abortion/070430foca .html.

11. Planned Parenthood, "Questions and Answers about FOCA," January 22, 2004, National Right to Life Committee, www.nrlc.org/foca/PPFAfoca-questions-12445 .pdf. Interestingly, as of January 2011, "Questions and Answers about FOCA" is no longer available on Planned Parenthood's website but continues to be available on several pro-life websites.

12. Justin Rigali, Letter to Members of Congress, United States Conference of Catholic Bishops, September 19, 2008, http://old.usccb.org/prolife/FOCArigaliltr.pdf.

13. Robert P. George, "Obama's Abortion Extremism," Witherspoon Institute, October 14, 2008, www.thepublicdiscourse.com/2008/10/133.

14. *Roe v. Wade*, 441 US 113 (1973).

15. See, e.g., Office of the General Counsel, Memorandum (on FOCA), United States Conference of Catholic Bishops, August 15, 2008, http://old.usccb.org/prolife/issues/ FOCA/analysis.pdf; and Human Life of Washington, "Stop FOCA (The Freedom of Choice Act)," November 26, 2008, www.humanlife.net/view_reports.htm?rpid=33.

16. *Webster v. Reproductive Health Services,* 492 US 490 (1989); see also *Harris v. McRae*, 448 US 297 (1980).

17. *Planned Parenthood v. Casey*, 505 US 833 (1992).

18. Secretariat of Pro-Life Activities, "The 'Freedom of Choice Act': Most Radical Abortion Legislation in US History," United States Conference of Catholic Bishops, September 30, 2008, http://old.usccb.org/prolife/issues/FOCA/FOCA_FactSheet08 .pdf; NOW, "FOCA Would Guarantee *Roe* Protections in US Statutes"; and Janet Benshoof, "Beyond *Roe*, after *Casey*: The Present and Future of a 'Fundamental' Right," *Women's Health Issues* 3 (1993): 162–70.

19. See, e.g., Kate Michelman, *Protecting the Right to Choose* (New York: Plume, 2007), 113–23.

20. FOCA, § 2(7): "The *Roe v. Wade* decision also expanded the opportunities for women to participate equally in society. In 1992, in *Planned Parenthood v. Casey* (505 US 833), the Supreme Court observed that, 'the ability of women to participate equally in the economic and social life of the Nation has been facilitated by their ability to control their reproductive lives.'"

21. *Gonzales v. Carhart*, 550 US 124 (2007).

22. See, e.g., *Harris v. McRae*, 448 US 297 (1980).

23. Omnibus Appropriations Act, 2009, Pub. L. 111-8, §§ 507–508, 123 Stat. 524, 802 (2009) (Hyde Amendment).

24. Joel Wm. Friedman, "Redefining Equality, Discrimination, and Affirmative Action under Title VII: The Access Principle," *Texas Law Review* 65 (1986): 41–99.

25. See Nancy Frazier O'Brien, "Rumors Aside, FOCA No Threat to Catholic Health Care," *Catholic News Service*, January 27, 2009, www.catholicnews.com/data/stories/ cns/0900402.htm.

26. See the Church Amendment, 42 USC § 300a-7 (2008); Coats Amendment, 42 USC § 238n (2008); and the Weldon Amendment, Pub. L. No. 108-447, § 508(d)(1), 118 Stat. 2809, 3163 (2004).

27. *Employment Division v. Smith*, 94 US 872 (1990); and Religious Freedom Restoration Act (RFRA), Pub. L. 103-141 (1993) (codified as later amended at 41 USC § 2000bb).

28. *Boerne v. Flores*, 521 US 507 (1997).

29. *United States v. Lopez*, 514 US 549 (1995).

30. *United States v. Morrison*, 529 US 598 (2000).

31. *Gonzales v. Raich*, 545 US 1 (2005). For an overview, see Ronald D. Rotunda and John E. Nowak, "The Commerce Clause and Restrictions on State Regulatory Powers," chap. 11 in *Treatise on Constitutional Law: Substance and Procedure* (St. Paul, MN: Thomson West, 2007). The continuing volatility of Commerce Clause jurisprudence is evident in the spate of litigation surrounding the federal health care reform legislation, the Patient Protection and Affordable Care Act (PPACA). More specifically, there is a split among the federal circuit courts about the constitutionality of PPACA. On the one hand, the US Court of Appeals for the Sixth Circuit rebuffed the claim that PPACA's "individual mandate" provision exceeded congressional authority under the Commerce Clause; see *Thomas More Law Center v. Obama*, 651 F.3d 529 (6th Cir. 2011). So did the DC Circuit; see *Seven-Sky v. Holder*, 661 F.3d 1 (DC Cir. 2011). On the other hand, the Eleventh Circuit held that the PPACA "individual mandate" exceeded congressional power under the Commerce Clause. See *Florida v. United States Department of Health & Human Services*, 648 F.3d 1235 (11th Cir. 2011). A federal district court in Virginia also found that the individual mandate exceeded congressional power; see *Virginia v. Sebelius*, 702 F.Supp. 2d 598 (E.D.Va. 2010). This judgment was reversed on appeal on procedural grounds; the Fourth Circuit held that the Commonwealth of Virginia did not have standing to challenge the individual mandate provision. See *Virginia v. Sebelius*, 656 F.3d 253 (4th Cir. 2011). In November 2011 the Supreme Court granted certiorari to the Eleventh Circuit case, agreeing to consider the constitutionality of the individual mandate as well as other legal issues raised by PPACA. For an academic analysis of the issue, see Mark A. Hall, "Commerce Clause Challenges to Health Care Reform," *University of Pennsylvania Law Review* 159 (June 2011): 1825–72. In June 2012, the Court upheld the constitutionality of the main provisions of the PPACA in *National Federation of Independent Business v. Sebelius*, 132 S.Ct. 2566 (2012). However, five of the nine justices (the four dissenting justices and the Chief Justice, who wrote the majority opinion) also expressed the view that the law was unconstitutional under the Commerce Clause. While their views on the Commerce Clause are certainly worthy of close scrutiny, they likely count only as dicta from a technical legal perspective, since they were not necessary to the actual resolution of the case.

32. David Alexander, "Obama Says Abortion Rights Law Not a Top Priority," Reuters, April 29, 2009, www.reuters.com/article/idUSN2946642020090430.

33. Amy Sullivan, "The Catholic Crusade against a Mythical Abortion Bill," *Time*, February 19, 2009, www.time.com/time/nation/article/0,8599,1880451,00.html.

34. Ibid.

༄

CHAPTER 5

Genetic Information and Razian Autonomy

A T A WHITE HOUSE PRESS CONFERENCE held in June 2000, President Bill Clinton announced that the first draft of the sequencing of the entire human genome had been completed two years ahead of schedule.[1] His announcement marked a major milestone of the Human Genome Project (HGP), an international collaborative effort whose scientific goals included sequencing the three billion DNA base units in the human genome and identifying the estimated thousands of genes that are located on the twenty-three pairs of human chromosomes.[2]

During the White House festivities President Clinton not only celebrated the scientific accomplishment but also looked forward to the new era of genetic medicine that it presaged. Clinton predicted that "decoding the human genome will lead to new ways to prevent, diagnose, treat, and cure disease."[3] More specifically, he suggested that in the not-so-distant future it would enable physicians to (1) "alert patients that they are at risk for certain diseases"; (2) "reliably predict the course of disease"; (3) "precisely diagnose disease and ensure the most effective treatment is used"; and (4) "develo[p] new treatments at the molecular level."[4] Clinton pledged his support for both privately and publicly funded genetic research as well as for "a strong structure to review the medical, ethical and other issues presented by the expected new power of genetic medicine."[5] In particular, he expressed his commitment to protect genetic privacy and ensure that "genetic information must never be used to stigmatize or discriminate against any individual or group."[6]

Did this genetic revolution materialize? In the first section of this chapter I review the scientific progress made by geneticists since Clinton's announcement, and I outline the state of medical genetics a decade later. In a nutshell, we know a great deal more about the genetic basis of diseases we or our progeny might eventually suffer, but we have scarcely begun the task of treating or preventing those diseases through gene therapy. We have long known that we are all destined for death, be it sudden or protracted. Genetics does not change that destiny. In its current state, genetics research simply gives us very limited insight into the particular dark pathways that might lie ahead for each of us—and yet the immediate moral and jurisprudential questions we face will require navigating the dimness with the faint beam provided by the current state of genetics. In the second section I outline the challenges many human beings face when confronted with probabilistic knowledge. In the third and fourth sections I propose that we deal with these moral and legal dilemmas in a manner that promotes autonomy as understood by Joseph Raz and as I outlined in the first chapter.

GENETIC MEDICINE: IT'S COMPLICATED

More than a decade has passed since we reached that milestone in our understanding of the "blueprint" of humanity with the first draft sequencing of the entire human genome. What are its practical fruits? When asked in 2010 by *Der Spiegel* how many medical benefits have ensued thus far from the HGP, Craig Venter was uncommonly blunt, replying "Close to zero, to put it precisely."[7] A decade ago many people were hopeful that unlocking the genome would provide the key to understanding a wide range of human characteristics in both healthy and sick people.[8] Venter, who sequenced his own genome, vividly dashed those hopes: "And what else have I learned from my genome? Very little. We couldn't even be certain from my genome what my eye color was. Isn't that sad? Everyone was looking for miracle 'yes/no' answers in the genome. 'Yes, you'll have cancer.' Or 'No, you won't have cancer.' But that's just not the way it is."[9]

Strikingly, time seems to have stood still on these genetic frontiers of medical progress.[10] To put it another way, medical advances that Clinton predicted as imminent a decade ago seem to have moved into the future in lockstep along with the horizon.[11] Some commentators have suggested that the widespread anticipation about the forthcoming medical benefits of genomics was a "social bubble" sustained by the enthusiasm of its participants rather than by hard analysis of expected social benefits and was bound to be burst in much the same way as "economic bubbles" such as investment in high-tech companies.[12]

Why the bleak assessment? Mainly because, while far from useless, the medical insights gleaned from the HGP have turned out to be extremely murky.[13] A recent study out of Brigham and Women's Hospital in Boston collected 101 genetic variants that had been statistically linked to heart disease in various studies scanning the human genome. After following 19,313 women for over twelve years, the study concluded that the variants had no predictive value.[14] The old-fashioned practice of taking a family history was a more helpful predictor of the disease than was the genetic testing.[15] Genetic testing was also not the best predictor of personal traits not related to disease, such as height. After studying the genomes of hundreds of thousands of people, three groups of scientists discovered more than forty genetic variants associated with height. The effect of these genetic variants, taken together, was minimal—they accounted for less than 5 percent of height's estimated 80–90 percent heritability. One could formulate a better prediction of height simply by asking people how tall their parents are.[16]

The problem of explaining genetic heritability, then, has proven to be far more difficult than anticipated a decade ago.[17] At that time researchers hypothesized that the human genome had a finite number of common variants—which could be easily identified—and that those variants were the key to understanding susceptibility to a number of diseases.[18] Now, however, there is increasing suspicion that some common diseases are caused not by a single powerful genetic variant but by a number of different variants, each of which is both powerful and rare.[19] If this is true, two patients might have the same presenting symptoms but the genetic causes of those symptoms could be different. Diseases may also be caused by common genetic variants that individually might be harmless but have a harmful effect when acting in concert.[20] In this scenario, a victim of a disease would be analogous to the unlucky loser of a "quick-pick" genetic lottery. Even with diseases that are known to be caused by a single variant, other variants evidently can exacerbate or mitigate the severity of the disease. For example, cystic fibrosis is generally caused by mutation of a single gene, but symptoms of cystic fibrosis can vary greatly from patient to patient, leading researchers to suspect that modifier genes might be one cause of the variability.[21]

In a rather maddening development, the knowledge gained in genetic studies has unsettled some prior understandings about how genes function in regulating cellular behavior. For example, genes—conventionally understood to be important—are apparently not all-important.[22] It appears now that much "non-coding DNA" also may play substantial roles in regulating gene expression.[23] Furthermore, the function of genes, as well as the proteins they code for, is not quite as straightforward as originally supposed. Tony Pawson, who studies cell biology at the University of Toronto, says, "Now we appreciate that the signaling information of cells is organized through networks of information rather than simple discrete pathways. It's infinitely more complex."[24]

What are the next steps? How are scientists going to move beyond these unknowns?[25] To make significant progress, some researchers believe that it will be necessary to sequence, analyze, and compare the full genomes of large numbers of individuals.[26] The 1000 Genomes Project, launched in 2008, is an international, multiphased effort to sequence the complete genome of thousands of patients who come from a number of different ethnic groups and suffer from an array of diseases.[27] Likewise, the Cancer Genome Atlas is attempting to collect more than twenty thousand tissue samples from more than twenty different types of cancers, with the hope of charting the relationship between genetic change and tumor growth.[28] Fortunately, technological advances have dramatically reduced the cost and increased the efficiency of sequencing a genome;[29] many researchers predict that the cost will be at or below one thousand dollars in the near future.[30] They also anticipate that the time required for sequencing will be cut to minutes using a single laboratory machine.[31] Ironically, faster, less expensive, and more accessible sequencing only engenders another hurdle: storing, processing, analyzing, and comparing the massive amounts of data produced by such sequencing. The National Human Genome Research Institute and other global research centers are aware of the emerging challenges in the realm of bioinformation and are attempting to address them.

Finally, and no less importantly, scientists have yet to unlock the relationship between genes and the environment, both inside and outside the cell. While a human body contains approximately one trillion cells, it houses between ten trillion and one hundred trillion microbes that can both help and hinder the well-being of their human hosts.[32] Understanding how genes interact with environmental agents to affect cellular processes is the task of another post-HGP endeavor, the Human Epigenome Project, which is attempting to investigate how certain environmental factors can affect whether and how certain genes are activated.[33]

Undeniably, the past two decades have brought dramatic advances in identifying genetic involvement in disease. In a speech at the 60th annual meeting of the American Society of Human Genetics in November 2010, Eric Lander, a distinguished geneticist at the Massachusetts Institute of Technology, summarized the progress: In 1990, only 70 genes causing Mendelian dominant or recessive disorders had been identified; currently they number more than 2,980. Most common disorders, however, are non-Mendelian; whereas scientists could identify only 25 genes contributing to common disorders in 2000, today they can point to more than 1,100 disease-associated genes, including those contributing to Alzheimer's disease, diabetes, heart disease, and age-related macular degeneration. Similarly, in 1990 only 12 genes were known to influence the development of cancer; now more than 240 have been isolated.

Ultimately, of course, geneticists hope to be able not only to treat diseases after they have appeared but also to use the techniques of gene therapy to cure them or even to forestall their appearance entirely.[34] Progress in gene therapy has been much slower than initially expected, even with monogenetic diseases such as cystic fibrosis.[35] But there are sundry signs of hope. According to a small French study, gene therapy has appeared to be successful for treating X-linked severe combined immunodeficiency disease;[36] a man with beta-thalassaemia was cured by gene therapy although physicians are not sure which gene was responsible;[37] and a new anti-HIV gene therapy appears to function by making T-cells resistant to infection.[38] Nonetheless, the field of gene therapy "is still at a fairly primitive stage."[39]

In the nearer term, genetic tests will be used to discern which patients are at higher risk of certain diseases (such as colon cancer or breast cancer) and therefore need more intensive monitoring.[40] Researchers also hope to develop "smart" drugs that target the precise diseases afflicting particular patients, or that avoid certain deleterious side effects of drug treatments such as chemotherapy or antiviral drugs.[41]

Those benefits, however, remain on the horizon. For the immediate future, most normative questions arising from the HGP will center on organizing and evaluating patterns of "knowing" rather than patterns of "doing."[42] More specifically, the moral and legal challenges of the current situation arise from a combination of two factors: the explosion of genetic information pertaining to an individual's health and medicine's relative inability to intervene to prevent or treat the diseases in which genetic components have been identified.

AUTONOMY AND PROBABILITY

At the close of his decennial anniversary editorial in *Nature*, Francis Collins quotes Antoine de Saint-Exupery's *The Wisdom of the Sands*: "As for the future, your task is not to foresee, but to enable it."[43] For those of us interested in the moral and legal challenges of the HGP, Saint-Exupery's charge might be reframed in terms of the following question: How do we enable a future whose contours we foresee only partially and probabilistically?

Before we can formulate an approach to dealing with the partial and probabilistic nature of currently available genetic information, we first must comprehend the nature and extent of the problem. Current testing may be able to tell an individual that he has a gene associated with a higher probability of developing diabetes, but the testing likely will not offer much information about the other circumstances that could affect whether that probability becomes actualized or how severe the disease will be.[44] Moreover, while such testing loudly calls attention to the person's risk of this particular disease, the results necessarily remain mute on other deleterious genetic proclivities that scientists have yet to identify. Finally, genetic testing may detract and distract from other ways in which human beings can be harmed by themselves or others. It is all very well and good to worry about an individual's increased danger of diabetes. Nonetheless, given that individual's daily commute, the more immediate threat to his life and health may be a teenage driver trying to text and change lanes simultaneously—especially if our driver also regularly texts while changing lanes.

A key theme of Sophocles's *Oedipus Rex* is often said to be the inexorability of fate; repulsed by the Delphic oracle's prophecy that he would kill his father and marry his mother, Oedipus left his homeland and built a life for himself far away—only to fulfill that prophecy in circumstances he could scarcely have imagined. The play, then, is also a testimony to the impossibility of predicting the course of the future. Even if one is told the ultimate outcome, the manner and circumstances in which it is realized can be entirely unexpected. If this testimony applies with respect to a fairly specific prophecy such as Oedipus's, it holds true a fortiori for the more general condition of human life: we will all die, and many of us will suffer from illnesses and disabilities before doing so. In its current state, genetic testing can give us some pieces of information relevant to our future; however, it cannot provide the whole picture. Genetic information conveys a certain type of information, which most often is not expressed as certainties but rather in probabilities. Consequently, the first question to be addressed is how well human beings process probabilistic information. According to a great deal of psychological and sociological data, the answer is not very well at all. For most people, probability is a slippery concept, both conceptually and mathematically.

It is not easy to define degrees of probability; moreover, it is not easy for agents accurately to assess the probable consequences of their actions. Not surprisingly, a recent study of one thousand Swiss citizens showed that "most [of them] reasoned appropriately in problems representing pure applications of probability theory, but failed to do so in approximations of real-world scenarios."[45] Many adults exhibit various other biases and difficulties with a range of concepts pertaining to ratios and probabilities, resulting in a worrisomely low numeracy—literacy with numbers.[46] Psychologists have begun to realize that "low numeracy distorts perceptions of risk and benefits of screening, reduces medication compliance, impedes access to treatments, impairs risk communication, limiting prevention efforts among the most vulnerable, and . . . appears to adversely affect medical outcomes."[47]

In addition, low numeracy means that when probabilistic data is presented, other factors—such as the way information is presented, the patient's mood, or decisional biases—disproportionately affect patient decision making.[48] One study argued that "statistical illiteracy (a) is common to patients, journalists, and physicians; (b) is created by nontransparent framing of information that is sometimes an unintentional result of lack of understanding but can also be a result of intentional efforts to manipulate or persuade people, and (c) can have serious consequences for health."[49] The study cites disturbing examples of common probabilistic mistakes in the medical context. Most people do not realize, for example, that the claim that mammography screening reduces the risk of dying from breast cancer by 25 percent means that one fewer woman out of a thousand will die of the disease.[50] Slicing the problem a different way, the study also examined how the framing of a probability risk can influence a decision maker. Patients who are told "If you have this test every two years, it will reduce your chance of dying from this cancer by about one-third over the next ten years" are far more likely to take the test than those who are told "If you have this test every two years it will reduce your chance of dying from this cancer from around 3 in 1,000 to around 2 in 1,000 over the next ten years."[51]

If low numeracy hampers normal medical decision making, we can predict, so to speak, that the problem will be exacerbated with respect to decision making around genetic information, even with respect to simple tests, given the fact that most people have only a shaky grasp of genetics itself. A recent clinical psychology study regarding women involved in maternal screening for Down syndrome suggests that "probabilistic screening information does not provide useable information and therefore does not promote informed choice."[52] According to surveys, women undergo these tests to get reassurance about the status of their unborn child; the study suggests that the tests "fail to offer reassurance, or offer false reassurance."[53] Why "false reassurance"? Testing can draw women's attention to highlighted risks and away from the many other potential anomalies for which there are no tests. Accordingly, in this study one in five women falsely believed that a negative test result guaranteed that the baby would be normal.[54]

Moreover, as cognitive psychologists note, most people, including many health care professionals, do not naturally assess risk in terms of statistics, which provides the vocabulary and conceptual framework of mathematical probability. "We don't quantify the risk of being hit by a bus before crossing the road, or of catching food poisoning at a particular restaurant. We know that there *are* risks, and these play a part in the choices we make, but knowing what they are numerically would probably add little to our decision-making process."[55] In our vocabulary, "risk" is far from a univocal term. In statistics, it refers to a probability; in everyday life, however, "risky" means "dangerous." For that reason, a test of statistical "risk" can be interpreted in lay terms to mean that the subject is "at risk." In another study of pregnant women tested for Down syndrome, the researchers found that "many women interpreted the at-risk status of their pregnancy not as a probability, but rather as indicating that their baby was in fact ill."[56] Part of the problem is that risk is mistakenly seen to be a property of an individual rather than of an aggregate of persons, even though "the grey areas of probability are not clearly meaningful at an individual level."[57] For example, while the risk of having a Down syndrome baby might be 1 in 151 for a particular cohort of women, for any individual woman the outcomes are best viewed in terms of the dichotomous probabilities of 0 percent or 100 percent; either the baby has Down syndrome or it does not; it is not afflicted "just a little bit."[58]

Most important, that same study revealed that health care providers and parents held different views of the purpose of genetic testing. The clinicians wanted to "identify and control potential problems in the pregnancy." In contrast, the patients were not focused on "identifying problems, but rather, in assuring the well-being of the baby." More specifically, "they did not compare relative risks, invoke specific numeric risk figures, or employ the clinicians' mundane analogies; instead, they responded to a generalized sense that their baby was in danger, and their decision-making reflected this logic, rather than the logic of risk assessment and risk reduction."[59]

Other studies raise the possibility that, if not managed appropriately, the gap between statistical risk and perceived risk will lead to counterproductive decision making. One exhaustive review article summarizes its findings in this way: "While evidence of the effects of perceived risk is limited and inconsistent, there is some evidence to suggest high risk estimations may adversely affect health and lead to inappropriate uptake of medical surveillance and preventative measures by some individuals."[60] In the end, the decision-making calculus reflects a host of factors about the assessors, including their perception of the level of risk (which may or may not be statistically accurate), their tolerance for uncertainty, their fear of certain outcomes, and other aspects of their character and emotional makeup.

Consequently, a key challenge of the current state of genetics is whether, when, and how it is possible for persons to incorporate the probabilistic information about their future health status into their practical reasoning here and now. Is it possible to argue, after all, that sometimes it is better *not* to know—especially if one can do nothing to change the outcome? Oedipus might have had a better life if he had not received the devastating oracle in the first place. Arguably, so too might people for whom genetic testing results point to Huntington's disease (which is genetically dominant and almost fully penetrant) or other devastating, incurable illnesses. At the same time, knowledge of the test results would be extremely useful in deliberating about matters affecting career and family, especially since in most cases symptoms do not appear until after those decisions have been made.

For the vast majority of people, however, the information they receive from the current state of genetic testing with respect to the vast majority of diseases is not likely to be as conclusive or as devastating as a Huntington's diagnosis. And, contrary to what might be expected, many people in fact do nothing or virtually nothing with this information.[61] Many others, however, may incorporate it into their decision-making process. Of course, the tested individual may not be the only person with an interest in the results; family members, researchers, insurance companies, and employers may also have a stake. The ethical and legal status of genetic information is a multifaceted question, and the thorny issues of genetic privacy and genetic discrimination were key concerns of the HGP's ELSI project—and they merit continued attention.[62] Here, however, I can concentrate only on one fundamental problem: considered from a Razian perspective, how does the availability of such personal genetic information enable or impede personal autonomy?

The massive resources dedicated to the discovery of genetic information and the far-reaching implications of that information for the ordering of individual and social life make it clear that the promotion and protection of individual autonomy must be, as Joseph Raz has argued, a communal project. How should access to increasing amounts of genetic information, which currently constitutes the ripest fruit of the HGP, shape legal promotion of the values and components of Razian autonomy? The question is relevant because genetic information is not generally information about the present but about the future. More precisely, it is about the possible future manifestations of one's constant genetic makeup. Autonomy, too, is about the future; it is the opportunity, in Raz's terms, to be the "part-author" of one's life.[63] Not sole author; just as human beings cannot determine all the circumstances of their societies, so they cannot entirely determine the form and function of their minds and bodies, both of which will shape the exercise of their freedom. Genetic information provides some insight, albeit limited and partial, into the current and future form and function of the minds and bodies of the individuals to whom it pertains.

PHYSICAL AND MENTAL WELL-BEING

Ideally, of course, genetic information ought to help us nurture and maintain the first component of Razian autonomy: the basic physical and psychological conditions necessary to exercise choice. Good physical health can enable a wider scope for the exercise of autonomy; good mental health provides the basic ability to steadily apprehend reality and appreciate in an undistorted fashion one's own (limited) power as a rational chooser. To the extent that genetic medicine can uncover and ameliorate the causes of debilitating mental illnesses such as schizophrenia and depression, it will ultimately contribute greatly to the social and personal virtue of autonomy. For reasons detailed earlier, however, those medical benefits are not on the near horizon. For the immediate future, it will not be possible to eliminate most genetic defects from the population without eliminating the people who carry them.[64]

In considering the implications of genetic information for individual autonomy, we need to also think about the mirror image of helping or healing, which, of course, is abandoning or killing. Many parents discover some aspects of the genetic makeup of their children through amniocentesis or other forms of prenatal testing. In some cases, the receipt of unwelcome results leads to a decision to terminate the pregnancy. Obviously, many people who consider unborn life to be fully human life will consider this action to be an unjustifiable form of homicide. One's views on the status of fetal life, however, are not dispositive. On the one hand, even those who consider abortion generally acceptable because the fetus is not a legally protectable "person" may have objections to certain instances of genetic abortion, such as sex-selective abortion.[65] On the other hand, in many cases involving fetal defect, the parents may recognize that they are killing their "baby" but see themselves as engaged in a justifiable form of euthanasia.

The topic of aborting genetically inferior fetuses inevitably raises the painful question of eugenics—literally, "genetic well-being"—and its connection with the explosion of genetic information. The experiments with eugenics in the twentieth-century West, not only in Nazi Germany but also in the United

States, are shameful.[66] Yet we cannot simply invoke these events as part of a blanket condemnation of the fruits of genetic counseling. In coming to terms with the past and its implications for the future use of genetic knowledge, we have to evaluate why these past events are so horrifying.[67] In my view, we need to examine four issues that are relevant to the moral evaluation of a particular genetics program.

First, the immediate purpose of the intervenors matters. There is a difference between the actions taken with the aim of eliminating genetic defects (genetic therapy) and those geared toward engineering a genetic "superman" (genetic enhancement).[68] This line is not always clear; for example, we could ask whether elevating someone from borderline mental handicap to the higher end of the normal scale is "therapy" or "enhancement." Nonetheless, therapeutic motives are more immediately consistent with the time-honored and traditional goals of medicine, in particular the elimination of suffering.

Second, the scope and coordination of the intervention matters. There is a difference between an approach that views genetics as a tool to foster the well-being of individuals and the families to which they belong and an approach that views it as a means for improvement of the performance profile of the nation as a whole. While it may still be morally objectionable, it is one thing for parents to try to create a genetically superior child. Regrettably, many parents already raise their children in ways that are morally objectionable, using "nurture" rather than "nature" to produce superior offspring that reflect well on the parents themselves. It is another thing entirely, however, for the state to lay claim to the reproductive potential of its entire citizenry for its own ends—that is, to create a genetically superior class of citizens. The moral problem with the latter is that it reduces individual human beings, who possess their own dignity and their own conceptions of life's purpose, to mere component parts of the larger political community. This radical reduction violates the values and virtues of autonomy and solidarity.[69]

Third, the assumptions underlying the interventions are crucial. For example, consider the personnel guiding a genetics program, large or small, public or private, who assume that the more beautiful and talented clients are inherently worth more as human beings. Those assumptions are not only inconsistent with the fundamental Christian belief in the equal dignity of all human beings as made in the image and likeness of God but also threaten the fundamental political equality posited by liberal democracies.[70] Such assumptions, furthermore, undermine the values and virtues of solidarity, in which all human beings work to recognize the fundamental worth of each of us, and work to further the flourishing of us all, individually and collectively.

Fourth, we must scrutinize the morality of any means we use to achieve our ends. Abortion and other forms of homicide are not the only problematic means in question here; involuntary sterilization is another less-publicized issue. It is one thing for a woman carrying a serious genetic defect to decide not to have children; it is another thing for the state to prohibit her from marrying or, even worse, to sterilize her against her will. Before enthusiasm for the project waned in mid-century (in part due to revelation of Nazi atrocities), more than sixty thousand individuals were involuntarily sterilized in the United States. More than thirty states adopted, at some point, a compulsory "eugenical sterilization" statute.[71] And the practice, while decried today, was ruled constitutional in the infamous 1927 Supreme Court case *Buck v. Bell*, in which Justice Oliver Wendell Holmes justified depriving Carrie Buck of her fertility on the grounds that "three generations of imbeciles are enough."[72]

The eugenics program of Nazi Germany was truly a moral atrocity.[73] However, it was not an atrocity merely because it pertained to eugenics. Rather, the moral flaws in the program relate to the four criteria identified earlier. The Nazis focused on eliminating genetic defects (and the suffering they caused) as well as on breeding genetically superior individuals. Their eugenics goals were systematically coordinated across the entire nation, not simply adopted by various individuals on a case-by-case basis. These goals incorporated a radically non-egalitarian idea that some life—because it potentially sapped the strength of the nation—was unworthy to live. Finally, the means used were deplorable; they were homicidal and radically coercive.

In sharp contrast, one can imagine two Ashkenazi Jews voluntarily seeking genetic testing and counseling before marrying in order to avoid having a child who suffered from the devastations of Tay-Sachs disease. Their decision, too, could be considered a type of "eugenics." Under the foregoing analysis, however, the couple's decision and actions can be sharply distinguished from the Nazi genetics program. The potential parents' recourse to genetic testing through morally acceptable means is an attempt to provide their future children with the physical and mental substrata necessary for becoming autonomous persons one day.

ABSENCE OF COERCION AND MANIPULATION

What are the implications of the recent explosion in genetic information for the two remaining components of Razian autonomy? Recall that the second component is independence, understood as the absence of coercion or manipulation, and the third component is having a range of morally worthwhile options from which to choose. In my view, the probabilistic state of genetic information, combined with the widespread inability of many people to grapple with probabilities, poses significant threats to both components of autonomy. These threats are compounded by the fact that information about the genetic makeup of individuals will likely be available first not to the individuals themselves but rather to those persons responsible for initially nurturing their capacity for autonomy in the first place: their parents.

In fact, the gravest danger that the current explosion of nearly indigestible genetic information poses is the opportunity for coercion or manipulation in raising children.[74] The motivations for seeking such information may well be natural and benign. Parents do, of course, shape their children's character, desires, commitments, and plans. At the same time, the peculiar nature of genetic information risks two distinct problems. First, the fact that the information has its source *in* the child herself may allow parents to obscure the fact that they themselves are in fact making an external decision about how to raise the child, and how to nurture her future. If a combination of three or four genes suggests that a child may have a particular talent for music, parents may steer the child toward piano lessons on the grounds that the child himself "wants" lessons, or that the decision is in some sense coming from "inside" the child and not from their own "outside" influence. The parents may deceive themselves into thinking that they are merely "uncovering" the child's fixed talents rather than shaping and directing those talents.

Second, and relatedly in our culture, the idea of genetic composition—of DNA—has a gravitational strength that is disproportionate to its highly selective and probabilistic nature. Some theorists have speculated that a person's DNA is the clearest window into her essence or even her "soul."[75] Genetic essentialism is a deeply mistaken but nonetheless powerful approach to discerning the meaning of genetic information.[76] It frequently is combined with genetic determinism, the view that a human being's future is inexorably written into his DNA.[77]

Given the difficulty of interpreting genetic test results, some parents may be inclined to adopt a certain type of genetic determinism, to make decisions about options available to their children according to narrow genetic indicators for talent (or the lack thereof) without examining more diffuse qualities such as temperament or character. Alternatively, parents may regard evidence of lack of significant talent or genetic ability in a particular area as a reason not to devote scarce time and financial resources to other talents or to other interests expressed by the child.

In my view, that would be a significant mistake. Children develop their self-identity through imagination as well as preparation. A key occupation of

childhood, at least in the West, is trying on as many identities as are imagina-
tively possible. Little boys and girls may see themselves as medieval knights and
princesses, astronauts, ballerinas, race-car drivers, doctors, firefighters, soldiers,
pilots, or Olympic ice skaters. One might respond that while imaginative play
is one thing, real preparation for the future is something different; such preparation ought to be guided by more sober assessments of talent. However, the
line is not so clear. A little girl whose genes do not yield the body type to be
an elite ballerina still may benefit from the discipline and balance conferred by
ballet lessons; a teenage boy whose predicted visual acuity and reflexes rule out
a career as a fighter pilot may still gain from the science courses and physical
training that are involved in the process of preparing to become one. A child
who aspires to become an FBI agent—or a space marshal—could profit-
ably cultivate a degree of the heroic determination to fight against injustice
demanded of such an official.

LIFE OPTIONS AND CHOICE

What about the autonomy and agency of the subjects of genetic information
themselves? Childhood training is certainly a means to a flourishing adulthood.
But it is a special kind of means. If used badly, genetic information can errone-
ously lead parents to treat their children's formative years as an instrumental
means, not a constitutive means, to the adult a child will become. The process
of self-discovery, of learning what one is good at rather than merely being told
what one is good at, is a key part of being a part-author of one's own life; self-
discovery is, therefore, preferable to the alternative of merely acting out a script
written and interpreted by someone else—even if, as many people believe, the
script is DNA and the author is God.

    The achievement of Razian autonomy requires that a subject have a rea-
sonable array of options about living life from which to choose. In my view, it
also requires a type of flexible imagination to select among and pursue those
options. To exercise my autonomy, to dare to become part-author of my own
life, I need to be able to imagine myself actively and effectively pursuing a
particular set of life goals, and flourishing within them. Furthermore, to sustain
the effort of the pursuit, I need the virtue of hope, which Thomas Aquinas
defined as a virtue whose object is a good that is difficult, although possible,
to obtain.[78] Hope and imagination are intertwined. As William Lynch argued,
hope entails an ability to foresee a future that is not bounded by the difficulties
that seem to overwhelm the present.[79] Having true but partial information
about one's future can distort the choices an agent makes because the agent

sees only one true thing most vividly, rather than all the true things in the balance necessary to make an informed decision.

Among the true things that we do not see at, say, age eighteen or twenty is how the choices we make will shape our character and commitments.[80] We may predict our future health status, or that of our loved ones; it is far more difficult to predict the stable moral personality—the nexus of knowing, valuing, and choosing—that will eventually shape our ability to respond effectively to that health status. The teenage boy who can carry on only a halting conversation with his high school guidance counselor will become the regional manager of a multi-million-dollar corporation. The teenage girl who can barely get out of bed to make a morning class will balance commitments to a busy family and a stressful job as a nurse practitioner. Here most human beings are hampered by a limited imagination. As an eighteen-year-old student, I may be able to imagine myself being an executive, a medical health professional, a lawyer—or a mature human being—from the outside, as it were. I can picture my future self doing the tasks that accompany those roles, almost as if I were watching a movie. It is far more difficult, however, to grasp the internal experience of actually having the perspective, judgment, balance, and experience that accompany such states of life. It may be virtually impossible to envisage what it would mean for me (as distinct from some other wise, older person) to respond to a personal crisis with courage and grace.

We have all read stories in the newspaper about men and women struck down in their prime by accident or illness. Consider a thirty-nine-year-old woman who dies of a cerebral hemorrhage, leaving behind her husband and three children. Let's say she had been the executive director of a homeless shelter and a pillar of the church and community. Suppose, however, that before she was married, she and her future husband were told that she was genetically predisposed to this problem. Would they have married? Would she have thrown herself into her work and community to the same degree? Perhaps. But perhaps not. And what about her husband? His younger self might have doubted his future capacity to raise a child as a widower. Yet twenty years later he has indeed developed personal and social resources that his younger self could scarcely have conceived. Moreover, while his younger self might have foreseen only the loss involved in marrying someone who died prematurely, his more mature self is able to look back at a rich life and relationship with his wife, a life and relationship that he would not have been able to envision as a younger man. His heartbreak at the loss of his wife is real, yet so is his love and pride in what they accomplished together through too short a time. Foresight and hindsight are not the same. Arguably, hindsight provides a truer perspective on this situation—perhaps even the perspective of wisdom.

Razian autonomy requires one to become the "part-author" of one's life, to have some possibility of shaping that life in the context of a range of certain personal and social "givens." Is it possible for a young father to incorporate information about his genetic information as "a given" without succumbing to genetic determinism—even if his genetic testing reveals that he will definitely (not merely probably) suffer from a devastating condition, such as Huntington's disease? Is there a way to receive this information and incorporate it into a life characterized by the exercise of Razian autonomy? Or in these circumstances is the only option for the young father to blind himself to the knowledge?

In a provocative article titled "Genetic Risk and the Birth of the Somatic Individual," Carlos Novas and Nikolas Rose argue that even in the face of devastating diseases, genetic knowledge can be "linked to the development of novel 'life-strategies,' involving practices of choice, enterprise, self-actualization and prudence in relation to one's genetic makeup."[81] Novas and Rose studied emerging websites created by and for persons suffering from Huntington's disease. They argue that "the practices of posting, reading and replying to messages in the webforums and chat rooms are techniques of the self, entailing the disclosure of one's experiences and thoughts according to particular rules, norms, values and forms of authority."[82] The sufferers develop a narrative to make sense of their affliction, and they deliberate upon key life decisions such as whether to marry, to have children, or to disclose the information to their families. As Novas and Rose rightly observe, these online deliberations among people grappling with the same diagnosis reflect a reconfigured view of authority: rather than automatically privileging the advice of experts such as genetic counselors, these exchanges honor the practical wisdom of experience. While the advice of actual experts is not irrelevant, theirs are not the only voices to be considered. In my own view, the opinions of those facing the same choices are particularly relevant because they bring the moral dimensions of the choices to be made to the foreground. While some experts may attempt to be "value-neutral" in the advice they provide to persons with Huntington's disease, no one who is confronted with the disease as his or her *own* disease can afford to pretend that the decisions to be made are anything other than thoroughly value-laden. Afflicted individuals will necessarily make choices about their own lives in light of their own options and their own values.

Novas and Rose propose that we think about the deliberations of such stricken individuals in terms of "life strategies," a concept that "attempts to give a name to the variable and multiple strategies that formulate in relation to particular directions that they would like their life to take." This concept of "life strategies," like Razian autonomy, is not abstract, disembodied, or completely open to constructive choices. It recognizes, in fact, that "only a finite set of forms of life are at our disposal; the practices and techniques that we have to shape the self and mould our lives are contoured by dominant cultural practices and are historically specific."[83] As we move on to the issue of regulating genetic information, the question we need to ask is whether and how we might, through certain information that will facilitate the productive development of "life strategies," instantiate the aims of Razian autonomy for people with particular genetic traits.

REGULATING ACCESS TO GENETIC INFORMATION

Genetic information provides only foresight—partial and probabilistic foresight, at that—into one's medical future. In light of this fact, how should we regulate such information? Nonregulation is of course an option. In that case, the market will determine availability of the information because where there is information to be had, there is money to be made. In May 2010 Pathway Genomics, a start-up company, announced that it would be selling a personalized genetic test at Walgreens for $20–$30; customers would provide saliva samples and would mail them to Pathway for analysis. Depending upon the specific testing package purchased (those separate packages costing an additional $79 to $249), the company would test for genetic markers associated with a range of conditions that affect the test subjects' own health or that of their progeny.[84] The response of the Food and Drug Administration (FDA) to the company's announcement was to question whether the product could be sold legally without its authorization. Rather than get involved in a dispute with the FDA over the necessity and scope of regulations, Walgreens backed out of the arrangement with Pathway.[85] Nonetheless, genetic testing marketed directly to consumers continues to be available through the Internet, although the FDA and at least one state have claimed that doing so without appropriate regulatory approval is illegal.[86]

Is there reason to be worried? Yes. In July 2010 a representative of the US Government Accountability Office (GAO) testified before a congressional subcommittee on the results of its undercover investigation of four direct-to-consumer (DTC) genetic tests.[87] Those results were a devastating indictment of the state of the market, for two reasons. First, the tests themselves are wildly unreliable: "Although the experts GAO spoke with believe that these tests show promise for the future, they agreed that consumers should not rely on any of the results at this time." As one expert said, "The fact that different companies, using the same samples, predict different directions of risk is telling and is important. It shows that we are nowhere near really being able to interpret [such tests]."[88] Second, the marketing for the tests was far from truthful. "GAO also found 10 egregious examples of deceptive marketing, including claims made by four companies that a consumer's DNA could be used to create personalized supplements to cure diseases." Two companies also suggested that the supplements available for purchase could "'repair damaged DNA' or cure disease, even though experts confirmed there is no scientific basis for such claims."[89]

What is the current state of regulation of DTC genetic tests? Spotty, at best. As Jeff Shuren of the FDA indicated in his congressional testimony at the same hearing, the FDA has not been as aggressive or comprehensive in dealing with DTC tests as it could or should be, despite the fact that it is the main regulatory body at the federal level.[90] In part, he admitted, the FDA has been overwhelmed by the explosion of both genetic tests and the diseases for which they purport to test. It was problematic, he acknowledged, that "although the FDA has cleared a number of genetic tests since 2003, none of the genetic tests now offered directly to consumers has undergone premarket review by FDA to ensure that the test results being provided to patients are accurate, reliable, and clinically meaningful."[91] The aggressive marketing of DTC genetic testing companies prompted the FDA to take more aggressive action by sending letters not only to Pathway but also to four other DTC genetic testing companies.[92]

Should DTC tests be available despite their evident flaws? If commitment to autonomy demands the maximum possible sphere of choice for all agents, then the tests should be permitted on the market. Buyers and sellers can negotiate on quality and price, perhaps drawing upon the assistance of independent quality-assessment services such as *Consumer Reports*. Let the buyer beware—and perform due diligence before buying. This radically individualistic approach to the marketplace was dominant in the United States in the era of laissez-faire capitalism of the nineteenth and early twentieth centuries.[93] The common law of contracts of that era posited roughly equal bargaining power between buyers and sellers as well as the equal ability of both parties to protect themselves in setting the terms of the deal. In particular, contract law of that era proceeded as if buyers were perfectly capable of investigating and assessing the quality of the product they were purchasing and of negotiating specific guarantees or warranties to protect themselves contractually. While those assumptions may have been valid in an era when farmers and artisans sold their produce and products at local markets, they no longer hold in an era where large companies sell products made off-site on a "take-it-or-leave-it" basis to their consumers.

Is there a better approach? Many contemporary commentators on medical ethics and law place a great deal of emphasis on informed consent.[94] This emphasis is consistent with a Feinbergian account of freedom, which could easily accommodate the view that each agent is entitled to true and relevant medical information before making a decision. A Feinbergian account, however, would have far more trouble restricting the commercial availability of such tests, provided that their nature and limits were fully disclosed. Such analysis would likely produce the claim that the choice to pursue information—even what most knowledgeable people consider useless information—should be protected because the value of that choice comes from the fact that it is chosen, not from any inherent worth.

A Razian understanding of autonomy is much more capable of accounting for the need for consumer protection regulation in an increasingly globalized marketplace. Recall that Raz's view of autonomy is rooted in a perfectionist liberalism that does not define autonomy primarily in negative and individualistic terms, or as personal freedom from external constraint. Instead, for Raz, autonomy is positive; it is the individual's decision to pursue one among a number of options for living that are widely recognized to be morally worthwhile. Autonomy is also social in both its inception and its goals. Society helps promote the physical and psychological conditions persons need to make autonomous choices, and it maintains and supports a sufficient range of options for that choosing. As Raz observes, no society is required to make morally objectionable options available to individuals; his observation can also be extended to assert that no society has to make available morally objectionable means to achieve those options.

Having access to defective or dangerous products—regardless of whether the flaws are disclosed—does not contribute to a consumer's ability to choose and execute a morally worthwhile life plan. What about the life plans of those employed by the seller of the genetic tests? As Raz explicitly recognizes, honoring autonomy does not entail the right to pursue immoral ends or to engage in immoral acts—particularly when those acts also interfere with the autonomous pursuit of worthy life plans by others.[95] Razian autonomy does not legitimate the right to sell useless and misleading products, let alone defective or dangerous ones. Furthermore, while appreciating the importance of informed consent, Raz's approach would not allow such consent to exhaust the realm of permissible governmental regulation. If certain genetic tests are not likely to provide practically helpful information, they ought not to be available for sale directly to consumers, especially given the difficulties most people have with processing probabilistic testing results. Regulators need not limit their interventions to requiring a complicated disclosure form in DTC packing materials.

In chapter 1 I argue that Raz's perfectionistic liberalism made more sense of key features of existing American law, such as the Americans with Disabilities Act and the Civil Rights Acts, than the more negative and individualistic liberalism of Joel Feinberg. Here I suggest that Raz's account of freedom also better accounts for the burgeoning law pertaining to American consumer protection measures, which extends from the Uniform Commercial Code's simple incorporation of implied and express warranties in contracts for the sale of goods to the complicated web of federal law and regulations. That legal web is designed to protect consumers against unsafe products and deceptive advertising and is administered by the FDA, the Federal Trade Commission, and a host of other state and federal regulatory bodies.[96]

From the earliest founding period, American constitutional law has recognized the "police power" of state governments to promote the common good as well as to protect the safety, health, and general morals of the people; in the last century, functionally analogous powers have also been extended to the federal government.[97] Some liberal legal theorists may object to some or all of these regulations (e.g., laws against smoking marijuana) on the grounds that these unjustified "paternalistic" invasions of an individual's freedom impose the regulator's values upon the subjects of the regulation. A perfectionist liberal such as Raz could reply that respecting autonomy does not mean that the state cannot restrict fruitless or immoral means by which some individuals might seek to achieve their goals. This rejoinder does not imply that any regulation is permissible. Perfectionist liberalism would simply focus the debate on the question of whether the prohibited project or prohibited means is in fact immoral or fruitless—whether the regulation is likely to be worthwhile given the restraints it imposes.

CONCLUSION

In this chapter I have grappled with the first fruits of the genetic revolution. For the foreseeable future, any medical insights yielded will be cast largely in terms of probabilities, not certainties. In light of the insights and criteria provided by Joseph Raz's conception of autonomy, I explored the possibilities—and the dangers—of relying on such probabilistic information in making decisions about one's life (or the life of one's children). The law on this topic is emerging; it likely will not keep pace with science. In formulating appropriate regulations, it is important not to be dazzled by the future promise of scientific breakthroughs. The overblown enthusiasm and predictions surrounding the 2000 White House announcement of the draft sequencing of the human genome should have taught us that lesson. There is no need to make genetic testing widely and directly available to consumers until they are able reasonably to rely upon those tests in making sound decisions.

NOTES

1. The White House, "President Clinton Announces the Completion of the First Survey of the Entire Human Genome," June 25, 2000, Human Genome Project: Information, www.ornl.gov/sci/techresources/Human_Genome/project/clinton1 .shtml. Accompanied by British Prime Minister Tony Blair, Clinton proclaimed that the worldwide race to sequence the genome had officially ended in a tie; the winners were the International Human Genome Project, a publicly funded endeavor under the directorship of Francis Collins, and Celera Genomics Corporation, a private company founded and controlled by Craig Venter.

2. An invaluable source of information on the project is the governmental Human Genome Project Information website. Information about post-HGP activities is at the National Human Genome Research Institute's website.

3. White House, "President Clinton Announces."

4. Ibid.

5. Ibid.

6. Ibid. Clinton had already signed an executive order prohibiting every civilian federal department and agency from using genetic information in hiring or promotion.

7. "Interview with Craig Venter," *Spiegel Online International*, July 29, 2010, www .spiegel.de/international/world/0,1518,709174,00.html.

8. See, e.g., G. J. B. van Ommen, E. Bakker, and J. T. den Dunnen, "The Human Genome Project and the Future of Diagnostics, Treatment, and Prevention," *Lancet* 354 (1999): S5–S10.

9. "Interview with Craig Venter."

10. See, e.g., Nicolas Wade, "A Decade Later, Genetic Map Yields Few New Cures," *New York Times*, June 12, 2010, A1; and Steve Sternberg, "The Human Genome: Big Advances, Many Questions," *USA Today*, July 7, 2010, www.usatoday.com/news/health/2010-07-08-1Agenome08_CV_N.htm. For the results of a recent poll of scientists about when they expect to see medical results, see Declan Butler, "Science after the Sequence," *Nature* 465 (2010): 1000–1001.

11. An editorial in the *Lancet* captures the state of the question:

> The Human Genome Project has been a scientific success. Cell biologists have found that human beings have surprisingly few genes (about 21,000 protein-coding sequences) compared with, for example, a roundworm with 20,000 such genes. The basic notions of gene expression in human beings have been shown to be far more complex than scientists had imagined. Population geneticists, through the International HapMap Project that catalogues common variants

in European, East Asian, and African genomes, have been able to reconstruct human population history and infer how particular populations on different continents have adapted to their environments.

However, the clinical benefits from the Human Genome Project are so far scarce. Although there has been some progress in targeting drugs to specific genetic defects in a few cancers and some rare inherited disorders, common diseases have turned out to be far more complex than originally thought. For example, of the 850 sites in the human genome implicated in common diseases, most are found near gene coding regions rather than within them. Additionally, common disease variants explain only a fraction of the genetic risk of disease. Most common diseases seem to be caused by large numbers of rare and unique variants that make one-size-fits-all therapeutic approaches almost impossible.

Editorial, "The Human Genome Project: 10 Years Later," *Lancet* 375 (2010): 2194. See also Ker Than, "Human Genome at Ten: 5 Breakthroughs, 5 Predictions," *National Geographic*, March 31, 2010, http://news.nationalgeographic.com/news/human-genome-project-tenth-anniversary; Geoffrey Carr, "The Human Genome Project: Turning Point," *The Economist*, June 19, 2010, 14–15; "The Human Genome at Ten" (special report), *Nature* 470 (2010): 649–50; W. Gregory Feero, Alan E. Guttmacher, and Francis S. Collins, "Genomic Medicine—An Updated Primer," *New England Journal of Medicine* 362 (2010): 2001–11; and Margaret A. Hamburg and Francis S. Collins, "Perspective: The Path to Personalized Medicine," *New England Journal of Medicine* 363 (2010): 301–30.

12. Philip Ball, "Bursting the Genomics Bubble," *Nature News*, March 31, 2010, www .nature.com/news/2010/310310/full/news.2010.145.html. See also Monika Gisler, Didier Sornette, and Ryan Woodward, "Exuberant Innovation: The Human Genome Project," Swiss Finance Institute Research Paper 10-12, SSRN, http://papers.ssrn.com/sol3/papers.cfm?abstract_id=1573682.

13. See, e.g., Stephen S. Hall, "Revolution Postponed," *Scientific American*, October 18, 2010, 60–67.

14. Nina Paynter, Daniel I. Chasman, Guillaume Paré, Julie E. Buring, Nancy R. Cook, Joseph P. Miletich, and Paul M Ridker, "Association between a Literature-Based Genetic Risk Score and Cardiovascular Events in Women," *Journal of the American Medical Association* 303 (2010): 631–37, doi:10.1001/jama.2010.119.

15. Nicole Ostrow, "Family Predicts Heart Disease Better than Gene Tests (Update 1)," Bloomberg Businessweek, February 16, 2010, www.bloomberg.com/apps/news?pid =newsarchive&sid=acOuo3qNWDaM.

16. Brendan Maher, "Personal Genomes: The Case of the Missing Heritability," *Nature* 456, no. 6 (2008): 8–21.

17. In February 2001, the journal *Nature* published the draft sequence of the human genome announced by President Clinton over six months earlier. In February 2011 that journal published several articles analyzing the current state and future promise of genomic science and medicine. Especially valuable is the review article by Eric S. Lander, "Initial Impact of the Sequencing of the Human Genome," *Nature* 470 (2011): 187–97; see also Elaine R. Mardis, "A Decade's Perspective on DNA Sequencing

Technology," *Nature* 470 (2011): 198–203; and Eric D. Green, Mark S. Guyer, and the National Human Genome Research Institute, "Charting a Course for Genomic Medicine from Base Pairs to Bedside," *Nature* 470 (2011): 204–13.

18. One of the most important post-HGP projects was the International HapMap Project, which aimed to map common human variants across populations. See International HapMap Project, http://hapmap.ncbi.nlm.nih.gov/whatishapmap.html.en. On the disappointments in the fruits of the HapMap, see Hall, "Revolution Postponed," 60–67.

19. As Hall details in "Revolution Postponed," not all scientists are skeptical about the common variant hypothesis; for example, Eric Lander, director of the Broad Institute, continues to emphasize its promise.

20. Carl Zimmer, "The Gene Puzzle," *Newsweek*, June 26, 2009, www.thedailybeast.com/newsweek/2009/06/26/the-gene-puzzle.html.

21. Maher, "Personal Genomes," 20.

22. Another post-HGP project, called the Encyclopedia of DNA Elements (ENCODE), is attempting to understand all functional elements in the human genome. See, e.g., "The ENCODE Project: ENCyclopedia of DNA Elements," *National Human Genome Research Institute*, www.genome.gov/10005107.

23. Erica Check Hayden, "Life Is Complicated," *Nature* 464 (2010): 664–67.

24. Quoted in ibid., 665. The area of systems biology has burgeoned in the past decade, attempting to model the network of interactions not only in human cells but also in the cells of other organisms, such as yeast and E. coli.

25. Butler, "Science after the Sequence."

26. See, e.g., Yudi Pawitan, Ku Chee Seng, and Patrik K. E. Magnusson, "How Many Genetic Variants Remain to Be Discovered," *PLoS One* 4, no. 12 (2009), doi:10.1371/journal.pone.0007969.

27. For an account of the results of the pilot phase, see The 1000 Genomes Project Consortium, "A Map of Human Genome Variation from Population-Scale Sequencing," *Nature* 467 (2010): 1061–73, doi:10.1038/nature09534.

28. National Cancer Institute, "Cancer Genome Atlas," http://cancergenome.nih.gov/.

29. "The Sequence Explosion," *Nature* 464 (2010): 671. See also "Biology 2.0," *The Economist*, June 17, 2010, 3–5.

30. Nicholas Wade, "Cost of Decoding a Genome Is Lowered," *New York Times*, August 10, 2009, D3. See also "NHGRI Funds Development of Third Generation DNA Sequencing Technologies," *National Human Genome Research Institute*, September 13, 2010, www.genome.gov/27541190; and "Low-Cost Ultra-Fast DNA Sequencing Brings Diagnostic Use Closer," *Science Daily*, May 22, 2010, www.sciencedaily.com/releases/2010/05/100519163840.htm.

31. "Your Genome in Minutes: New Nanotechnology Could Slash Sequencing Time," *PhysOrg.com*, December 20, 2010, www.physorg.com/news/2010-12-genome-minutes-nanotechnology-slash-sequencing.html.

32. *Newsweek*, "The Gene Puzzle." The editorial refers to the Microbe Project (www.microbeproject.gov/), which is investigating the relationship of microbes and genes in cellular functions.

33. The focus is on methylation patterns because "methylation is the only flexible genomic parameter that can change genome function under exogenous influence. Hence

it constitutes the main and so far missing link between genetics, disease and the environment that is widely thought to play a decisive role in the aetiology of virtually all human pathologies." Human Epigenome Project, www.epigenome.org/index .php?page=project.

34. See J. K. Räty, J. T. Pikkarainen, T. Wirth, and S. YläHerttuala, "Gene Therapy: The First Approved Gene-Based Medicines, Molecular Mechanisms and Clinical Indications," *Current Molecular Pharmacology* 1 (2008): 13–23.

35. Helen Pearson, "One Gene, Twenty Years," *Nature* 460 (2009): 164–69. For a sample of articles detailing progress in gene therapy, see Wolfgang Poller, Roger Hajjar, Heinz-Peter Schultheiss, and Henry Fechner, "Cardiac-Targeted Delivery of Regulatory RNA Molecules and Genes for the Treatment of Heart Failure" *Cardiovascular Research* 86 (2010): 353–64, doi:10.1093/cvr/cvq056; Yuko Miyagoe-Suzuki and Shin'ichi Takeda, "Gene Therapy for Muscle Disease," *Experimental Cell Research* 316 (2010): 3087–92; D. Sheyn, O. Mizrahi, S. Benjamin, Z. Gazit, G. Pelled, and D. Gazit, "Genetically Modified Cells in Regenerative Medicine and Tissue Engineering," *Advanced Drug Delivery Reviews* 62 (2010): 683–98; J. R. Naegele, X. Maisano, J. Yang, S. Royston, and E. Ribeiro, "Recent Advances in Stem Cell and Gene Therapies for Neurological Disorders and Intractable Epilepsy," *Neuropharmacology* 58 (2010): 855–64; and Siyu Cao, Allan Cripps, and Ming Q. Wei, "New Strategies for Cancer Gene Therapy: Progress and Opportunities," *Clinical and Experimental Pharmacology and Physiology* 37 (2010): 108–14.

36. At the same time, however, patients were at risk of developing acute leukemia. Salima Hacein-Bey-Abina, Julia Hauer, Annick Lim, Capucine Picard, Gary P. Wang, Charles C. Berry, Chantal Martinache, Frédéric Rieux-Laucat, Sylvain Latour, Bernd H. Belohradsky, et al., "Efficacy of Gene Therapy for X-Linked Severe Combined Immunodeficiency," *New England Journal of Medicine* 363 (2010): 355–64. The issue of the safety and efficacy of treatment is important, although not dissimilar to those problems raised by other types of clinical testing. In 1999 Jesse Gelsinger died while participating in a gene therapy trial pertaining to liver disease at the University of Pennsylvania. Some linked the 2007 death of Jolee Mohr to her participation in a clinical trial of the uses of gene therapy to alleviate symptoms of rheumatoid arthritis, although the NIH Recombinant DNA Advisory Committee found that link to be unlikely. Stephanie Cajigal, "Gene Therapy Trial to Resume Despite Patient's Death," *Neurology Today* 8, no. 2 (2008): 32.

37. Andy Coghlan, "Blood Disorder Cured—A First for Gene Therapy," *New Scientist* 207, no. 2778 (2010): 1.

38. "New Anti-HIV Gene Therapy Makes T-Cells Resistant to HIV Infection," *ScienceDaily*, January 26, 2011, www.sciencedaily.com/releases/2011/01/110126121059.htm.

39. Ana P. Cotrim and Bruce J. Baum, "Gene Therapy: Some History, Applications, Problems, and Prospects," *Toxicologic Pathology* 36 (2008): 97–103. Consequently, while the moral questions surrounding the appropriate uses of gene therapy are riveting and crucial, they do not loom large from a practical perspective. A good overview of the distinct moral issues raised by gene therapy is LeRoy Walters and Julie Gage Palmer, *The Ethics of Human Gene Therapy* (New York: Oxford University Press, 1997). In particular, they explore the distinctions between therapeutic genetic intervention

and genetic enhancement, on the one hand, and genetic alterations to somatic cells and germ line alterations, on the other.

40. Elizabeth Morris, "Routine Colonoscopies May Become Obsolete: Simple DNA Tests Detect Early Cancer," *Boston Examiner*, November 1, 2010, www.examiner .com/health-news-in-boston/routine-colonoscopies-may-become-obsolete-simple-dna-tests-detect-early-cancer; Mandy Kendrick, "Could a Genetic Test on Stool Samples Make Colonoscopy Unnecessary Someday," *Scientific American Blog*, June 23, 2009, www.scientificamerican.com/blog/post.cfm?id=could-a-genetic-test-on-stool-sampl-2009-06-23. For an account of some of the challenges involved, see Shobita Parthasarathy, *Building Genetic Medicine: Breast Cancer, Technology, and the Comparative Politics of Health Care* (Cambridge, MA: MIT Press, 2007).

41. For a sample of information provided to the general public, see, e.g., "A Smarter Way to Treat Cancer," *Massachusetts General Hospital*, July 9, 2010, www.mgh.harvard .edu/about/newsarticle.aspx?id=2275. For a more theoretical overview, see, e.g., I. H. Tarner, U. Müller-Ladner, and C. G. Fathman, "Targeted Gene Therapy: Frontiers in the Development of 'Smart Drugs,'" *Trends in Biotechnology* 22, no. 6 (2004): 304–10. See also "Frequently Asked Questions about Pharmacogenomics," *National Human Genome Institute*, www.genome.gov/27530645; and Martha Lynn Craver, "Genetic Medicine Finally Is Hitting Its Stride," *Kiplinger*, July 12, 2010, www.kiplinger.com/ businessresource/forecast/archive/genetic-medicine-finally-hitting-its-stride.html. On side effects of drug treatments, see Shelley D. Smith, "The Human Genome Project 10 Years Out: Reviewing the Past, Present, and Future of Genomic Medicine," *Medscape Today*, January 4, 2011, www.medscape.com/viewarticle/735196.

42. Zoe Bianchi, "The Current Status of Gene Therapy: Therapeutic Gene Treatments— Reality or Dream," *Suite101*, January 21, 2010, www.suite101.com/content/ the-current-status-of-gene-therapy-a192095.

43. Francis Collins, "Has the Revolution Arrived?," *Nature* 464 (2010): 674–75.

44. "Many highly predictive genes will be required to identify substantial numbers of subjects at high risk of cancer." Margaret S. Pepe, Jessie W. Gu, and Daryl E. Morris, "The Potential of Genes and Other Markers to Inform about Risk," *Cancer Epidemiology, Biomarkers & Prevention* 19 (2010): 655–65. See also Robin M. Hallett, Anna Dvorkin, Christine M. Gabardo, and John A. Hassell, "An Algorithm to Discover Gene Signatures with Predictive Potential," *Journal of Experimental & Clinical Cancer Research* 29 (2010): 120, doi:10.1186/1756-9966-29-120.

45. Ralph Hertwig, Monika Andrea Zangerl, Esther Biedert, and Jürgen Margraf, "The Public's Probabilistic Numeracy: How Tasks, Education and Exposure to Games of Chance Shape It," *Journal of Behavioral Decision Making* 21, no. 4 (2008): 457–70, doi:10.1002/bdm.611.

46. Valerie F. Reyna and Charles J. Brainerd, "Numeracy, Ratio Bias, and Denominator Neglect in Judgments of Risk and Probability," *Learning and Individual Differences* 18 (2008): 89.

47. Ibid.

48. Valerie F. Reyna, Wendy L. Nelson, Paul K. Han, and Nathan F. Dieckmann, "How Numeracy Influences Risk Comprehension and Medical Decision Making," *Psychological Bulletin* 135 (2009): 943.

49. Gerd Gigerenzer, Wolfgang Gaissmaier, Elke Kurz-Milcke, Lisa M. Schwartz, and Steven Woloshin, "Helping Doctors and Patients Make Sense of Health Statistics," *Psychological Science in the Public Interest* 8, no. 2 (2008): 53–96.

50. Ibid., 53.

51. Ibid., 65.

52. Helen West and Ros Bramwell, "Do Maternal Screening Tests Provide Psychologically Meaningful Results? Cognitive Psychology in an Applied Setting," *Journal of Reproductive and Infant Psychology* 24 (2006): 61.

53. Ibid.

54. Ibid., 63.

55. Ibid., 65.

56. Linda M. Hunt, Heide Castañeda, and Katherine B. De Voogd, "Do Notions of Risk Inform Patient Choice? Lessons from a Study of Prenatal Genetic Counseling," *Medical Anthropology* 25 (2006): 193–219.

57. Ibid., 212.

58. Ibid.

59. Ibid., 213.

60. S. Sivell, G. Elwyn, C. L. Gaff, A. J. Clarke, R. Iredale, C. Shaw, J. Dundon, H. Thornton, and A. Edwards, "How Risk Is Perceived, Constructed and Interpreted by Clients in Clinical Genetics, and the Effects on Decision Making: Systematic Review," *Journal of Genetic Counseling* 17 (2008): 30.

61. See, e.g., J. T. Heshka, C. Palleschi, H. Howley, B. Wilson, and P. S. Wells, "A Systematic Review of Perceived Risks, Psychological and Behavioral Impacts of Genetic Testing," *Genetics in Medicine* 10 (2008): 19–32.

62. In 2008 the Genetic Information Nondiscrimination Act (GINA), Pub. L. 110-233, 122 Stat. 881, was enacted into federal law.

63. Joseph Raz, *The Morality of Freedom* (Oxford: Clarendon Press, 1986), 204.

64. On embodiment, see James F. Keenan, SJ, "Genetic Research and the Elusive Body," in *Embodiment, Medicine, and Morality*, ed. Margaret Farley and Lisa Sowle Cahill, 59–73 (Dordrecht, Netherlands: Kluwer, 1995).

65. For a discussion of the ethical dilemma over prenatal testing and abortion among pro-choicers, see Amy Harmon, "Abortion + Genetic Testing = ???," *New York Times*, May 13, 2007, C1.

66. See, e.g., Edwin Black, *War against the Weak: Eugenics and America's Campaign to Create a Master Race* (Washington, DC: Dialog Press, 2008); and Alexandra Minna Stern, *Eugenic Nation: Faults and Frontiers of Better Breeding in Modern America* (Berkeley: University of California Press, 2005).

67. Alison Bashford and Philippa Levine, *The Oxford Handbook of the History of Eugenics* (New York: Oxford University Press, 2010).

68. For a helpful introduction and discussion of this particular distinction as well as the numerous ethical questions that derive from it, see President's Council on Bioethics, *Beyond Therapy: Biotechnology and the Pursuit of Happiness* (New York: Harper, 2003). For my commentary on the deliberative function of bioethics commissions, see M. Cathleen Kaveny, "Diversity and Deliberation: Bioethics Commissions and Moral

Reasoning," *Journal of Religious Ethics* 34, no. 2 (2006): 311–37. For more concrete discussions, see James F. Keenan, SJ, "'Whose Perfection Is It Anyway?': A Virtuous Consideration of Enhancement," *Christian Bioethics* 5, no. 2 (1999): 104–20; and Gerald P. McKenny, "Technologies of Desire: Theology, Ethics, and the Enhancements of Human Traits," *Theology Today* 59, no. 1 (2002): 90–103. In 1999 *Theological Studies* devoted part of its annual "Notes on Moral Theology" to the question of genetics. See James J. Walter, "Theological Issues in Genetics," *Theological Studies* 60, no. 1 (1999): 111–23; Thomas A. Shannon, "Ethical Issues in Genetics," *Theological Studies* 60, no. 1 (1999): 124–34; and M. Cathleen Kaveny, "Jurisprudence and Genetics," *Theological Studies* 60, no. 1 (1999): 135–47.

69. There is an emerging literature on theology, genetics, and disability that is relevant to the articulation of solidarity's requirements in the realm of genetics: John Swinton and Brian Brock, eds., *Theology, Disability, and the New Genetics: Why Science Needs the Church* (London: T & T Clark, 2007); and Mary Jo Iozzio, "Genetic Anomaly or Genetic Diversity: Thinking in the Key of Disability in the Human Genome," *Theological Studies* 66, no. 4 (2005): 862–81. Also relevant to solidarity are broad conceptions of social and cultural identity. See, e.g., Christian Scharen and Aana Marie Vigen, *Ethnography as Christian Theology and Ethics* (New York: Continuum, 2011); and Jonathan Tran, "Transgressing Borders: Genetic Research, Immigration, and Discourses of Sacrifice," *Journal of the Society of Christian Ethics* 28, no. 2 (2008): 97–116.

70. For more specifically Christian evaluations of the ethical dilemmas posed by gene therapy, enhancements, and access to genetic information, see Celia Deane-Drummond, *Genetics and Christian Ethics* (Cambridge: Cambridge University Press, 2006); Lisa Sowle Cahill, "Germline Genetics, Human Nature, and Social Ethics," in *Design and Destiny: Jewish and Christian Perspectives on Human Germline Modification*, ed. Ronald Cole-Turner (Cambridge, MA: MIT Press, 2008), 145–66; Lisa Sowle Cahill, *Theological Bioethics: Participation, Justice, and Change* (Washington, DC: Georgetown University Press, 2005); Lisa Sowle Cahill, ed., *Genetics, Theology, and Ethics: An Interdisciplinary Conversation* (New York: Crossroad, 2005); Jack Mahoney, SJ, "Christian Doctrines, Ethical Issues, and Human Genetics," *Theological Studies* 64, no. 4 (2003): 719–49; and Gerald P. McKenny, "Religion and Gene Therapy: The End of One Debate, the Beginning of Another," in *A Companion to Genethics*, ed. Justine Burley and John Harris (Oxford: Blackwell, 2002), 287–301. For a survey of official Catholic teaching on the question, see Thomas A. Shannon, "The Roman Catholic Magisterium and Genetic Research: An Overview and Evaluation," in *Design and Destiny: Jewish and Christian Perspectives on Human Germline Modification*, ed. Ronald Cole-Turner, 51–72 (Cambridge, MA: MIT Press, 2008).

71. Philip R. Reilly, *The Surgical Solution: A History of Involuntary Sterilization in the United States* (Baltimore: Johns Hopkins University Press, 1991), 94. See also Victoria F. Nourse, *In Reckless Hands: Skinner v. Oklahoma and the Near-Triumph of American Eugenics* (New York: W. W. Norton, 2008).

72. *Buck v. Bell*, 274 US 200 (1927). Subsequent investigation of the facts of the case suggested that neither Carrie Buck nor her child was, in fact, mentally handicapped.

Her family had her committed in order to hide the fact that her pregnancy was the result of rape by the nephew of her adoptive mother. See Paul A. Lombardo, "Three Generations, No Imbeciles: New Light on *Buck v. Bell*," *New York University Law Review* 60 (1985): 50–62.

73. See, e.g., Robert Jay Lifton, *The Nazi Doctors: Medical Killing and the Psychology of Genocide* (New York: Basic Books 2000). For an interesting attempt to relate Nazi genetics to our own times, see Robert E. Pollack, "The Religious Obligation to Ask Questions of Nature and the State: Bonhoeffer on the Protection and Dignity of Human Life, in the Context of DNA-Based Genetic Medicine Today," *Union Seminary Quarterly Review* 60, nos. 1–2 (2006): 78–110. For recent Jewish reflections on genetic ethics, see Mark Popovsky, "Coping with Multiple Uncertainties: A Jewish Perspective on Genetic Testing for Breast Cancer and Prophylactic Interventions," *Journal of the Society of Christian Ethics* 29, no. 1 (2009): 127–51; and Jeffrey H. Burack, "Jewish Reflections on Genetic Enhancement," *Journal of the Society of Christian Ethics* 26, no. 1 (2006): 137–61.

74. See, e.g., Karen Peterson-Iyer, *Designer Children: Reconciling Genetic Technology, Feminism, and Christian Faith* (Cleveland: Pilgrim Press, 2004); and Lisa Sowle Cahill, "Genetics, Ethics, and Feminist Theology: Some Recent Directions," *Journal of Feminist Studies in Religion* 18, no. 2 (2002): 53–77. For the argument that parents have the right to design their children, see, e.g., John A. Robertson, *Children of Choice: Freedom and the New Reproductive Technologies* (Princeton, NJ: Princeton University Press, 1994).

75. Notably, Francis Crick, the codiscoverer of DNA, argued that he has identified the group of cells responsible for what we have called the "soul." See Francis Crick, *The Astonishing Hypotheses: The Scientific Search for the Soul* (New York: Touchstone, 1995).

76. See, e.g., Paul Brodwin, "Genetics, Identity, and the Anthropology of Essentialism," *Anthropological Quarterly* 75 (2002): 323–30; Anne Scott, "Like Editing Bits of Ourselves: Geneticisation and Human Fate," *New Genetics and Society* 25 (2006): 109–24. For an assessment of human nature in light of the closely related question of evolution, see Stephen J. Pope, *Human Evolution and Christian Ethics* (Cambridge: Cambridge University Press, 2007).

77. See, e.g., Ilan Dar-Nimrod and Steven J. Heine, "Genetic Essentialism: On the Deceptive Determinism of DNA," *Psychological Bulletin*, December 13, 2010, doi:10.1037/a0021860. See Harold W. Baillie and Timothy K. Casey, eds., *Is Human Nature Obsolete? Genetics, Bioengineering, and the Future of the Human Condition* (Cambridge, MA: MIT Press, 2005). For theological assessments, see Allen Verhey, *Nature and Altering It* (Grand Rapids, MI: Eerdmans, 2010); Celia Deane-Drummond, Bronislaw Szerszynski, and Robin Grove-White, eds., *Reordering Nature: Theology, Society, and the New Genetics* (London: T & T Clark, 2003); Gerald P. McKenny, *To Relieve the Human Condition: Bioethics, Technology, and the Body* (Albany: State University of New York Press, 1997); Ted Peters, *Playing God? Genetic Determinism and Human Freedom* (New York: Routledge, 1997); and Ted Peters, *For the Love of Children: Genetic Technology and the Future of the Family* (Louisville, KY: Westminster/ John Knox Press, 1996).

78. Thomas Aquinas, *Summa theologica*, 3 vols., trans. Fathers of the English Dominican Province (New York: Benziger Bros., 1948), II-II, q. 17, art. 1.

79. William Lynch, *Images of Hope* (Notre Dame, IN: University of Notre Dame Press, 1990). See also M. Cathleen Kaveny, "Cultivating Hope in Troubled Times: Catholic Colleges," *Origins* 35 (2005): 376–79.

80. See James F. Keenan, SJ, "What Does Virtue Ethics Bring to Genetics?," in *Genetics, Theology, Ethics: An Interdisciplinary Conversation*, ed. Lisa Sowle Cahill, 97–113 (New York: Crossroad, 2005).

81. Carlos Novas and Nikolas Rose, "Genetic Risk and the Birth of the Somatic Individual," *Economy and Society* 29 (2000): 485–513.

82. Ibid., 502.

83. Ibid., 507.

84. See, e.g., Rob Stein, "Company Plans to Sell Genetic Testing Kit at Drugstores," *Washington Post*, May 11, 2010, www.washingtonpost.com/wp-dyn/content/article/2010/05/10/AR2010051004904.html.

85. Rob Stein, "Walgreens Won't Sell Over-the-Counter Genetic Test after FDA Raises Questions," *Washington Post*, May 13, 2010, www.washingtonpost.com/wp-dyn/content/article/2010/05/12/AR2010051205156.html.

86. See "FDA to Regulate Direct-to-Consumer Genetic Tests," *Journal of the National Cancer Institute* 102 (2010): 1610–17; and Alexis Madrigal, "California Health Department Licenses Big DNA Testing Companies," *Wired Science*, August 20, 2008, www.wired.com/wiredscience/2008/08/california-heal/.

87. "Direct-to-Consumer Genetic Tests: Misleading Test Results Are Further Complicated by Deceptive Marketing and Other Questionable Practices," *General Accounting Office*, July 22, 2010, www.gao.gov/new.items/d10847t.pdf.

88. Ibid. For an overview of the hearings from a perspective more sympathetic to the industry, see Dan Vorhaus, "From Gulf Oil to Snake Oil": Congress Takes Aim at DTC Genetic Testing, *Genomics Law Report*, July 22, 2010, www.genomicslawreport.com/index.php/2010/07/22/from-gulf-oil-to-snake-oil-congress-takes-aim-at-dtc-genetic-testing/.

89. Ibid.

90. Other agencies with responsibility for oversight include the Federal Trade Commission, which has authority to restrict unfair or deceptive trade practices; and the Centers for Disease Control (CDC) and the Centers for Medicare and Medicaid Services (CMMS), which oversee and certify laboratories that provide medical testing services. In addition, comparatively few states offer regulation of DTC tests. For a fuller explanation, see Katherine Drabiak-Syed, "Baby Gender Monitor: Class Action Litigation Calls Attention to a Deficient Federal Regulatory Framework for DTC Genetic Tests, Politicized State Statutory Construction, and a Lack of Informed Consent," *Michigan State University Journal of Medicine & Law* 14 (2010): 71–92.

91. Jeffrey Shuren, "Direct-to-Consumer Genetic Testing and the Consequences to the Public," US Food and Drug Administration, July 22, 2010, www.fda.gov/NewsEvents/Testimony/ucm219925.htm.

92. Ibid.

93. See Howard J. Sherman, E. K. Hunt, Reynold F. Nesiba, Philip A. O'Hara, and Barbara A. Wiens-Tuers, *Economics: An Introduction to Traditional and Progressive Views*, 7th ed. (Armonk, NY: M. E. Sharpe, 2008), 133–36.

94. The best overview of the topic continues to be Ruth R. Faden and Tom L. Beauchamp, *A History and Theory of Informed Consent* (New York: Oxford University Press, 1986).
95. See Raz, *Morality of Freedom*, 213–16.
96. See Charles L. Knapp, Nathan M. Crystal, and Harry G. Prince, *Problems in Contract Law*, 6th ed. (New York: Aspen Publishers, 2007), 498–99. Also relevant are key developments in tort law, such as the recognition of class action suits conjoined with the development of products liability law.
97. The Ninth Amendment to the Constitution is normally considered to protect the "police power" of the states. The federal right to regulate in these matters is more tenuous; it is generally anchored in the Commerce Clause of Article One. However, this matter may be in flux. Chief Justice John Roberts cast the decisive vote upholding the constitutionality of the health care reform law under Article I's Taxing Clause. Along with four other justices, he rejected the law's constitutionality under the Commerce Clause.

CHAPTER 6

❧

Dying Gracefully

I N NOVEMBER 1996, just two weeks before he died, Joseph Cardinal Bernardin finished his book *The Gift of Peace*, in which he offers his meditations on three widely publicized events that punctuated the last years of his life: the false accusation of sexual abuse and his eventual reconciliation with his accuser; the diagnosis of an extremely aggressive form of cancer and his initially successful medical battle, which won him fifteen months of remission; and finally, the return of the disease and his decision to live fully for the remaining span of time allotted to him.[1] Bernardin recounts how all three events brought him to death and resurrection. In each event, he was called to let go of his own views of the proper course of his life and to grow ever more radical in his trust in Jesus Christ. While he could have made "letting go" seem peaceful, Bernardin does not flinch from describing the pain and uncertainty embedded in the arduous process of dying. In the end, we see how in the midst of his trials he embraced God's "gift of peace." His story inspires readers bearing the burdens of their own crosses to hope and pray for the same gift.

The challenge of grappling with the pain and uncertainty of dying is, of course, nothing new to humanity in general, nor to Christians in particular. In fact, religious writing about dying was extremely popular from the late Middle Ages through the Catholic Reformation, when premature death loomed as an omnipresent threat. The focus of most works in this tradition, known as the *ars moriendi*, or the "art of dying [well]," is pastoral and practical. The overarching purpose of this literature is to advise and assist persons as they prepare to relinquish their hold on this life and embark upon the next.[2] Of course, the specific focus of such assistance varies from era to era as different aspects of dying become more acute problems in different cultural contexts. The primary existential difficulty for those living during the time when the *ars moriendi* achieved its greatest prominence was the constant tension people experienced between hope of salvation and fear of eternal damnation.[3]

As we enter the third millennium, however, it is clear that we face a very different problem. The distinctive questions regarding death and dying that confront today's Western cultures involve a crisis of meaning, not a crisis of salvation. In many ways, the contemporary crisis is far more radical than the medieval one; rather than probing whether we have successfully conformed our hearts and minds to the deep metaphysical order of the universe, the foremost question is whether there is any discernible order calling for such conformity in the first place. Not surprisingly, questions of meaning become most acute when one is faced with the reality of death and dying. For persons who find themselves in the midst of it, is there any possible value in the dying process? What about for their loved ones, or for society? Is it possible for persons to continue living while at the same time dying—by growing in some way personally, spiritually, or socially in the midst of their physical diminishment? Or is dying an inexorable, impersonal, biological event best completed as quickly and easily as possible?

Woody Allen famously remarked, "It's not that I'm afraid to die. I just don't want to be there when it happens."[4] This line captures a prominent, perhaps even dominant, American sensibility toward death and dying.[5] Many people living in the United States today, including many Catholics, would say that the ideal death is a swift and sharp transition from vigorous existence to nonexistence—a death that circumvents the process of dying altogether. For example, a qualitative study of geriatric outpatients revealed that "the most frequently mentioned themes associated with good deaths were to die without pain, in one's sleep, quickly, without suffering, and without knowledge of impending death."[6] In a different survey of terminally ill men, a respondent described a good death in the following manner: "Oh, just going to sleep one night and not waking up. It would be a very easy, fast way to go, no drugs, no side effects, so to me that would be real easy."[7] Not everyone who expressed these preferences did so for the same reasons. For example, some thought that dying in one's sleep was preferable because it avoided consciousness of death's final approach, while others thought a sleeping death meant a painless, quick, peaceful, or easy exit from this world. Even in this variation it is clear that, overall, many people do not see dying as a stage in life that can both express and shape important personal commitments as well as strengthen key social and familial bonds.[8]

In this chapter I turn to the topic of end-of-life decision making. My focus here is the vexing questions regarding which treatments and procedures, if any, individuals are morally obliged to use in order to prolong their lives. The Roman Catholic moral tradition offers a long and rich history of reflection upon these questions, articulating a helpful distinction between "ordinary" means to preserve one's life, which are morally required, and "extraordinary" means of life preservation, which are not morally required and in some cases may be morally prohibited.

That tradition, however, is subject to distortion in two key ways. First, it wrongly can be reduced to a set of rules specifying lists of "required" and "optional" treatments that apply to all patients, no matter what their condition, social situation, or personal commitments. Second, those lists of rules can be misrepresented as a self-contained body of norms, intelligible even apart from a larger normative vision of the nature and purpose of human life, including living in the shadow of death. In my view, these two distortions are intimately related. It is precisely because the Catholic framework on end-of-life decision making is not always firmly situated within the tradition's broader view of a good death that it becomes easier to view that framework as a one-size-fits-all set of rules prescribing always-required and always-optional treatments.

Consequently, the most important step to take in communicating the wisdom of the Catholic medical-moral tradition about making decisions at the end of life is to explicitly relate the tradition to its larger goal of helping people deliberate and discern how to live well while dying. By drawing upon Cardinal Bernardin's reflections about his own impending death in *The Gift of Peace*, I situate, illustrate, and contextualize the Catholic normative framework regarding medical care in the shadow of death. More broadly, I also show how that framework can facilitate the exercise of Razian autonomy on the part of dying patients, and solidarity on the part of those surrounding them. In so doing, I lay the groundwork for the consideration of legal issues surrounding end-of-life decision making in the next chapter. I realize, of course, that many people, if not most people, do not die in the same manner that Cardinal Bernardin did, possessing his deliberative faculties until fairly close to the end of his life. A full consideration of the art of dying well would need to go on to consider what that might look like in cases of patients who suffered from mentally incapacitating illnesses for months or years before their death. In these cases patients do not make end-of-life decisions for themselves; they are subject to the decisions of third parties. Nonetheless, I think it important to begin by looking at the central case of how competent individuals ought to think about their own decision making at the end of life.[9]

THE GIFT OF PEACE

In *The Gift of Peace*, Bernardin depicts the period during which a person directly and concretely confronts mortality as a very important component of life, and he offers a vision of what constitutes a good death that is very different from the viewpoint encapsulated in Woody Allen's quip. The cardinal's book, in short, is an *ars moriendi* for our time. Bernardin describes his struggles with cancer in terms of his lifelong relationship with Christ and with the brothers and sisters in Christ whom he was called to the priesthood to serve. In keeping with his deepest values, his medical decision making was not an exercise in abstract moral reasoning but a prayerful discernment of the continually unfolding shape of his life and vocation.

From the perspective of Catholic Christianity, the life of a human being is not simply a flicker of consciousness "marking time" before being extinguished by the same cycle of creation and destruction that formerly brought that life into existence.[10] Rather, each person is born with a purpose: to grow in knowledge and love of the God in whose image she was created and to serve her fellow human beings, who are equally made in the image of God. Earthly human existence, therefore, is a gift of inestimable value. As Pope John Paul II emphasizes in his encyclical *Evangelium vitae*, "the Gospel of God's love for man, the Gospel of the dignity of the person and the Gospel of life are a single and indivisible Gospel."[11] Nonetheless, for Christians, our earthly human existence is not an absolute value. Our destiny extends beyond mortal existence to eternal life. Through the incarnation, crucifixion, and resurrection of Christ Jesus, we have been called to fellowship with God and with one another—a fellowship that breaks the barriers of sin and death in a way that we can barely and imperfectly imagine. In the words of the Apostle John, "Beloved, we are God's children now; what we will be has not yet been revealed. What we do know is this: when he is revealed, we will be like him, for we will see him as he is" (1 John 3:2).

Put another way, after Easter Sunday, death remains an evil afflicting human experience but not an absolute evil to be avoided at all costs. It can cruelly cut short the plans we have carefully and prayerfully made for our own lives and for those of our loved ones, and it can painfully stretch the bonds of love and friendship. But death cannot eradicate those bonds, nor can it even render meaningless a life that seems to end long before its time, as when a baby is born dying or a teenager is killed in a car accident the night of the senior prom. That bond of love is the promise of the resurrection.

What stance should human persons who believe in the promises of Jesus Christ take toward their embodied, mortal lives? The appropriate model is not one of dominion but of stewardship. As stewards of our own earthly existence, we are called to make decisions about all aspects of our life—how we live as well as how we die—in light of our common vocation to know, love, and serve the God who has created and redeemed us in Jesus Christ. In their pastoral statement on end-of-life issues, the Ohio Catholic bishops observe that stewardship has three components: creativity, humility, and compassion.[12] Creativity recognizes that good stewardship requires active engagement, not mindless submission. Each individual, within the concrete circumstances in which she finds herself, is called to discern what God is calling her to be and to do. Humility highlights the fact that our creativity is circumscribed by our status as creatures whose ultimate nature and purpose are determined not by ourselves but by the creator in whose image we are made. The third element of stewardship, compassion, honors the essential relationship of all persons. We are called to be one another's keepers and to bear one another's burdens as brothers and sisters in Christ.[13]

As *The Gift of Peace* illustrates, this framework of meaning is not meant to apply narrowly to decision making about death and dying. Rather, it is designed to shape all of the decisions we make over the course of our lives. Bernardin writes of how he had always "prayed and struggled constantly to be able to let go of things more willingly, to be free of everything that keeps the Lord from finding greater hospitality in my soul or interferes with my surrender to what God asks of me."[14] God had been calling him to this struggle all of his life. He found that calling in his attempts to reconcile the demands of conflicting political groups in the Church, in his efforts to free himself from any attachments to financial security, and, most radically of all, in his struggle to deal with the false charges of sexual abuse. His initial diagnosis of cancer and the inexorable return of the disease after a brief reprieve did not mark a change in the nature of God's call to him but instead were invitations to pursue his vocation even more deeply.

In the cardinal's account of "letting go" of his earthly existence, the most striking feature of that period of his life is its rich intensity. Invoking Charles Dickens, he wrote that "it has been the best of times, it has been the worst of times."[15] Bernardin viewed it as "the *best* because of the reconciliation, love, pastoral sensitivity and peace that have resulted from God's grace and the support and prayers of so many people."[16] Far from being a passive victim of his fate, Bernardin discerned that God was calling him to begin a new ministry to the terminally ill. He recognized that he had a task to accomplish in his dying. "I told the media that probably the most important thing I could do for the people of the Archdiocese—and everyone of good will—would be the way I prepare for death."[17]

Remaining true to his vocation to speak the truth about dying, Bernardin did not ignore what made the final three years of his life the worst of times: "the humiliation, physical pain, anxiety and fear."[18] He reflected on the "purpose and redemptive value" of suffering[19]—words that can seem utterly hollow, if not unspeakably cruel, when uttered as pious truisms by the healthy and powerful to those overcome by the weakness and pain of physical or emotional affliction. Yet in his case the words ring true; they are written in the blood and tears of his own weakness. He reflected that "in the final analysis, our participation in the paschal mystery—in the suffering, death, and resurrection of Jesus—brings a certain *freedom*: the freedom to let go, to surrender ourselves to the living God, to place ourselves completely in his hands, knowing that ultimately he will win out!"[20] The concrete power of that rather abstract promise is not only manifest in the vivid details of Bernardin's own struggles to move through suffering to surrender but also in the paradoxical fact that the vitality of his witness as Christ's priest grew in proportion to his own suffering and physical weakness.

ASSISTED SUICIDE AND EUTHANASIA

The vision of life, death, and resurrection to which Cardinal Bernardin was so radically committed undergirds the approach to end-of-life decision making developed over the centuries by Catholic moralists. The wisdom of that approach becomes vividly clear when it is set in the context of the Cardinal's own journey toward death and resurrection.

That Catholic tradition, most importantly, has consistently maintained that it is wrong to perform any action with the aim of taking innocent life, whether one's own life or that of another.[21] On that basis, the tradition has rejected euthanasia, which it defines as intentionally killing another human being in order to put her out of her suffering. It has also rejected physician-assisted suicide, which occurs when the patient takes a lethal dose of medicine prescribed for that purpose by her physician. At the same time, and equally crucially, the tradition clearly repudiates any claim that patients have an obligation to employ each and every medical means that they foresee will prolong their lives. It explicitly recognizes, in fact, that patients can on occasion forgo life-prolonging treatment without being charged with suicide. Moreover, it affirms that patients can legitimately choose certain medical interventions that will foreseeably shorten their lives, such as the use of powerful narcotics to control otherwise intractable pain.

To many people the foregoing distinctions seem arbitrary and unjustifiable.[22] If, for example, euthanasia is morally wrong, why distinguish between administering a shot of morphine with the intention of shortening a dying patient's life, on the one hand, and doing so while merely foreseeing the life-shortening effects of the morphine, on the other? If it is morally acceptable for one patient to forgo open-heart surgery because she cannot bear the thought of yet another surgery, why is it not similarly acceptable for another to do so in order to get a hard life over and done with? Is the Catholic approach to end-of-life decision making merely a set of arbitrary rules? In my judgment, no.

To see the point of this approach, however, we have to begin by putting ourselves in the perspective of the acting agent—the patient making decisions about his or her own course of treatment. At its heart, the Catholic framework is a guide for discernment, meant to aid those struggling with hard choices about medical care to make those choices in a way consistent with the Good News of Christ's life, death, and resurrection. Consequently, the first question to be asked in applying that framework is what the particular patient's own purpose is in refusing a particular life-saving treatment, or in obtaining a particular treatment that may shorten life.

The prohibitions against assisted suicide and euthanasia are prohibitions against acting with a particular purpose—the purpose of ending one's own life or that of another, either as an end in itself or as a means to another end.[23] In short, the Catholic tradition teaches that it is morally impermissible for a human agent to aim to eradicate herself or another person from this earthly life. To do so is to fail to appreciate life's goodness and to fail to trust in God's goodness and mercy. To discern whether a person is acting with that impermissible purpose, however, we cannot merely look at the external characteristics of the action. Nor can we examine solely the consequences of the action, or particular aspects of its structure. We have to put ourselves in the mind-set of the acting person and ask what their immediate and more remote purposes are in pursuing or rejecting a particular treatment option.[24]

It is important, in particular, not to regard a patient's choice in accepting or refusing a particular treatment as suicidal solely on the grounds that death was a certain (or likely) outcome of that choice.[25] We need to distinguish between an agent's intended effects in acting and the foreseen-but-unintended side effects of the action. While this distinction is philosophically and legally controversial, it is nonetheless already embedded in our ordinary way of evaluating actions.[26] We routinely distinguish, for example, between taking a healthy dose of codeine-infused cough medicine in order to get high and taking the same dose but accepting the resulting feeling of disassociation as an inevitable side effect of an attempt to quell the symptoms of a chest cold. The same distinction operates in matters of life and death as well. Consider the heroic passengers of the doomed United Airlines Flight 93, who apparently crashed the plane into the Pennsylvania countryside on September 11, 2001, rather than allowing terrorists to crash it into the White House or the Capitol. Although the passengers likely knew that the immediate result of their actions would be their own deaths, no one labels those actions as suicide.

It is also important to avoid assessing the agents' purposes solely in terms of whether the agents engage in a positive action or simply refrain from acting. Sometimes we make deliberate choices *not* to do a particular thing or *not* to follow a particular course of action. Not-doing, in other words, can be as purposeful as doing and can therefore be evaluated on the same basis.[27] For example, I can choose not to pay the cashier for my items before walking out the door; in most instances, the purpose of this nonaction is so clear that it is often redescribed in active terms as "theft." This phenomenon also occurs in matters of life and death. Consider the case of parents who, with the goal of ridding themselves of the burden of parenthood, do not feed their child. Not only do we easily recognize that the immediate purpose of this action is to bring about the child's death but we also redescribe the omission in active terms by saying that the parents *starved* their child.

In general, then, our purposes in acting cut across the distinctions between acts and omissions. Those purposes, however, cannot be invariably equated with the foreseen consequences of our actions. This observation also holds true in the particular realm of medical decision making at the end of life. A physician can give narcotics with the aim of suppressing respiration to cause death, or with the aim of relieving pain. The first is an act of euthanasia; the second is not. A diabetic patient can refuse insulin either because he does not consider life worth living after his wife's death or because it no longer makes sense to fight the diabetes in light of his end-stage cancer. The former refusal is suicidal, but the latter is not.

What, ultimately, is objectionable about euthanasia or assisted suicide? This question is always troublesome, particularly when the person asking such a question is suffering from a terminal illness. Within the Catholic framework, the short answer is that in aiming to end my own life or someone else's life, I am attempting to exercise an absolute dominion over human life that belongs only to God, and in so doing I am abandoning the duty of creative stewardship over life that is appropriate to human beings.[28] Viewed as a moral rule detached from a broader account of a good death, this response can easily seem too abstract and heartless. A more persuasive answer about why euthanasia and assisted suicide are prohibited kinds of actions must draw upon a broader account of what constitutes a good death.[29] Consider, for example, Cardinal Bernardin's own account of living and dying with cancer. It would have been simply inconceivable for the cardinal to choose to end his own life. Why?

First, because Bernardin viewed the purpose of his whole life as learning to subordinate his own will to God's will, he knew that ending his sojourn on earth at the time and place of his choosing would have been an act of self-assertion rather than submission. Accordingly, he writes of how his prayer life and relationship with God grew during this time. Second, such an act would have presupposed that there was no meaning or purpose in his dying, that there was no way that he could offer the process of letting go of earthly existence in service to Christ and his brothers and sisters in Christ. From his prayer and discernment, Bernardin knew this presupposition to be utterly false. In fact, after his diagnosis, he quickly recognized that he was being called to extend his priesthood in an entirely different direction by ministering to the dying. He recognized that he was a "priest first, a patient second."[30] Walking among other terminal patients as their true brother, Bernardin could offer words and deeds with a special credibility and power to comfort. Third, choosing assisted suicide or euthanasia would have denied others the gift of being able to give and minister to him. Cardinal Bernardin writes simply and movingly of how he was sustained in difficult times by the support of his friends, family, and fellow priests. He cannot but have known how much that opportunity to care for him meant to them.

TREATMENT DECISIONS

At the same time that the Church teaches that we should never practice actions aimed at death, such as euthanasia or assisted suicide, it also recognizes that we are not required to take every action aimed at preserving our earthly existence. More specifically, we are obliged to take "ordinary" but not "extraordinary" means to preserve our lives.[31] How do we decide whether a particular course of medical treatment is ordinary or extraordinary? The judgment must be made on a case-by-case basis, taking into account not only the potential benefits of the treatment but also its burdens and inconveniences, its likelihood of success, and its cost, not in the abstract but in terms of the likely effects on the particular patient in question and her family members.[32] A treatment that is ordinary for one patient may be extraordinary for another, taking into account all the circumstances of that patient's life. The National Conference of Catholic Bishops' *Ethical and Religious Directives for Catholic Health Care Facilities* emphasizes that the individual patients, if they are competent, should themselves make these judgments. Recognizing the need to balance numerous factors, the *Health Care Directives* refer to proportionate and disproportionate means of preserving life interchangeably with ordinary and extraordinary means.[33]

Three aspects of the distinction between ordinary and extraordinary means are worth stressing. First, in evaluating the benefits and burdens of a particular treatment, the proper basis for the evaluation is the whole patient, not merely the particular disease that the treatment is targeting. A person afflicted with kidney failure and cancer makes a decision about whether to continue with dialysis not only by looking narrowly at whether it continues to compensate for his renal function but also by considering more broadly its effect upon his total health.

Second, the assessment of benefits and burdens must encompass medical issues as well as the full range of personal and social concerns. The Catholic tradition on end-of-life decision making is personalized; it is not narrowly medicalized. In addition to factors such as the difficulty of obtaining treatment, pain, and expense, the analysis also recognizes that patients can legitimately fear and recoil from either the execution or the aftermath of some treatments. In his now-classic survey of the tradition, Daniel Cronin observed that some patients' legitimate objections to amputation included the painfulness of the procedure itself and the anticipation of living with a mutilated body.[34]

Third, some of the judgments involved in deciding between ordinary and extraordinary measures are complex and heartbreaking. Furthermore, they can be made under pressure or for the wrong reasons. Nonetheless, *abusus non tollit usum*: the potential abuse of the categories must not be allowed to obscure the fact that they can be properly applied in many situations. It is certainly the case, for example, that adult children, in order to preserve their inheritance, can pressure elderly parents to forgo reasonable courses of treatment. It is also the case, however, that elderly parents might reasonably decide not to expend enormous sums of money to access treatments not covered by their insurance, particularly if the treatments are of uncertain effectiveness or burdensome in other ways.[35]

One consequence of this distinction between ordinary and extraordinary means, therefore, is that sometimes patients will rightly refuse medical treatment that might otherwise have prolonged their lives. What is the difference between refusing a treatment option knowing that the result will be death and choosing death intentionally? Although this question can be hard to answer persuasively in the abstract, the difference is apparent in many (but not all) concrete cases. For example, after his initial diagnosis, Cardinal Bernardin underwent a long, grueling operation to remove the cancerous tumor, followed by a demanding regimen of chemotherapy and radiation. His physicians cautioned him that even with the operation, he had a one in four or five chance of surviving for five years. Nonetheless, he decided to go ahead with the operation. Life is a great good, and at sixty-seven, Cardinal Bernardin had a great deal he still wanted to accomplish; for him, the surgery was a proportionate means enabling him to fulfill God's purposes for him. We can easily imagine, however, a person who would find the very same treatment that Bernardin underwent to be disproportionate. For example, an individual who was twenty-five years older than Bernardin and had completed all the tasks he needed or wanted to accomplish in life might well decide to forgo surgery. For such a person, the difficulty of undergoing an operation and its aftermath might not be counterbalanced by the benefit of a slim chance for an extended life.

When the cardinal's cancer returned fifteen months after the surgery, he faced an entirely different set of circumstances. His physicians told him that there was no further treatment likely to work against his disease; he essentially had no choice but to prepare for death. God was calling him home. In his own words, he came to view death as a friend. Suppose, however, that Bernardin had been presented with an option of choosing a prolonged experimental treatment for which the chances for success were essentially unknown. Or suppose, hypothetically, that a treatment very likely to work would cost the Archdiocese of Chicago many millions of dollars, funds otherwise marked for charity. We can easily imagine that he would have refused such options, not in order to choose death but in order to preserve other values that would be sacrificed by a decision to continue treatment. In the first option, he would have been required to undergo an onerous treatment plan with very little hope of success; in the second, his decision to struggle on would have prevented the Archdiocese from fulfilling its other responsibilities. In refusing to fight to prolong his life under such hypothetical conditions, the cardinal would not be setting himself against God's sovereignty over life and death but simply discerning from all the facts and circumstances confronting him that God was drawing his life to a close.[36]

SUFFERING, AUTONOMY, AND SOLIDARITY

For most of us, the difficult part of confronting a terminal illness is the ominous prospect of pain and suffering. Although the terms are often used interchangeably, physical pain and suffering are not the same thing. Specialists in the area tell us that most physical pain associated with dying can be brought down to tolerable levels while maintaining a satisfactory level of consciousness in the patient. In a very few cases, satisfactory pain control can be established only by sedating the patient to the level of unconsciousness.[37] Most of the time the drugs necessary for effective pain management do not shorten a patient's life; however, in some instances, they could suppress respiration in a manner that brings about death more rapidly than would otherwise occur.[38]

The Catholic tradition does not prohibit physicians from taking measures that are truly intended to control otherwise uncontrollable pain. Just as we are not obligated to take any and every measure that might prolong our lives, no matter the burden to ourselves or to others, so we are not required to forgo every measure that might alleviate our pain, despite the fact that pain medications might have the side effect of shortening our lives. As with the identification of proportionate and disproportionate means, the appropriate decision about how to balance consciousness with effective pain control must be made on a case-by-case basis by the patients themselves, if they are competent to do so. Some dying patients might, in order to say farewell to a loved one, decide to forgo optimum pain medication in order to preserve consciousness. A rare few might decide to do so in order to express their solidarity with the crucified Christ. But the decision to bear more physical pain than necessary is one that a dying individual must make for herself. When we are asked to make decisions for dying patients who are not competent to make them for themselves, our obligation to care mercifully for them requires that we decide in favor of effective pain control.

Physical pain, despite its worrisome issues, is a relatively simple phenomenon compared to the complexities of suffering. Lawyers in tort suits tend to use the phrase "pain and suffering" almost as if the two terms were synonymous. But the philosopher Eric Cassell reminds us that "pain" and "suffering" are distinct concepts.[39] We can suffer immeasurably without experiencing any physical pain (such as when we watch a loved one die). We can also be racked with significant physical pain without any accompanying suffering (such as when a woman delivers a long-hoped-for baby). Although separable, it is important to acknowledge the overlap between the two experiences; in many cases, severe physical pain—or the prospect of such pain—is a major cause of human suffering. By examining the nature and meaning of suffering and its relationship to pain, we can make progress in understanding the roles of autonomy and solidarity at the end of life.

What is suffering, exactly? Cassell, who in my view has written most profoundly on the topic, defines it as "the distress brought about by the actual or perceived impeding threat to the integrity or continued existence of the whole person."[40] He recognizes that the threat at issue is not merely a threat to the physical integrity of persons, for "while they may be identified with their bodies, [they] cannot be whole in body alone." Nor is suffering a purely "quantitative matter" in which a certain amount of unpleasant physical stimuli or tissue damage, or even an objectively assessable threat level uniformly triggers suffering in all persons. Fundamentally, suffering is a threat to an individual's sense of personal identity, the narrative account that one gives of oneself, uniting the past and future events, circumstances, relationships, and purposes into a coherent life project. Purposes are key; as Cassell notes, "to be whole and able to suffer is to have aims or purposes."[41] Suffering is prompted by the prospect of disintegration of one's personal identity, which is in turn triggered by the realization (or the strong fear) that one will no longer be able to pursue one's accustomed or expected range of purposeful activity. The matrix of purposeful actions through which human beings define and affirm their identities include mundane and routine tasks as well as grand plans. Cassell writes movingly of a young woman whose legs were mangled in a terrible motorcycle crash. Lying on the highway, her first deliberate action was to pull her skirt down to cover herself. As Cassell notes, she "was still involved in the purposes of her usual self"; her suffering would arise from her realization that those quotidian purposes would never again play the same role in her life.[42]

Suffering, then, can be seen as a significant threat to a person's identity, as the latter is understood in terms of the fruits of Razian autonomy. Recall that for Raz "the ideal of personal autonomy is the vision of people controlling, to some degree, their own destiny, fashioning it through successive decisions throughout their lives."[43] Decisions build one upon the other, long-term plans are made, and an autonomous person attempts to live those decisions and plans with a certain stable commitment. "The autonomous person has or is gradually developing a conception of himself, and his actions are sensitive to his past. A person who has projects is sensitive to his past in at least two respects. He must be aware of having the pursuits he has, and he must be aware of his progress in them."[44] Integrity is a key aspect of autonomy for Raz; he believes an autonomous person identifies with her choices and is loyal to them.[45] Being a part-author of one's own life means fidelity to the life that one is, in part, responsible for creating.

In Raz's terms, then, suffering is such a wrenching experience because it disintegrates previously autonomous persons, cleaving them from the plans and purposes with which they have defined themselves as part-authors of their own lives. A mother who loses a child to an accident and a family that loses its home to a tsunami are both forced to abandon previously constant conceptions of their lives. "A person who feels driven by forces which he disowns but cannot control . . . does not lead an autonomous life. The life he has is not his own. He is thoroughly alienated from it."[46] Suffering persons, as they struggle to make sense of the shards of their lives, may even experience their inability to pursue their previous goals as a frustrating type of self-betrayal. "Loyalty to one's projects and relationships" is a key aspect of autonomy.[47] If it becomes impossible or impracticable to pursue those relationships, many reflective persons begin to question themselves and their judgment, reviewing the choices that led to the source of the suffering.

We are now in a position to see the relationship between physical suffering and pain more clearly. Severe physical pain can so overwhelm a human being that the pursuit of all the goals entwined with personal identity becomes impossible, and this is so for at least two reasons. First, all pain, particularly if it is severe or chronic, is enervating; it drains its sufferers of the physical and psychological resources to formulate, evaluate, revise, and carry out many of the immediate purposes and more remote goals that constitute one's life. Moreover, as Elaine Scarry so brilliantly argues, severe pain unmakes the self as an agent by destroying the ability to reflect upon and to articulate one's experiences. "It is the intense pain that destroys a person's self and world, a destruction experienced spatially as either the contraction of the universe down to the immediate vicinity of the body or as the body swelling to fill the entire universe. Intense pain is also language-destroying: as the content of one's world disintegrates, so the content of one's language disintegrates; as the self disintegrates, so that which would express and project the self is robbed of its source and its subject."[48] Furthermore, the sense of self-disintegration is magnified as a sense of self-betrayal; "the person in great pain experiences his own body as the agent of his agony."[49]

Second, and related, the overarching goal of many persons afflicted with significant pain is to find some way to make it go away. One might object that this goal is clearly worthy and is one that will likely require the planning and execution of many intermediate steps, such as the identification of and consultation with appropriate specialists and the experimentation with various techniques of pain management. The problem is, however, that this goal is experienced not as freely chosen but as overwhelmingly imposed by exigent circumstances. Consequently, it is analogous to Raz's example of the Hounded Woman, who is trapped on a small island with a wild animal who is perpetually hunting her. Her mental and physical resources are devoted entirely to attempting to escape its deadly bite. Raz denies that the Hounded Woman can really exercise autonomy, despite the fact that "we can further develop her story to provide her with medium and long-term options all dominated by her one overpowering need and desire to escape being devoured by the beast."[50] In Raz's view, "a choice between survival and death is no choice"; consequently, autonomy's criterion of having an adequate range of options must be understood to mean that one's choices cannot be "dominated by the need to protect the life one has."[51] In my view, a similar point holds about a choice between relative ease in one's own body and severe pain—it, too, is no choice at all.

OVERCOMING SUFFERING

If suffering involves disintegration of one's self-identity, then overcoming suffering involves finding a way forward toward reintegration, toward a new life that somehow also incorporates a narrative about the old life. New purposes are found; new commitments are made. In some instances, the new is in some way deeply continuous with the old purposes; for example, athletes, confronted unexpectedly with physical handicaps, may learn how to adjust to their limitations and pursue their goals through other means, such as the Paralympics. In other situations, the disintegration prompts a thorough reevaluation of the course of one's life, yielding a dramatic restructuring along the lines of a conversion experience.[52]

Is it possible to overcome suffering in the face of one's own death, with the entailing loss of self and agency? Without denying the likelihood of suffering in such a context, Cassell suggests that it is not always inevitable. Moreover, he believes that physicians and caregivers can be taught to recognize and alleviate suffering, and he identifies three types of knowledge needed to cultivate those skills. First, we need to have specific and rich understanding of the suffering person as a unique human being; we need to be able to appreciate the details of her individual personality and social context. Armed with that understanding, the caregiver can see that what looks like icy noncommunication for one family is actually quiet supportiveness in another. Second, we need to have some sense of the values and projects of the dying person. What urgent tasks will be left undone? Is the person incorporated into the dying process as an agent, and not merely as the occasion for the agency of others? Third, and most provocatively, Cassell invokes an aesthetic factor: is there some discernible harmony in the person's living-while-dying that exhibits continuity with the values of the life lived earlier? To make his point, Cassell uses the example of an Albanian man, dying from metastatic cancer of the lung, who experienced a sense of fittingness about dying from the same disease that had taken his father and brothers before him.

Cassell's model calls for the development of detailed and discerning knowledge of another person in order to discern whether and why that person is suffering. That knowledge, in my view, is integrally related to the practice of solidarity as understood in the terms of Pope John Paul II precisely because solidarity calls for active relationship to individual persons in their particular strengths and weaknesses.[53] Detailed knowledge of a person's history and social context is not only necessary to identify whether he or she is suffering but also to help alleviate that suffering. Given sufficient knowledge, we can offer those who are suffering ways of reinterpreting their past purposes that will allow them some continuity, even in circumstances—such as chronic illness or disability—that have significantly changed for the worse. If we know them well enough, we can help them deal with the challenges of dying by helping them look back upon and reassess their lives, both what they did and what happened to them, in a way that will allow them some closure. Solidarity, in other words, supports autonomy by helping persons find a way to transcend suffering by reaffirming, reassessing, or reconfiguring their own purposes amidst tremendous pain and affliction.

Frequently, however, victory over suffering can only be glimpsed through a glass, darkly. This bleak prospect holds for all manner of suffering: terminal illness, poverty, violence, loss, or betrayal in deep personal relationships. But Christians, by inscribing their narratives within the story of the life, death, and resurrection of Jesus Christ, have a way of both recognizing and transcending suffering. As Bernardin noted, "the essential mystery of the cross is that it gives rise to a certain kind of loneliness, an inability to see clearly how things are unfolding, an inability to see that, ultimately, all things will work for our good, and that we are, indeed, not alone."[54]

Bernardin recognized how difficult it is to be with others whose suffering we cannot eliminate. "Whenever we are with people who suffer, it frequently becomes evident that there is very little we can do to help them other than be present to them, walk with them as the Lord walks with us. The reason this is so frustrating is that we like to be 'fixers.'"[55] We need to overcome our own urge to "fix" a situation that is not fixable, or to flee our own impotence by fleeing from them. "It's precisely in letting go, in entering into complete union with the Lord, in letting him take over, that we discover our true selves. It's in the act of abandonment that we experience redemption, that we find life, peace, and joy in the midst of physical, emotional, and spiritual suffering."[56]

CONCLUSION

In this chapter I situated Catholic teaching on end-of-life decision making in its rightful, broader context of purposeful decision making about life as a whole. By taking Joseph Cardinal Bernardin's *The Gift of Peace* as a touchstone, I showed why the distinction between ordinary and extraordinary means of preserving life is not an arbitrary set of rules externally imposed upon seriously ill persons but a set of guidelines for sufferers to use in discerning how to remain faithful to their own commitments and purposes in light of their mortality. The guidelines are part, but only part, of the Christian tradition of the *ars moriendi*.

What about the prospect of pain and suffering so associated with dying for most people? In most circumstances, pain can be controlled medically. Suffering, on the other hand, is a far more complex phenomenon. Understanding its causes and its potential amelioration requires us to delve more deeply into the intertwined requirements of autonomy and solidarity. Suffering, in essence, is a blow to the fruits of Razian autonomy; alleviation from suffering generally is facilitated by the exercise of solidarity as understood by Pope John Paul II. Even when suffering cannot be eradicated, it can be borne more easily when it is not borne alone.

In the next chapter I turn to the jurisprudential questions around death and dying, focusing on the constitutional framework that provides the basic structure for other laws. Given the values of autonomy and solidarity, and the wide range of morally worthwhile lives that they serve in this pluralistic nation, how should we configure the legal framework that governs such issues as assisted suicide and euthanasia as well as the decisions to withdraw medical treatment? As always, the law needs to take into account not only fundamental matters of moral pedagogy but also more pragmatic questions such as feasibility and acceptability in light of the current social and political consensus of a nation's citizenry.

NOTES

This chapter has its seeds in M. Cathleen Kaveny, "Last Rights: Dying Gracefully," *Church* 14, no. 2 (Summer 1998), 11–17.

1. Joseph Bernardin, *The Gift of Peace* (Chicago: Loyola Press, 1997).
2. N. F. Blake, "Ars moriendi," in *Dictionary of the Middle Ages*, ed. Joseph R. Strayer (New York: Scribner, 1982), 1: 547–48. The primary literature is extensive. For one example, see Robert Bellarmine, "The Art of Dying Well," in *Spiritual Writings*, trans. Ronald J. Teske, SJ (Mahwah, NJ: Paulist Press, 1989), 231–386. See also Paul Binski, *Medieval Death* (Ithaca, NY: Cornell University Press, 1996); Nancy Lee Beaty, ed., *The Craft of Dying: A Study in the Literary Tradition of the Ars Moriendi in England* (New Haven, CT: Yale University Press, 1970); Carlos M. N. Eire, *From Madrid to Purgatory: The Art and Craft of Dying in Sixteenth-Century Spain* (New York: Cambridge University Press, 1995); and Austra Reinis, *Reforming the Art of Dying: The*

Ars Moriendi *in the German Reformation* (1519–28) (Aldershot, England: Ashgate Publishing, 2006). More contemporary works include Christopher P. Vogt, *Patience, Compassion, Hope, and the Christian Art of Dying Well* (Lanham, MD: Rowman & Littlefield, 2004); and Peter Fenwick and Elizabeth Fenwick, *The Art of Dying* (New York: Continuum, 2008).

3. See, e.g., the preface to Bellarmine's *Ars moriendi*: "No one who is willing to consider attentively that in death one must render an account to God of all we have done, said, and thought, even of one idle word uttered, while the devil is our accuser, conscience is our witness, God is our judge, and the punishment of eternal death or an everlasting reward is awaiting us, will deny that the art of dying well is the most important of all the arts." Bellarmine, *Spiritual Writings*, 235.

4. Woody Allen, *Without Feathers* (New York: Ballantine Books, 1983), 106.

5. See K. E. Steinhauser, N. A. Christakis, E. C. Clipp, M. McNeilly, S. Grambow, J. Parker, and J. A. Tulsky, "Preparing for the End of Life: Preferences of Patients, Families, Physicians, and Other Care Providers," *Journal of Pain and Symptom Management* 22 (2001): 727.

6. Elizabeth K. Vig, Nathaniel A. Davenport, and Robert A. Pearlman, "Good Deaths, Bad Deaths, and Preferences for the End of Life: A Qualitative Study of Geriatric Outpatients," *Journal of the American Geriatrics Society* 50 (2002): 1541–48.

7. Elizabeth K. Vig and Robert A. Pearlman, "Good and Bad Dying from the Perspective of Terminally Ill Men," *Archives of Internal Medicine* 164, no. 9 (2004): 98. See also a UK study by Charles Leadbeater and Jake Garber, *Dying for Change* (London: Demos, 2010), which also recognized that "many people say they would like to die without warning and in their sleep." Ibid., 25.

8. For an interesting articulation and defense of the view that dying is an important stage of life, see Alasdair MacIntyre, "The Right to Die Garrulously" in *Death and Decision*, ed. Ernan McMullin (Colorado: Westview Press, 1978), 75–84.

9. For a vivid account of what happens when individuals die of different causes by a medical doctor, see Sherwin B. Nuland, *How We Die: Reflections on Life's Final Chapter* (New York: Knopf, 1994).

10. For two recent broader visions of Catholic bioethics, see Lisa Sowle Cahill, *Theological Bioethics: Participation, Justice, and Change* (Washington, DC: Georgetown University Press, 2005); and Anthony Fisher, OP, *Catholic Bioethics for a New Millennium* (Cambridge: Cambridge University Press, 2012). For a well-regarded textbook, see Benedict M. Ashley, OP, Jean deBlois, CSJ, and Kevin D. O'Rourke, OP, *Health Care Ethics: A Catholic Theological Analysis*, 5th ed. (Washington, DC Georgetown University Press, 2006).

11. Pope John Paul II, *Evangelium vitae* (*Gospel of Life*) (1995), para. 2. See, more broadly, Christopher Tollefsen, ed., *John Paul II's Contribution to Catholic Bioethics* (Dordrecht, Netherlands: Springer, 2010).

12. Catholic Bishops of Ohio, "Pastoral Reflections: Euthanasia, Assisted Suicide," *Origins* 23 (1993): 373–78. For a scholarly overview of some of the issues, see Lisa Sowle Cahill, "Bioethical Decisions to End Life," *Theological Studies* 52, no. 1 (1991): 107–27.

13. Diana Fritz Cates and Paul Lauritzen, eds., *Medicine and the Ethics of Care* (Washington, DC: Georgetown University Press, 2001).

14. Bernardin, *Gift of Peace*, 6.
15. Ibid., ix.
16. Ibid.
17. Ibid., 136.
18. Ibid., ix.
19. Ibid., 47.
20. Ibid., 48.
21. See, e.g., John Paul II, *Evangelium vitae*, para. 57:

> If such great care must be taken to respect every life, even that of criminals and unjust aggressors, the commandment "You shall not kill" has absolute value when it refers to the innocent person. And all the more so in the case of weak and defenceless human beings, who find their ultimate defence against the arrogance and caprice of others only in the absolute binding force of God's commandment.
>
> In effect, the absolute inviolability of innocent human life is a moral truth clearly taught by Sacred Scripture, constantly upheld in the Church's Tradition and consistently proposed by her Magisterium. This consistent teaching is the evident result of that "supernatural sense of the faith" which, inspired and sustained by the Holy Spirit, safeguards the People of God from error when "it shows universal agreement in matters of faith and morals."

22. See, e.g., Ronald Dworkin, *Life's Dominion: An Argument about Abortion, Euthanasia, and Individual Freedom* (New York: Knopf, 1993). For an excellent anthology on the broader questions that is not dependent upon theological claims, see John Keown, ed., *Euthanasia Examined: Ethical, Legal, and Clinical Perspectives* (Cambridge: Cambridge University Press, 1995). Included in this volume is the fascinating debate between John Finnis (who opposes euthanasia) and John Harris (who defends it): John Harris, "Euthanasia and the Value of Life," 6–22; John Finnis, "A Philosophical Case against Euthanasia," 23–35; John Harris, "The Philosophical Case against the Philosophical Case against Euthanasia," 36–45; John Finnis, "The Fragile Case for Euthanasia: A Reply to John Harris," 46–55; John Harris, "Final Thoughts on Final Acts," 56–61; John Finnis, "Misunderstanding the Case against Euthanasia: Response to Harris's First Reply," 62–71.
23. This is the operative definition of euthanasia found in Vatican declarations on the subject. See Sacred Congregation for the Doctrine of the Faith, *Declaration on Euthanasia* (1980).
24. In the technical terms of Catholic moral theology, the immediate purpose of an acting agent is the "object" of the action. "*The morality of the human act depends primarily and fundamentally on the "object" rationally chosen by the deliberate will.* . . . In order to be able to grasp the object of an act which specifies that act morally, it is therefore necessary to place oneself *in the perspective of the acting person*." Pope John Paul II, *Veritatis splendor* (*The Splendor of Truth*) (1993), para. 78. Not surprisingly, the definition of the "object" of an action, and John Paul II's understanding of it "in the perspective of the acting person," has been subject to vigorous debate. See, for example, Martin Rhonheimer, *The Perspective of the Acting Person: Essays in the*

Renewal of Thomistic Moral Philosophy, ed. William F. Murphy (Washington, DC: Catholic University of America Press, 2008). For representative positions contrary to Rhonheimer's interpretation of the encyclical, see Stephen L. Brock, "*Veritatis splendor* §78, St. Thomas, and (Not Merely) Physical Objects of Moral Acts," *Nova et vetera* 6, no. 1 (2008): 1–62; and Lawrence Dewan, "St. Thomas, Rhonheimer, and the Object of the Human Act," *Nova et vetera* 6, no. 1 (2008): 63–112.

25. See John Finnis, "Intention and Side-Effects," in *Intention & Identity*, vol. 4 of his *Collected Essays* (Oxford: Oxford University Press, 2011), 173–97.

26. I deal with some of the issues in my analysis of the *mens rea* requirement in murder in English law in M. Cathleen Kaveny, "Inferring Intention from Foresight," *Law Quarterly Review* 120 (2004): 81–107.

27. For defense of this point, see Thomas Aquinas, *Summa theologica*, 3 vols., trans. Fathers of the English Dominican Province (New York: Benziger Bros., 1948), I-II, q. 6, art. 3; and G. E. M. Anscombe, "The Two Kinds of Error in Action," *Journal of Philosophy* 60 (1963): 393–400.

28. See Kevin Wildes, SJ, "Ordinary and Extraordinary Means and the Quality of Life," *Theological Studies* 57 (1996): 500–512, at 500–01.

29. The first chapter of Bellarmine's *ars moriendi* explicates "the first rule for dying well, which is that one who desires to die well should live well." Bellarmine, *Spiritual Writings*, 239.

30. Bernardin, *Gift of Peace*, 75.

31. See, e.g., United States Conference of Catholic Bishops, *Ethical and Religious Directives for Catholic Health Care Services*, 5th ed. (Washington, DC: United States Conference of Catholic Bishops, 2009), ERDs 56 and 57 (hereafter cited as *Health Care Directives*).

32. For a good summary of the history, see Wildes, "Ordinary and Extraordinary Means." Also see Gilbert C. Meilaender, "Ordinary and Extraordinary Treatments: When Does Quality of Life Count?" *Theological Studies* 57, no. 3 (1997): 527–531, for a response to Wildes's presentation. Wildes's rejoinder can be found at "When Does Quality of Life Count? A Response to Gilbert Meilaender," *Theological Studies* 59, no. 3 (1998): 505–8. See also Gilbert Meilaender's *Bioethcs: A Primer for Christians*, 2nd ed. (Grand Rapids, MI: Eerdmans, 2005).

33. See *Health Care Directives*, ERDs 57–59.

34. Daniel A. Cronin, "The Moral Law in Regard to the Ordinary and Extraordinary Means of Conserving Life," in Russell E. Smith, ed., *Conserving Human Life* (Braintree, MA: Pope John XXIII Medical-Moral Research and Education Center, 1989), 111. Obviously, the development of better prosthetic devices eliminates much (although perhaps not all) of the grounds for objection.

35. On a theology of aging, see James F. Keenan, SJ, "Dualism in Medicine, Christian Theology and the Aging," *Journal of Religion and Health* 35 (1996): 33–45. For many Americans, the most expensive aspect of caring for an elderly loved one is not the medical treatment itself but the nursing services and other assistance necessary to keep them in their own homes. Much of inpatient care is covered by Medicare; most people, however, do not have the insurance or other resources necessary to subsidize round-the-clock in-home care. See U. Piamjariyakul, V. M. Ross, D. M. Yadrich, A. R. Williams, L. Howard, and C. E. Smith, "Complex Home Care: Part I—Utilization

and Costs to Families for Health Care Services Each Year," *Nursing Economics* 28 (2010): 255–63; Ubolrat Piamjariyakul, Donna Macan Yadrich, Vicki M. Ross, Carol E. Smith, Faye Clements, and Arthur R. Williams, "Complex Home Care: Part II—Family Annual Income, Insurance Premium, and Out-of-Pocket Expenses," *Nursing Economics* 28 (2010): 323–29; Carol E. Smith, Ubolrat Piamjariyakul, Donna Macan Yadrich, Vicki M. Ross, Byron Gajewski, and Arthur R. Williams, "Complex Home Care: Part III—Economic Impact on Family Caregiver Quality of Life and Patients' Clinical Outcomes," *Nursing Economics* 28 (2010): 393–414; and Karen Buhler-Wilkerson, "Care of the Chronically Ill at Home: An Unresolved Dilemma in Health Policy for the United States," *Milbank Quarterly* 85 (2007): 611–39.

36. There are, of course, hard questions—most notably the question of artificial nutrition and hydration. Catholic moralists are divided on the issue, and an intervention by Pope John Paul II did not serve to settle the debate, since it generated dispute about its proper interpretation. For an overview of the issue, see Lisa Sowle Cahill, "Bioethics," *Theological Studies* 67, no. 1 (2006): 120–42. See Pope John Paul II, "Address to the Participants in the International Congress on 'Life-Sustaining Treatments and Vegetative State: Scientific Advances and Ethical Dilemmas,'" March 20, 2004, www.vatican.va/holy_father/john_paul_ii/speeches/2004/march/documents/hf_jp-ii_spe_20040320_congress-fiamc_en.html. See also the 2007 commentary on the question issued by the Congregation for the Doctrine of the Faith, www.vatican.va/roman_curia/congregations/cfaith/documents/rc_con_cfaith_doc_20070801_nota-commento_en.html. On the interpretation of the papal allocution, see John J. Paris, SJ, James F. Keenan, SJ, and Kenneth R. Himes, OFM, "Did John Paul II's Allocution on Life-Sustaining Treatments Revise Tradition," *Theological Studies* 67, no. 1 (March 2006): 163–68; and Thomas A. Shannon and James J. Walter, "Reply to Professors Paris, Keenan, and Himes," *Theological Studies* 67, no. 1 (2006): 169–74. For a range of perspectives on the underlying questions, see Ronald P. Hamel and James J. Walters, eds., *Artificial Nutrition and Hydration and the Permanently Unconscious Patient: The Catholic Debate* (Washington, DC: Georgetown University Press, 2007); and Christopher Tollefsen, ed., *Artificial Nutrition and Hydration: The New Catholic Debate* (Dordrecht: Springer, 2010).

37. See New York State Task Force on Life and the Law, "Clinical Responses to Pain and Suffering," in *When Death Is Sought: Assisted Suicide and Euthanasia in the Medical Context* (Albany, NY: Health Education Services, 1994), 35–47. For a comprehensive approach to pain management, see Mark V. Boswell and B. Eliot Cole, eds., *Weiner's Pain Management* (Boca Raton, FL: Taylor & Francis, 2006); for pain management at the end of life, see George J. Taylor and Jerome E, Kurent eds., *A Clinician's Guide to Palliative Care* (Malden, MA: Blackwell, 2003).

38. Needless to say, depriving someone of consciousness in the last hours of life is not a decision to be made lightly. See *Health Care Directives*, ERD 61: "Patients should be kept as free of pain as possible so that they may die comfortably and with dignity, and in the place where they wish to die. Since a person has the right to prepare for his or her death while fully conscious, he or she should not be deprived of consciousness without a compelling reason. Medicines capable of alleviating or suppressing pain may be given to a dying person, even if this therapy may indirectly shorten the person's

life so long as the intent is not to hasten death. Patients experiencing suffering that cannot be alleviated should be helped to appreciate the Christian understanding of redemptive suffering." See also Sacred Congregation for the Doctrine of the Faith, *Declaration on Euthanasia* (1980).

39. Eric J. Cassell, *The Nature of Suffering and the Goals of Medicine*, 2nd ed. (New York: Oxford University Press, 2004), chap. 5.
40. Eric J. Cassell, "Recognizing Suffering," *Hastings Center Report* 21 (1991): 24.
41. Ibid., 25.
42. Ibid.
43. Joseph Raz, *The Morality of Freedom* (Oxford: Clarendon Press, 1986), 369.
44. Ibid., 385.
45. Ibid., 382–83.
46. Ibid., 382.
47. Ibid., 384.
48. Elaine Scarry, *The Body in Pain: The Making and Unmaking of the World* (New York: Oxford University Press, 1985), 35.
49. Ibid., 47.
50. Raz, *Morality of Freedom*, 374–77.
51. Ibid., 376.
52. See, e.g., Laura Petrecca, "Health Scare Can Inspire Start of Business," *USA Today*, February 22, 2011, www.usatoday.com/money/smallbusiness/2011-02-22-sicknesstohealth22_CV_N.htm, for a description of how three individuals started their own businesses after having health issues. For a more theoretical perspective on the adaptability of persons to drastic changes in their physical and mental state, see President's Council on Bioethics, *Taking Care: Ethical Caregiving in Our Aging Society* (Washington, DC: US Executive Office of the President, 2005), 80–89.
53. Pope John Paul II, *Sollicitudo rei socialis* (*On Social Concern*) (1987), para. 39.
54. Bernardin, *Gift of Peace*, 46. In this thought, he echoes the views of the great Protestant moralist Paul Ramsey in *The Patient as Person*, 2nd ed. (New Haven, CT: Yale University Press, 2002), a pioneering text in bioethics that is still relevant today. See especially chap. 3, "On (Only) Caring for the Dying."
55. Ibid., 47.
56. Ibid., 48–49.

CHAPTER 7

❦

Dying Well, Assisted Suicide, and Constitutional Law

E ACH YEAR JUNE 26 COMES AND GOES peaceably and uneventfully at the Supreme Court of the United States. Tourists pose for photographs on the imposing marble steps while political reporters wait impatiently for the last decisions of the Court's current term. The Capitol police and US marshals are always vigilant; nonetheless, the annual arrival of that particular day poses no special challenges to them. In short, June 26 in Washington, DC, is nothing like January 22, the anniversary of *Roe v. Wade*.[1] And therein lies an important jurisprudential lesson.

On June 26, 1997, the Supreme Court handed down two historic decisions on end-of-life issues, *Washington v. Glucksberg* and *Vacco v. Quill*.[2] Holding that the Constitution does not protect a right to commit suicide that itself entails a right to assistance in committing the act, the majority opinions then relegated assisted suicide and euthanasia to the "'laboratory' of the states."[3] Without dissent, the Court overturned the decisions of the Second and Ninth Circuit Courts that conferred Fourteenth Amendment protection upon the choice of competent, terminally ill adults to end their own lives with medication prescribed by their physicians.[4] In a nutshell, the Supreme Court held that the Constitution does not protect the "right to die"—but neither does the Constitution prevent states from legalizing assisted suicide should they deem it in the best interests of their residents to do so.[5]

In the fifteen years since *Glucksberg* and *Quill* were handed down, physician-assisted suicide has not developed into a neuralgic constitutional problem dividing the country in the way that abortion long has been. One might be tempted to say that the Court, by deferring to the states and refusing to intervene, contributed nothing to the national debate over assisted suicide. In my view, however, that assessment is inaccurate. It is simply incorrect to claim that these two decisions have nothing to say about death with dignity, despite the fact that the Court ultimately refused to create a broad new constitutional right on the topic. Consequently, we must grapple with the way in which these two decisions actually helped shape our society's ongoing debate about the entangling ethical and legal questions in end-of-life decision making.

As legal theorist and literary critic James Boyd White reminds us, courts do not simply issue abstract judgments that impersonally and mechanically guide the behavior of individual and institutional agents in our society. Rather, those who play a role in the legal enterprise are engaged in a type of "constitutive rhetoric" that actually helps mold the community's moral identity. Moreover, the community-constituting character of law does not inhere solely in the results that issue from particular cases but also in the very way the questions are framed for decision. A lawyer arguing a client's position, and, a fortiori, a judge writing an opinion "is always saying not only, 'Here is how this case should be decided,' but also 'Here—in this language—is the way this case and similar cases should be talked about. The language I am speaking is the proper language of justice in our culture.'"[6]

Assuming that White is correct, if we are to understand the full import of the Supreme Court decisions on any issue, including assisted suicide, we cannot fix our gaze solely on the legal conclusions. We must also scrutinize the language of the justices—how they frame the issues at stake, what communal hopes and fears they invoke, which modes of argument they find persuasive and which they discount, and how they parse the particular words and phrases through which they convey all these things. By exercising the authority to interpret the constitutive document of our nation—a task that has ultimately rested in the Court's hands since *Marbury v. Madison* in 1803[7]—the justices inevitably wield a tremendous power of moral formation. In effect, they are moral teachers.

How, then, do the opinions in *Glucksberg* and *Quill* refocus the discussion regarding our communal obligations to persons in our midst who are confronting the momentous and often terrifying task of relinquishing their earthly existence?[8] In the initial sections of this chapter I examine the issues on which these two decisions exert significant pedagogical influence: the tension between general rules or classifications and the particular needs of individuals; the interrelations among pain, dignity, and equality; and the limits of philosophical theory and the correlative importance of practical experience in making good law. In the final section I examine the moral pedagogy of an earlier US Supreme Court decision about end-of-life decision making, *Cruzan v. Director, Missouri Dept. of Health.*[9] As previously noted, *Glucksberg* and *Quill* hold that there is no constitutionally protected right to assisted suicide (and, by extension, euthanasia). *Cruzan*, however, assumed without deciding that there is a constitutionally protected right for competent persons to refuse all forms of medical treatment, including life-preserving interventions such as artificial nutrition and hydration.

Taken together, these three decisions limn a jurisprudential success story regarding one of the most controversial medical-moral questions of our time. The Court is fully cognizant that our nation is divided about the moral issues surrounding end-of-life decision making. At the same time, the justices recognize that no individual or family makes these choices in a vacuum. People rightly worry about having access to good medical care and adequate pain control; in addition, they do not want to bankrupt their families emotionally or financially with the burdens of a protracted illness.

In virtually no other context is the socially conditioned nature of autonomy clearer than in end-of-life decision making. On the one hand, those who defend the legalization of assisted suicide and euthanasia point out that the laws against such practices impede the autonomous choice of some patients to end their lives with the aid of a physician's expertise. On the other hand, opponents to legalization also have an autonomy-based argument at their disposal: if assisted suicide (and euthanasia) is legalized, the possibility that other patients will be coerced or manipulated into making that fateful choice for the benefit of third parties (such as family members) is substantially increased. Some might object that patients can always rebuff any attempts at coercion or manipulation. But while the young, healthy, and independent might undertake that battle, those whose physical and mental strength are quickly waning might not have the same ability to do so.

Moreover, while less obvious, the socially conditioned nature of autonomous decision making is also evident at the level of social policy. As we learned from Joseph Raz, the paths persons follow in the exercise of their autonomy are deeply conditioned by the options available to them in the broader society. To return to a crude but apt example, no matter how much a modern teenage boy wishes to commit himself to the vocation of a Knight Templar, he cannot do so; that is simply not a socially supported option in our time and place. Less crudely, we can nonetheless easily see how various approaches to end-of-life decision making can be encouraged or discouraged by broader social policies. For example, studies show significant shifts over the past several decades in the location of death for most people.[10] In 1958 about 61 percent of deaths took place in hospitals; in 2005 that number dropped to about 37 percent.[11]

Furthermore, in many cases dying persons are not physically or mentally able to make treatment decisions on their own behalf. Most states have elaborate legal frameworks that allow individuals to identify surrogate decision makers who will make treatment decisions for them when they are incapacitated.[12]

Where and how one dies is a social practice affected by many other social practices.[13] How comprehensively are pain management techniques taught to family practitioners in medical school? How generously are in-home nursing services covered by public and private insurance? How deeply are religious groups committed to visiting the sick and comforting the dying, particularly those who have no family? If the policies and practices recommended by the hospice movement are in place, then the demand for assisted suicide and euthanasia might be reduced. Conversely, if assisted suicide is legalized, the change in law might abate the urgency of providing other forms of end-of-life assistance.[14] Over the long term, therefore, it is very possible that the choices available to patients will be reduced rather than enhanced by a change in law initially and ironically motivated by the need to promote patient autonomy. How, then, does one promote autonomy in end-of-life decision making? How does one encourage the sort of solidarity with those who are dying that many people, whether or not they are religious, see as an admirable personal and social virtue?[15] These questions of morality, law, and policy are not easy to address—and even less easy to resolve. To a large extent, their resolution depends upon the accuracy of our assumptions about how the changes in law will shift incentives, thereby shifting individual decisions and social practices.

Rather than using the Constitution to impose a one-size-fits-all solution upon the nation as a whole, the Court leaves significant room for the states to formulate their own varying answers. Under this model, the "laboratories of the states" tender and implement different policies based on the states' disparate assessments of the likely consequences of changes in law. If a state, after appraising the implemented policies for their relative strengths and drawbacks, want to tinker with the relevant laws, revision would be relatively straightforward (amendment of a state law being a more simple matter compared to making a shift in federal constitutional jurisprudence). And, in keeping with the nation's tradition of democratic persuasion, activists on both sides of the issue in each state, at every point in the process, have both the opportunity and the responsibility to persuade their fellow citizens as to the merits of their various arguments.[16] By deciding the assisted-suicide cases in the manner that it did, the Court fulfills Isidore of Seville's injunction that good law ought to be substantively "suitable to place and time," enacted "according to the custom of the country, " and generally "virtuous, just, [and] possible to nature."[17]

EQUALITY, RULES, AND EXCEPTIONS

What moral lessons did the Court teach in the assisted-suicide cases?[18] The *Glucksberg* opinion communicates its most notable moral lesson in the way that it frames the legal claim at stake. The Court could simply have adopted the lower court's framing of the issue; the Ninth Circuit, in an en banc opinion, held that a competent, terminally ill adult has a constitutionally protected liberty interest in ending her own life with a dose of lethal medication prescribed by her physician. But in reversing the Ninth Circuit, the Supreme Court pointed to the fact that the Washington statute at issue in the case enacted a generally applicable prohibition against aiding another person to commit suicide. That observation led the Court to describe the issue before it in *Glucksberg* as "whether the 'liberty' specially protected by the Due Process Clause includes a right to commit suicide which itself includes a right to assistance in doing so."[19]

What vision of society does the Court affirm and from what vision does it distance itself in adopting this characterization of the issue? By defining the question in terms of the constitutional validity of a generally applicable rule against aiding suicide, the Court refuses to carve out a separate class of persons—the class of competent, terminally ill adults—for treatment that is significantly different from that accorded to everyone else in the society. In so refusing, the Court recognizes that the most important thing to be said about the dying is that they are still among the living, for however short a period of time. With that step, the Court helps to instantiate the virtue of solidarity. The dying, in other words, ought not to be seen as a different class of human beings who do not merit the same protections against unjust killing because they are soon to leave this world. In the words of Paul Ramsey, "acts of caring for the dying are deeds done bodily for them which serve solely to manifest that they are not lost from human attention, that they are not alone, that mankind generally and their loved ones take note of their dying and mean to company with them in accepting this unique instance of the acceptable death of all flesh."[20]

Moreover, the Court's urgent concern to protect the equal status of those who are terminally ill as well as other vulnerable members of society, such as those who are poor, elderly, and disabled, has molded our future deliberations on end-of-life decision making. Fully aware of the law's pedagogical force in shaping the mores of society, the Court unequivocally affirms that the state "has an 'unqualified interest in the preservation of human life'" that is "symbolic and aspirational as well as practical."[21] Most significantly, the Court recognizes that the state's interest is more comprehensive than preventing the "abuse, neglect, and mistakes" that impede an individual's autonomous choice for or against assisted suicide.[22] According to the Court, "the State's interest here goes beyond protecting the vulnerable from coercion; it extends to protecting disabled and terminally ill people from prejudice, negative and inaccurate stereotypes, and 'societal indifference.'"[23] Even Justice Stevens—whose concurrence draws a macabre analogy between assisted suicide and capital punishment in order to show that "a State does have the power to place a lesser value on some lives than others"[24]—goes out of his way to pay explicit respect to the equal status of those who are dying. Attempting to sidestep the inconsistencies in his argument, Stevens denies that permitting only those who are terminally ill and disabled to choose their own deaths implies that their lives "have less value than the lives of those who are healthy."[25]

Thus, one community-constituting lesson we might take from *Glucksberg* is that protecting the equality of our most vulnerable members should be at the center of every effort to rethink current policy on assisted suicide and euthanasia. Are there any circumstances under which permitting assisted suicide would not threaten that equality? Some of the concurring opinions suggest that there may be situations in which it would be unconstitutional for the state to enforce its general prohibition against assisted suicide. By scrutinizing the justices' admittedly compressed descriptions of these situations, we might glean some hint of the circumstances in which they believe permitting assisted suicide might be reconciled with maintaining the equality of all persons.

Most important, it appears that cases raising a valid constitutional claim would likely arise as true exceptions to a general rule rather than as a basis for a new rule. Justice Stevens's concurrence, for example, suggests that individual patients or physicians might find themselves in circumstances where it would be unconstitutional for the state to enforce the general prohibition against assisting suicide in their case. In a footnote, even the majority opinion acknowledges that such a situation might arise, but the opinion goes on to caution that a successful plaintiff "would need to present different and considerably stronger arguments" than those presented in the instant cases.[26]

Not surprisingly, at the heart of the assisted-suicide question we find a specifically legal problem: the perennial tension between enforcing rules whose general applicability indisputably furthers the common good versus making particularized exceptions to those rules in cases where enforcement would cause excessive hardship to specific persons. One problem is that proponents on both sides of this tension make their claims in rhetorical terms, as illustrated by the numerous lower court opinions in both *Glucksberg* and *Quill*.[27] Invariably, the opinions declaring assisted suicide to be a constitutionally protected choice describe the plight of the particular patients who sought to make that choice in vivid, heart-wrenching detail; at the same time, these opinions downplay the possibility that legalizing assisted suicide could erode necessary protections for the vulnerable. By contrast, the opinions denying the existence of a "right to die" allude to the circumstances of those patients only briefly and in the most abstract terms. Instead, these rulings focus on the importance of preserving the longstanding rule against private killing.

Neither rhetorical approach is wrong in itself. But each approach alone is incomplete. In *Persons and Masks of the Law*, John Noonan reminds us that rules and persons are equally essential components of the legal system, and they are destined to remain in constant tension with each other.[28] In some cases, focusing too rigidly on rules can create masks that hide the humanity (and the pain) of the specific persons to whom they apply. In others, concentrating too narrowly on the particular circumstances of the individuals before the bench can betray the more general demands of a just social order. Noonan does not go so far, but one could argue that the most appropriate way to view rules is as protecting those persons whose faces are not vividly before the bench.

Both rules and exceptions, if their nature and function are properly understood and applied, can work together to benefit the common good. Contrary to conventional wisdom, exceptions do not necessarily erode a legal rule; in fact, recognition of a true exception can function as a "safety valve" that enables the rule to maintain its force in the vast majority of cases for which it was designed to apply.[29] Precisely because such recognition must be focused on the specific needs of specific persons, analyzing a true exception requires exacting sensitivity to the unique constellation of facts and circumstances arising in an extraordinary situation. Unlike a rule, which directs us to compare one situation with another in order to treat similar cases similarly, an exception discourages such comparison by claiming to govern only a narrowly defined case or set of cases.[30]

Keeping in mind this proper relationship between rules and exceptions, one can interpret both the Court's support of the general rule against assisted suicide and its recognition of the possibility of a narrow range of exceptions as correcting a fundamental deficiency in the balance the lower courts opinions struck between persons and rules. Both circuit court opinions rightly allowed the pleas of the dying patients before them to be heard; the judges did not mask the faces of the suffering in search of relief. Yet in their desire to respond to the pleas of those patients, the circuit courts did not simply make an exception for the undeniably hard individual cases before them. Instead they created an entirely new rule for *all* competent, terminally ill people—without paying proper heed to the persons whose faces they could not see but whose lives would also be affected by the rule's existence.

What type of legal framework does the ideal of "legal rules qualified by compelling exceptions" suggest? I believe that it supports the framework currently in place in most American states, in which physician-assisted suicide and euthanasia are illegal but very rarely prosecuted.[31] Needless to say, significant objections from a number of competing vantage points can be levied against the current legal situation in most states. To those who believe that the moral prohibition against intentionally taking innocent life is absolute, the present enforcement levels may appear too lax. To those who worry that the secrecy shrouding the current "exception-making" process leads to abuses such as those of Jack Kevorkian, legalizing and regulating assisted suicide might look like a way to minimize the risks. To those who fear that even the remote threat of prosecution has a chilling effect on physicians' decision making, it might seem that outright legalization is the only way to ensure access to a lethal prescription. These objections are weighty and merit ongoing consideration by legislators and citizens. Unlike in *Roe*, in which the Court minimized competing concerns of law, morality, and policy, in *Glucksberg* and *Quill* the Court emphasizes that its decisions "permit the debate to continue, as it should in a democratic society."[32] However, it did not leave the nation entirely without guidance. As we accept the Court's directive to continue our national debate, let us also heed its implicit invitation to scrutinize the way in which the rules and exceptions we formulate may affect the equal status of all persons in the community.

PAIN, DIGNITY, AND EQUALITY

The Court's contribution in realigning our national discussion of assisted suicide and euthanasia went beyond reconstituting the proper relationship between rule and exception in order to preserve the equality of all persons in society. Important as well are the glimpses that the concurring opinions provide of features likely to be required of a compelling exception. While Justices Stevens and Souter appear more open to arguments supporting assisted suicide that are based on preserving the "dignity" of the dying patient, Justices O'Connor, Ginsburg, and Breyer would set a more stringent standard. In surveying the justifications for assisted suicide, they put the desire to eliminate severe and unremitting physical pain in a class by itself. More specifically, Justice O'Connor stakes her support of the majority position on the fact that "a patient who is suffering from a terminal illness and who is experiencing great pain has no legal barriers to obtaining medication, from qualified physicians, to alleviate that suffering, even to the point of causing unconsciousness and hastening death."[33] While Justice Breyer writes of a "right to die with dignity," he hastens to add that in his view, "the avoidance of severe physical pain (connected with death) would have to constitute an essential part of any successful claim."[34]

As I argued in the last chapter, some moral traditions, including the Catholic tradition, do not believe that Justice O'Connor's scenario actually violates the moral prohibition against murder because the act in the circumstances described does not aim at taking life but only at alleviating pain. However, that action may violate a legal prohibition against killing, depending upon how such a prohibition is formulated and applied by the various states. Physicians who might refrain from giving some patients adequate medication for fear of being held criminally liable if that medication shortens the patient's life should find welcome reassurance in Justice O'Connor's concurrence. As she points out, the Due Process Clause—if it protects any aspect of the physician–patient relationship at all—surely protects a physician who takes an action with the intention of alleviating her patient's severe pain.

The justices' broader emphasis on preserving the equal status of vulnerable members of society suggests that any exception to the prohibition against assisted suicide should be stringently conditioned on the requirement of unbearable pain. Most of us recognize that determinations regarding physical pain must be made on a case-by-case basis. First, no one can truly feel the pain of another, although we may be able to learn a great deal about its source and severity from observation, study, and conversation. Second, individuals can have different pain thresholds and often respond to pain medications with varying degrees of success and speed. Third, a disease may not follow precisely the same course in one person that it does in another, which results in different levels of physical discomfort for the respective patients. Consequently, the fact that one person afflicted with stage IV lung cancer suffers from intense pain cannot be straightforwardly extended to arrive at a judgment about the pain suffered by another person with the same diagnosis.

In contrast, fundamental human dignity is not a purely individual matter; it is the common moral currency of the community. An individual can no more define and apply her own unique conception of fundamental dignity than she can design and print her personal, boutique conception of legal tender. Judgments about fundamental dignity must be universalizable; they cannot be made about particular persons suffering from particular deficiencies without also implying the same judgment regarding others who are similarly situated. A particularly vivid remark from the Ninth Circuit's reversed opinion in *Glucksberg* confirms this assessment: "A competent, terminally ill adult, having lived nearly the full measure of his life, has a strong liberty interest in choosing a dignified and humane death rather than being reduced at the end of his existence to a childlike state of helplessness, diapered, sedated, incontinent."[35] Such a statement immediately places all those living in such a state in the rhetorical position of having to justify why choosing *not* to die would preserve their dignity.

Thus the Supreme Court suggests that a society committed to maintaining the equality of all its members cannot honor exceptional claims to assisted suicide that are based on maintaining fundamental human dignity; at the same time, however, the *Glucksberg* opinion might be more open to exceptional cases based on the avoidance of severe physical pain. These two justificatory claims lie at opposite poles of a broad spectrum of reasons why mentally competent persons might seek to end their own lives with medical assistance. The range of that spectrum is evoked by Eric Cassell's brilliant analysis of suffering. As I discussed in the last chapter, Cassell defines suffering as "the distress brought about by the actual or perceived impending threat to the integrity or continued existence of the whole person."[36] Severe physical pain is one source of suffering but not the only source. For those who are chronically ill or disabled, suffering may also be rooted in an inability to pursue long-held plans and achieve the goals they had set for their lives. Individuals can even suffer without experiencing any threat at all to their physical well-being, such as when catastrophe strikes family members or close friends.

As the public discussion of assisted suicide and euthanasia continues, advocates of legalization and those who find themselves "exception-makers" under the current legal framework will face an ever-increasing need for line drawing. To which types of suffering is physician-assisted death a legitimate response? Does our attitude toward suffering (in ourselves and in others) depend solely on the severity of the suffering and the prospects for its relief, or also upon its source and character? For purposes of legitimating assisted suicide, are some types of suffering more appropriately classed as great physical pain (and therefore possible candidates for an exception to the general legal prohibition), while other types are better viewed as analogous to claims of loss of fundamental dignity (and therefore rejected as exceptions because incompatible with fundamental equality)?

These questions elicit no easy answers. What is clear, however, is that American Christians who endorse the tradition's rejection of assisted suicide and euthanasia have a task that is made even more imperative in light of the Supreme Court's decisions. We must show our fellow citizens that, in many if not all situations, solidarity is an effective and appropriate response to suffering.

By standing with those who suffer, we can potentially help them reconstruct their identities, find a new wholeness in their lives, and ultimately transcend the loss of their previous integrity. This challenge has both individual and social dimensions. At the individual level, nothing can replace spending time with those who are suffering; the Christian tradition has long commended this practice as part of the spiritual works of mercy. But beyond this spiritual aid lie many practical and policy-oriented considerations. As I argued earlier, the Americans with Disabilities Act helped to ameliorate the suffering of those who would not otherwise be able to participate in our common life by mandating measures that improved access to public spaces and accommodations for persons with disabilities. Similarly, advances in computer technology have enabled vision-impaired citizens to continue reading and writing and thereby to maintain their self-identities as readers and writers. If those of us in religious communities begin to think in strategic, practical terms about providing creative ways for people to reintegrate their lives after significant loss, we will be on the right track.

PHILOSOPHICAL THEORY AND PRACTICAL EXPERIENCE

The Supreme Court's assisted-suicide opinions helpfully exemplify this beneficial blend of sympathetic concern and tangible practicality. Eschewing abstract arguments of political theory, the two majority opinions place their trust in the far more concrete wisdom supplied by empirical data and historical practice. Public debate might follow the lead of this model.

Not one opinion, not even those of Justices Stevens and Souter, praises or criticizes the highly publicized "Philosophers' Brief," which was submitted to the Court by the "dream team" of liberal political theorists (Ronald Dworkin, Thomas Nagel, Robert Nozick, John Rawls, Thomas Scanlon, and Judith Jarvis Thomson).[37] The brief is not even mentioned, much less cited as support. Also given short shrift is the famous "Mystery Passage" from *Planned Parenthood v. Casey*, which proclaims that "at the heart of liberty is the right to define one's own concept of existence, of meaning, of the universe, and of the mystery of human life. Beliefs about these matters could not define the attributes of personhood were they formed under compulsion of the State."[38] In responding to this passage, which furnished a major component of the Ninth Circuit's argument in favor of a constitutionally protected right to die, the Supreme Court does not match philosophical abstraction with philosophical abstraction. The majority opinion does not proffer a Kantian disquisition on why a proper understanding of autonomy cannot support assisted suicide or euthanasia. Instead, the justices simply maintain that the fact "that many of the rights and liberties protected by the Due Process Clause sound in personal autonomy does not warrant the sweeping conclusion that any and all important, intimate and personal decisions are so protected."[39] For this Court, historical continuity, not theoretical consistency, is decisive. Because "the history of the law's treatment of assisted suicide in this country has been and continues to be one of the rejection of nearly all efforts to permit it," assisted suicide is "not a fundamental liberty interest protected by the Due Process Clause."[40]

Furthermore, if historical experience can truly trump demands for philosophical consistency, then that same analysis can also apply to save a philosophical concept—a concept that is of utility in the vast majority of cases but at times has proven problematical to apply. In the *Quill* majority opinion, the Court rejects the respondents' claim that the distinction between assisted suicide and refusing life-saving treatment is so arbitrary and irrational as to violate the Due Process Clause. Significantly, the Court does not descend to the trenches of the philosophical debate over the existence of a meaningful distinction between "killing" and "letting die." After emphasizing that the distinction generally "comports with fundamental legal principles of causation and intent" that are firmly rooted in American law, the Court simply remarks that "granted, in some cases, the line between the two may not be clear, but certainty is not required, even were it possible."[41]

The Court's studied indifference to the philosophical arguments in *Glucksberg* veers into a preoccupation with the concrete, as demonstrated by the prominent role played by the information available on the Dutch practice of assisted suicide and euthanasia. In legitimating the state's fear that legalizing assisted suicide would simply be the first step on a slippery slope leading to involuntary euthanasia, the majority opinion relies heavily on Dutch statistics showing that a high proportion of patients in the Netherlands were killed without their explicit request or consent.[42]

But this same Dutch data is put to its most rhetorically powerful—and surprising—use in Justice Souter's concurrence. After a detailed analysis of the Due Process Clause, followed by a careful and sympathetic presentation of the arguments in favor of legalizing assisted suicide, Souter concludes that the "importance of the individual interest here, as within that class of 'certain interests' demanding careful scrutiny of the State's contrary claim . . . cannot be gainsaid."[43] Souter sidesteps and, all but dismissing the state's general interests in preserving life and discouraging suicide, focuses instead on the state interest in avoiding the slippery slope. He recounts the state's position that legalizing assisted suicide could lead to involuntary suicide and euthanasia as well as the respondents' rejoinder that stringent regulation will prevent such difficulties.

At this point in the concurrence, Souter's theoretical sympathies clearly favor constitutional protection for assisted suicide. As he presents them, the pragmatic arguments are in equipoise. What, then, finally turns the tide in favor of the majority viewpoint? For Souter, it is the Dutch situation. He observes that the regulatory proposals set forth by the respondents are very similar to the guidelines already in use in the Netherlands. Unwilling to adopt the majority's conclusion that the Dutch data demonstrates outright abuse, Souter does concede that "the capacity of the State to protect the others if respondents were to prevail is, however, subject to some genuine question, underscored by the responsible disagreement over the basic facts of the Dutch experience."[44] After acknowledging that the legislative branch is better equipped than the judiciary to deal with "an emerging issue as to which facts currently unknown could be dispositive," he concludes that the Court should "stay its hand" for the time being, if not for all time.[45] Thus for Souter, the Dutch data functions as a deus ex machina that in the end enables him to accept the majority's judgment, despite his clear philosophical sympathies for the opposing position. In a close case, empirical information trumps philosophical conviction. On this point, Souter's opinion is emblematic of the Court's entire outlook.

What are we to make of the Court's decision to dodge the philosophical arguments surrounding assisted suicide in favor of the tangible data furnished by history and empirical evidence? Obviously, this is a pressing question for those whose commitments to the value of autonomy have convinced them that the decisions should have gone the other way. But making sense of the Court's actions should be equally pressing for those who believe that the current prohibition against assisted suicide and euthanasia should be maintained not simply because the prohibition is a valuable safeguard against abuse, or because it reflects the way we Americans have always done things, but also because barring suicide and euthanasia is justifiable in a deeper sense as a matter of law and morality.[46] The discussion about assisted suicide and euthanasia is at once a discussion about what constitutes a good life in this community, what constitutes a good way to take one's leave from life, and what our collective obligations are to those in the midst of their leave-taking. Ultimately the Court rightly diverts the decisions about these issues to the people, but we should not interpret any reluctance to deal with these issues as a sign of their lack of importance. The justices' refusal to decide the answers for themselves does not imply that the questions were in any way unworthy; rather, the Court was simply acknowledging the limits of its role, not only as the ultimate representative of the judicial branch of our government but also as a moral teacher to our nation. Like any good teacher, the Court has honored the fact that the student herself must ultimately control the formation of her own character.

CRUZAN: BATTERY AND MEDICAL TREATMENT

While the Court may be relatively indifferent to philosophical matters in the assisted-suicide decisions, we as a society do not have that luxury; we must, I think, articulate a sound moral and legal basis for distinguishing between assisted suicide and euthanasia, on the one hand, and withdrawal of medical treatment, on the other. As I noted earlier, the Supreme Court's 1990 *Cruzan* opinion assumed without deciding that a competent adult has a constitutionally protected "liberty interest" to refuse all medical treatment, even life-saving treatment or artificial nutrition and hydration.[47] Both the Ninth and the Second Circuits unsuccessfully argued, in opinions that were later overruled by the Supreme Court in *Glucksberg* and *Quill*, that it did not make sense to grant constitutional protection to refusals of life-saving treatment while at the same time refusing such protection to assisted suicide. Does the Supreme Court's distinction between withdrawing treatment and assisted suicide make sense on moral and legal grounds, as well as on grounds of public policy and history? I believe that it does. To see why, we must grapple more closely with the arguments that the Court rejected.

In his en banc opinion for the Ninth Circuit in *Compassion in Dying v. State of Washington* (later overruled in *Glucksberg*), Judge Stephen Reinhardt argues that the Supreme Court's *Cruzan* opinion is easily extended to encompass assisted suicide.[48] He correctly notes that the *Cruzan* majority assumed without deciding that a competent adult has a constitutionally protected liberty interest in refusing unwanted medical treatment, including artificial nutrition and hydration.[49] He also rightly observes that in some cases, including that of Nancy Cruzan herself, refusal of medical treatment will lead inexorably to the patient's demise. Working from these two premises, he concludes: "*Cruzan*, by recognizing a liberty interest that includes the refusal of artificial provision of life-sustaining food and water, necessarily recognizes *a liberty interest in hastening one's own death*" (emphasis added). In my view, this leap is unwarranted, both in logic and in law.

First, a fair reading of *Cruzan* demonstrates that the right to refuse treatment is firmly grounded in the longstanding common law prohibition against battery, which is generally if somewhat loosely defined as "unconsented touching." The liberty interest assumed by *Cruzan* is designed to protect each individual's bodily integrity against unwanted invasion in the name of medical science. To put the matter bluntly, *Cruzan's* assumption ensures that a competent individual will not be strapped to a gurney, intubated, sedated, and medicated without her consent, no matter how strongly her physicians believe such treatment to be necessary for her own well-being.

Accordingly, the fundamental concern of the liberty interest assumed by *Cruzan* is not the right to die but the right to live unencumbered by unwelcome medical treatment. In some but by no means all cases, a competent individual's decision to refuse such treatment may result in the "hastening of her death," sometimes intentionally so. In still fewer instances the refusal of treatment will allow the patient actually "to determine the time and manner" in which she dies. Judge Reinhart recharacterizes *Cruzan* as providing a liberty interest in the right to die by assisted suicide. In so doing, he illegitimately supplants the twin purposes of the liberty interest—the fundamental concern that it furthers (the right to live unencumbered by unwelcome medical treatment) and the larger purposes intended to be promoted by acknowledging it (the protection of bodily integrity)—in favor of particular effects that obtain only when the liberty is exercised in certain circumstances (the hastening of one's own death).

This type of recharacterization is a jurisprudentially perilous way of developing new rights. First, in some cases, the effect in question might be antithetical to the very purpose of the right at stake. In these cases, such a redescription will conflate the exercise of a right with the abuse of that same right. For example, the "free speech rights of the media" cannot be redescribed as the "right negligently to print false statements about public figures," even though the Supreme Court has interpreted the First Amendment as forbidding successful libel suits in such situations.[50]

Second, although the effect in question might not directly conflict with the purpose of the liberty interest, the effect might nonetheless be socially undesirable on other grounds. For example, the right to diplomatic immunity is inappropriately redescribed as the "right to flout the law," despite the fact that one result of the right may be that some foreign diplomats indeed flout the law openly and frequently.

Third, in some instances the terms used to delineate a right may on their face encompass behavior that implicates other complicated issues of social importance. To recharacterize this behavior as a right itself would be to settle those issues prematurely. At the very least, Reinhardt's recharacterization of the *Cruzan* liberty interest involves the third type of mistake, given the ramifications that the social practice of "aid-in-dying" may have for weak and vulnerable members of society.

The confusion in the aftermath of *Cruzan* is also reflected in the Second Circuit's *Quill v. Vacco* opinion, which was later reversed by the Supreme Court. The Second Circuit not only considers the distinction between assisted suicide and withdrawal of treatment unsound but also goes so far as to hold that the distinction lacks a rational basis entirely.[51] More specifically, the Second Circuit asserts that "the New York statutes prohibiting assisted suicide . . . do not serve any of the state interests . . . in view of the statutory and common law schemes allowing suicide through the withdrawal of life-sustaining treatment."[52] Amazingly, *Quill* here charges the state of New York with irrationality for honoring a basic tenet of jurisprudence: the best can be the enemy of the good. A state legislature must make hard choices about how far to pursue certain goals with the recognition that full implementation might require too many scarce social resources or impinge too heavily upon other important values.

To see where the Second Circuit goes wrong, we must begin by seeing what it gets right. In fact, both the instant Second Circuit opinion and the foregoing Ninth Circuit ruling, despite being subsequently overruled by the Supreme Court, rightly observe that the distinction between "actively" taking steps likely to result in a patient's death and "passively" declining to provide treatment likely to forestall death cannot be decisive from either a logical or an ethical perspective. Unfortunately, the opinions fail to recognize that the agent's intention in deciding what course of action to pursue *can* be defended as morally decisive. As I argued in the previous chapter, the line of intention cuts across the "active/passive" distinction. Just as it is possible either to withhold a medical intervention or to provide a medical intervention with the aim of causing the patient's death, so it is equally tenable either to refuse life-saving medical treatment or to furnish treatment that foreseeably shortens a patient's life (such as some types of painkillers) without aiming at death.[53]

The line drawn by *Cruzan*, however, does not precisely track the logic of intention outlined in the previous paragraph. Instead, *Cruzan* assumes that a competent adult patient has a liberty interest in refusing any medical treatment, including life-sustaining interventions. Consequently, from a moral perspective that rejects intentionally taking one's own life, the legal framework adopted by *Cruzan* might initially appear overinclusive in the protections it confers. The *Cruzan* liberty interest encompasses decisions to withdraw medical treatment that aim at death as well as those decisions to withdraw that aim at avoiding treatment's burdens. From a moral perspective, the first group of decisions is suicidal. Why not respond to the Second Circuit's challenge—that is, the finding that there is no rational basis for distinguishing between assisted suicide and withdrawal of treatment—by cutting back the right to refuse care so as to protect only those decisions not made with the intent of causing one's own death? Why not eliminate constitutional protection for suicide entirely?

To answer this question, we must contend with the differences between morality and law. While it suffices for moralists to affirm the decisive nature of an agent's intention, lawmakers must also take into account the practical difficulties involved in discerning that intention. In the vast majority of cases involving competent, gravely ill individuals deciding to forgo medical treatment, identifying and assessing the intentions motivating those decisions is a very difficult and time-consuming task. We saw in the last chapter how the application of the distinction between "ordinary" and "extraordinary" means of prolonging life can vary greatly from person to person. Human beings differ substantially in their capacities to bear the pain and uncertainty associated with medical treatment, as well as in their evaluations of the monetary and nonmonetary costs associated with a continued battle against illness. For one person, a decision not to pursue a course of chemotherapy may truly be taken in order to pursue death, while for another person the same decision may simply be made in order to avoid the pain and inconvenience of the treatment. In cases of doubt, it is appropriate for the law to allow the individuals most affected by an outcome the freedom to make the decision themselves.

Moreover, it is important to recognize that there are in reality two moral questions raised by lawmaking in this area. The first is whether a patient may morally refuse life-sustaining treatment. As we saw earlier, the answer to this question depends upon the intention of the patient in making such a refusal. The second question is equally crucial. Assume that a competent, adult patient has decided to forgo treatment precisely to bring about death. How far can the state go to stop her from carrying through with her plan? The simple fact that one individual intends to follow an illicit course of action does not entitle other members of the community to do anything and everything necessary to prevent her from so doing. As noted, to prevent a competent adult patient from deliberately killing herself by refusing necessary medical care, we would need to strap her down and force treatment upon her. By recognizing the liberty interest to refuse medical treatment, *Cruzan* can be read as saying that the end, however beneficial, does not justify such means.

CONCLUSION

In this chapter I argue that in our pluralistic liberal democracy the current constitutional status quo on end-of-life decision making is a successful integration of moral and practical concerns. It is often assumed that advocates for the legalization of assisted suicide are the defenders of autonomy. I suggest, however, that there is reason to worry that legalization would in fact pose certain threats to autonomy by increasing the danger of coercion or the risk of manipulating vulnerable patients to "choose" death prematurely. Furthermore, it is often argued that assisted suicide is the most compassionate response to those plagued with significant pain or other types of suffering associated with the end of life. I propose, however, that resorting too quickly to assisted suicide to deal with suffering that is defined overbroadly can undermine human dignity. Extending my discussion of Eric Cassell's work from the last chapter, I argue that the practice of solidarity could help dying patients overcome suffering by offering them ways of reintegrating their lives that both acknowledge and transcend their new limitations.

I do not pretend that assisted suicide and euthanasia are not difficult questions, upon which thoughtful Americans of goodwill have a range of opinions. Furthermore, while there is no denying that liberalizing the law has potentially troublesome ramifications, the precise nature of those ramifications is speculative. It is true that we have some data about the assisted-suicide practice from Oregon and, to a lesser degree, Washington. But drawing any lessons from this data for other states, which currently have varying levels of medical benefits, would be of questionable validity.[54] Also unclear is the way the recent financial crisis or the upcoming health care reform program will shape the incentives of American patients and their families to seek assisted suicide.

In this situation it was jurisprudentially wise for the Supreme Court in both *Glucksberg* and *Quill* to let the "laboratory of the states" resolve the question of whether to legalize assisted suicide. It was equally prudent of the Court in *Cruzan* to uphold the right of competent patients to reject unwanted medical treatment, even if such treatment will save or extend their lives. Given the highly individualized nature of health care decisions, rejecting treatment is not necessarily tantamount to suicide. Furthermore, even if it is suicidal, that does not end the inquiry. The follow-up question is what can be done to prevent suicide. The Anglo-American legal tradition's commitment to bodily integrity has yielded an abhorrence of battery, or unconsented touching. A government cannot order a health care facility to strap down competent patients and force treatment upon them—even to prevent suicide. That end does not justify those means.

The states, then, have a great deal of power regarding the legal status of physician-assisted suicide. How should voters think about their moral responsibilities in selecting those officials who will make, enforce, and interpret the law at the state level? How should the electorate think about analogous responsibilities at the federal level? I turn now to these and related questions.

NOTES

This chapter draws upon M. Cathleen Kaveny, "Assisted Suicide, the Supreme Court, and the Constitutive Function of the Law," *Hastings Center Report* 27, no. 5 (September/October 1997): 29–34; and M. Cathleen Kaveny, "Assisted Suicide, Euthanasia, and the Law," in the "Notes on Moral Theology 1996," *Theological Studies* 58, no. 1 (March 1997): 124–48.

1. *Roe v. Wade*, 410 US 113 (1973).
2. *Washington v. Glucksberg*, 521 US 702 (1997); and *Vacco v. Quill*, 521 US 793 (1997).
3. *Glucksberg, Quill* 521 US at 737 (O'Connor, J., concurring in the judgments). This phrase is a favorite of Justice O'Connor's; it appears not only in her concurring opinion for the assisted suicide cases but also in her concurrence in *Cruzan v. Director, Missouri Dept. of Health*, 497 US 261, 292 (1990).
4. *Quill v. Vacco*, 80 F.3d 716 (2d Cir. 1996); *Compassion in Dying v. State of Washington*, 79 F.3d 790 (9th Cir. 1996) (en banc).
5. Currently physician-assisted suicide is legal in three states. Oregon and Washington enacted specific legislation legalizing the practice; see Wash. Rev. Code Ann. §§ 70.245.010–70.245.904 (West Supp. 2011); and Ore. Rev. Stat. §§ 127.800–127.995 (2009). In Montana, the state Supreme Court has held that physician-assisted suicide did not violate the state's statutory framework; see *Baxter v. State*, 224 P.3d 1211 (Mont. 2009). In 2006 the Supreme Court upheld Oregon's assisted-suicide law against the Bush administration's efforts to undermine it by treating physicians who complied with its provisions as violating the Federal Controlled Substances Act. See *Gonzales v. Oregon*, 546 US 243 (2006).
6. James Boyd White, *Heracles' Bow: Essays on the Rhetoric and Poetics of Law* (Madison: University of Wisconsin Press, 1985), 34.
7. *Marbury v. Madison*, 5 US (1 Cranch) 137 (1803). The case has come to stand for the proposition that the judiciary branch has the final say in matters of constitutional interpretation and that the Constitution is the supreme law of the land.
8. For theological engagement with legal cases, the classic text is Paul Ramsey, *Ethics at the Edges of Life: Medical and Legal Intersections* (New Haven, CT: Yale University Press, 1978). On Ramsey's case analysis, see Gilbert Meilaender, "'Love's Casuistry': Paul Ramsey on Caring for the Terminally Ill," *Journal of Religious Ethics* 19, no. 2 (1991): 133–56. See also Lisa Sowle Cahill, "Bioethics," *Theological Studies* 67, no. 1 (2006): 120–42; and Cahill, "Bioethical Decisions to End Life," *Theological Studies* 52, no. 1 (1991): 107–27; John Paris, "Active Euthanasia," *Theological Studies* 53, no. 1 (1992): 113–26; John F. Kilner, *Life on the Line: Ethics, Aging, Ending Patients' Lives, and Allocating Vital Resources* (Grand Rapids, MI: Eerdmans, 1992); and James

F. Walter and Thomas A. Shannon, eds., *Quality of Life: The New Medical Dilemma* (Mahwah, NJ: Paulist Press, 1990). The English legal case analogous to *Cruzan* is *Airedale NHS Trust v. Bland* [1993] AC 789; see John Finnis, "Bland: Crossing the Rubicon," *Law Quarterly Review* 109, no. 3 (1993): 329–37.

9. *Cruzan*, 497 US at 292. The *Cruzan* case involved the removal of artificial nutrition and hydration from a patient in a persistent vegetative state. Another case of this type came to national attention in 2004–5 in the Terri Schiavo controversy. For helpful links to key state and federal documents, see "Euthanasia: Legal Documents in the Terri Schiavo Case," *ProCon.org*, http://euthanasia.procon.org/view.additional-resource.php?resourceID=001464. For a good anthology on the case, see Arthur L. Caplan, James J. McCartney, and Dominic A. Sisti, eds., *The Case of Terri Schiavo: Ethics at the End of Life* (Amherst, NY: Prometheus Books, 2006). See also Kenneth W. Goodman, ed., *The Case of Terri Schiavo: Ethics, Politics, and Death in the 21st Century* (New York: Oxford University Press, 2010).

10. Place of death varies according to numerous variables, including region of the country, race, marital status, underlying disease, financial and insurance status. See, e.g., N. Muramatsu, R. L. Hoyem, H. Yin, and R. T. Campbell, "Place of Death among Older Americans: Does State Spending on Home- and Community-Based Services Promote Home Death," *Medical Care* 46 (2008): 829–38; A. Gruneir, V. Mor, S. Weitzen, R. Truchil, J. Teno, and J. Roy, "Where People Die: A Multilevel Approach to Understanding Influences on Site of Death in America," *Medical Care Research and Review* 64 (2007): 351–78; S. L. Mitchell, J. M. Teno, S. C. Miller, and V. Mor, "A National Study of the Location of Death for Older Persons with Dementia," *Journal of the American Geriatric Society* 53 (2005): 299–305; James Flory, Yinong Young-Xu, Ipek Gurol, Norman Levinsky, Arlene Ash, and Ezekiel Emanuel, "Place of Death: US Trends since 1980," *Health Affairs* 23 (2004): 194–200; and Ezekiel J. Emanuel, Arlene Ash, Wei Yu, Gail Gazelle, Norman G. Levinsky, Olga Saynina, Mark McClellan, and Mark Moskowitz, "Managed Care, Hospice Use, Site of Death, and Medical Expenditures in the Last Year of Life," *Archives of Internal Medicine* 162 (2002): 1722–28. See also Robert H. Blank and Janna C. Merrick, eds., *End-of-Life Decision Making: A Cross-National Study* (Cambridge, MA: MIT University Press, 2005).

11. National Center for Health Statistics, "Worktable 309: Death by Place of Death, Age, Race, and Sex: United States, 2005," Centers for Disease Control and Prevention, April 10, 2008, www.cdc.gov/nchs/data/dvs/Mortfinal2005_worktable_309.pdf.

12. See Nancy M. P. King, *Making Sense of Advanced Directives*, 2nd ed. (Washington, DC: Georgetown University Press, 2007); Lawrence P. Ulrich, *The Patient Self-Determination Act: Meeting the Challenges in Patient Care* (Washington, DC: Georgetown University Press, 1999); and Cristiano Vezzoni and John Griffiths, *Advance Treatment Directives and Autonomy for Incompetent Patients: An International Comparative Survey of Law and Practice, with Special Attention to the Netherlands* (Ceredigion, UK: Mellen Press, 2008).

13. For example, the invention of "intensive care" has changed the way people die, raising questions of distributive justice. See M. Cathleen Kaveny, "Developing the Doctrine of Distributive Justice: Methods of Distribution, Redistribution, and the Role of Time in Allocating Intensive Care Resources," in *Allocating Scarce Medical Resources: Roman Catholic Perspectives*, ed. H. Tristram Engelhardt Jr. and Mark J. Cherry, 177–99 (Washington, DC: Georgetown University Press, 2002).

14. See, e.g., this volume from the founder of the modern hospice movement, Cicely Saunders, Dorothy H. Summers, and Neville Taylor, *Hospice: The Living Idea* (Philadelphia: Saunders, 1981). No one has done more to grapple with the challenges of dying well in the contemporary American health care system than Daniel Callahan. See Daniel Callahan, *The Troubled Dream of Life: In Search of a Peaceful Death* (Washington, DC: Georgetown University Press, 2000); Callahan, *Setting Limits: Medical Goals in an Aging Society with "A Response to My Critics"* (Washington, DC: Georgetown University Press, 1995); and Callahan, *What Kind of Life? The Limits of Medical Progress* (Washington, DC: Georgetown University Press, 1995).

15. For example, Mother Teresa, who dedicated her life to ministering to the dying poor in India, was named by Gallup News Service as the "Most Admired Person of the Century." See Frank Newport, "Mother Teresa Voted by American People as Most Admired Person of the Century," Gallup, December 31, 1999, www.gallup .com/poll/3367/mother-teresa-voted-american-people-most-admired-person-century.aspx.

16. Needless to say, the experience of those states that have legalized physician-assisted suicide will be extremely relevant to other states considering the option. The state of Oregon now has more than a decade's worth of data on the practice. See K. Hedberg, D. Hopkins, R. Leman, and M. Kohn, "The 10-Year Experience of Oregon's Death with Dignity Act: 1998–2007," *Journal of Clinical Ethics* 20 (2009): 124–32. As the article notes, a tiny but growing proportion of the deaths in the state are attributable to lethal prescriptions under the Death with Dignity Act. In 1998 16 deaths were attributable to such prescriptions (11.3 per 10,000 total deaths); in 2007, there were 49 deaths so attributable (15.6 per 10,000 total deaths). Patients with cancer accounted for 82.1 percent of the total deaths from lethal medication. Patients choosing physician-assisted suicide were disproportionately white, highly educated, and urban dwellers. The two most common reasons for requesting lethal medication were loss of autonomy and decreasing ability to engage in enjoyable activities. The article identifies several worrying trends in the data, including patient concern about inadequate (current or future) pain control and a decline in physician referrals for formal psychiatric evaluation before acceding to a patient's request for a lethal prescription.

17. Thomas Aquinas, *Summa theologica*, 3 vols., trans. Fathers of the English Dominican Province (New York: Benziger Bros., 1948), I-II, q. 95, art. 3 (citing Isidore of Seville, *Etymologies* vol. 21).

18. See M. Cathleen Kaveny, "Assisted Suicide, the Supreme Court, and the Constitutive Function of the Law," *Hastings Center Report* 27, no. 5 (1997): 29–34.

19. *Glucksberg*, 521 US at 723.

20. Paul Ramsey, *The Patient as Person*, 2nd ed. (New Haven, CT: Yale University Press, 2002), 153.

21. *Glucksberg*, 521 US at 728, 729 (quoting *Cruzan*, 497 US at 282).

22. Ibid., 731.

23. Ibid., 732 (quoting *Compassion in Dying*, 49 F.3d at 592).

24. *Glucksberg, Quill*, 521 US at 738 (Stevens, J., concurring in the judgments).

25. Ibid., 746.

26. *Quill*, 521 US at 809, n13; see also *Glucksberg*, 521 US at 751, n24.

27. While no longer legally controlling, these opinions continue to merit examination by

ethicists. I analyze them in M. Cathleen Kaveny, "Assisted Suicide, Euthanasia, and the Law," *Theological Studies* 58, no. 1 (1997): 124–48.

28. John T. Noonan Jr., *Persons and Masks of the Law*, 2nd ed. (Berkeley: University of California Press, 2002).

29. Elizabeth Anscombe makes a similar comment with regards to borderline cases in ethics. See G. E. M. Anscombe, "Modern Moral Philosophy," in *Ethics, Religion and Politics: Collected Papers Volume III* (Minneapolis: University of Minnesota Press, 1981), 36.

30. The relationship of rules to exceptions is, of course, difficult to explicate. As Paul Ramsey argues, sometimes exceptions can be identified and specified with sufficient clarity that they can become part of a more nuanced rule. See Paul Ramsey, "The Case of the Curious Exception," in *Norm and Context in Christian Ethics*, ed. Gene H. Outka and Paul Ramsey, 74–93 (New York: Charles Scribner's Sons, 1968). In my judgment, however, it is not always possible to specify all exceptions to a rule in advance; the exception arises from the totality of the circumstances and their interaction with each other. See M. Cathleen Kaveny, "Between Example and Doctrine: Contract Law and Common Morality," *Journal of Religious Ethics* 33 (2005): 669–95.

31. Unfortunately, I have been unable to find reliable estimates on the number of unreported instances of physician-assisted suicide and euthanasia in the United States. There are estimates about the Netherlands and Belgium, where euthanasia is legal under some circumstances. See Mette L. Rurup, Hilde Buiting, H. Roeline W. Pasman, Paul J. van der Maas, Agnes van der Heide, and Bregje D. Onwuteaka-Philipsen, "The Reporting Rate of Euthanasia and Physician-Assisted Suicide: A Study of the Trends," *Medical Care* 46 (2008): 1195–97; Tinne Smets, Johan Bilsen, Joachim Cohen, Mette L Rurup, Freddy Mortier, and Luc Deliens, "Reporting of Euthanasia in Medical Practice in Flanders, Belgium: Cross Sectional Analysis of Reported and Unreported Cases," *British Medical Journal* 341 (2010), doi:10.1136/bmj.c5174; Bregje D. Onwuteaka-Philipsen, Agnes van der Heide, Martien T. Muller, Mette Rurup, Judith A. C. Rietjens, Jean-Jacques Georges, Astrid M. Vrakking, Jacqueline M. Cuperus-Bosma, Gerrit van der Wal, and Paul J. van der Maas, "Dutch Experience of Monitoring Euthanasia," *British Medical Journal* 331 (2005): 691–93; and Judith A. C. Rietjens, Paul J. van der Maas, Bregje D. Onwuteaka-Philipsen, Johannes J. M. van Delden, and Agnes van der Heide, "Two Decades of Research on Euthanasia from the Netherlands: What Have We Learnt and What Questions Remain?" *Bioethical Inquiry* 6 (2009): 271–83. This last article argues that while 18 percent of cases of euthanasia were reported in 1990, that number rose to 80 percent in 2005. Obviously, the definition of the term "euthanasia" is key; the study suggests that many of the doctors who did not report their cases did not consider their actions to be euthanasia. To better discern the mind of physicians in end-of-life decision making, the authors did not use the term "euthanasia" in the anonymous questionnaire distributed to physicians. The questionnaire focused instead on documenting the physician's purpose in acting and on identifying the consequences he or she foresees would occur. Some suggest that the reluctance to prosecute may be slowly changing. See, e.g., Ann Alpers, "Criminal Act or Palliative Care: Prosecutions Involving the Care of the Dying," *Journal of Law, Medicine, & Ethics* 26 (1998): 308–26; and Lewis Cohen, Linda Ganzini, Christine

Mitchell, Stephen Arons, Elizabeth Goy, and James Cleary, "Accusations of Murder and Euthanasia in End-of-Life Care," *Journal of Palliative Medicine* 8 (2005): 1096–1104. While the number of prosecutions is still extremely small, the statistics nonetheless suggest the importance of educating lawyers (especially prosecutors) as well as physicians about the permissibility of taking aggressive steps to control pain when necessary, even if so doing will shorten the patient's life.

32. *Glucksberg*, 521 US at 735. Attitudes toward voluntary euthanasia vary according to a number of factors. For example, blacks are more opposed to the practice than whites; see, e.g., William L. MacDonald, "The Difference between Blacks' and Whites' Attitudes toward Voluntary Euthanasia," *Journal for the Scientific Study of Religion* 37 (1998): 411–26. Social liberals are more likely to support legalization; see, e.g., John Strate, Timothy Kiska, and Marvin Zalman, "Who Favors Legalizing Physician-Assisted Suicide? The Vote on Michigan's Proposal B," *Politics and the Life Sciences* 20 (2001): 155–63. Religion also correlates with opposition to these practices; see Benjamin E. Moulton, Terrence D. Hill, and Amy Burdette, "Religion and Trends in Euthanasia Attitudes among US Adults, 1977–2004," *Sociological Forum* 21 (2006): 249–72.

33. *Glucksberg, Quill*, 521 US at 736–37 (O'Connor, J., concurring in the judgments). The degree to which this exception would be necessary is a matter of dispute. On the one hand, it appears that in all but a very few cases, controlling physical pain while preserving a patient's consciousness is medically possible. On the other hand, many American physicians appear to be both inadequately familiar with available pain control techniques and reluctant to use some medications (e.g., opioids) for fear of engendering addiction. See, e.g., Brenda Breuer, Ricardo Cruciani, and Russell K Portenoy, "Pain Management by Primary Care Physicians, Pain Physicians, Chiropractors, and Acupuncturists: A National Survey," *Southern Medical Journal* 103 (2010): 738–47; L. Leong, J. Ninnis, N. Slatkin, M. Rhiner, L. Schroeder, B. Pritt, J. Kagan, T. Ball, and R. Morgan, "Evaluating the Impact of Pain Management (PM) Education on Physician Practice Patterns—A Continuing Medical Education (CME) Outcomes Study," *Journal of Cancer Education* 25 (2010): 224–28; and Marla Z. Wolfert, Aaron M. Gilson, June L. Dahl, and James F. Cleary, "Opioid Analgesics for Pain Control: Wisconsin Physicians' Knowledge, Beliefs, Attitudes, and Prescribing Practices," *Pain Medicine* 11 (2010): 425–34.

34. *Glucksberg, Quill*, 521 US at 790, 791 (Breyer, J., concurring in the judgments).

35. *Compassion in Dying*, 79 F.3d at 814.

36. Eric Cassell, "The Nature of Suffering," *Hastings Center Report* 21, no. 3 (1991): 24.

37. Ronald Dworkin, Thomas Nagel, Robert Nozick, John Rawls, Judith Jarvis Thomson, and T. M. Scanlon, "Assisted Suicide: The Philosopher's Brief," *New York Review of Books*, March 27, 1997, 41–47.

38. *Planned Parenthood v. Casey*, 505 US 833 (1992), 851. *Casey* is the most important recent case on abortion rights.

39. *Glucksberg*, 521 US at 727.

40. Ibid., 728.

41. *Quill*, 521 US at 801, 807–8.

42. See Charles T. Canady, "Physician-Assisted Suicide and Euthanasia in the Netherlands," 104th Cong., 2nd Sess., 1996, Comm. Print, 10–11. The best analysis of the Dutch

data is John Keown, "Euthanasia in the Netherlands: Sliding Down the Slippery Slope?," in John Keown, ed. *Euthanasia Examined: Ethical, Clinical, and Legal Perspectives* (Cambridge: Cambridge University Press, 1995); and Keown, "Down the Slippery Slope?: Further Reflections on Euthanasia in the Netherlands in the Light of the Remmelink Report and the van der Maas Survey," in Luke Gormally, ed. *Euthanasia, Clinical Practice and the Law* (London: Linacre Centre, 1994) 219–40. Keown has integrated analysis of the Oregon data into his analysis; see his "Considering Physician-Assisted Suicide: An Evaluation of Lord Joffe's Assisted Dying for the Terminally Ill Bill," pamphlet for the Care Not Killing Alliance, London, 2006. See also John Keown, *Euthanasia, Ethics, and Public Policy: An Argument against Legislation* (Cambridge: Cambridge University Press, 2002).

43. *Glucksberg, Quill* 521 US at 782 (Souter, J., concurring in the judgments).

44. Ibid., 787.

45. Ibid., 788, 789.

46. On assisted suicide and vulnerable populations, see M. Cathleen Kaveny, "Managed Care, Assisted Suicide, and Vulnerable Populations," *Notre Dame Law Review* 73 (1998): 1275–1310. Others argue that the data give no reason to worry that vulnerable persons will be adversely affected by the legalization of assisted suicide or euthanasia. See, e.g., Margaret P. Battin, Agnes van der Heide, Linda Ganzini, Gerrit van der Wal, and Bregje D Onwuteaka-Philipsen, "Legal Physician-Assisted Dying in Oregon and the Netherlands: Evidence concerning the Impact on Patients in 'Vulnerable' Groups," *Journal of Medical Ethics* 33 (2007): 591–97.

47. *Cruzan,* 497 US at 278. Building upon common expectations, the law generally presumes that incompetent persons would consent to life-saving medical treatment if they were able to do so, e.g., in the case of accident victims found lying unconscious by the side of the road. The narrow legal issue decided by *Cruzan* is that it is not unconstitutional for a state to require clear and convincing evidence rebutting that presumption before permitting life-saving treatment to be withheld or withdrawn from incompetent patients.

48. *Compassion in Dying,* 79 F.3d at 814–15 (citing *Cruzan,* 497 US at 278, 287, 289).

49. *Cruzan* actually speaks more strongly of "a constitutionally protected right to refuse lifesaving hydration and nutrition." *Cruzan,* 497 U.S. at 279.

50. *New York Times Co. v. Sullivan,* 376 US 254 (1964).

51. *Quill,* 80 F.3d at 729–31.

52. Ibid., 730.

53. If taken at its face, *Quill's* unqualified dismissal of the distinction between intention and foresight may be the most jurisprudentially radical aspect of the case. While not always firm, this distinction runs indispensably throughout the American legal system.

54. What it would take to "prove" the policy case for (or against) physician-assisted suicide is disputed. See, e.g., Bonnie Steinbock, "The Case for Physician Assisted Suicide: Not (Yet) Proven," *Journal of Medical Ethics* 31 (2005): 235–41; and Edgar Dahl and Neil Levy, "The Case for Physician Assisted Suicide: How Can It Possibly Be Proven?" *Journal of Medical Ethics* 32 (2006): 335–38. See also Katrina Hedberg and Susan Tolle, "Putting Oregon's Death with Dignity Act in Perspective: Characteristics of Decedents Who Did Not Participate," *Journal of Clinical Ethics* 20 (2009): 133–35.

PART III

Voting, Morality, and the Law

CHAPTER 8

∽

Voting and Faithful Citizenship

I N 2007 THE UNITED STATES CONFERENCE OF CATHOLIC BISHOPS
(USCCB) issued "Forming Consciences for Faithful Citizenship," a guide
for American Catholics to use in discerning their political responsibilities in the
face of the upcoming 2008 national elections.[1] In 2011 the bishops reissued the
same document for the 2012 elections, along with a new introductory note.[2]
No one doubts that the ballots cast by Roman Catholics are key in determining the results of national elections in the United States, although their role
as "swing voters" is often overstated.[3] The actual impact of the bishops' guide
upon the political choices made by Catholic voters is not apparent; in fact,
a 2011 poll suggests that only a small minority of American Catholics read
"Faithful Citizenship" in preparation for the 2008 election.[4] Nonetheless, few
political commentators are willing to dismiss its influence entirely.[5] American
journalists, politicians, political strategists, and political scientists rightly take
the document seriously as a potentially significant intervention in American
political life made by the religious leaders of a powerful segment of voters.[6]

But how should "Faithful Citizenship" be situated within the context
of Catholic moral and political thought?[7] The answer to this question is not
entirely clear. While several Catholic theologians, ethicists, and legal scholars
have offered important commentary on the 2008 document, most have tended
to engage various particular aspects of the document rather than assessing it
more holistically.[8] They do not delve deeply into such foundational issues
as what citizens actually do when we vote in a particular election, or how a
document such as "Faithful Citizenship" might function to shape a Catholic

citizen's decision to vote. In my view, addressing these fundamental issues is essential to understanding the document itself as a piece of practical political theology in the Catholic tradition.[9]

In the first two parts of this book, I examined a range of matters about the proper relationship of law and morality in a pluralistic society such as our own. That examination, however, has been largely theoretical. While I have proposed judgments about how the law ought to respond to several contemporary moral issues, I have not discussed how citizens who agree with those judgments ought to go about implementing them in the political realm. In a representative democracy such as our own, the most concrete step that ordinary citizens can take to affect the course of their city, state, and country is to vote. The goal of this last part of the book, then, is to look more closely at the act of voting, with a view toward the ways in which this particular political activity has a direct bearing on the common good.[10]

In this chapter I sketch a holistic moral analysis of the act of voting in and through a critical conversation with "Faithful Citizenship." In particular, I concentrate on the relationship between developing a proper view of the "issues," on the one hand, and casting one's vote for a particular candidate in a particular election, on the other. Building upon and fleshing out that analysis, I focus on more particular questions raised for American Catholic voters in recent years, specifically examining whether issues involving "intrinsic evils" deserve more attention from voters as well as whether voting involves impermissible "cooperation with evil."

I begin with the bishops' election guides because they are the most widely distributed episcopal directives to American Catholics about how to bridge the duties of faith and the obligations of citizenship.[11] Since the nation's bicentennial in 1976, the bishops' conference has issued guides prior to each presidential election.[12] They do not, by and large, make new and original proclamations but rather repackage and represent current Catholic teaching in a form appropriate for voters who are turning their attention to the upcoming political contests. The statements draw upon magisterial teaching from Rome, along with other teaching documents produced by the American bishops themselves, who have a long and honorable history of offering their collective moral and political reflection upon the challenges facing this country.[13]

What, exactly, is the purpose of these guides, which are often casually referred to as voting guides? The answer depends upon the definition of the term. On the one hand, the guides do not endorse any particular candidates or even present a list of approved candidates. Indeed, the USCCB cannot endorse candidates without running afoul of federal tax law, upon pain of losing their tax-exempt status.[14] On the other hand, no one can doubt that the bishops do mean to influence the Catholic voters by shaping their consciences in accordance with Catholic teaching. Furthermore, while the guides all acknowledge that key components of Catholic social teaching are enduring, the emphasis of each guide clearly reflects the bishops' perception of the challenges facing the American people during a particular national election. One might more properly say, then, that the bishops' guides are "issue" guides since they are largely dedicated to articulating Catholic teaching on key controverted issues in a particular election.[15]

But "issue spotting" is not enough. There is a significant gap between developing a proper view of timely moral and political issues considered in the abstract and casting one's vote for a particular candidate in a particular election in a particular polity. Voting in a morally responsible manner requires not merely a proper view of the issues but also a proper understanding of at least three additional matters: the meaning and function of voting for a political official in general; the nature, responsibilities, and limits of a particular political office; and the purposes of the particular political body holding the election. While the bishops' guides cannot endorse or oppose specific candidates, there is no reason why they cannot articulate, in general terms, the moral meaning of voting and the criteria that voters ought to use to evaluate candidates for political office. Nor is there any reason that they cannot encourage reflection upon the way in which voters ought to assess the nexus between candidates and issues.

CONTINUITY AND EVOLUTION: A COMPARATIVE PERSPECTIVE ON "FAITHFUL CITIZENSHIP"

While the most recent guide, "Forming Consciences for Faithful Citizenship" (2007) (FC-2007), is worth analyzing on its own terms, it is more instructive to compare it to the first guide, "Political Responsibility: Reflections on an Election Year" (1976) (PR-1976).[16] The comparison reveals in capsule form how dramatically the years have shifted the perceptions of the Church leadership about the place of Catholics in American political life and in the United States more generally. More important, the comparison also uncovers a striking pattern of change: Over the years, the bishops have vastly increased the number of issues they wish voters to note while simultaneously greatly reducing the number they wish voters to emphasize. In the most recent guide, abortion is far from the only issue, but it is clearly the dominant issue.

Audience

Whereas PR-1976 explicitly addressed itself to all Americans, FC-2007 is directed primarily to Catholics.[17] PR-1976 presumes that many people will be interested in its reflections; moreover, it assumes that the concerns, responsibilities, and perspectives of Catholics are broadly consonant with the responsibilities of all Americans of good will, particularly those who are religious. It specifies that "we specifically do not seek the formation of a religious voting bloc."[18] That line (and sentiment), in contrast, is missing from FC-2007, which manifests a pervasive desire to shape the Catholic population toward a distinctly Catholic type of political engagement "to apply authentic moral teaching in the public square."[19]

Desired Response

The difference in audience is accompanied by a difference in the expected response; whereas PR-1976 hopes that its words "will provide an opportunity for thoughtful and lively debate," FC-2007 invites deference, if not obedience: It stresses "the moral responsibility of each Catholic to hear, receive and act upon the Church's teaching in the lifelong task of forming his or her own conscience." One might say that the drafters of FC-2007 suspect there has been too much debate over the past few decades and not enough effort on the part of Catholics to appropriate and act upon magisterial teaching about controverted moral and political issues.

Predominant Fear

As its title "Political Responsibility" intimates, the major worry of PR-1976 is widespread political apathy and cynicism, resulting in "the abandonment of political participation."[20] In contrast, the predominant worry of FC-2007 is moral skepticism and relativism; it is vexed more about the human capacity to recognize the moral truth rather than the motivation to act upon the truth it recognizes. In response, it emphasizes the Church's capacity to teach the moral truth relevant to political society. "What faith teaches about the dignity of the human person and about the sacredness of every human life helps us see more clearly the same truths that also come to us through the gift of human reason."[21] As its title indicates, FC-2007 is concerned about *faithful* citizenship—citizenship exercised in accordance with the truths recognized by the Catholic faith.

Excluded Voices

In reflecting on the political situations they respectively confront, both documents highlight voices that might be missing from the discussion in large part because of political marginalization and ensuing discouragement. PR-1976 identifies these voices with the poor and socially sidelined, whereas FC-2007 identifies the politically marginalized with devout Catholics, particularly those who oppose abortion.[22]

Relative Optimism

While PR-1976 does not flinch from the problems facing American society at that time, it tacitly presupposes that effort and commitment in favor of the common good will be rewarded with results. Moreover, it presumes that the Church's political efforts will be joined—or at least appreciated—by people of good will.[23] There is a natural, almost youthful energy in its call for all Christians to "join together in common witness and effective action to bring about Pope John's vision of a well-ordered society based on truth, justice, charity, and freedom."[24] In contrast, the tone of FC-2007 is decidedly battle-weary, almost lamenting. The bishops present the United States as a nation on the brink of great difficulties arising from political crises and a deep level of moral self-contradiction verging on hypocrisy.

Content

The most immediately striking difference between the two documents, however, is their content. PR-1976 is pithy, including three tightly written sections: (1) an analysis of political responsibility and the electoral process, which calls for a "committed, informed, and involved citizenry to revitalize our political life";[25] (2) an account of the Church and the political order, which defends Catholic participation in American political life and articulates the role of the Church in the political discussion; and (3) an identification of key issues the bishops believe "are central to the national debate this year."[26] In contrast, although it too encompasses three substantive sections, FC-2007 is at least twice as long as PR-1976; each section includes several subsections.[27] Clearly the work of a drafting committee rather than a single individual, it is also far more loosely organized, even redundant. Different passages in the document are not harmonized; in fact, at points they verge on contradicting each other. Several passages appear to be inserted to furnish "pull quotes" to various political constituencies rather than to provide coherent guidance to all readers.

Treatment of Issues

The key difference between the documents, however, is not the issues themselves but the way in which they are treated. PR-1976 identifies eight issues for the reader's consideration: abortion, the economy, education, food policy, housing, human rights and US foreign policy, mass media, and military expenditures. The policy proposals that the bishops advocated with respect to education and food policy are spelled out in slightly more detail, but PR-1976 is content to offer "brief summaries" and to refer its readers to other documents listed at the end of the text for a fuller explanation.

In contrast, FC-2007 not only identifies many more issues, it also circles around them again and again. They are addressed in two of the four substantive subsections of part 1 and dominate parts 2 and 3.[28] A key subsection of part 1 organizes the issues under seven key themes: (1) the right to life and the dignity of the human person, (2) the call to family, communion, and participation, (3) rights and responsibilities, (4) the option for the poor and vulnerable, (5) the dignity of work and the rights of workers, (6) solidarity, and (7) caring for God's creation.[29] Part 2, titled "Applying Catholic Teaching to Major Issues: A Summary of Policy Positions of the United States Conference of Catholic Bishops," is entirely devoted to grouping fifty-seven (!) issues presented in bold type under four broader themes: human life, family life, social justice, and global solidarity.[30] Finally, part 3 identifies ten "policy goals that we hope will guide Catholics as they form their consciences and reflect on the moral dimensions of their public choices."

Strikingly, the verbs associated with the policy goals in part 3 are both ambitious and vague. For example, we are enjoined to "address" the requirement to protect the weak; "keep" the nation from turning to violence; "define" marriage in a traditional way; "achieve" comprehensive immigration reform; "help" people overcome poverty, particularly children; "provide" health care to those who lack it; "continue to oppose" prejudice and discrimination; "encourage" social stakeholders to work together to overcome poverty; "establish and comply" with moral limits in the use of force; and "join with others around the world" to promote peace, human rights, religious liberty, and justice.[31] In part 3 of FC-2007, the framing of the issues points to underlying values identified in Catholic social thought. While these verbs focus attention on the values they highlight, they provide virtually no guidance in moving toward practical and effective implementation of those values. They simply remind

Catholics of their importance, and trust that Catholic voters will work out the practical details with respect to specific elections themselves. In this respect, part 3 of FC-2007 resembles the entirety of PR-1976, which also functioned largely to remind Catholics to engage key aspects of Catholic social thought as they fulfilled their civic duties. To say that reminder is not specific, however, is not to say that it is not important; FC-2007 explicitly cautions voters against making up their minds solely on the basis of their own self-interest.[32]

The Overriding Issue: Abortion

The most obvious contrast between PR-1976 and FC-2007, however, is in their prioritization of the issues. PR-1976 deliberately does not do so. It begins with abortion, but only because it is presenting the issues in alphabetical order. In contrast, FC-2007 does not merely begin with abortion; it treats the topic repeatedly and pervasively. Doubtless, some of the disparity between the two documents is due to the changing political circumstances; countering the effects of *Roe v. Wade* would have seemed a less daunting task in 1976 than it has come to be seen nearly four decades later. As I noted earlier, a clear sense of discouragement, even weariness, accompanies FC-2007's initial discussion of the question.

It is evident that affirming the status of the unborn has not only acquired pride of place in the years since the bishops' first electoral missive; it has also acquired a certain organizational force and power. FC-2007 treats the right to life for the unborn as the "preeminent" issue from a practical perspective, and it repeatedly uses the right to life to provide the touchstone for the theoretical evaluation of other issues, both explicitly and implicitly. Quoting Pope John Paul II, FC-2007 goes so far as to say that any concern for human rights is "false and illusory" if it does not include an antiabortion program.[33] Moreover, the document regularly mentions the plight of the unborn in connection with other issues to which it is not commonly linked, such as the preferential option for the poor and marginalized, and the need to combat violence.[34]

It would be accurate but incomplete to say that FC-2007 embraces a "consistent ethic of life" that sees the "life issues" and the issues of social justice as interconnected. The document not only connects them, it also reorganizes them conceptually to present the right to life as standing at the center of all other rights. Functionally, it holds them as lexically ordered, requiring that the first issue be addressed satisfactorally before moving on to the next. In comparison to the overriding importance of protecting the right to life of the unborn by prohibiting abortion (ideally, by constitutional amendment), all other social and political issues are relativized. For the bishops, there is no doubt that the right to life is the fundamental issue of social justice.

This lexical ordering of issues, moreover, clearly shapes the bishops' most specific advice regarding voting, found in paragraphs 34–36. Taken together, these paragraphs limn a clear path for the conscientious Catholic voter, with the barest sketch of an alternative route that is morally acceptable. Paragraph 34 states: "A Catholic cannot vote for a candidate who takes a position in favor of an intrinsic evil, such as abortion or racism, if the voter's intent is to support that position." It then goes on to say, "a voter should not use a candidate's opposition to an intrinsic evil to justify indifference or inattentiveness to other important moral issues involving human life and dignity." Note the contrast: we have here a clear prohibition (voting for a candidate in order to support abortion rights) set over against a vague admonition against "indifference or inattentiveness" to other important moral issues. Note, as well, that FC-2007 could easily (and just as correctly) have made the point in the reverse way, with a clear prohibition of voting for someone with an unacceptable stance on other moral issues, set over against an admonition against "indifference or inattentiveness" to abortion. For example, reversing the elements, the passage would read: "A Catholic cannot vote for a candidate who takes a position in favor of a policy that undermines human life and dignity if the voter's intent is to support that position. . . . A voter should not use a candidate's opposition to other policies that undermine human life and dignity to justify indifference or inattentiveness to abortion." It did not do so. The logical structure of the passage prioritizes abortion.

When *can* a Catholic legitimately vote for a pro-choice candidate? According to paragraph 35, "a Catholic who rejects a candidate's unacceptable position" may vote for him or her "only for truly grave moral reasons, not to advance narrow interests or partisan preferences or to ignore a fundamental moral evil." Moreover, in the context of the bishops' discussion, the morally "grave" reasons for voting for a pro-choice candidate alluded to in paragraph 35 seem only to contemplate a situation where there is no pro-life candidate available. In fact, paragraph 36 goes on explicitly to suggest as much: "When all candidates hold a position in favor of an intrinsic evil, the conscientious voter faces a dilemma. The voter may decide to take the extraordinary step of not voting for any candidate or, after careful deliberation, may decide to vote for the candidate deemed less likely to advance such a morally flawed position and more likely to pursue other authentic human goods."[35]

In the context of the sustained emphasis on the importance and uniqueness of abortion, what does it mean for the bishops to affirm that "As Catholics we are not single-issue voters," as they do in paragraph 42? In this framework, to say that Catholics are not single-issue voters is most plausibly interpreted as saying that other moral issues become important after the candidates successfully pass the hurdle of the abortion question. This reading is supported by paragraph 42 itself, which continues: "A candidate's position on a single issue is not sufficient to guarantee a voter's support. Yet a candidate's position on a single issue that involves an intrinsic evil, such as support for legal abortion or the promotion of racism, may legitimately lead a voter to disqualify a candidate from receiving support."[36] Nowhere does the document straightforwardly allow a conscientious voter to select a pro-choice candidate if there is a pro-life candidate in the race. In contrast, as I have shown above, on numerous occasions FC-2007 affirms the decision to refuse to cast a vote for a pro-choice candidate, even if the only alternative is to refrain from voting altogether. FC-2007 treats the issues as lexically ordered: First consider abortion and then consider everything else.

FROM ISSUES TO CANDIDATES: VOTING AS A MORAL ACT

Consequently, unlike PR-1976, FC-2007 does not merely identify a range of issues to keep in mind while voting, it also strongly encourages its audience to walk into the polls with one particular issue at the top of the list—and by clear implication, of all lists, for every single election. Only after emphasizing again that "the moral obligation to oppose intrinsically evil acts has a special claim on our consciences and our actions" does paragraph 37 gesture to the other factors involved in electing a candidate: "These decisions should take into account a candidate's commitments, character, integrity, and ability to influence a given issue." Read in context, the brief reference to other factors involved in voting seems little more than an afterthought. Ironically, despite their focus on the life issue, the bishops do not even raise the possibility that a particular candidate (or party) might be fabricating a commitment to end abortion for strategic political reasons. It does not caution voters to evaluate the sincerity with which a candidate holds a particular position; rather, it seems to assume candidates will act according to their platforms if elected to office.

How, then, do we move from considering issues to selecting candidates? There is, alas, no straight path forward; instead, I think that we must go back to the beginning. We must ask ourselves a fundamental set of questions: What is "voting" as a moral act? How ought we to deliberate about a particular instance of voting? How does the broader political and social context affect the way we cast our votes?

What do we do when we vote in an American political election? Most fundamentally, we exercise our responsibility as citizens in a representative democracy, in a polity in which we are both sovereigns and subjects. We select those individuals who will exercise political authority on our behalf, in accordance with the limits on role and term length specified in the community's foundational documents (e.g., the federal and state constitutions). We participate in the choice of those persons to whose judgment we will defer during their appointed time in office.

Why should we vote? Political scientists have devoted a great deal of attention to this question because the odds are overwhelming that no individual vote will make any appreciable difference, particularly in national elections.[37] Because they do not think they will change the outcome, many people decline to participate in the process.[38] While understandable, a voter's decision to opt out is, in my view, deeply mistaken; more specifically, it reduces the purpose of the practice of elections to crude, consequentialist terms.

It is true, of course, that the primary function of an election is selective; one member of a field of candidates is chosen by the electorate to lead the community by serving in a particular office. There are, however, other purposes for which one can cast a vote. For example, voting can also be expressive. By their votes citizens can "send a message" about their general attitude about the course of the community to those who assume or remain in power. This message may result in policy change; in fact, we frequently see how such messages may yield midterm course corrections. Most importantly, however, voting is contributive. Given the structure of the government, (adult) citizens share joint responsibility for selecting our own leaders. The contributive function of voting cannot be neatly captured in crude, consequentialist terms because it is the electoral process that matters, not merely the result. One might go so far as to say that voting is an act of political solidarity with one's community.

It is worth remembering that many civic duties have no crudely identifiable "consequences" if they are considered in a narrow, individualistic manner. If, for example, a defendant is acquitted, that does not mean in and of itself that a prosecutor failed to do his or her job. The prosecutor is not a lone minister of justice; the causal power of the role is contextualized and limited by the roles and responsibilities of other people, not least the members of the jury. In the American system, balancing the scales of justice is a social, even a collaborative, project. Those involved in the process contribute to its integrity even if their view on the merits of a particular case does not ultimately prevail.

The practice of holding elections is also a social, collaborative project. We cast our votes as individuals. The direct political import of those votes, however, is forged in a context that is doubly social; it is determined by who else is running for a particular office, and who else is voting in that particular election. The indirect political import of voting is also socially determined. If large numbers of people refuse to vote, or if large, identifiable groups of people (e.g., minorities and women) are prevented or discouraged from voting, the viability and stability of the electoral system is threatened. Each of us may go into the voting booth alone, but voting is anything but a solitary act.

On a practical level, what do we do when we vote? As I noted earlier, most fundamentally and straightforwardly, we select a particular candidate to assume or retain public office, and to serve the relevant political community by assuming a distinct array of political duties. The selection is not unrestricted. In order to be eligible for office, candidates frequently have to meet certain official criteria (e.g., pertaining to age and residency); they also must be willing to assume the responsibilities of the office to which they are elected. Very often the range and number of eligible candidates in a general election has been narrowed by the primary system; voting for a candidate outside that system is a "waste" of one's vote with respect to the selective function of voting, although it may have significant import with respect to its expressive and contributive functions.

Selecting a candidate for public office is an exercise of practical reason that itself incorporates judgment about a candidate's probable exercise of practical reason over the sphere of his responsibilities while in office. Therefore, voting involves a combination of judgment (about the merits of the candidate) and prediction (about the nature of the challenges that the individual holding the office will face during the upcoming term). In assessing candidates for a particular office, four considerations are paramount:

- *Competence*—Does the candidate have the intellectual capacity, the experience, the temperament, and the judgment to do the job?
- *Character*—Does the candidate have a good set of moral values and the integrity to pursue them in situations of temptation and fear?
- *Collaboration*—Can the candidate work well with other people, both political allies and opponents?
- *Connections*—What are the moral and practical ramifications of the candidate's political and financial connections for the manner in which he or she will carry out the job? Politicians do not act alone; they take their place within networks of political power, including party affiliations, lobbyists, and big corporate and individual donors.

The point of electing candidates to an office, after all, is to empower and enable them to accomplish a set of tasks, both specified and unspecified, in service of the common good. In evaluating candidates, the foregoing considerations point to various factors involved in being an "empowered and enabled" political servant. These factors are not fungible. Moreover, there is a certain minimum level of achievement that is indispensable with respect to each consideration;

saintly demeanor does not make up for lack of experience or intelligence; strategic brilliance does not compensate for antisocial behavior. Moreover, precisely because politics is not a solitary activity, the same criteria for holding political power ought to be applied with respect to the key party leaders with which a particular candidate is affiliated. In some cases, in fact, it is the voter's view of the party leadership that ought to be decisive. Depending upon the situation in a particular political community, "voting the party" rather than a particular candidate may be a strategy that is morally justified. If party politics are strong, then voters in a general election often find themselves choosing between already assembled political teams with competing governing strategies and priorities.

The opposite of empowering and enabling, of course, is thwarting and hindering. In some cases, perhaps too many cases, a voter may exercise the selective function of the ballot in a negative rather than a positive way. Voting is a crude instrument for setting a community's social and political direction; sometimes the best one can do is try to prevent a deadly crash here and now, in the hope of setting a better course down the road. There are instances in which a responsible voter will describe what he or she is doing as casting a clear vote against one candidate or party rather than voting for that candidate's or that party's opponent. Sometimes, of course, the situation facing a voter is far more ambiguous. Suppose none of the candidates score particularly well on the four criteria identified earlier; the best one can do is to pick the candidate whom one believes, overall, to be the least inadequate leader. In this situation, sometimes too common, voters are not selecting leaders for their virtues but for their relative lack of key vices.

The expressive function of voting is extremely important from a practical perspective but logically secondary to the selective function. It comes into play when voters want to send a message to those seeking to hold office, or to influence those in office. A vote can function as a crude form of communication to those newly elected to office and to incumbents who will stand for election in the future. In our political era, of course, the meaning of a vote is debated, fleshed out, and perhaps altered by the auxiliary forces of the political system, including incessant polling and political commentary.

The contributive function of voting is fulfilled by participation in the process of choosing the community's political leadership. It also, generally, requires that each citizen educate himself or herself on the state of the community, the candidates available to lead it, and the various political programs offered as overarching plans of government. Does the contributive function also require that one refrain from voting if one has not come to an informed, independent view of each and every issue and each and every candidate? In my view, no.[39] It seems to me that a citizen could reasonably decide to rely upon the advice of those they trust about key issues and leading candidates in particular elections. Furthermore, it seems to me that a citizen could reasonably make a global decision to support a cohesive political organization or party on the view that the coordination is necessary to efficiently and effectively achieve particular goals. Such reliance does not need to be a wholesale abdication of political judgment, provided that citizens periodically review and critically assess their political alliances and their actual achievements.

THE RELATIONSHIP OF ISSUES AND CANDIDATES

In the foregoing paragraphs I have argued that citizens vote primarily for candidates—individuals running for particular offices, who are to be assessed in the context of their political collaborators—not for "issues." What, then, is the relationship between candidates and issues? The answer to this question depends upon the answer to a prior question: what exactly is an "issue"? The term is general, even imprecise. A quick perusal of the *Oxford English Dictionary* definition of the word reveals that it can refer to some sort of product, result, or decision, as well as to the underlying matter that demands some sort of result or decision. In common usage, it gestures vaguely toward a topic or a question that is currently the subject of discussion or controversy. In our current political climate, the term can refer to a complex problem with many causes, both natural and social (hunger, global warming, illegal immigration); it can refer to the working of an entire sector of social life (the economy); it can refer to a morally objectionable practice, whether legal or illegal (abortion, drug use); it can refer to a particular legislative proposal (authorizing gay marriage, banning capital punishment); it can refer to a deliberate policy or decision by a governing body (sending troops to the Middle East, authorizing "enhanced interrogation"); and it can refer to a fundamental value that operates through many spheres of life, public and private, political and social (free exercise of religion).

Given the imprecision surrounding the meaning of the term "issue," how do we begin to pin down a candidate's relationship to the issues, or to one issue in particular? We frequently say that a candidate has a "stance" on an issue. What does that mean? At a minimum, it means that he or she has a judgment that a particular situation poses a problem for the common good, a view about what has caused that situation, and a proposal for doing something to remedy the problem. Each of these factors can incorporate both moral and factual considerations, sometimes in extremely complicated ways. One may think that global warming does not pose a problem because one is unconvinced by the scientific data proffered to support the theory, or because one believes that the end of the world is imminent as God prepares to punish humanity for our sins. One may think that abortion in a particular society is a problem because one judges that it counts as the intentional killing of human beings, or because it hinders the nationalist ambitions of a "superior" race (e.g., the view of some Nazis). In assessing a candidate's stance on the "issues," then, voters need to consider all three factors identified in the preceding paragraph. Many times they are interrelated; very frequently, one's view of the reason a particular situation harms the common good will affect one's view of its cause, and that view, in turn, will significantly determine the proposal to remedy it.

Why should a candidate's stance on key issues be important? A candidate's stance reveals important aspects of that candidate's suitability for office, including information important to assessing the candidate's character, competence, collaboration, and connections. Obviously, something about a candidate's character may be revealed by his or her stance on particular issue. At the same time, we must tread cautiously in moving from a candidate's position on an issue to a wholesale judgment of moral probity or aptitude for leadership, particularly in mixed questions of fact and value. We need to ask ourselves whether the factual judgment embedded in a particular moral position is "reasonable, but wrong." Moreover, in assessing a candidate's stance, it is also important not to take everything she says at face value. Politicians are not always truthful about their positions, or honest about the depth of commitment with which they hold them. A candidate's moral character, however, is not the sole factor illuminated by a stance on key issues. Competence, connections, and collaborative possibilities are revealed as well. The candidate's diagnosis of the problem and proposed solutions sheds light on her intellectual and practical competence, as well as her ability to marshal collective resources and to work together with political allies and opponents to address particular threats to the community.

Assessing the relationship between a candidate for a particular office and a given issue begins, but does not end, with considering a candidate's stance on key issues in the abstract. An election is not a seminar; voters should not evaluate candidates' stances on the issues solely from a purely academic vantage point but also in direct relationship to their ability to affect them. Perspective in assessing candidates' stands on issues is important in determining how to cast one's ballot. Voters, after all, rightly care about the issues not merely because they reveal something about the character and qualifications of the candidate. They also care because it matters, in a fundamental way, what is done about them.

Consequently, evaluating a candidate's stance on issues must not be performed from on high but from an action-oriented and pragmatic perspective.

First, issues should loom larger to the extent that they are within the purview of the office to which the candidate aspires. From an action-oriented, pragmatic perspective, the views of a potential school board member on peace in the Middle East are not particularly salient, although the issue itself is crucial.[40] Second, voters ought to pay particular attention to the final component identified earlier regarding a candidate's stance on an issue: his or her concrete proposal for addressing it, thereby remedying the threat it poses to the common good. In some cases, a voter rightly supports candidates who adopt the soundest policy, even if they do so for less-than-sound reasons.

ISSUES AND PRIORITIES

Looking at the relationship between issues and candidates from an action-oriented, pragmatic perspective is instructive about how we should think about issues more generally. Recall that the several meanings of the word "issue" hold together both a situation and its outcome; a problem *at* issue, so to speak, begs for a resolution *to* issue from the relevant debate and discussion. Evaluating and prioritizing issues in the context of elections, then, more generally requires us to assess the threat each problem poses for the common good—and to also consider the possibility and necessity of ameliorating those problems through governmental intervention.

Because political issues tend to press us to formulate an action plan, they are susceptible to being ranked in different ways that are at least partially incommensurable. On the one hand, some issues are important, even fundamental; they go to the basic structure, values, and political arrangements of the country. Who counts as an equally protectable person? Who gets to vote in elections? What are basic due-process requirements that must be followed by law enforcement officials? On the other hand, some issues are urgent: the problem they pose must be addressed now or the immediate well-being of the nation, its stability, and the welfare of the people is seriously threatened. Natural or man-made disasters, such as a catastrophic earthquake, a meltdown at a nuclear plant, or a widespread famine, fall into this category.

Much of the difficulty in ranking issues stems from the fact that the fundamental and the urgent may compete for time, attention, and limited resources. Upon reflection, this competition is not surprising; action items in the two categories compete in similar fashion in nearly every area of human activity, from work responsibilities to child rearing. Time management experts and strategists tell us that, as agents, most people face the danger of miscategorizing too many tasks as urgent, thereby consistently putting off consideration of more fundamental issues.[41] At the same time, however, there is such a thing as an urgent problem. Maintaining the foundation of a house is important— indeed, fundamental—to the well-being of the entire building. At the same time, if the roof is leaking, or lightning has set it afire, those problems must be addressed first.

By virtue of their urgency, some issues cannot be assessed and addressed in predictable ways. Sometimes urgent issues arise or mature to a crisis point unexpectedly. Holders of higher office may be remembered by their responses to issues that were wholly or largely unanticipated at the time they were elected. No one expected George W. Bush's presidency to be defined by his response to terrorism; the attacks on the Twin Towers in 2001 reconfigured the entire nation's priorities. Responsibly electing national leaders always involves some assessment of their ability to address new and unexpected challenges and situations.

Finally, the action-eliciting, resolution-oriented nature of political issues generates an additional criterion according to which they must be evaluated: amenability to improvement. Some issues involve problems that are easily and quickly solvable; others do not. As I argued earlier in this chapter, "issue" is a somewhat amorphous concept; a political issue usually includes an identifica- tion of a problem threatening the political common good, a diagnosis of its cause, and a proposed solution. In one set of cases, issues point to problems that simply cannot be solved. From a theological perspective, of course, the ultimate issue for human community is sin and its consequences; short of the Second Coming, there is no fully acceptable remedy for it. In a second set of cases, issues cannot be solved using generally acceptable tools of government intervention. Shoddy and inaccurate reporting on the part of the press is a deep issue for our political life, but the government cannot directly target this set of problems without running afoul of the First Amendment. Of course, it is possible to argue that a particular issue is solvable if more extreme means are employed. In the mid-nineteenth century, many people in the North judged (rightly or wrongly) that the issue of slavery in the South was not solvable without war. The question then becomes whether one is willing to employ the necessary means. In a third set of cases, issues cannot be resolved by our community's political actors because the responsibility for the underlying problem belongs to other actors and agents. To a large extent, the situation in the Middle East falls into that category.

In prioritizing issues, therefore, it is important to consider both the pos- sibility and the likelihood of solving (or significantly ameliorating) the problem associated with the issue by the morally acceptable means at hand. This claim is actually a generalization of a more specific claim I made earlier in the chapter, which is that in evaluating the significance of a candidate's stance on an issue, voters need to take into account the candidate's ability to affect it by holding a particular office. If a particular problem cannot be addressed by acceptable political measures, it ought not to be considered a political issue.

One might object that one can redefine an issue to pick out a subset of the problem that is addressable in this manner. We do not, after all, consider sin as such a political issue but we do treat one subset of sins—serious violations of the rights of others—as a political matter in our tort and criminal law. This objection, which has a great deal of merit, suggests two responses. First, particularly in the context of elections, citizens ought to take care to define political issues in ways that are tied fairly closely to the identification of a politically cognizable problem, a diagnosis of its cause, and a proposed solution. This circumscribed definition of an issue is not necessary for all purposes, or even for all political purposes. The venerable American tradition of the jeremiad, a stylized speech by a politician or a preacher decrying the failings of the people and calling for repentance, demonstrates that there is a time and a place for general allusions to the social and moral problems of the country.[42] Nonetheless, at the time of a national election, issues should be described in circumscribed terms that are geared to appropriate political intervention. So, for example, a crucial political issue might be defined "violent crime" or "cybercrime," not the vices of injustice, excessive anger, greed, and dishonesty more generally.

Second, this last example makes clear that problems are overlapping. These vices may not be narrowly definable as political issues but they point to problems to be addressed by different realms of civil society, including families, churches, synagogues, and mosques. State and federal law may not be able to target these vices directly but they can make indirect progress by enabling and encouraging the appropriate bodies to do so. Furthermore, as I argue repeatedly in this book, through its pedagogical role, state and federal lawmaking can make it clear that violent crimes and cybercrimes are problematic not merely because they violate justice but also because they are the fruits and exemplification of morally disturbing patterns of activity.

"FAITHFUL CITIZENSHIP": A SECOND LOOK

The foregoing analysis of candidates and issues, I think, allows us to gain some critical perspective on "Faithful Citizenship." It would have been wise for the bishops to focus on what it means to vote for a candidate rather than an issue. The bishops' tax-exempt status prevents them from endorsing or opposing particular candidates; it does not, however, prevent them from reflecting on general qualifications of a candidate, in terms of his or her competence, collaborative abilities, connections, and character. What are the virtues of a good public servant? Western political philosophy includes a number of reflections on this question—some profound, and some troubling.[43] Recent Catholic moral theology has witnessed a resurgence of interest in the role of virtue in the moral life; it would make sense to extend the analysis to the virtues necessary for political leadership, particularly in a pluralistic liberal democracy such as our own. In my view, exposition of the necessary virtues would also highlight the capacities necessary to promote the virtues of autonomy and solidarity in the populace, as developed in other chapters in this book. I realize, of course, that in suggesting that the bishops' guides give new emphasis to the qualities of candidates, I am calling for substantial new work on the part of both the bishops themselves and moral and political theologians in order to better assist Catholics in fulfilling their moral obligations to vote. That work will need to be done with a view toward elections to come.

At the same time, I also want to make a few comments about how the bishops might have added some necessary nuance and distinctions to their treatment of issues, including the issue of abortion. When historians of Catholicism and American politics examine FC-2007, what will be most striking to them, I believe, is what it leaves out—not what it includes. Written to the voters of a country experiencing the greatest economic downturn since the Great Depression of the 1930s, FC-2007 pays scant attention to the matter of the economy. This oversight is doubly surprising because the immediate triggers for the economic meltdown were fraudulent and flagrantly irresponsible lending practices in the financial industry, and the increasing securitization of real estate lending.[44] The 2011 "Introductory Note" does little to rectify the omission. In the list of six issues to which the bishops call the voters' attention, the economic crisis appears in fourth place—behind abortion, conscience protection for Catholic ministries, and the defense of traditional marriage—and ahead of immigration and war.

The effects of the Great Recession were clearly devastating by the time of the 2008 election, both nationally and internationally. Consequently, the state of the economy at that time was an urgent issue; arguably, given the depth of the crisis, it was also a fundamental issue. In FC-2007 the bishops called upon citizens to vote for the common good, not merely for their own economic self-interest. A reasonable concern on the part of voters for the basic economic well-being of one's family, including both their children and their elderly parents, however, is not censurable self-interest. It is one thing not to be able to afford another European vacation; it is another thing entirely to lose the roof over one's head.[45] Furthermore, given the gravity of the situation, it was reasonable for voters to focus on the potential for the Great Recession to trigger political instability around the globe.[46]

A second distinction the bishops might have helpfully drawn was between those issues that were ripe for intervention by those serving in higher political office and those that were not. The prospect of health care reform was politically ripe in the 2008 national election, for example, in a way that it had not been for the previous fifteen years. The issue of "enhanced interrogation" and its relationship to prohibited torture was also ripe. The issue was raised by the policies of the outgoing Bush administration; the bishops could have noted that it would be possible for an incoming administration to change course. Moreover, the bishops could have observed that the same changeability attached to the issue of federal funding for embryonic stem cell research; what Bush prohibited by his own authority, his successor could permit in the same fashion.

We are now in a position to return to the issue of abortion, which FC-2007 treats as the primary issue for Catholic voters. Let me begin with the relationship between issues and character. Is someone who does not support overturning *Roe* by that very reason possessed of a defective moral character that renders them unfit to lead the country? In my view, it very much depends upon the reasons underlying the position. As I noted earlier, living in a pluralistic society requires citizens to develop not only a sense of moral right and wrong but also a sense of which views fall within the category of "reasonable, but wrong." Different people, of course, will have different views about what counts as a "reasonable, but wrong" position with respect to matters related to abortion jurisprudence. Nonetheless, in evaluating character and fitness for office, the category itself is valuable. In employing the category, voters need to ask what the underlying normative values expressed by the candidate's position are, and what the merits of the factual judgments embedded in that position are. So, for example, the character of a candidate who thinks that unborn life has no value whatsoever at any stage in pregnancy should be evaluated differently from one who thinks that the American society is too divided over the issue to make fundamental alterations to American constitutional law.

What about abortion as an issue considered in the abstract? The bishops justifiably consider the legal status of abortion a fundamental issue in that it goes to the basic question of who counts as an equally protectable member of our political society. Why not, then, make it an absolute priority in voting? A key difficulty with doing so stems from the fact that changing that status does not score nearly as high on the scales of urgency, amenability to improvement, or ripeness, at least at the federal level.[47]

By suggesting that abortion is not an urgent federal issue, let me emphasize again that I am not implying that it is not important or even fundamental. I mean only to say that its status does not threaten the current stability of the government or the society's ability to function. In fact, part of the reason abortion is such an intractable issue for the pro-life movement is that social patterns have crystallized around the fact that abortion is a readily available and widely used option—a legal option—with which to address an unwanted pregnancy.[48] Consequently, those who are opposed to legalized abortion must grapple with the likelihood that, if successful, they will precipitate social change and instability. Indeed, I suspect that a widespread inchoate uneasiness about the practical ramifications of such a change largely accounts for the unwillingness of many Americans to take this step, even if they are theoretically convinced of the humanity of the unborn.

In addition to urgency, I have argued that amenability to improvement is key to voters' assessment of issues in voting. Here, again, abortion is problematic. The fundamental legal status of abortion is not subject to significant immediate change by any elected official, including the president of the United States. Because the Supreme Court has conferred constitutional protection upon a woman's right to choose abortion, it will take the Supreme Court to reverse its own holding—or a constitutional amendment. It is true that the president appoints Supreme Court justices who then go on to serve life terms. No president, however, can control how many appointments he or she will have to the Supreme Court, and no president can control whether the Senate will confirm his or her nominees. No president can control how a justice votes after being appointed to the Court. Moreover, no president can control whether the Court will actually agree to hear a case that raises the issue, or to decide that case in a way that undercuts the central holding of *Roe v. Wade*. Finally, there is good reason to think that the justices are acutely aware that overturning *Roe* could be as destabilizing to the legal system as the original opinion was some forty years ago.[49]

I also suspect that the legal status of abortion was not a ripe issue in the 2008 federal election, particularly in the context of the economic meltdown. In fact, studies have shown relative stability in American attitudes toward abortion extending over decades. Roughly speaking, most believe it is a morally problematic procedure but do not want to make it illegal, especially early in pregnancy, when the vast majority of abortions take place.[50] At the same time, most do not want to fund it with tax dollars, except in exceptional cases. And in fact, there have been stringent restrictions on government funding of abortion for many years now.[51] In short, at least at the federal level, the status quo seems to be fairly stable. Abortion is neither broadly prohibited nor broadly subsidized with federal funds. The 2008 elections presaged no serious move on the part of either party to disturb this status quo.[52]

Do the foregoing observations suggest that a candidate's stand on legal abortion ought not to be treated as significant? Absolutely not. They do suggest that the problem is far more complicated than simply correlating a politician's stand on *Roe v. Wade* with a vote for or against him or her. For example, assuming that the "issue" of abortion also includes not merely changing its legal status but also reducing the number of abortions, then the economy becomes a key pro-life concern. Studies have shown that the number of abortions is correlated, among other things, to the economic and social circumstances of women facing crisis pregnancies.[53] Not surprisingly, US abortion rates, after years of steady decline, began to rise slightly in 2008 and 2009; many experts attributed it to the deteriorating economic situation.[54] Of course, it is also important to remember that abortion is not the only "life issue" on the table. Given the growing elderly population of the United States, the staggering growth in health care costs, and the fragile state of the economy, renewed pressures to legalize physician-assisted suicide and euthanasia are to be expected.[55] The state-by-state struggle to convince Americans to retain or reintroduce legal prohibitions against these practices will involve a different set of challenges from those involved in the national struggle to overturn *Roe v. Wade*.[56]

CONCLUSION

What does it mean to vote? In this chapter I have suggested that the act of voting has several functions in a pluralistic representative democracy such as our own. First, voting entails a selective function; the primary task of voters is to choose those who will lead a particular political community for a specified period of time. Voting also has an expressive function; citizens use their ballots to communicate messages to those in office about the direction in which the political community appears to be heading. Finally, and most important, voting has a contributive function; by exercising their right to suffrage, citizens fulfill their responsibilities as sovereign subjects in their respective political communities within the framework of a representative democracy.

How, morally, should citizens cast their votes? Proper moral analysis of the act of voting must take into account not only the three functions of the act of voting but also the structure of the act itself. To put it bluntly, apart from referenda items, voters are asked to select among people, not positions. So, in casting their ballots, voters must make a direct choice between or among candidates running for a given office, not between or among issues.

In my view, this fundamental feature of casting a ballot should serve as a touchstone for recalibrating our reflections on the moral implications of the act of voting. Election guides, for example, would do well to place more emphasis on assessing the fitness of candidates for a particular office in a contextual, comparative way. In general, voters ought to evaluate a candidate's general suitability in terms of the requirements for the particular office that is sought. That evaluation should include scrutiny of both the candidate's moral character—paying particular attention to the virtues and vices most likely to be involved in the elected post—and the candidate's social and political networks. With whom will the candidate work? To whom will the candidate be loyal? These are key questions. Many election guides, however, do not concentrate on describing virtues and vices of candidates; they emphasize instead the issues they perceive to be (or hope to be) relevant to the voters. The election guides issued over the years by the United States Conference of Catholic Bishops are no exception to this generalization.

How, then, should citizens think morally and practically about the issues relevant to casting their ballots for a particular candidate in a particular election? I have suggested that the term "issue" is too vague to be helpful for practical decision making because too often the word simultaneously encompasses a diagnosis of a problem, an account of its cause, and a proposed solution. Evaluating a candidate's stand on the issues requires careful attention to each of these three factors. Further complicating the matter, political issues and the underlying problems they highlight claim our attention in different ways. Some are important, even fundamental, because they go to the basic structure of the political community. Others are urgent because the mandate to protect the well-being of the community demands that they be addressed here and now. Issues, then, are not abstract propositions about the community; they are action items in that they are the problems that can be addressed by the tools available to political officeholders. Consequently, voters should not to evaluate the relative significance of issues in the abstract but should instead consider the specific context of whether and to what degree the problems identified by the issues can be ameliorated by the particular candidate seeking a particular office.

The enduring challenge faced by the pro-life movement is that the current legal status of abortion is not immediately susceptible to any sort of significant change at the federal level. For nearly forty years now, abortion has been a constitutionally protected but not federally funded option available to women facing crisis pregnancies. To change this situation in any substantial way, the constitutional protection afforded to abortion by *Roe v. Wade* would need to be removed. The most direct way to accomplish this goal, of course, would be to pass an amendment to the Constitution that, at the very least, directly overturns *Roe*. The procedural hurdles of such an amendment are specified in the Constitution itself, and they are—in the name of political stability—

exceedingly onerous.[57] Efforts to amend the Constitution rarely succeed; of the thousands of amendments that have been surfaced, only thirty-three have received the necessary two-thirds votes of both houses of Congress to rise to the level of a proposal. Of these thirty-three, only twenty-seven amendments (including the ten encompassed by the Bill of Rights) have been ratified.[58]

The difficulty of passing a constitutional amendment that directly overturns *Roe v. Wade* has led large segments of the pro-life movement, including the US bishops' conference, to concentrate on achieving that same goal indirectly, by electing a series of presidents who will over time remake the Supreme Court with justices able and willing to overturn *Roe*. It seems to me that the divisions in the country that make the direct strategy practically impossible also tell against the effectiveness of the indirect strategy. Moreover, the indirect strategy also has significant moral problems that do not plague the amendment process, however impractical the latter may be.

Supporting a constitutional amendment directly targeted at undoing *Roe* conflicts with few, if any, of a voter's other duties to promote the common good. While any change to the fundamental law of the country is potentially destabilizing, the prospect of such a narrowly targeted amendment merits serious consideration by anyone who believes that equally protectable human life begins at any time before birth; who thinks *Roe* itself was badly decided; or who judges more generally that controversial questions ought to be decided by the elected officials in the legislatures, not by the courts. But the pro-life movement's indirect strategy of making abortion a litmus-test issue for voters, with the expectation that they will elect officials who will somehow overturn *Roe*, does raise red flags. The duty of a voter is to promote the common good by selecting the best candidate for a political office in light of the range of factors I have outlined in this chapter. Given that most office-holders have multifaceted responsibilities, voters cannot consider only one issue—even a fundamental issue—in casting their ballots. Presidential elections are no exception.

FC-2007 rightly says that Catholics are not to be single-issue voters.[59] It does not elaborate, however, on why that is the case. In this chapter I have attempted to make a case for that position, centering my analysis on the nature and purpose of the act of voting. Voting is a role-related moral obligation incumbent upon qualified citizens who are both sovereigns and subjects in our representative democracy. The moral obligation of citizens in their roles as voters to promote the common good necessarily requires consideration of a number of competing responsibilities.

More specifically, citizen-voters rightly take into account their other role-related obligations in casting their votes. It is not selfish to help build a society in which individuals can fulfill their moral and religious responsibilities to others. Moreover, no one disputes that these responsibilities of voters are, like those of office-holders, multifaceted. For example, parents have a duty to provide for their children; therefore, it is morally correct for a mother or father to work at a job that will materially provide for their sons and daughters rather than to donate all their time to a pro-life lobbying group. Analogously, in threatening economic circumstances, it can be equally morally correct for parents to vote for candidates most likely to protect the jobs by which they provide for their children, even if those candidates are pro-choice. To take another example, surely it is morally permissible to direct some of one's surplus funds toward the victims of Hurricane Katrina rather than donating everything to the local crisis pregnancy center. But as our government has the basic obligation to provide for victims of national disasters, it follows that voters are morally obliged to consider which governmental candidates will best fix the broken disaster-response system. In certain elections, that consideration may be decisive.

There is no easy way to undo the legal effects of *Roe v. Wade*. For pragmatic reasons, the pro-life movement, including the bishops' conference, has sidelined the straightforward, direct, and morally less-complicated route of passing a constitutional amendment. Instead, it has prioritized an indirect route, urging voters to choose presidential candidates who will appoint Supreme Court justices who will overturn *Roe*. That strategy, too, has its drawbacks and limitations, moral as well as practical. The voters, with their multifaceted obligations, should not blinder themselves and focus single-mindedly on one issue in the abstract, even if the issue is abortion. Voters must select among candidates, not among issues—and they are morally required to do so in light of the concrete challenges and possibilities for the common good posed by a specific election at a specific time.

NOTES

1. The bishops overwhelmingly approved the guide with a 221–4 vote. Nancy Frazier O'Brien, "Bishops Overwhelmingly Approve Politics Document, Bulletin Insert," *Catholic News Service*, November 15, 2007, www.catholicnews.com/data/stories/cns/0706456.htm.
2. USCCB Administrative Committee, New Introduction for "Forming Consciences for Faithful Citizenship," *Origins* 41 (2011): 293–95.
3. See, e.g., the very helpful analysis by CARA (Center for Applied Research in the Apostolate) at Georgetown University, released in the summer before the 2008 presidential election. CARA, "Election '08 Forecast: Democrats Have Edge among US Catholics," June 20, 2008, http://cara.georgetown.edu/pro61808.pdf.

4. Mark M. Gray, CARA, Georgetown University, "CARA Poll 2011: Fordham Center on Religion and Culture Questions," August 2011, www.fordham.edu/images/undergraduate/centeronreligionculture/faith_citizen_poll%20crc-cara.pdf. The poll showed that only 16 percent of the polling subjects had even heard about "Faithful Citizenship"; 71 percent of those who were not aware of the document said that it would have had "no influence at all" on the way they cast their ballots. More surprisingly, however, 74 percent of those who were aware said that the document had "no influence at all" on their votes.

5. See Patricia Zapor, "Catholic Voters Mirror General Election in Support for Obama," *Catholic News Service*, November 6, 2008, www.catholicnews.com/data/stories/cns/0805649.htm.

6. See, e.g., Neela Banerjee, "Catholic Bishops Offer Voting Guide, Allowing Some Flexibility on Issues of Abortion," *New York Times*, November 15, 2007, A30; Robin Toner, "With Faith in the Spotlight, Candidates Battle for Catholic Votes," *New York Times*, April 15, 2008, A1; and E. J. Dionne Jr., "A Catholic Shift to Obama?" *Washington Post*, October 21, 2008, A17.

7. On the broader question of the political common good, see David Hollenbach, SJ, "The Common Good and Issues in US Politics: A Critical Catholic Approach," *Journal of Religion and Society* supp. no. 4 (2008): 33–46.

8. See articles by legal scholars Michael A. Simons, Robert John Araujo, SJ, Elizabeth F. Brown, Robert J. Delahunty, David L. Gregory, Susan J. Stabile, and Amelia J. Uelmen in a symposium, "Catholic Teaching, Catholic Values, and Catholic Voters: Reflections on *Forming Consciences for Faithful Citizenship*" in the *Journal of Catholic Legal Studies* 47 (2008): 205–342. For analysis by theologians and ethicists, see Dennis Hamm, SJ, and Gail S. Risch, eds. "Faithful Citizenship: Principles and Strategies to Serve the Common Good," *Journal of Religion & Society* supp. no. 4 (2008). In addition to the article by David Hollenbach, SJ, cited in note 7, and the article by John Carr cited in note 16, the issue includes pieces by David O'Brien, Julia Fleming, Bryan N. Massingale, and William R. O'Neill, SJ, among others.

9. For wider perspective, see John Langan, SJ, "The Individual and the Collectivity in Christianity," in *Religious Diversity and Human Rights*, ed. Irene Bloom, J. Paul Martin, and Wayne L. Proudfoot (New York: Columbia University Press, 1996). See also John Langan, SJ, "Hope in and for the United States of America," *Journal of the Society of Christian Ethics* 25, no. 2 (2005):3–16; and John Langan, "Contrasting and Uniting Theology and Human Rights," *Journal of Religious Ethics* 26, no. 2 (1998): 249–55.

10. For a review of the broader religious and political context at the time of the 2008 election, see Lisa Sowle Cahill, "Religion and Politics: USA," *Theological Studies* 70, no. 1 (2008): 186–91.

11. On the broader responsibilities of Catholics in political life, see Gregory A. Kalscheur, SJ, "Catholics in Public Life: Judges, Legislators, and Voters," *Journal of Catholic Legal Studies* 46, no. 2 (2007): 211–58; and Robert E. Rodes Jr., "On Lawyers and Moral Discernment," *Journal of Catholic Legal Studies* 46, no. 2 (2007): 259–76.

12. United States Catholic Conference Administrative Board, "Political Responsibility: Reflections on an Election Year," *Origins* 5 (1976): 565–70 [hereafter PR-1976]; see also United States Catholic Conference, "US Bishops' Resolution on Political

Responsibility," *Origins* 6 (1976): 7; United States Catholic Conference Administrative Board, "Statement on Political Responsibility," *Origins* 9 (1979): 349–55; United States Catholic Conference Administrative Board, "Political Responsibility: Choices for the '80s," *Origins* 13 (1984): 732–36; United States Catholic Conference Administrative Board, "Political Responsibility: Choices for the Future," *Origins* 17 (1987): 369–75; United States Catholic Conference Administrative Board, "Political Responsibility: Revitalizing American Democracy," *Origins* 21 (1991): 313–23; United States Catholic Conference Administrative Board, "Political Responsibility: Proclaiming the Gospel of Life, Protecting the Least among Us, and Pursuing the Common Good," *Origins* 25 (1995): 369–75; United States Conference of Catholic Bishops Administrative Board, "Faithful Citizenship: Civic Responsibility for a New Millennium," *Origins* 29 (1999): 309–18; United States Conference of Catholic Bishops Administrative Committee, "Faithful Citizenship: A Catholic Call to Political Responsibility," *Origins* 33 (2003): 321–31; and United States Conference of Catholic Bishops, "Forming Consciences for Faithful Citizenship," *Origins* 37 (2007): 389–403 [hereafter FC-2007].

13. Camilla J. Kari, *Public Witness: The Pastoral Letters of the American Catholic Bishops* (Collegeville, MN: Liturgical Press, 2004).

14. Assuming they are organized as tax-exempt charitable corporations under federal law, religious bodies are prohibited from engaging in certain political behavior such as endorsing candidates. Section 501(c)(3) of the Internal Revenue Code states that such an organization cannot "participate in, or intervene in (including the publishing or distributing of statements), any political campaign on behalf of (or in opposition to) any candidate for public office." After Catholic Answers produced its first voting guide, Catholics for a Free Choice challenged the group's tax-exempt status; in 2008 the IRS ruled that the guide did not constitute a prohibited political campaign intervention because it did not support or oppose a specific candidate. In response to the controversy, however, Catholic Answers formed a separate corporation under a different section of the Internal Revenue Code (501[c][4]), Catholic Answers Action, to handle its political activities.

15. For an older but still helpful perspective, see John Langan, "The Morality of Single Issue Voting," *Christian Century* 99 (1982): 818–22.

16. For historical reflection on the bishops' guides by someone deeply involved in the process of producing them, see John Carr, "Faithful Citizenship: History, Context, Direction, Dangers," *Journal of Religion and Society* supp. no. 4 (2008): 6–19.

17. "As pastors and teachers, we address this Statement on political responsibility to all Americans in hopes that the upcoming elections will provide an opportunity for thoughtful and lively debate on the issues and challenges that face our country as well as decisions on the candidates who seek to lead us." (PR-1976, para. 1). "This statement highlights the role of the Church in the formation of conscience, and the corresponding moral responsibility of each Catholic to hear, receive, and act upon the Church's teaching in the lifelong task of forming his own conscience." (FC-2007, para. 5.)

18. PR-1976, para. 16.

19. FC-2007, para. 16.

20. PR-1976, para. 4.

21. FC-2007, para. 10.
22. PR-1976, para. 3; and FC-2007, para. 16.
23. "We wish to point out that these issues are not the concerns of Catholics alone; in every case we have joined with others to advocate these concerns." PR-1976, para. 19.
24. PR-1976, para. 17.
25. Ibid., para. 4.
26. Ibid., para. 19.
27. FC-2007's sections are part 1: "Forming Consciences for Faithful Citizenship: The US Bishops' Reflection on Catholic Teaching, and Political Life," part 2: "Applying Catholic Teaching to Major Issues: A Summary of Policy Positions of the United States Conference of Catholic Bishops (USCCB)," and part 3: "Goals for Political Life: Challenges for Citizens, Candidates, and Public Officials."
28. In addition to abortion, other issues identified in part 1 ("How Does the Church Help the Catholic Faithful to Speak about Political and Social Questions?") include racism and unjust discrimination, the death penalty, unjust war, torture, war crimes, hunger, access to health care, and immigration policy (FC-2007, para. 29).
29. "What Does the Church Say about Catholic Social Teaching in the Public Square?— Seven Key Themes," ibid., paras. 40–62.
30. A few particular issues are listed under more than one theme.
31. FC-2007, para. 90.
32. Ibid., para. 41.
33. "Above all, the common outcry, which is justly made on behalf of human rights—for example, the right to health, to home, to work, to family, to culture—is false and illusory if *the right to life*, the most basic and fundamental right and the condition for all other personal rights, is not defended with maximum determination." Ibid., para. 26 (quoting Pope John Paul II, *Christifideles laici* (1988), para. 38).
34. FC-2007, paras. 51, 90.
35. Ibid., para. 36.
36. In examining paragraph 42, one might object that the use of the word "may," rather than "must," provides some room for maneuver. In my judgment, however, the word "may" provides only the tiniest of loopholes to those who believe it is best to support a pro-choice candidate rather than a pro-life candidate for a given office, despite (not because of) the candidates' respective stands on abortion. It is consistent with the point in paragraph 36, discussed earlier, that one may be forced to choose between pro-choice candidates in a particular election.
37. See, e.g., André Blais, *To Vote or Not to Vote: The Merits and Limits of Rational Choice Theory* (Pittsburgh: University of Pittsburgh Press, 2000); and Jocelyn A. J. Evans, *Voters and Voting: An Introduction* (London: Sage Publications, 2004).
38. See, e.g., Pew Research Center, "Who Votes, Who Doesn't, and Why: Regular Voters, Intermittent Voters, and Those Who Don't," October 18, 2006, http://people-press .org/2006/10/18/who-votes-who-doesnt-and-why/; and California Voter Foundation, "California Voter Participation Survey: Survey Summary Report—Importance of Voting," January 27, 2006, www.calvoter.org/issues/votereng/votpart/summaryreport .html#2.
39. Jason Brennan takes the contrary view in his provocative new book, *The Ethics of*

Voting (Princeton, NJ: Princeton University Press, 2011). He argues that citizens have a duty to vote well, or not to vote at all. "Voting well," in his view, means being epistemologically justified in believing a person or policy will promote the common good. Brennan also maintains that vote buying or selling can be morally permissible, provided that the practice does not violate his other criteria for voting well. In my view, Brennan's criteria for what counts as being epistemologically justified in voting are too stringent. I also do not think his argument for the acceptability of vote selling is persuasive because I am worried about turning political power into a market commodity.

40. Even here, of course, matters are complicated. With some exceptions (e.g., celebrity candidates), most politicians build a career in a deliberate, step-by-step fashion. Some attention must be given to nurturing young candidates with sound views, even if those views are not immediately relevant to their entry-level positions in politics.

41. See, e.g., Peter Turla, "Time Management Tips for Setting Priorities," www.time man.com/Articles/timemanagementtipsforprioritysetting.shtml; and Hillary Chura, "Entrepreneurs Take Time to Organize Their Time," *New York Times*, August 10, 2006, C7.

42. See, e.g., Sacvan Bercovitch, *The American Jeremiad* (Madison: University of Wisconsin Press, 1978).

43. See, e.g., Aristotle, *The Politics*, trans. Carnes Lord (Chicago: University of Chicago Press, 1985); Thomas Aquinas, *Commentary on Aristotle's Politics*, trans. Richard J. Regan (Indianapolis: Hackett, 2007); and Aquinas, *Summa theologica*, 3 vols., trans. Fathers of the English Dominican Province (New York: Benziger Bros., 1948), II-II (treatise on the virtues); Niccolò Machiavelli, *The Prince*, trans. George Bull (New York: Penguin, 2005); and Thomas Hobbes, *Leviathan* (New York: Penguin, 1985).

44. Financial Crisis Inquiry Commission, *The Financial Crisis Inquiry Report* (Washington, DC: Government Printing Office, 2011).

45. Some of the dire articles widely available to the American public around the time of the election include the following: Daniel Gross, "Why It's Worse Than You Think," *Newsweek*, June 16, 2008, 20; John Maggs, "What's the Worst That Could Happen to the Economy?" *National Journal*, October 4, 2008, 25; Bill Powell, "Life without Credit," *Time*, November 3, 2008, 54; Tara Siegel Bernard and Jenny Anderson, "Downturn Drags More Consumers into Bankruptcy," *New York Times*, November 15, 2008, A1; and Kelly Evans and Jeff Bater, "Americans' Gloom Reverberates—Third Quarter GDP Is Revised Downward as House Prices Continue Descent," *Wall Street Journal*, November 26, 2008, A2.

46. Peter S. Goodman, "US and Global Economies Slipping in Unison," *New York Times*, August 24, 2008, A1.

47. State elections may be a different story. *Planned Parenthood v. Casey*, 503 US 833, 856 (1992) "chipped away" at *Roe* by relaxing the standard under which abortion regulation would be evaluated. Instead of treating abortion as a "fundamental right" whose infringement would be strictly scrutinized, *Casey* recast it as a "liberty interest" that could not be subject to an "undue burden." Because *Casey* also jettisoned the rough "trimester" framework used by *Roe*, the ruling made it easier for states to enact legislation pertaining to early abortions, such as informed consent and waiting period

requirements. For an argument that *Casey* stabilized the legal situation, see Neal Devins, "How *Planned Parenthood v. Casey* (Pretty Much) Settled the Abortion Wars," *Yale Law Journal* 118 (2009): 1318–54. The state regulations permitted by *Casey* may have some effect on the incidence of abortions; see Michael J. New, "Analyzing the Effect of Anti-Abortion US State Legislation in the Post-*Casey* Era," *State Politics & Policy Quarterly* 11 (2011): 28–47.

48. "To eliminate the issue of reliance that easily, however, one would need to limit cognizable reliance to specific instances of sexual activity. But to do this would be simply to refuse to face the fact that for two decades of economic and social developments, people have organized intimate relationships and made choices that define their views of themselves and their places in society, in reliance on the availability of abortion in the event that contraception should fail." *Planned Parenthood v. Casey*, 503 US at 856.

49. "A decision to overrule *Roe*'s essential holding under the existing circumstances would address error, if error there was, at the cost of both profound and unnecessary damage to the Court's legitimacy, and to the Nation's commitment to the rule of law. It is therefore imperative to adhere to the essence of *Roe*'s original decision, and we do so today." *Casey*, 505 US at 869.

50. For example, Gallup has long asked the question, "Do you think abortions should be legal under any circumstances, legal only under certain circumstances, or illegal in all circumstances?" In April 1975 21 percent said "legal under any circumstances," 54 percent said "legal only under certain circumstances," and 22 percent replied "illegal in all circumstances." Another 3 percent had no opinion. In May 2010 24 percent said "legal under any circumstances," and 19 percent said "illegal in all circumstances." The other two numbers were the same in 2010 as they were in 1975. See Gallup, "Abortion," www.gallup.com/poll/1576/abortion.aspx.

51. The most important restriction is found in the Hyde Amendment, first passed in 1976, which broadly prohibits federal funding of abortion except in a narrow range of cases. For a more recent version, see Omnibus Appropriations Act, Pub. L. 111-8, §§ 507–8, 123 Stat. 524, 802 (2009) (Hyde Amendment). The 2009 version allows for exceptions in the case of rape, incest, and danger to the mother's life.

52. The widely quoted remark of Democratic candidate Barack Obama to a Planned Parenthood audience in July 2007 that, once inaugurated, the "first thing he would do" would be to sign the Freedom of Choice Act into law was campaign puffery. As I argued in chapter 4, no Congress had ever passed the bill, and given its nature, no Congress was ever likely to do so. Even the abortion-related debate about health care did not pertain to the normative question about whether federal funds should subsidize abortion but rather to the complicated factual question about whether they actually would do so under the health care reform legislation. See, e.g., Annenberg Policy Center, "Abortion: Which Side Is Fabricating?," *FactCheck.org*, www.factcheck.org/2009/08/abortion-which-side-is-fabricating/.

53. A recent study found that, of US women who obtain abortions, 42 percent have incomes below 100 percent of the federal poverty level ($10,830) for a single woman with no children, and 27 percent had incomes between 100 percent and 199 percent of the federal poverty level. Rachel K. Jones, Lawrence B. Finder, and Susheela Singh,

"Characteristics of US Abortion Patients, 2008," *Guttmacher Institute*, www.gutt
macher.org/pubs/US-Abortion-Patients.pdf.

54. For the survey, see Rachel K. Jones and Kathryn Kooistra, "Abortion Incidence and Access to Services in the United States, 2008," *Perspectives on Sexual and Reproductive Health* 43, no. 1 (2011): 41–50; for commentary, see, e.g., Rob Stein, "Falloff in Abortion Rate and in Number of Procedures Stalls," *Washington Post*, January 11, 2011, A1; and David Crary, "Rise in Abortions during Recession Stalls Longtime Drop," *Washington Times*, January 10, 2011, A1.

55. There is evidence that suicide rates in the United States are correlated to the economy. See Feijun Luo, Curtis S. Florence, Myriam Quispe-Agnoli, Lijing Ouyang, and Alexander E. Crosby, "Impact of Business Cycles on US Suicide Rates, 1928–2007," *American Journal of Public Health* 101, no. 6 (June 2011): 1139–46, http://ajph.aphapublications.org/doi/pdf/10.2105/AJPH.2010.300010.

56. In 2011 the US bishops issued their first full statement on end-of-life issues, "To Live Each Day with Dignity: Statement on Physician-Assisted Suicide," *Origins* 41, no. 8 (June 30, 2011): 113–17.

57. Amendments must first be proposed and then ratified. In the most common approach, the votes of two-thirds of the members of both the House of Representatives and the Senate are required to propose an amendment. In an alternate method that has never been used, two-thirds of state legislatures can ask Congress to call a national convention to propose amendments. After being proposed, a prospective amendment must be ratified by three-fourths of the states. Generally, state ratification is accomplished by votes of the state legislatures. Alternatively, three-fourths of the states can approve the amendment in ratifying conventions. This second method has been used only once, to pass the Twenty-First Amendment repealing Prohibition.

58. John Vile, *A Companion to the United States Constitution and Its Amendments* (Westport, CT: Greenwood Publishing, 2006), 112.

59. "As Catholics we are not single-issue voters." FC-2007, para. 42.

CHAPTER 9

❧

Intrinsic Evil and Political Responsibility

I N CHAPTER 8 I ARGUE THAT, in our American representative democracy, any moral analysis undertaken by voters must center on the candidates, whom voters need to evaluate in terms of their competence, character, collaborative potential, and political connections. This is not to say that issues are irrelevant—far from it. However, voters do need to evaluate issues in a strategic and action-oriented manner, not in an abstract way. Voters should prioritize issues not merely on the basis of their importance (meaning their significance within the basic political framework of the society) but also their urgency (meaning their immediate potential to destabilize the political community). Furthermore, voters must discern whether the problem identified by a given issue is amenable to solution, or at least to amelioration, by the political tools available to those elected to a particular office. In short, instead of casting a ballot solely on the basis of issues in the abstract, voters ought to examine the quality of the candidates, their stance on the issues, and their ability to affect those issues if elected to office.

In this chapter I consider a possible objection to this line of argument. From the standpoint of the voters, are there issues that deserve separate and heightened consideration because they are morally different in degree or kind? In recent years some American Catholics, including the US bishops, in "Forming Consciences for Faithful Citizenship" (2007) (FC-2007), have claimed that issues dealing with "intrinsic evil" deserve priority attention from voters.

220 VOTING, MORALITY, AND THE LAW

At first blush this claim has a certain appeal. After all, "intrinsic evil" suggests wrongdoing of an entirely different magnitude than run-of-the-mill wrongdoing; it connotes great and contaminating evil that we take inside ourselves simply by associating with it, evil that ruins everything that it touches. If this is the case, one might argue that intrinsic evils pose great moral dangers to both individuals and society at large, and these dangers ought to dwarf all other considerations in casting one's vote. FC-2007 reinforces this impression, claiming that intrinsically evil actions "must always be rejected and opposed and must never be supported or condoned" because "they are always opposed to the authentic good of persons." The position of FC-2007 on intrinsic evils was reiterated by and expanded upon in statements issued by some individual bishops.[1] In that same vein, several Catholic political commentators during the 2004 and 2008 presidential elections complained about Catholics supporting candidates who did not, in the judgment of these commentators, adequately oppose such intrinsic evils as abortion, euthanasia, and homosexual acts (the last being implicated by the legal recognition of gay marriage).[2]

The foregoing is meant to note how the term "intrinsic evil" is used in the passionate give-and-take that characterizes many Catholic discussions about voting for a pro-choice politician. That interpretation of the term, however, is in significant tension with the great weight of the Church's long moral tradition. The term "intrinsic evil" does not have its roots in the expansive imagery of the Church's prophetic witness but rather in the tightly focused analysis of its moral casuistry. It is not a rhetorical flourish; instead, it is a highly technical term of Catholic moral theology with roots in scripture as well as in the action theory of St. Thomas Aquinas.[3]

How, then, did "intrinsic evil" become a catchword in the political debate among American Catholics? Is the new use of the term a coherent and helpful development of the moral tradition? I hope to shed some light on these questions. In the first section of this chapter I sketch the traditional, technical meaning of the term "intrinsic evil" as it has come to be understood within Catholic moral theology. Defining what this term means—and does not mean—is essential to properly understanding the responsibilities of the Catholic voter. In short, the mere fact that an action is labeled "intrinsically evil" within the traditional rubric of Catholic moral theology tells us very little about its status as a moral or political issue in American life, and even less about how to evaluate the political position of candidates running for office. The second section attempts to account for and analyze the emerging political use of the term "intrinsic evil" in American debates. To do so I look to two sources whose rationale and force were intermingled in the discussions surrounding American elections: Pope John Paul II's encyclicals that prophetically condemned moral evil at the level of both individual acts and social practices and the long-standing amenability of American public life to the rhetoric of prophetic denunciation.

WHAT "INTRINSICALLY EVIL" MEANS

From the perspective of the long tradition of Catholic moral theology, the fact that an act is called an intrinsic evil tells us two and only two things. First, it tells us why an action is wrong—because the acting agent's "object" or immediate aim or purpose is wrong. Second, the fact that an act is intrinsically evil tells us that it is always wrong to perform that type of act, regardless of the agent's larger motive or the other circumstances of the act. But characterizing an act as intrinsically evil says nothing about the comparative gravity of the act. Some acts that are not intrinsically evil (e.g., driving while intoxicated) can on occasion be worse both objectively and subjectively than acts that are intrinsically evil (e.g., telling a jocose lie). As I will illustrate, some homicides that are not intrinsically evil are worse than some intrinsically evil homicides. Furthermore, the fact that an act is intrinsically evil does not by itself tell third parties anything at all about their duty to prevent that act from occurring.

Unpacking the technical meaning and role of the term "intrinsic evil" within the Catholic moral tradition requires us to step back and contemplate the general framework for analyzing the morality of human acts.[4] Reflecting the enduring influence of Aquinas's approach to this task (which was itself indebted to Aristotle), the tradition holds that three aspects of each act merit moral analysis: its object, its larger end (sometimes called motive), and its circumstances.[5] For an act to be morally good, it needs to be good in all these respects; that is, the agent needs to do the right thing for the right reason in the right situation. For an act to be morally unacceptable, however, a defect in any of these elements suffices. For example, an act can be flawed because it is performed for the wrong motive; if I give alms solely to earn fame, then my act is morally wrong despite the fact that the giving of alms is itself praiseworthy.[6] Or an otherwise virtuous action can be rendered defective if performed under the wrong circumstances. Thus, while it is entirely good for a newly wedded couple to consummate their union to become one flesh, doing so in the church vestibule immediately following the ceremony is not morally acceptable.

Most significantly for our discussion, the immediate purpose or "object" of the acting agent can be disordered or defective. The object is the immediate goal for which that person is acting; it is "the proximate end of a deliberate decision."[7] In the vast majority of cases, identifying the object of an act is not difficult. Eliciting from an acting agent an honest answer to the question "What are you doing?" is usually sufficient. "I am studying math" or "I am cleaning the house" provides the needed information. Sometimes, of course, agents lie. Very few murderous nephews would be likely to say, "I am murdering my uncle," even if caught red-handed pouring a lethal dose of poison into the unfortunate man's drink. In such cases, we infer the agent's object from the context and surrounding circumstances of the action (e.g., a forged amendment to Uncle Rodney's will in favor of the penniless nephew and the nephew's gambling debts to the mob). We may be wrong on occasion. Many times, however, our inferences are correct.

But in some cases it can be genuinely difficult to identify correctly the object of an action—not only for the observers but also for the agents themselves. These hard situations strain the boundaries of the Catholic tradition's action theory in ways that have generated much controversy. Moralists and journalists alike tend to be attracted to difficult scenarios, where the component parts of an ethical framework are pressed to their breaking point. In this chapter, however, I deal with more ordinary cases, where the object of the agent's act is not in question. Most of the time we have no trouble identifying an agent's object in acting or its relationship to broader purposes and plans: this woman is "stealing" the stereo to exchange it for drugs; that man is committing adultery because he is bored and lonely; those teenagers are "lying" about their whereabouts last night because they didn't want to get into trouble.[8]

Because an act takes its identity primarily from its object, Catholic moralists say that an act with a defective or disordered object is "intrinsically" evil, meaning that the disorder afflicts the innermost structure of the act itself. Intrinsically evil acts, therefore, are acts that are wrong by reason of their object, not by reason of their motive or their circumstance. In *Veritatis splendor*, Pope John Paul II states that such acts are "'incapable of being ordered' to God, because they radically contradict the good of the person made in his image."[9] Consequently, intrinsically evil actions can never be morally good, no matter what the intended outcomes.

In Catholic teaching, what are some examples of acts considered to be intrinsically evil? It is always wrong to act with the immediate purpose of killing an innocent human being, no matter what the context or larger motivation. This prohibition rules out not merely contract killing but also intentional killing of the dying to end their suffering, intentional killing of unborn children, and saturation bombing of cities in wartime. But not all intrinsically evil acts involve mortal assault. Sex also provides fertile ground for them. Masturbation, homosexual acts, and contracepted heterosexual acts are all, according to official Catholic moral teaching, intrinsically evil, in part because "they close the sexual act to the gift of life."[10] It is never morally acceptable for a married couple to contracept, even if a pregnancy would threaten the life of the woman and the baby she carried. Official Church teaching says that if natural family planning does not provide sufficiently reliable protection, the couple should refrain from sex until menopause rather than use contraception even once.[11]

Over the centuries Catholic moralists have also identified other acts as intrinsically evil. For example, lying (generally defined as making a false assertion with the intent of deceiving) has often been identified as an intrinsically evil act. Consequently, it too is always wrong, no matter what the consequences. Many Catholic moralists have argued, for example, that it is never morally permissible to tell a lie, even to save a life. Under this view, if a Nazi storm trooper knocks on the door asking whether Jews are hiding in the attic, homeowners are not morally permitted to respond with a lie; the only morally acceptable alternative is to evade or to refuse to answer the question.[12]

It is often said that the Catholic moral tradition teaches that the end does not justify the means. This statement is imprecise. In the vast majority of instances, the end does justify the means—for what else would do so? Agents act for a purpose, for a larger end. We study all night to pass the medical boards, we go to work at an unpleasant job to earn money, and we take the bitter medicine to feel better. In some cases, such as the last example, the means are purely instrumental; if we could feel better without that awful medicine, we would gladly skip it. In other cases, the means may be at least partially constitutive of the end; studying not only allows future doctors to pass the exams that are required for certification; it also imparts the knowledge necessary for them to care for patients properly.

More precisely, the admonition "the end does not justify the means" is meant to highlight that even an end of pressing importance does not justify using a means that is morally wrong. By definition, intrinsically evil acts are morally wrong—therefore agents may never rightly choose to use them, no matter what might be gained by doing so.

Why not do evil so that good might result? In my view, the most compelling answer to this question comes from a virtue-oriented account of the relationship between one's character and one's acts. According to such an account, doing evil is never without consequence to the agent.[13] One might object that many evildoers in fact manage to escape punishment; there is no doubt that the wicked prosper, at least in earthly terms. That may be true. Nonetheless, the greatest harm suffered by the wrongdoing agent does not take the form of penalties imposed by third parties but of psychic wounds that are self-inflicted.

How is this the case? The Catholic understanding of Christian morality is teleological; it is oriented toward an understanding of what friendship with God and friendship with one another in God would look like in light of the decisive but still incomplete victory of Jesus Christ over sin and death. The habits that allow one to understand and experience flourishing as friendship with and in God are virtues while the habits that impede such understanding and experience are vices.

Deliberately performing an evil act warps an agent's character, distorting his capacity to identify, make, and follow through on good choices in the future. As virtue-oriented accounts of morality remind us, acts create habits, and habits in turn shape the way we perceive and deliberate about other acts.[14] Moral fitness is roughly analogous to physical fitness. Eating only junk food and shunning exercise leads to a loss of the taste for more nutritious food as well as to diminished capacity for quick and graceful movement. So a couch potato addicted to pizza and soda would be unlikely to embark upon a strenuous hike to reach a remote and beautiful place. Similarly, regularly performing acts that are inconsistent with the virtues—those habits that characterize human flourishing within the Christian framework—can make one less able to recognize morally virtuous acts, and less able to perform them when they are required.

If we accept the premise that immoral acts have a deleterious impact on the agent's character, then we also need to consider the implications of that premise for the distinction we are trying to make between intrinsically evil acts and ordinary wrongful acts.[15] Alasdair MacIntyre supplies a helpful connection:

> Imagine a community which has come to recognize that there is a good for man and that this good is such that it can only be achieved in and through the life of a community constituted by this shared project. We can envisage such a community requiring two distinct types of precepts to be observed in order to ensure the requisite kind of order for its common life. The first would be a set of precepts enjoining the virtues, those dispositions without the exercise of which the good cannot be achieved, more particularly if the good is a form of life which includes as an essential part the exercise of the virtues. The second would be a set of precepts prohibiting those actions destructive of those human relationships which are necessary to a community in which and for which the good is to be achieved and in which and for which the virtues are to be practiced.[16]

Intrinsically evil acts are acts that are flatly inconsistent with human flourishing. Further, a strong stream of the Western moral and legal tradition teaches that it is never morally permissible to perform an intrinsically evil act for a good end. Intrinsic evils, however, do not exhaust the category of wrongdoing.

Performing an act that is wrong by reason of its circumstances or its motive is also never right. All wrongful acts ultimately impair an agent's ability to participate in the practices constituent of human flourishing; consequently, they too ought never to be performed. Many wrongful acts also violate the rights of other persons or otherwise impinge upon their legitimate claims and expectations of how they will be treated, so these acts thereby interfere with the flourishing of others. In sum, some acts that are not intrinsically evil are, nonetheless, very wrong indeed.

WHAT "INTRINSICALLY EVIL" DOES NOT MEAN

Understanding the meaning of the term "intrinsically evil" requires situating it within a broader context of wrongdoing more generally. It also requires considering with some specificity what the term does not mean, a topic to which I now turn.

Intrinsically Evil Does Not Mean Gravely Evil

The fact that lying is intrinsically evil means that the prohibition against it extends across the range of human activities; it is always and everywhere wrong. It is wrong to lie to the FBI when the agency is pursuing a suspected terrorist, even if the suspected terrorist is your brother. It is also wrong to tell your Aunt Edna that her purple sunflower hat is fabulous if you think it is hideous, even if she has a heart condition. The latter would be an intrinsically evil act. At the same time, it would not be a serious evil. Why not? Following Augustine, Aquinas clearly states that telling a lie—which he defines as speaking what one believes to be a falsehood with the intention to deceive—is always sinful.[17] But he recognizes that not every lie is a mortal sin.[18] By proposing that the essence of a mortal sin is its opposition to the theological virtue of charity, Aquinas avoids lumping all lies together. Some lies, such as the lie to Aunt Edna, do not violate charity.[19] To say that an act is intrinsically evil does not necessarily mean that it is a grave evil, either objectively or subjectively. Objectively speaking, lying is not always seriously wrong, although it is always wrong.

Even with respect to acts that the official Catholic tradition has long held to be seriously wrong as an objective matter, there is room for nuance and distinction. For example, few moralists would deny that contraception, which separates the unitive and procreative goods of the sexual act, is a less grave matter than abortion, which involves the taking of human life.[20] Adultery, which involves a violation of marital vows, is more morally troubling than fornication, which does not. Moreover, while the Church has long taught that all sexual misdeeds, including masturbation, are objectively serious, it has also recognized that subjective culpability can vary from case to case.[21]

For numerous reasons, not all intrinsically evil acts are fit for prohibition by positive law. No serious candidate for national office maintains that masturbation, homosexual acts, or contraception should be outlawed in the United States today; most Catholic legal theorists since the Second Vatican Council, whether conservative or progressive, would agree.[22] Why, exactly, should we refrain from criminalizing these acts? As I described in the first chapter, liberal legal theorists such as Joel Feinberg would say that they are "harmless" immoralities and therefore beyond the proper scope of the criminal law. Feinberg further asserts that even if the agents performing such acts are harmed, they consented to the harm and therefore are not wronged in a way the law ought to consider.

A virtue-oriented account of law takes a different tack; it posits that no immorality is truly "harmless" because immorality of any degree invariably distorts the character of the agent. Obviously, many persons, both Catholic and non-Catholic, would contend that some acts included in the tradition's list of intrinsic evils are not morally wrong, are consequently not in fact inconsistent with a virtuous life, and therefore ought not to be criminalized. However, for those who do agree with official Catholic teaching on the immorality of these acts, the Thomistic view of law as a teacher of virtue gives reasons to nonetheless refrain from targeting these acts with legal prohibitions.

Even as it rejects the notion that immoral acts are harmless per se, a virtue-oriented account of law can still acknowledge that a subset of those acts are consistent with justice as an externally oriented virtue in that they do not directly infringe the rights of an innocent third party. Furthermore, as I argue in the first two chapters, good lawmaking has to take into account what is realistically possible in any particular time and place. It is not a sound jurisprudential strategy to prohibit actions that are widely practiced in a particular population. As Aquinas writes, "Now human law is framed for a number of human beings, the majority of whom are not perfect in virtue. Wherefore human laws do not forbid all vices, from which the virtuous abstain, but only the more grievous vices, from which it is possible for the majority to abstain; and chiefly those that are to the hurt of others, without the prohibition of which human society could not be maintained: thus human law prohibits murder, theft and such like."[23] And Aquinas would surely add, law has to be regularly and fairly enforced to be effective. Precisely because most sexual acts take place behind closed doors, broad enforcement of the prohibitions would require highly invasive enforcement procedures. Good lawmakers, when considering a proposed law, will weigh its cost of enforcement against its benefits to the common good—and will take into account as well the law's effect upon those called to enforce it and upon those suspected of violating it.[24]

Faced with the practical and moral difficulties of enforcing wholesale prohibitions against intrinsically evil acts, lawmakers often rightly target such acts selectively. Consequences, motives, and circumstances cannot elevate intrinsically evil acts into morally acceptable ones. However, these factors do have an impact on how such acts ought to be treated by legislators and courts. So, for example, we do not outlaw all lying; instead, we concentrate only on certain forms of lying, such as perjury (lying under oath) or making false statements on official documents. We no longer deem private consensual acts between adults to be illegal but we do prohibit public sexual activity, sexual activity between adults and minors, nonconsensual sexual acts between adults, and prostitution (sexual acts performed for money).

An Intrinsically Evil Homicide Is Not Always Worse Than Every Other Wrongful Homicide

At this point someone might object: "The foregoing reflections may be true about intrinsically evil acts in general, but that class of intrinsically evil acts involving the taking of life—particularly innocent life—constitutes human behavior at its worst and represents injustice of the gravest kind. Surely the law needs to condemn these acts most harshly." But even this claim does not hold up under closer scrutiny, for intrinsically evil acts do not necessarily make for the most egregious form of homicide with respect either to the subjective culpability of the killer or to the objective wrong done to the innocent victim. The following two examples ought to make that point clear.

Consider first a man who burns down his own building for the insurance money, foreseeing but not intending that his employee, a single mother, will die in the blaze. He does not want her to die; her death forms no part of his purpose or plan. He simply does not care whether she dies. This heinous act reveals great depravity on the part of the perpetrator and causes unspeakable pain and tragic harm to the victim. The act is not, however, intrinsically evil. The object of his act, to burn down his own building, is not inherently wrong. The act is wrong only because of its motive (fraud) and because of its circumstances (the likelihood that an innocent woman would lose her life).

Contrast this hypothetical with a situation involving an elderly man suffering from Lou Gehrig's disease. Fearful of undergoing a protracted and difficult death, he begs his wife to kill him. Finally, she acquiesces to his pleas and kills him painlessly with an overdose of barbiturates. The wife has committed an intrinsically evil act. She has intentionally killed a helpless, innocent person.

Her act is seriously wrong, yet her personal blameworthiness is mitigated by her motive of alleviating suffering. And, as a matter of objective injustice, the victim's actions (begging for and consenting to the killing) surely diminish the severity of the offender's actions.

In these two examples, the law has reason to prohibit the taking of both lives because private killing invariably harms the common good. At the same time, however, the legal system ought to recognize that the employer's act, which is not intrinsically evil, is morally worse, both subjectively and objectively, than the wife's act, which is intrinsically evil. In fact, while most district attorneys would be eager to prosecute the death-dealing defrauder to the full extent of the law, many would decline to press a murder case against the wife whose love and loyalty to her suffering husband took a deeply misguided form.[25]

Preventing Intrinsically Evil Acts Is Not Always Our Top Moral Priority

According to some commentators, third parties have an overriding duty to prevent intrinsically evil acts and to protect their potential victims—and for that reason, voters ought to prioritize opposition to gay marriage and abortion.[26] But this argument is incorrect. Of all the harms that require prevention by third parties, those harms caused by intrinsically evil acts are not necessarily the most critical to control. Sometimes preventing harm caused by other kinds of wrongdoing, or even harm caused by natural disasters, can take priority.

Let us return to the earlier examples. Suppose a third party had to choose between saving the single mother about to die as a result of her boss's setting the fire (an evil act but not an intrinsically evil one) and protecting the man with Lou Gehrig's disease who is about to be voluntarily euthanized by his wife (an intrinsically evil act). Faced with this dilemma, the third party could legitimately opt to prioritize the victim of the nonintrinsically evil act (the mother). Likewise, choosing to protect a person endangered by a natural disaster over coming to the rescue of a victim of human wrongdoing is defensible in some circumstances. For example, a toddler about to drown in a flash flood—a death not attributable to human wrongdoing—is as deserving of protection as is a potential victim of euthanasia.

More generally, one's obligation to intervene in order to prevent harm to others, whether or not that harm is directly caused by an intrinsically evil act, depends upon a number of factors. Is the intervenor in any way responsible for the harm about to occur? Does the intervenor have a special responsibility for either the perpetrator (if there is one) or the victim? What is the likelihood that the intervenor's efforts will succeed? And if the efforts are unsuccessful, will they make matters worse? By devoting her efforts to this particular rescue effort in lieu of another, what good will the intervenor fail to do and what other evil will she fail to prevent? Is intervening in this situation incompatible with performing other duties?

The Motive and Circumstances of Particular Actions also Deserve Moral Scrutiny

Some Catholic commentators maintain that because intrinsically evil acts are so undeniably wrong, we should give priority to preventing them over preventing acts that may or may not be wrong, depending upon the circumstances. Their argument seems to run like this: According to the teaching of the Church, abortion, euthanasia, and homosexual acts are always wrong, whereas war and capital punishment are only sometimes wrong. Therefore, good Catholics ought to focus their political efforts on preventing acts they know to be wrong, and ought to remain agnostic about the rest. Another related view describes intrinsic evils as "nonnegotiable issues" that are in contrast with other issues on which "Catholics are permitted leeway."[27] Still another stance in this family suggests that the Church gives us "wiggle room" for prudential judgment on issues that do not involve intrinsically evil acts.[28] Those who hold such views urge Catholic voters to prioritize opposition to intrinsic evils in voting precisely because intrinsic evils are always wrong.

The foregoing interpretations of a Catholic approach to the morality of human action are deeply mistaken. The error lies in treating the Catholic moral tradition as an arbitrary code with strictures that are purely external impositions. Under this faulty notion, once every clear requirement or prohibition is fulfilled, the agent operates in a field of pure unfettered discretion—a field in which no further moral judgments about her action are relevant. In taking absolute moral rules as mandatory and context-dependent moral rules as mere suggestions, this approach implies that reasonable people can disagree about the application of context-dependent moral rules in each and every case, and that the existence of good-faith disagreement about the application of the rule means the dispute ought not to be relevant to decision making. But none of these assumptions are true.

"Do not intentionally kill the innocent" is an absolute moral rule, while "Do not speed" is context-dependent. Since speeding affects the common good, we cannot simply agree to disagree about what constitutes "driving at an excessive speed" when determining the speed limit or when thinking about what reasons justify exceeding the limit. The fact that there is some disagreement at the margins of the injunction against speeding does not mean that there are no clear cases. For example, driving ninety miles per hour in a busy school zone is seriously violating the requirements of justice by exposing children to unnecessary risk. Furthermore, the fact that "speeding" is a relative term—and there is some (even significant) dispute about its application—does not mean that responsible citizens can ignore the relationship between speed and highway safety. In the end, we ask our public officials to look at the pattern of fatal motor accidents and adjust our traffic laws accordingly.[29]

More broadly, it is essential to recognize that the Catholic tradition is a guide that must be actively appropriated and applied by each moral agent in the context of making particular decisions. The tradition teaches that intrinsically evil acts are always wrong. But while moral analysis of particular acts and policies begins with that teaching, it most definitely does not end there. More specifically, the tradition also teaches that acts can be wrong because of their object, motive, or circumstances. Even if a particular act is not wrong by reason of its object, we have a positive duty to further consider its motive and circumstances before performing or endorsing it, particularly if the consequences might bring great harm to other people (as, for example, collateral damage in war).

To offer an illustration, some wars are just and some wars are unjust. Yet this dichotomy does not mean we can be agnostic about the justice of a particular war being waged by our own government in our names. We have a duty to evaluate each particular military conflict according to the criteria that the tradition has developed for distinguishing just wars from unjust ones. In *The Challenge of Peace: God's Promise and Our Response*, their pastoral letter on war and peace, the US Catholic bishops offered a helpful summary of these criteria.[30] To justify the decision to go to war (*jus ad bellum*), seven criteria must be met: just cause, competent authority, comparative justice, right intention, last resort, probability of success, and proportionality of expected good to be achieved in light of the damage likely to be inflicted. We cannot defend indifference to or agnosticism about a particular war on the grounds that waging war in general is not "intrinsically evil." Under these criteria, if we judge a war to be just (e.g., World War II), we ought to support it. Likewise, a war judged to be unjust (e.g., the Vietnam War) ought to be opposed. As morally serious citizens, we can neither hide behind a veil of culpable ignorance nor seek the nonexistent "wiggle room" on such questions.

Furthermore, the just war tradition places stringent restrictions on the manner in which war is conducted (*jus in bello*) and rejects "total war," even for a just cause.[31] Among the criteria applied to the waging of war are the principle of discrimination, which prohibits intentionally targeting noncombatants (an intrinsically evil act), and the principle of proportionality, which requires that a cost–benefit analysis be performed with respect to particular military options, not merely with respect to the war as a whole. Precisely what counts as a violation of the principle of discrimination is sometimes highly contested, as *The Challenge of Peace* notes. Among other things, people of goodwill can dispute what military actions count as the intentional killing (sometimes called "direct" killing) of noncombatants or how to calculate whether military battles inflict damage grossly disproportionate to their immediate strategic benefits. Nonetheless, such controversies do not excuse citizens from the obligation to make their own informed judgments about the quality of a particular military altercation, and to act on that basis.

Intrinsic Evil Is Not the Only Useful Category in Deciding One's Vote

Given the preceding analysis, how much help is the category of "intrinsic evil" in deciding whom to vote for in an important national election? In my view, it is hardly any help at all. As I argue in chapter 8, voters select among candidates, not among issues. In making that selection, they must examine various aspects of a candidate's fitness for office, including character, competence, collaborative abilities, and connections. A candidate's stance on key issues matters, but so does the likelihood that the candidate will be able to make a difference with respect to those issues.

A defender of the category's usefulness might say that a candidate who does not disapprove of an intrinsic evil reveals an unworthy character. That may be the case, but so does callousness toward the foreseen (but unintended) consequences of an unjust war, particularly toward the children who are orphaned, maimed, or killed—and so does indifference toward starving children in this country and in the world as a whole, many of whom are done an injustice not by individual Americans but by American policy as a whole. Moreover, as chapter 8 argued, in this fallen world, a candidate's moral character alone is not enough; political competence and other practical skills are also required. The person with the best moral character may not be the best president.

Another possible justification for the usefulness of the category of "intrinsic evil" is that it helps us prioritize our actions. On that basis, politicians have an obligation to oppose intrinsic evils before addressing other sorts of evils. As I have argued earlier, however, the duty of citizens—and candidates—to oppose wrongful actions depends not on an assessment that the actions constitute intrinsic evils but on a finding about the degree to which those actions harm the common good. The related duty of candidates to enact laws prohibiting wrongful acts depends on how seriously those acts violate the demands of justice as well as on other factors, such as whether the proposed laws will be effective and enforceable. The fact that an act to be addressed by a proposed law is intrinsically evil tells us nothing about how it rates on these important criteria.

Alternatively, one could say that the category of "intrinsically evil acts" rightly prompts citizens to target wrongdoing at home before worrying about evildoing abroad. The trouble with this argument is that it focuses on the wrong element—the location of the wrongdoing—rather than the identity of the wrongdoer. Because the United States is a representative democracy, the acts implementing our foreign policy are carried out in our name and performed in our interest.[32] Precisely because these harms generated by that policy are inflicted on our behalf, we have a duty as citizens and voters to work against American policies that unjustly harm the inhabitants of other countries.

Finally, giving priority to opposing intrinsically evil acts might be defended on strategic, political grounds. If all Catholics ought to recognize intrinsically evil acts as strictly impermissible, then it ought to be possible to develop a consensus to politically oppose such acts. Because the reality is that it will never be possible to develop a broad consensus to fight against evils whose wrongfulness depends upon motives and circumstances, adherents to this view argue that the best way for Catholics to express their ecclesial unity in the political realm is to focus their attention upon battling intrinsic evils in the public square.

In my judgment, this argument is flawed. Even Catholics who agree with the teaching that intrinsically evil acts are always wrong may reach different conclusions about which situations pose the greatest immediate threat to the common good, and the best way to alleviate the danger. Threatening situations can be posed by intrinsic evils (e.g. abortion), nonintrinsic evils (the threat of war, escalating to nuclear conflagration), or even natural evils (a catastrophic tsunami or major earthquake). In a representative democracy, disagreement about the nature of threats to the common good, and the appropriate response to those threats, will lead to political divisions. It should not lead, however, to ecclesiastical divisions. To suggest that Catholics must politically prioritize opposition to intrinsically evil acts simply because we should all agree that those acts are wrong comes dangerously close to substituting political unity for ecclesiastical unity.

INTRINSIC EVIL AS PROPHETIC LANGUAGE

Finally, we must reckon with the position that, if the concept of intrinsically evil acts has any utility whatsoever in political considerations, it might be in relation to that one issue of overriding importance: abortion. Let me lay out this argument. For more than three decades, the regime of legalized abortion has claimed well over a million unborn lives a year.[33] The Supreme Court of the United States not only permits this regime but also honors it as the instantiation of a constitutionally protected liberty interest.[34] In this circumstance, the term "intrinsic evil" helps evoke why abortion deserves prime consideration in voting. Abortion happens inside a woman's womb, inside what should be the safest relationship of all: that between mother and child. Abortion also happens inside our society; it is estimated that about one in three American women will have an abortion in her reproductive lifetime.[35]

Within the context of abortion, the term "intrinsic evil" has moved far beyond the technical use traditionally employed in Catholic action theory: it is evocative, not analytical. More generally, much of the language the pro-life movement wields with regard to abortion is prophetic language. By this I mean that it evokes the tone of the great Hebrew prophets in reflecting on the failings of God's chosen people. As Abraham Joshua Heschel observed, "The prophet was an individual who said No to his society, condemning its habits and assumptions, its complacency, waywardness, and syncretism."[36] As I have described elsewhere, the language of prophetic indictment is deeply embedded in American political culture. The Puritans who migrated to New England saw themselves as the "New Israel," a people called by God to special responsibilities and blessed by God with special riches.[37] Puritan clergymen regularly availed themselves of a particular form of preaching known as the "jeremiad." As its name suggests, the jeremiad recalls the urgent call to moral repentance found most strikingly in the book of the prophet Jeremiah but also prevalent in the other prophetic books of the Hebrew Bible, the Christian Old Testament.[38]

Social and ethnic groups who claimed their place in this increasingly pluralistic nation also appropriated prophetic discourse in their own way and for their own purposes.[39] And in the late twentieth century, spurred on by Pope John Paul II's prophetic imagery of the dichotomy between the "culture of life" and the "culture of death," Catholics began to cast the battle against legalized abortion in prophetic terms.[40] Consider, for example, Francis Cardinal George's response to a question from the journalist John Allen on whether the need to overturn *Roe v. Wade* was merely a matter of prudential judgment: "It can't be. If you've got an immoral law, you've got to work to change that. You've got children being killed every day. It goes on forever. That's the great scandal, and that's why there's such a sense of urgency now. There's no recognition of the fact that children continue to be killed, and we live, therefore, in a country drenched in blood. This can't be something that you start playing off pragmatically against other issues."[41]

Similarly, in an interview with the *New York Times*, Archbishop Charles Chaput hybridized the technical meaning of intrinsic evil from moral theology by adopting a prophetic approach in applying the term to abortion.

> You know some moral issues, all moral issues are moral issues, and it's good to be on the right side of them all the time, but some are dependent on the basic principles of human life. The dignity of human life. You never violate it. Whether it's the creation of embryos for embryonic stem cell research or abortion, [these] are violations of the dignity of human beings, from our perspective. And you can never justify it. You can sometimes justify going to war. You may think that the Iraq war is horrible, but there may be sometimes when you can justify [going to war]. It doesn't have the same moral weight. And, it's not calculating 40 million abortions against 40,000 deaths in Iraq. That's not how you do the calculus. The calculus is on the intrinsic act itself. You know, and abortion is never, ever, ever right. And so to elect someone who has no respect for unborn human life . . . or has a . . . what kind of respect? . . . a kind of respect that is wobbly . . . it doesn't make any sense. Why would you trust someone with your life, if that person is willing to let unborn babies die?[42]

This turn toward the prophetic use of "intrinsic evil" is not a purely American phenomenon; it also is clearly visible at the highest levels of the ecclesial hierarchy. In a 2005 speech Pope Benedict remarked, "Everyone must be helped to become aware of the intrinsic evil of the crime of abortion. In attacking human life in its very first stages, it is also an aggression against society itself. Politicians and legislators, therefore, as servants of the common good, are duty bound to defend the fundamental right to life, the fruit of God's love."[43]

How did the hybridized use of "intrinsic evil" come about? In my view, it is in large part attributable to Pope John Paul II, who, in his 1993 encyclical *Veritatis splendor*, not only defends the traditional understanding about the existence and definition of intrinsically evil acts but also prophetically emphasizes their incompatibility with human flourishing. More specifically, he insists that "the Church teaches that 'there exist acts which per se and in themselves, independently of circumstances, are always seriously wrong by reason of their object.'"[44] Pope John Paul II points to "a number of examples" from a particularly prophetic passage from *Gaudium et spes*, Vatican II's Pastoral Constitution on the Church and the Modern World:

> Whatever is opposed to life itself, such as any type of murder, genocide, abortion, euthanasia or willful self-destruction, whatever violates the integ-

rity of the human person, such as mutilation, torments inflicted on body or mind, attempts to coerce the will itself; whatever insults human dignity, such as subhuman living conditions, arbitrary imprisonment, deportation, slavery, prostitution, the selling of women and children; as well as disgraceful working conditions, where men are treated as mere tools for profit, rather than as free and responsible persons; all these things and others of their like are infamies indeed. They poison human society, but they do more harm to those who practice them than those who suffer from the injury. Moreover, they are a supreme dishonor to the Creator.[45]

As it happens, however, many of the items on this list are not, in fact, straightforward intrinsic evils. In some cases, the object of the prohibited act stands in need of more careful definition before we can make any judgment about its status. For example, the passage claims that "mutilation" violates the integrity of the body. But what about the amputation of a gangrenous limb or responsible organ donation? Both acts are physical violations of bodily integrity but both can be morally acceptable because the object of these acts is not immoral. In other cases, however, it is virtually impossible to see the prohibited acts as intrinsically evil—that is, wrong by reason of the object. "Arbitrary imprisonment" is another clearly context-dependent moral wrong. What counts as "arbitrary" depends upon assumptions about the specific requirements of due process, which are not universal. "Deportation" is a wrong in some circumstances but not in others. In still other cases, such as "disgraceful working conditions," or "slavery," or treating people as "mere tools for profit," we are not dealing with specific acts at all but with complicated social patterns and practices for which many agents are responsible.

Why, then, did *Gaudium et spes* describe these practices as "intrinsically evil" (*intrinsece malum*)? Actually, it did not do so. It said, rather, that they (and others things like them) were "disgraces" or "infamies."[46] It was Pope John Paul II who introduced the term "intrinsically evil" to categorize the items on the list without explicitly noting the terminological shift or taking stock of its implications. In my view, his choice is both ironic and troubling. A central purpose of *Veritatis splendor* is to defend the tradition's moral tripartite analysis of human acts in terms of objects, ends, and circumstances rather than more holistic or consequentialist approaches. By suggesting that Vatican II's list of "infamies" are intrinsically evil acts, Pope John Paul II not only cast his own painstaking account of the proper moral analysis into confusion, he also opened the door again to the very consequentialism and proportionalism he previously rejected. As the terms "infamies" and "disgraces" suggest, the practices identified by *Gaudium et spes* are great evils, but they are not all intrinsic evils. By gathering them all under the label "intrinsic evil," *Veritatis splendor* ironically reintroduced the idea that the magnitude of the evil is all that matters.

The Church teaches that abortion is both an intrinsic evil and an infamy. It is not, however, an infamy because it is an intrinsic evil. In my view, it is essential to keep these two concepts distinct. Some skeptics might ask why: if the "prophetic" use of the term "intrinsic evil" is helpful in eradicating entrenched social practices such as abortion, why not use it to that end? In my view, such a strategy wrongly reduces the Catholic moral tradition to a set of merely rhetorical tools when it should more properly be seen as a guide for substantive moral decision making. Effective rhetoric, of course, has an important place, particularly in the public square. Yet the rhetorical sense of this specific term should not be so widely separated from its substantive meaning, particularly when other rhetorically effective possibilities are ready at hand. Vatican II's language of "infamy" and "disgrace" already provides more than ample material for the rhetoric of prophetic condemnation of practices harmful to the common good, without compromising the meaning of a key term from the Catholic moral tradition. Honoring these distinctions also helps us to think more broadly about the range of social practices to which the term "intrinsic evil" applies, as exemplified by the range of practices *Gaudium et spes* identifies as deeply destructive to the common good.

CONCLUSION

In this chapter I considered the claim that some issues, such as abortion and same-sex marriage, deserve priority attention from voters because they deal with intrinsically evil acts. I have argued that the technical meaning of the term does not support such a claim, although the emerging prophetic meaning may do so. In my view, it would be a mistake for the tradition to jettison the technical meaning of the term. Eliminating the technical meaning, moreover, will not eliminate political debate. Like the use of the clearly prophetic word "infamies" in *Gaudium et spes*, the prophetic use of "intrinsic evil" is meant to start an urgent discussion among people of goodwill about grave injustices in the world. Labeling an act as an "intrinsic evil" does not provide a detailed blueprint for action. Identifying infamies is one thing; deciding upon a strategy to deal with them is something altogether more difficult, as I showed in more detail in chapters 2 and 3.

NOTES

This chapter has its seeds in M. Cathleen Kaveny, "Intrinsic Evil and Political Responsibility," *America*, October 27, 2008, 15–19.

1. See, e.g., Bishop Kevin Farrell and Bishop Kevin Vann, "Joint Statement to the Faithful of the Dioceses of Dallas and Fort Worth," October 8, 2008, *Catholic Pro-Life Committee*, www.prolifedallas.org/pages/Joint_Statement: "Forming Consciences for Faithful Citizenship clearly teaches that not all issues have the same moral equivalence. Some issues involve 'intrinsic evils'; that is, they can never under any circumstance or condition be morally justified. Preeminent among these intrinsic evils are legalized abortion, the promotion of same sex unions and 'marriages,' repression of religious liberty, as well as public policies permitting euthanasia, racial discrimination or destructive human embryonic stem cell research." As I will describe later, their articulation of "intrinsic evil" owes a great deal to the Catholic Answers voting guide, which stresses "non-negotiable issues." See also Archbishop John Naumann and Bishop Robert Finn, "Our Moral Responsibility as Catholic Citizens," *Catholic Diocese of Kansas City-St. Joseph*, September 12, 2008, www.diocese-kcsj.org/_docs/JointPastoral-Moral-Cons-09-08.pdf; and "Blunt Statements for US Bishops: Voting for Pro-Abortion Candidates is Gravely Sinful," *CatholicCulture.org*, November 4, 2008, www.catholicculture.org/news/features/index.cfm?recnum=60228. This emphasis on "intrinsic evils" continued into the 2010 election season; see, e.g., "Election Year Questions and Answers," *Kansas Catholic Conference*, www.kscathconf.org/wp-content/uploads/2010/07/Election-Year-Questions-Answers.pdf.

2. George Weigel, "Pro-Life Catholics for Obama," *Newsweek*, October 14, 2008, www.thedailybeast.com/newsweek/2008/10/13/pro-life-catholics-for-obama.html; Michael Novak, "Catholics for Obama?" *American Enterprise Institute for Public Policy Research*, August 8, 2008, www.aei.org/article/28445.

3. Thomas Aquinas, *Summa theologica*, 3 vols., trans. Fathers of the English Dominican Province (New York: Benziger Bros., 1948), I-II, qq. 6–21. Aquinas himself did not use the term "intrinsic evil" (*intrinsece malum*) in developing his action theory; however, he provided the framework within which the term would be developed by later moralists. For examinations of the development of the concept, see James Murtagh, *Intrinsic Evil: An Examination of This Concept and Its Place in Current Discussions on Absolute Moral Norms* (Rome: Tipografia di Patrizio Graziani, 1973); and John F. Dedek, *Intrinsic Evil: The Invention of an Idea* (Elk Grove, IL: St. Julian, 1977). According to Dedek, the concept originated with Durandus of St. Pourçain, OP, (d. 1332), a critic of Aquinas.

4. The Catholic moral tradition is often called "casuistical" because of its focus on specific cases and controversies. This tradition has largely disappeared after Vatican II. In my judgment, however, it has great value; it ought to be retrieved, reformed, and revived rather than left behind. See M. Cathleen Kaveny, "The Marginalization of Casuistry," in *The Crisis of Authority in Catholic Modernity*, ed. Michael J. Lacey and Francis Oakley, 225–58 (Oxford: Oxford University Press, 2011).

5. Compare Aquinas, *Summa theologica*, I-II, q. 18, arts. 2–4 with *Catechism of the Catholic Church*, 2nd ed. (Washington, DC: US Catholic Conference, 2000), para. 1755.

6. Aquinas considers this example; see *Summa theologica*, I-II, q. 18, art. 4., ob. 3 and reply.

7. Pope John Paul II, *Veritatis splendor* (*The Splendor of Truth*) (1993), para. 78.

8. The Catholic moral tradition was forged in the process of providing manuals to assist priests in hearing confessions. For a good history of this tradition, see John Mahoney, *The Making of Moral Theology: A Study of the Roman Catholic Tradition* (New York: Oxford University Press, 1989). A point of commonality between the "proportionalists" (e.g., Richard McCormick, SJ, and Charles Curran) and the "new natural lawyers" (e.g., Germain Grisez, John Finnis) is a dissatisfaction with the physicalist way in which the manualist tradition defined the object of an act. A good way to begin to see the difficulties involved in specifying the object of an intrinsically evil act is by examining the different definitions of "lying" in the first and second editions of the *Catechism of the Catholic Church*. The first edition (1994) defined lying as "to speak or act against the truth in order to lead into error someone who has the right to know the truth." The second edition, based upon the official Latin text (1997), defined it as "to speak or act against the truth in order to lead someone into error" (para. 2483; see also corresponding pages in 2508). For reflections on lying from different perspectives, see Charles E. Curran, *The Catholic Moral Tradition Today: A Synthesis* (Washington, DC: Georgetown University Press, 1999), 155–64; and John Finnis, *Aquinas* (Oxford: Oxford University Press, 1999), 154–63.

9. John Paul II, *Veritatis splendor*, para. 80.

10. *Catechism of the Catholic Church*, para. 2357. Not every act that foreseeably results in infertility is "contraception" (e.g., a hysterectomy to remove a cancerous uterus). The purpose of the act must be to deprive the sexual act of its life-giving potential in order to qualify.

11. See, e.g., Pope Paul VI, *Humane vitae* (*Of Human Life*) (1968), para. 14.

12. The Catholic tradition's position on lying is deeply indebted to St. Augustine, who wrote two treatises on the subject: *De mendacio* (395) and *Contra mendacium* (420). For a contemporary discussion of the morality of lying along Thomistic lines, see Alexander Pruss, "Lying and Speaking Your Interlocutor's Language," *Thomist* 63, no. 3 (1999): 439–53; and Lawrence Dewan, OP, "St. Thomas, Lying, and Venial Sin," *Thomist* 61 (1997): 279–300.

13. In response to this objection, many religious believers have invoked divine punishment, claiming that divine omniscience and omnipotence will ensure that evildoers will stand before the bar of justice in the next life, if not this one. Certainly, the idea of divine judgment and punishment are central to the Christian tradition. It is important, however, not to interpret those terms too extrinsically. Unlike in the human realm, divine punishment is not the infliction of an unpleasant restriction or sensation that can be removed just as easily as it was applied. In theological terms, the ultimate punishment is being intrinsically unable to perceive and appreciate God's presence. By committing sinful acts, persons wound themselves, thereby rendering themselves

less able to bear the power and beauty of that presence. According to Aquinas, God's grace is necessary for human beings to enjoy divine presence in the first place; our natural abilities do not render us "strong enough" to do so on our own. Such grace is doubly necessary in the case of human sin. Thanks to the sacrificial love of Jesus Christ, divine grace heals our self-inflicted wounds before going on to strengthen us beyond our natural capacities to appreciate God's presence. According to Aquinas, grace is actually a type of divinization; we can be "friends" with God only if God communicates some share of divine likeness to us so that we have a common basis for the friendship. Aquinas, *Summa theologica*, I-II, q. 109.

14. The resurgence of virtue theory in both theological and philosophical contexts in the last few decades has led to a voluminous literature. Key elements in the discussion include: Elizabeth Anscombe's classic 1958 essay, "Modern Moral Philosophy," in *The Collected Philosophical Papers of G. E. M. Anscombe, Ethics* (Oxford: Blackwell, 1981), 3:26–42; Alasdair MacIntyre, *After Virtue*, 3rd ed. (Notre Dame, IN: University of Notre Dame, 2007), 69; and Stanley Hauerwas, *Character and the Christian Life: A Study in Theological Ethics* (San Antonio, TX: Trinity University, 1975). A helpful, although somewhat dated, survey of the literature can be found in William Spohn, SJ, "Notes on Moral Theology 1991: The Return of Virtue Ethics," *Theological Studies* 53 (1992): 60–75. The degree to which the contemporary resurgence of virtue theory among Christian ethicists is, in fact, an accurate reflection of Aquinas's work is an interesting question. See Thomas F. O'Meara, OP, "Virtues in the Theology of Thomas Aquinas," *Theological Studies* 58 (1997): 254–85. See also Alasdair MacIntyre, "The Return to Virtue Ethics," in *The Twenty-Fifth Anniversary of Vatican II: A Look Back and a Look Ahead*, ed. Russell E. Smith (Braintree, MA: The Pope John Center, 1990), 239–49. James Keenan, SJ, has dedicated considerable energy to articulating more broadly accessible accounts of the virtues in Christian life. See, e.g., Daniel J. Harrington, SJ, and James F. Keenan, SJ, *Jesus and Virtue Ethics: Building Bridges between New Testament Studies and Moral Theology* (Lanham, MD: Sheed & Ward, 2002).

15. This is not to say, of course, that moral theologians have not vigorously disputed how to describe particular intrinsic acts (e.g., lying, adultery), or even whether particular acts are rightly named intrinsically evil at all (e.g., contraception). In at least one case, the Church has decided that an act previously treated as intrinsically evil is not so. Usury, defined as lending money at interest, was long considered by the tradition as always wrong. Now, its wrongness depends upon the circumstances, including the interest rate, the relative needs and resources of lender and borrower, and the nature of the economic system. For an account of how Church teaching has developed on moral issues, see John T. Noonan Jr., *A Church That Can and Cannot Change* (Notre Dame, IN: University of Notre Dame Press, 2005). For reflections that take into account the shift over time, see John T. Noonan Jr., "Experience and the Development of Moral Doctrine," in *Proceedings of the Fifty-Fourth Annual Convention* (Washington, DC: Catholic Theological Society of America, 1999), 54:43–56; and M. Cathleen Kaveny, "A Response to John T. Noonan Jr.," in *Proceedings of the Fifty-Fourth Annual Convention* (Washington, DC: Catholic Theological Society of America, 1999), 54:57–64.

16. Alasdair MacIntyre, "Theology, Ethics, and the Ethics of Medicine and Health Care: Comments on Papers by Novak, Mouw, Rach, Cahill, and Hartt," *Journal of Medicine and Philosophy* 4 (1979): 437.

17. Aquinas follows Aristotle in dividing lies into the three categories of officious, jocose, and malicious—subsuming Augustine's identification of eight kinds of lies in the *Contra mendacium.*

18. Aquinas, *Summa theologica*, II-II, q. 110, art 4.

19. "As regards the end in view, a lie may be contrary to charity, through being told with the purpose of injuring God, and this is always a mortal sin, for it is opposed to religion; or in order to injure one's neighbor, in his person, his possessions or his good name, and this also is a mortal sin, since it is a mortal sin to injure one's neighbor, and one sins mortally if one has merely the intention of committing a mortal sin. But if the end intended be not contrary to charity, neither will the lie, considered under this aspect, be a mortal sin, as in the case of a jocose lie, where some little pleasure is intended, or in an officious lie, where the good also of one's neighbor is intended. Accidentally a lie may be contrary to charity by reason of scandal or any other injury resulting therefrom: and thus again it will be a mortal sin, for instance if a man were not deterred through scandal from lying publicly." Ibid.

20. While regarding them as "fruits from the same tree," Pope John Paul II also acknowledges their differences: "Certainly, from the moral point of view contraception and abortion are specifically different evils: the former contradicts the full truth of the sexual act as the proper expression of conjugal love, while the latter destroys the life of a human being; the former is opposed to the virtue of chastity in marriage, the latter is opposed to the virtue of justice and directly violates the divine commandment 'You shall not kill'." Pope John Paul II, *Evangelium vitae* (*The Gospel of Life*) (1995), para. 13.

21. See, e.g., the *Catechism of the Catholic Church*, para. 2352.

22. See, e.g., John Courtney Murray, SJ, "Memo to Cardinal Cushing on Contraception Legislation," Woodstock Theological Center Library, http://woodstock.georgetown .edu/library/murray/1965f.htm; and John M. Finnis, "Law, Morality, and 'Sexual Orientation,'" *Notre Dame Law Review* 69 (1994): 1049–76. While I agree with his conclusion, I also think Murray's argument that contraception is a matter of "private morality" is too indebted to liberal legal theory and not enough to Aquinas.

23. Aquinas, *Summa theologica*, I-II, q. 96, art. 2.

24. More broadly, the way in which some law enforcement assignments adversely affect the character of the agents who take them would be an interesting subject for ethical and sociological analysis. Even those who oppose the constitutional jurisprudence of *Roe v. Wade* are willing to make some distinctions regarding its precedents. It is possible to support the right to privacy as articulated in *Griswold v. Connecticut*, 381 US 479 (1965) while opposing its extension in *Eisenstadt v. Baird*, 405 US 438 (1972). *Griswold* struck down a law prohibiting the use of contraceptives even by married couples; as Justice Douglas noted in the majority opinion, enforcing this law would involve invading the privacy of the marital bedroom. At issue in *Eisenstadt*, by contrast, was a law prohibiting the sale of contraceptives to unmarried people; enforcing this law would not involve a similar invasion of the home. See, e.g., Finnis, "Law, Morality, and 'Sexual Orientation,'" 1076.

25. The mental state required for the crime of murder is somewhat confused. The Model Penal Code (1962, revised 1981), developed by the American Law Institute as a template for the standardization and revision of state criminal law, defines murder not only as purposefully killing another human being but also as knowingly killing "under circumstances manifesting extreme indifference to the value of human life." Model Penal Code, § 210.2 (1). The second prong of the definition resonates with the common law category of "depraved heart murder," in which the defendant exhibits a "callous disregard for human life." For a dated but still helpful analysis, see Ann Alpers, "Criminal Act or Palliative Care? Prosecutions involving the Care of the Dying," *Journal of Law, Medicine & Ethics* 26 (1998): 308–31. Prosecuting someone who killed violently is probably easier than trying to convict a person who dispenses an overdose of lethal medication already prescribed to the dying patient. In May 1985, seventy-six-year-old Roswell Gilbert was convicted by a Florida jury of murdering his wife by firing two bullets into her brain. Gilbert claimed he was euthanizing his wife, who suffered from Alzheimer's disease and a painful bone condition. The governor granted him clemency after he served five years of a twenty-five-year sentence without the possibility of parole. See his obituary, "Roswell Gilbert, 85, Who Killed His Ill Wife and Went to Prison," *New York Times*, September 8, 1994, D19.

26. See, e.g., paragraph 4 of Farrell and Vann, "Joint Statement to the Faithful": "But let us be clear: issues of prudential judgment are not morally equivalent to issues involving intrinsic evils. No matter how right a given candidate is on any of these issues, it does not outweigh a candidate's unacceptable position in favor of an intrinsic evil such as abortion or the protection of 'abortion rights.'"

27. This approach was spearheaded by Catholic Answers, a group engaged in Catholic apologetics. See their *Voting Guide for Serious Catholics*, 2nd ed. (El Cajon, CA: Catholic Answers Action, 2006), 5: "Thus, to the greatest extent possible, Catholics must avoid voting for any candidate who intends to support programs or laws that are intrinsically evil." The guide's identification of intrinsically evil actions was highly selective: abortion, euthanasia, embryonic stem cell research, cloning, and same-sex marriage. See also ibid., 15.

28. The phrase was used by numerous commentators on Catholic blogs around the time of the 2004 and 2008 presidential elections. See, e.g., "Morally Justifying Immoral Voting Behavior," *The Cranky Conservative*, February 25, 2008, http://crankycon.politicalbear .com/2008/02/25/morally-justifying-immoral-voting-behavior/. Its most prominent use was by Michael J. Sheridan, bishop of Colorado Springs, in an interview with the *New York Times*. See Laurie Goodstein, "Bishop Would Deny Rite for Defiant Catholic Voters," *New York Times*, May 14, 2004, A16. Goodstein writes, "In the interview, the bishop said that his aim was to clarify the standards for Catholic voters and that he hoped they applied them in their choice of candidates. He said that on the 'basic moral teachings of the church,' there is no 'wiggle room.'" See also Religious News Service, "Catholic Democrats Scolded on Abortion," *Washington Post*, March 11, 2006, www .washingtonpost.com/wp-dyn/content/article/2006/03/10/AR2006031001845.html.

29. According to the National Highway Traffic Safety Administration, in 2009 there were 13,636 Americans who were murder victims, while in that same year, 30,797 Americans died in motor vehicle crashes. National Highway Traffic Safety Administration,

Fatality Analysis Reporting System, http://www-fars.nhtsa.dot.gov/Main/index.aspx. A 2005 report estimated that one-third of all traffic fatalities are related to speeding. Cejun Liu, Chou-Lin Chen, Rajesh Subramanian, and Dennis Utter, "Analysis of Speeding-Related Fatal Motor Vehicle Traffic Crashes," National Highway Traffic Safety Administration, Technical report DOT HS 809 839, June 2005, http://www-nrd.nhtsa.dot.gov/Pubs/809839.pdf.

30. USCCB, *The Challenge of Peace: God's Promise and Our Response* (Washington, DC: United States Catholic Conference, 1983), paras. 85–100.

31. Ibid., paras. 101–10.

32. In contrast, while the *Roe* regime permits abortion, one cannot say that the abortions themselves are carried out in the public name and interest. They are state-licensed private killing, not state-authorized killing, as in the case of war.

33. In 2008 1.21 million abortions were performed; approximately nine out of ten occurred in the first twelve weeks of pregnancy. Guttmacher Institute, "Facts on Induced Abortion in the United States," May 2011, www.guttmacher.org/pubs/fb_induced_abortion.html.

34. While *Roe v. Wade*, 410 US 113 (1973), described abortion as a constitutionally protected "right," *Planned Parenthood v. Casey*, 505 US 833 (1992) categorized it as a "liberty interest," a term that on its face is more consistent with the Court's refusal to recognize a woman's claim on the state to pay for it. See *Harris v. McRae*, 448 US 297 (1980).

35. Rachel K. Jones and Megan L. Kavanaugh, "Changes in Abortion Rates between 2000 and 2008 and Lifetime Incidence of Abortion," *Obstetrics & Gynecology* 117 (2011): 1358–66.

36. Abraham Joshua Heschel, *The Prophets* (New York: Perennial Classics, 2001), xxix.

37. M. Cathleen Kaveny, "Prophetic Discourse in the Public Square," 2008 Santa Clara Lecture, Ignatian Center for Jesuit Education, Santa Clara University, Santa Clara, CA, November 11, 2008. http://www.scu.edu/ignatiancenter/events/lectures/archives/upload/w-09_Kaveny_Lecture-2-pd-2.pdf.

38. See Perry Miller, *The New England Mind: From Colony to Province* (Cambridge, MA: Belknap Press of Harvard University Press, 1981).

39. See, e.g., James Darsey, *The Prophetic Tradition and Radical Rhetoric in America* (New York: New York University Press, 1997).

40. John Paul II, *Evangelium vitae*.

41. John L. Allen Jr., "Synod: Interview with Cardinal Francis George," *National Catholic Reporter*, October 15, 2008, http://ncronline.org/node/12198.

42. "All the News That's Fit to Print . . . Sort of—Transcript of *New York Times* interview with Archbishop Charles J. Chaput, OFM Cap.," Archdiocese of Denver, October 6, 2004, www.archden.org/archbishop_writings_discourses/addresses/addresses_Oct06_04_NYTimesInterview.pdf, 6.

43. Pope Benedict XVI, "Address at a Meeting on Family and Life Issues in Latin America," Vatican, December 3, 2005, para. 5.

44. John Paul II, *Veritatis splendor*, para. 80 (citations omitted).

45. *Gaudium et spes* (*Pastoral Constitution on the Church in the Modern World*) (1965), para. 27.

46. "haec omnia et alia huiusmodi probra quidem sunt, . . . " Ibid.

CHAPTER 10

Voting and Complicity
in Wrongdoing

I N CHAPTER 8 I SKETCH A MORAL ACCOUNT of the act of voting in the context of the American political system. In my view, the crucial aspect of most
American elections is that they present voters with choices about candidates,
not choices about issues. Consequently, the voters' main task is to evaluate
the various candidates in terms of their potential to serve the common good
with competence and integrity. This is not to say that substantive issues do not
matter. In casting their ballots, however, voters must not evaluate issues merely
in the abstract but rather in concrete relation to the way in which those issues
intersect with the particular candidates running for office.

In chapter 9 I address one possible objection to the moral framework for
voting that I outline in chapter 8. In this chapter I continue my analysis by
examining a second objection to that framework. It charges that citizens who
vote for politicians with morally flawed positions on key issues are complicit
in the wrongs done by such politicians after they assume office. Framed in the
technical terms of Catholic moral theology, this objection charges that such
voters are wrongfully "cooperating with evil" by facilitating the wrongdoings
of those holding political office.

A reader may reasonably assume that this "cooperation with evil" objection
is nothing more than a slight verbal variation on the "intrinsic evil" objection
considered in chapter 8. Indeed, from a purely rhetorical perspective, both
terms convey a deep and somewhat amorphous sense of wrongness, particularly
to those who are not well versed in the manualist tradition of pre–Vatican
II Catholic moral theology. Both terms have in fact been used by American

Catholics to condemn their coreligionists who vote for candidates that support the right to abortion or same-sex marriage. Some commentators have even combined the labels "intrinsic evil" and "cooperation with evil" in an apparent effort to augment the gravity of their condemnation. For example, in an incident that was widely publicized in both the religious and secular press immediately after the 2008 presidential election, a South Carolina priest bluntly told the members of his congregation who had voted for Obama to refrain from presenting themselves for communion. The angry tone of prophetic indictment permeates the letter that Rev. Jay Scott Newman wrote to his parishioners: "Voting for a pro-abortion politician when a plausible pro-life alternative exists constitutes material cooperation with intrinsic evil, and those Catholics who do so place themselves outside of the full communion of Christ's Church and under the judgment of divine law. Persons in this condition should not receive Holy Communion until and unless they are reconciled to God in the Sacrament of Penance, lest they eat and drink their own condemnation."[1]

While rhetorically effective, this concatenation of "intrinsically evil" and "cooperation with evil" is conceptually unsound. It mistakenly implies that the two qualities, when added together, yield some sort of Total Moral Monstrosity Quotient. A compelling appeal, to be sure—but it is just not true. As I outline in the previous chapter, the term "intrinsic evil" only indicates *why* it is wrong for an agent to perform a particular action; it says nothing at all about the gravity of the wrongful act at issue.

The definition of "intrinsic evil" supplies part, but only part, of the answer to a first-order moral question: how do we determine what sorts of actions are right (or wrong) for a human person to do (or to refrain from doing)?

In contrast, the term "cooperation with evil" refers to a second-order moral question. Once we have discerned that it is wrong for one person to perform a particular act (because of motive, circumstances, or object), we frequently then need to ponder a second question: is it morally permissible for another person to act in a way that furthers the first person's wrongdoing? This is a second-order question because it kicks in only when the primary agent's action is indeed wrongful. In fact, a discussion of cooperation with evil cannot get off the ground unless both parties to the discussion are in accord about the wrongfulness of the primary agent's act. Suppose two friends are conversing about whether they should give a third friend a ride to the store to buy a carton of cigarettes. Unless the pair agrees that it is wrong for their friend to smoke, there will be no discussion of cooperation with evil, for anyone who considers smoking to be entirely a matter of personal preference is unlikely to appreciate the moral dilemma in giving a friend a lift to buy cigarettes.

Because "intrinsic evil" and "cooperation with evil" refer to very different problems within the framework of Catholic moral theology, their impact upon the ethical analysis of voting must be examined separately. In my view, such an examination yields different ultimate verdicts about the two concepts. As I argue in chapter 9, the traditional, technical use of "intrinsic evil" offers very little help to the Catholic voter weighing her obligations at the ballot box. Likewise, as a technical concept, "cooperation with evil" is also relatively useless to voters. It does, however, point to a real moral problem insufficiently addressed in Catholic moral theology: how to deal with wrongdoing that does not have one identifiable large, single cause but thousands, perhaps millions, of small causes, each of which is insignificant when taken by itself, but many of which are decisive when taken together.

In the first section of this chapter I set the stage with an overview of the problem of complicity, both in more general terms and within the framework of Catholic moral theology. In the second section I focus on the topic of voting, showing why the concept of cooperation with evil is inadequate to address the questions of complicity that voting raises. In the concluding section I highlight some of the areas in which Catholic moral theology and social thought need to be developed to address the moral challenges of living in a pluralistic liberal democracy and an increasingly globalized culture.

COMPLICITY AND COOPERATION WITH EVIL: A BRIEF PRIMER

When is it wrong to facilitate or to make use of the wrongful acts of another? The problem of complicity is one of the most difficult and pervasive questions in the moral life. Should a low-level drug dealer in Arizona be responsible for the far more numerous and grave illegal acts committed by his suppliers in California? This and related questions are addressed by the criminal law through doctrines such as accessory liability and conspiracy.[2] Should a corporation be civilly responsible for the harm caused intentionally or negligently by its employees? This question is addressed in tort law within the framework of *respondeat superior*, among other doctrines.[3] The twentieth century has presented ample cause for philosophers, sociologists, and anthropologists to dig into questions of how broadly to attribute responsibility for horrendous acts physically committed by (relatively) few people. To take the most obvious example of the Holocaust or other instances of mass killing or genocide, these experts ask how ordinary people, by a series of more or less ordinary acts or omissions, can facilitate monstrous evil.[4]

In Christian theology the broadest framework for contemplating the question of complicity with evil is the doctrine of original sin.[5] The venerable *New England Primer*, the first reading textbook used in the American colonies, illustrated the first line of the alphabet with the line "In Adam's Fall We sinned all," which nicely captures the dual nature of original sin: all living human beings are complicit in Adam's original sin by endorsing it, activating it, and extending it in the commission of our own sins.[6] At the same time, our first parents are complicit in our sins by opening a weakness in the human soul to act in ways that violate the requirements of human flourishing. Sin spreads; it seems to be easily transmitted; it presents itself as an inescapable and lamentable aspect of the human condition. In our own era, sexual abuse furnishes an example of the phenomenon. A number of those people who are abused as children grow up to be become abusers themselves, engendering a self-perpetuating, destructive social pattern.[7] And so we should understand that the biblical narrative of Adam, Eve, and the serpent highlights through metaphor the ubiquity, seeming contagiousness, and apparent senselessness of sin.[8]

Some contemporary Christian thinkers, such as Reinhold Niebuhr, grapple with sin's pervasiveness by locating it largely outside the individual and more in the society as a whole.[9] While the idea of collective wrongdoing has permeated modern Catholic social teaching, recent magisterial documents have been wary of overly expansive accounts of social sin on the grounds they tend to minimize the fundamental nature of sin as a personal act.[10] As Christine Firer Hinze observes, "undergirding this discussion of social sin is a Catholic anthropology that locates moral responsibility in persons, and an implicit social theory which, despite a penchant for images of organic unity, remains 'actionist' rather than 'structurist': groups never exert agency completely apart from the intentions and decisions of members."[11]

This anthropology and social theory is consonant with the particular context in which Catholic moral theology found its home for centuries—the context of the sacrament of penance.[12] The sacrament requires individual penitents to confess particular sins, identified according to both number and species, to a priest, who acts *in persona Christi*. In addition to absolution, the priest-confessor is obliged to issue a penance that serves as both punishment and medicinal remedy for the penitent. From the Council of Trent until the Second Vatican Council, Catholic moral theology largely developed around facilitating the practice of sacramental confession. Seminary professors wrote "manuals" that enabled confessors to judge the nature and gravity of the acts committed by penitents—and even to assess whether the acts confessed were sinful at all. Because individuals were required to personally confess each particular sin that they committed, manualist moral theology tended to be both individualistic and particularistic.[13]

Naturally enough, this focus exerted significant influence upon the development of the framework for analyzing cooperation with evil, which is frequently defined as "concurrence with another person in a sinful act."[14] More specifically, questions falling under the rubric of cooperation with evil are often framed in terms of whether it is morally permissible for one individual—the cooperator—intentionally or knowingly to contribute to the wrongful act of another individual—the primary agent. Not surprisingly, the types of cases addressed by the manuals over the years reflect the realities of everyday life in the time and place of their various authors. The most famous cooperation case addressed by the magisterium is whether a manservant can carry the ladder or open the window so that his master can enter the second-floor bedroom of a virgin in order to rape her.[15] In more recent times, questions considered by manualists include whether a cab driver can deliver a customer to a house of prostitution, whether a head-of-household can work at a munitions plant making weapons of mass destruction, and whether a physician or a counselor can refer a patient for an abortion.

As these examples suggest, many (although not all) of the cases involve workers struggling to reconcile their consciences with the demands of their workplace, a struggle that may be more urgent because of the need to support minor children.[16] The confessors hearing these cases understood the difficulty faced by many of their penitents; on the one hand, losing a job meant losing a livelihood and the ability to fulfill family obligations while, on the other, committing a mortal sin risked the loss of eternal happiness. To instruct such persons to avoid all cooperation with evil, just to be on the safe side, would be wrongly dismissive of their positive obligations to act in order to fulfill their role-related responsibilities.

The Catholic moral tradition has developed an elaborate, technical matrix for evaluating cooperation with evil in order to take due account of the complexity of these situations.[17] The matrix is not a computer program; it is not meant to generate undebatable answers to what are undeniably complicated questions, as James Keenan has repeatedly pointed out. Rather, its function is to illuminate some of the salient issues that potential cooperators should consider in evaluating the moral status of their actions.

Most crucial is whether the contribution to the wrongdoing is intentional; in other words, whether the cooperator actually intends, either as an end in itself or as a means to some other end, the wrongdoing designed by the principal agent. The tradition calls such intentional furtherance of the illicit activity of another "formal cooperation"; precisely because it involves intentional evildoing on the part of the cooperator, it is never permissible.

While formal cooperation is always prohibited, the permissibility of material cooperation is determined on a case-by-case basis and depends upon a variety of factors. Material cooperation involves a situation in which the cooperator foresees but does not intend that his or her action will facilitate the wrongful action of the primary agent. The factors used to evaluate material cooperation include the following:

- Does the act of the cooperator overlap physically with the wrongful act of the primary agent?[18]
- If the acts do not overlap physically, how much distance is there between the two acts in terms of time, space, and causal connection?[19]
- Will the wrongful act take place anyway, regardless of whether the cooperator goes forward with his or her act of material cooperation?[20]
- What loss will be avoided or gain achieved by cooperating?
- How grave is the wrongful act in question?
- Is the cooperation an isolated act or an ongoing pattern of involvement?
- Will the cooperation unavoidably cause "scandal" by leading other people to mistakenly think the primary agent's wrongdoing is really nothing to worry about?[21]

In the decades following the Second Vatican Council, the manualist tradition of moral theology largely fell into desuetude and, with it, the traditional matrix for analyzing problems of cooperation with evil. In the early 1990s, however, that framework was retrieved and refurbished to address a new set of problems. Faced with new financial pressures, Catholic health care facilities were forced to consider mergers or other types of affiliations with non-Catholic partners in order to survive. Some of these potential partners performed procedures prohibited by Catholic teaching, such as sterilizations or abortions. Under what circumstances were such partnerships morally proper?[22] Addressing this question required extending the cooperation with evil matrix in at least three ways.

First, the matrix needed to apply not merely to individual cooperators but also to corporate agents. Understandably enough, the manualists had not devoted extensive consideration to this matter since sacramental confession is an individual matter in which each person takes responsibility for his or her own sins.

Second, considering the cases of hospitals required more attention to the good that could be achieved by cooperation, not merely the evil that could be avoided. As I noted earlier, most individuals presenting with cooperation problems face the prospect of serious loss to themselves and their family members if they decide not to cooperate for moral reasons. In contrast, a corporate agent cannot suffer analogous direct loss, even if failure to cooperate means going out of business. However, a corporate agent can lose the opportunity to do good works that may be essential to the vulnerable populations it serves.

Third, the background context had changed, substantially increasing the danger of scandal. More specifically, most of the cooperation cases considered by the manuals assumed a society in which there was substantial agreement about the first-order moral judgments involved, such as the wrongness of fornication, sterilization, or abortion. In contrast, in an increasingly pluralistic American context, those first-order judgments were highly contested, even among Catholics. Consequently, any sort of contribution, no matter how remote, by an identifiably Catholic cooperator could more easily lead people to conclude that these actions were not really morally objectionable.

Ultimately, most American theologians—and most bishops—judged that the matrix of cooperation with evil could be stretched to cover cases of institutional cooperation centrally, but not exclusively, involving Catholic health care facilities. After some discussion (and some controversy), the bishops revised the *Ethical and Religious Directives for Catholic Health Care Services* to address the emerging questions involved in corporate affiliations. On the one hand, these revisions acknowledged the positive benefit provided by Catholic health care as a manifestation of the corporal and spiritual works of mercy; on the other hand, they noted the potential for scandal involved in becoming too entangled in practices prohibited by Church teaching but increasingly acceptable in society at large.[23]

One new provision, ERD 70, stated that "Catholic health care organizations are not permitted to engage in immediate material cooperation in actions that are intrinsically immoral, such as abortion, euthanasia, assisted suicide, and direct sterilization." I suspect that this directive has furnished a ready springboard for more sweeping public statements condemning cooperation in intrinsically evil acts as never permissible—statements of the sort I quoted at the beginning of this chapter. The difficulty with these statements is that they make a general moral principle out of a directive that combines moral analysis and prudential judgment.

Note first that ERD 70 does not prohibit all cooperation with intrinsically evil acts; rather, it bars only immediate material cooperation, which is the technical term for instances of cooperation where the external act of the cooperator virtually merges with the external act of the wrongdoer. The manualists generally prohibited immediate material cooperation in any wrongful act, except in the case of duress. Why? Because, from an external perspective, the cooperator appears to be not merely cooperating but actually doing wrong.

Understandably enough, the manualists were too often captured by this external perspective. Their goal, after all, was to assist confessors who themselves approached their penitents externally as both judges and priests. Confessors had very little time to actually enter into the practical reasoning of those confessing in order to assess their actions from an internal point of view. Moreover, the manualists were writing manuals, not advanced treatises; they sought to provide their brethren in the trenches—who often were not well educated but were nonetheless responsible for the care of their parishioners' souls—with clear guidance on separating sinful from nonsinful actions. A situation of duress makes it abundantly clear to an external observer, such as a confessor, that the cooperator is not actually choosing to engage in wrongdoing. If the teller held at gunpoint opens the safe and turns over the money, she is clearly not executing her own act of theft but rather immediately materially cooperating with someone else's act.

While the motivation to restrict justifiable immediate material cooperation to cases of duress is understandable given the purposes of the manuals, the result is not philosophically justified. Provided that we use the correct theory of human action—a theory that focuses on the immediate and more remote purposes for which the agent is acting and that is not dominated by an externalist and physicalist account of the object of the act—we have no reason to limit justification for immediate material cooperation to duress alone. Other good reasons, such as protecting the common good from an immediate threat, can serve as sufficient justifications. For example, an undercover agent who pretends to buy state secrets from a rogue spy is not under any form of duress but is justifiably and immediately materially cooperating in the spy's act of treason.

Second, ERD 70 prohibits immediate material cooperation in intrinsically evil acts. Bearing in mind the technical definition of the latter term, do we really want to say that immediate material cooperation in intrinsically evil acts is by itself more troublesome than immediate material cooperation in acts that are not wrong by reason of motive or circumstance? No. The gravity of the wrongful act committed by the primary agent is far more important than the reason why it is wrong. That distinction also needs to be preserved in evaluating the moral permissibility of material cooperation in evil, even *immediate* material cooperation with evil. At the same time, the issue of immediate material cooperation in intrinsically evil acts only raises in a heightened fashion the more general question about immediate material cooperation: is the cooperator actually doing evil, rather than merely cooperating with it?

Third parties are more likely to be able to quickly identify intrinsically evil acts as wrong precisely because they do not need to first consider the agent's broader motive or other circumstances. While it is important to acknowledge this point, it is also essential not to make too much of it. Accurately identifying an intrinsically evil act does require understanding the object or immediate purpose of the act from the agent's point of view; it also demands an awareness of the circumstances that enter into defining the object of an intrinsically evil act. For example, one cannot judge whether a physician giving a large dose of morphine to a patient is committing the intrinsically evil act of "euthanasia" without first knowing whether he intends to shorten the patient's life or whether he merely foresees that consequence.

In light of these three observations, how do we understand the ERD 70's prohibition against Catholic health care services engaging in immediate material cooperation with intrinsically evil acts such as abortion, sterilization, or contraception?[24] The key is to remember that the document is a set of practical directives, not an academic treatise on moral theology. These directives are not meant to track a precise moral distinction; they are meant to provide clear institutional guidance. They are designed to address a situation in which Catholic health care institutions will be involved on a close and ongoing basis with other entities that do not completely share their values. The medical context affects both the content and interpretation of the directives. ERD 70, for example, is not concerned about the whole range of intrinsically evil acts but rather with those likely to be performed or requested in American hospitals: abortion, sterilization, and euthanasia. Moreover, in the American context, where the nature of these three acts as intrinsically evil is hotly contested, the bishops made the strategically understandable choice to prohibit Catholic health care facilities from engaging in immediate material cooperation with any of the three acts.

The danger of scandal—as well as the risk that the hospitals would too easily slip from cooperation to commission of such acts—can justify the bishops' decision to enact such a pragmatic prohibition. The prohibition cannot, however, legitimately be extended to articulate a general moral principle against immediate material cooperation in all intrinsically evil acts, or to all forms of material cooperation with abortion, euthanasia, or sterilization by all persons in all circumstances. More specifically, the prohibition does not stretch to encompass formulating a general moral principle against voting for a candidate who supports the legalization of intrinsically evil acts, as we will see in the following. The guidelines appropriately governing the behavior of Catholic health care facilities cannot be applied automatically to direct the behavior of Catholic citizens.

VOTING AND COOPERATION WITH EVIL

Some Catholics have claimed that abortion and a few other issues such as embryonic stem cell research and same-sex marriage deserve special consideration from voters because they involve intrinsic evils. After explicating the meaning of the term in traditional Catholic moral theology, I argue that the mere fact that an issue pertains to an intrinsic evil does not justify priority treatment from voters. Why, then, have some people claimed that it does? I suggest that their claim reveals an emerging prophetic use of the term "intrinsic evil." Consistent with the rhetoric of prophetic indictment used by American moral reformers since Puritan times, those who use the term this way direct the moral energies of all good-willed people to the issues that they highlight. Unfortunately, while this language of moral indictment effectively calls attention to entrenched wrongdoing, it utterly fails to offer practical guidance about how to address it. In other words, the mere use of the label "intrinsic evil" does nothing to inform voters about how to translate their attention into an effective program of change and reform. To put it another way, if every foreseen and foreseeable consequence of the act of voting rises to the level of a cooperation with evil problem, then virtually every other act an agent performs entails a similar cooperation with evil problem. Many, if not most, of our acts contribute in some attenuated way to the wrongdoing of others.

At some point Catholic moralists draw a line and speak not of cooperation with evil but of background conditions of original sin and human sociality. If we do not draw such a line, we will feed into an expanded account of human responsibility comparable to that endorsed by the most extreme utilitarians. For example, no one says that employers should use the cooperation with evil matrix to decide whether to pay their employees, who may use the money to fund seriously evil acts. Still less do we hear the claim that an emergency room doctor's decision about whether to save the life of a patient should turn upon an assessment of the patient's future risk of harm to others. An employer has a general obligation to pay his employees, and a physician has an obligation to cure her patients; we do not encourage employers or physicians to make case-by-case judgments of their actions on the basis of a cooperation with evil analysis.[25]

Like paying one's employees and caring for one's patients, a citizen's responsibility to vote is a role-related obligation. In my view, it is an obligation that sounds in justice. Voters have a duty to assess and select candidates in light of the criteria set forth in chapter 8. These candidates are likely very morally imperfect; some are even corrupt. Their newly acquired power will allow them to do some bad things. We do not generally apply a cooperation with evil matrix to hold physicians responsible for what patients foreseeably do with renewed health, or hold employers responsible for what employees foreseeably do with a paycheck. Why is it more appropriate to apply a cooperation with evil matrix to hold particular voters responsible for the morally unsavory laws and policies they foresee (but do not intend) will be supported by the candidates for whom they vote? I see no reason.

There are two additional threshold problems with treating voting as a classical cooperation with evil problem.[26] First, and most important, as the manualists recognize, there is a general presumption against avoiding situations involving cooperation with evil, a presumption that, frankly, would cut against anyone ever voting in most American elections. Indeed, some Catholic commentators have proclaimed that they will not vote at all to avoid enmeshing themselves in cooperation problems. Voting, however, is a duty, a positive obligation to further the well-being of one's community through the exercise of practical judgment about its future leadership. Abstaining from voting on the grounds of avoiding cooperation with evil seems worrisomely animated by the sectarian impulse that has long led certain branches of Christianity to withdraw from society with the goal of avoiding all contribution to or benefit from worldly corruption. This sensibility, however honorable in itself, is not in line with the main lines of Catholic political thought, which has always operated on the Augustinian assumption that the wheat and tares will grow together until the end of time.[27]

Second, if voting counts as cooperation with evil with respect to abortion rights, it also counts as cooperation with evil with respect to each and every wrong that we can predict office holders will perpetrate. The cooperation with evil matrix is indiscriminate; it does not pick out some wrongful actions as more worthy of its attention than others. How to run such a matrix in light of all the bad acts that a politician may engage in—factoring in questions of likelihood, causality, and degree of closeness—boggles the mind. To trigger a cooperation with evil problem, there ought to be a clear and direct causal line between the act of the cooperator, on the one hand, and the wrongful act of the primary agent, on the other.

Nevertheless, many American Catholic commentators and members of the clergy do believe it is appropriate to treat voting as a cooperation with evil problem, at least with respect to voting for pro-choice candidates. For example, in an interview with the *New York Times* on the eve of the 2004 election, Archbishop Charles Chaput stated that it was a sin to vote for a pro-choice candidate. "'If you vote this way, are you cooperating in evil?' he asked. 'And if you know you are cooperating in evil, should you go to confession? The answer is yes.'"²⁸ Raymond Burke, formerly the Archbishop of St. Louis and now Cardinal Prefect of the Supreme Tribunal of the Apostolic Signatura, has repeatedly made similar pronouncements. In a widely publicized interview with radical pro-life activist Randall Terry in 2009, Burke maintained, "And so if you, knowing that abortion is a grave crime against human life—is killing of an innocent, defenseless human life—and you vote for the candidate who says that he intends to make that more available—that practice of infanticide—you bear a responsibility. That is, you have cooperated in the election of this person into office, there's no question about it."²⁹

In making these claims, however, Chaput and Burke were being more rigorist than the current pope. When asked whether Catholics could vote for pro-choice politicians, Joseph Cardinal Ratzinger answered "sometimes" instead of "never." Like Chaput and Burke, Ratzinger does treat voting for a pro-choice politician as a cooperation with evil problem, which I find problematic. Nonetheless, his approach does not support either their analysis or their conclusions. In fact, Ratzinger's brief remarks can be used to illuminate the way in which the two American prelates significantly distort the traditional cooperation matrix in their efforts to muster unconditional Catholic opposition to pro-choice politicians.

At the end of a text considering the question whether Catholic politicians who were pro-choice should be denied communion, Ratzinger appended the following footnote, which applies cooperation with evil analysis in a very different way than the two American prelates: "[N.B. A Catholic would be guilty of formal cooperation in evil, and so unworthy to present himself for holy communion, if he were to deliberately vote for a candidate precisely because of the candidate's permissive stand on abortion and/or euthanasia. When a Catholic does not share a candidate's stand in favor of abortion and/ or euthanasia but votes for that candidate for other reasons, it is considered remote material cooperation, which can be permitted in the presence of proportionate reasons.]"³⁰

To unpack Ratzinger's statement, three points need to be kept in mind. First and foremost, in cases of material cooperation—unlike that of formal cooperation—the cooperators do not intend to further the wrongdoing of other agents. Instead, the cooperators act for their own legitimate ends, foreseeing but not intending that their action will facilitate that wrongdoing. However, material cooperators *do* foresee that facilitation, a fact that Chaput has not always clearly grasped. For example, in the full transcript of his interview with the *New York Times*, which is available on the Archdiocese of Denver's website, Chaput reflects: "Now, if the person does something wrong, are we responsible for that? Well, if we didn't know they were going to [do] something wrong, our participation is remote, but if we knew they were going to do something wrong and we approved of it, our responsibility would be really be close, even if we knew they were going to do something wrong and we voted for them for another reason, we would still be responsible in some ways."[31] Chaput here confuses the applicable analysis, wrongly suggesting that in order to qualify as remote cooperation, the cooperator can have no knowledge of the wrongful action to be committed by the primary agent. He also unhelpfully elides formal and material cooperation, rather than distinguishing them, as Ratzinger properly does.

Second, Ratzinger's footnote draws upon the traditional analysis holding that while formal cooperation is always prohibited, the permissibility of material cooperation is determined on a case-by-case basis. As I outlined in the previous section, that analysis is contingent upon a number of factors: Does the act of the cooperator overlap physically with the act of the wrongdoer? If not, how much distance is there between the two acts in terms of time, space, and causal connection? Will the wrongful act take place anyway, regardless of whether the cooperator goes forward with the act of material cooperation? Ratzinger's answer to these questions is what generates his conclusion that the act of voting is one of "remote material cooperation." Clearly, there is no physical overlap between a citizen's act of selecting a candidate for office and morally problematic acts of the office holder. In other words, we are not dealing with immediate material cooperation but instead with mediate material cooperation. Moreover, the act of voting is remote mediate material cooperation because it is extremely removed in terms of time, space, and causation from the wrongful act in question (enacting permissive abortion laws), and even further removed from the underlying wrong (the act of abortion itself). Finally, while Ratzinger does not say so, it is clearly free cooperation, not necessary cooperation, since no single voter can reverse the legalization of abortion or prevent any woman from having an abortion by refusing to vote. As Ratzinger indicated, remote material cooperation can be justified by "proportionate reasons." Just as remote material cooperation is the most attenuated type of cooperation, so the level of justification is the most lenient.

Some Catholics have insisted that nothing is proportionate to the great evil of abortion, functionally turning Ratzinger's qualified permission to vote for pro-choice politicians into an absolute prohibition. For example, in their joint pastoral letter, Archbishop Joseph Naumann of Kansas City, Kansas, and Bishop Robert Finn of Kansas City, Missouri, ask, "What could possibly be a proportionate reason for the more than 45 million children killed by abortion in the past 35 years? Personally, we cannot conceive of such a proportionate reason."[32] This approach, however, misapplies the criterion. In assessing proportionate reason, the focus should stay on the particular act of cooperation and its particular consequences; the analysis should not migrate to the global evil with which the act of cooperation is associated. We cannot simply set 1.5 million annual abortions on the negative side of the equation as if they are entirely caused by one elector's vote. Still less can we count abortions that occurred in the past as consequences of that sole vote. (Nor, for that matter, can we attribute moral responsibility for an unjust war to a single taxpayer's contribution to the public coffers.) A solitary vote for a pro-choice politician is not likely to make any significant difference to any particular woman's decision for or against abortion, given that abortion has long been a constitutionally protected right in this country. In fact, voters might well judge that voting for a candidate who supports a large safety net for mothers and dependent children would be a better way to increase the number of children brought to term, especially at the state level.[33]

In response, some pro-lifers might argue that while a vote for a pro-choice politician may not cause many new abortions, a vote for a pro-life politician, particularly a pro-life president, is the better way to prevent abortions. Even here, however, the causal chain is tenuous. A president may not have the opportunity to make appointments to the Supreme Court; even if he or she does, no president has control over how justices vote once they are seated. If the Supreme Court overturns *Roe v. Wade*, many states will simply legalize the procedure on their own. It is not at all clear that voting for a pro-life president will prevent abortions in any significant number, particularly if other executive policies make it harder for women facing crisis pregnancies to have children. These women can always travel to a state where abortion is legal.[34]

COOPERATION WITH EVIL AND THE COMMON GOOD

What, then, *would* count as proportionate reasons to justify voting for a pro-choice candidate, foreseeing but not intending to advance or maintain abortion rights? In my view, voters would be justified in selecting a pro-choice candidate if they discerned that such a candidate best served the common good in accordance with the framework I set forth in chapter 8. Cardinal Burke would doubtless respond by saying that there is no proportionate reason for voting for a pro-choice candidate if a pro-life candidate is available. He would, I think, have two interrelated reasons for this response, one based in his interpretation of Pope John Paul II and the other based in his conception of the common good. I will examine them in turn.

First, in a 2009 speech at the National Catholic Breakfast, Burke extended *Evangelium vitae's* moral analysis of legislators voting for pro-choice abortion legislation to cover the situation of citizens voting for pro-choice legislators. He writes:

> [Pope John Paul II] offers as an example the case of a legislator who has the possibility of voting for a law which would restrict the evil of procured abortion, even though it would not eradicate it completely. He concludes that the legislator could vote for the legislation, while his own opposition to procured abortion remains clear, for his vote does not in fact represent an illicit cooperation with an unjust law, but rather a legitimate and proper attempt to limit its evil aspects. [citation omitted] In an analogous manner, as voters, we are often faced with a choice among candidates who do not fully oppose unjust laws. In such a case, we must choose the candidate who will most limit the evil effects of unjust laws.[35]

But voting for a particular piece of legislation dedicated solely to abortion is not analogous to voting for a candidate for public office. The hypothetical law considered by the pope explicitly raises only one issue: abortion. Furthermore, it does not raise countervailing sets of concerns about abortion; in the pope's example, it appears that the law in question will effectively both restrict abortion and lower the incidence of the procedure. In contrast, as I argued in chapter 8, voting for a candidate for office involves making a judgment about a person who will have to handle many issues and balance many different sets of concerns. Moreover, a candidate's effect upon abortion rates is not necessarily congruent with his or her pro-choice policies; social and economic circumstances also interact with law to influence abortion rates.

Burke would doubtless immediately rejoin that voting for abortion legislation and voting more generally for a candidate are indeed analogous because abortion is, in our time, the single most important issue affecting the common good. His speech continues:

> But, there is no element of the common good, no morally good practice, which a candidate may promote and to which a voter may be dedicated, which could justify voting for a candidate who also endorses and supports the deliberate killing of the unborn, euthanasia or the recognition of a same-sex relationship as a legal marriage. The respect for the inviolable dignity of innocent human life and for the integrity of marriage and the family are so

fundamental to the common good that they cannot be subordinated to any other cause, no matter how good it may be.[36]

In my estimation, Burke's view of the common good is deeply inadequate. First, he assumes that the components of the common good are layered, or lexically ordered; that is, the first or "fundamental" level must be secured completely before we can turn to the second, and so on. His approach suggests, for example, that we must begin by ensuring that all human beings are legally protected to the fullest extent possible before going on to ensure that the community is protected against outside threats (for example, from terrorists) or inside disasters (such as flood or famine). But this cannot be the case. It was not wrong for the voters to prioritize fighting terrorism in 2001, nor was it wrong for them to prioritize strengthening the global economy in 2008. The government, furthermore, does not have to dedicate its funds to prosecuting every crime or feeding every hungry child before apportioning some money to art museums and colleges.

Burke's image for the common good appears to be like the layers of a rock wall. In my view, however, the elements of the common good are not simple block layers as much as they are an intricate herringbone pattern. Various elements, such as the status of the members of the community, their immediate physical needs for food and shelter, the education of the next generation, and the opportunity for meaningful work, must all be integrated tightly into the pattern for the wall to stand upright. All elements of the pattern must receive due attention, even if not full attention, in order to extend the wall through space and time.

In fact, all elements *have* received some attention in the American context. Human life is generally protected against attack in this country. Even unborn human life has some protections; it is not entirely vulnerable. The state does not force women to have abortions. No one can authorize the termination of a pregnancy but the woman who carries the fetus. There are stringent (if not absolute) protections against experimentation on fetuses, both within and outside the womb.[37] Abortions can be restricted or outlawed after viability. No matter how unjust the situation is, we are not in a Hobbesian state of nature that destroys the integrity and viability of the political community.

Burke might reply that I misunderstand his analogy; in his view, the political community is not like making a simple rock wall but like building a house. We need a good foundation before putting up the walls, good floors before moving in the furniture. The difficulty with this analogy is that our community is not building a house from scratch. We are living in an older house, with additions and renovations from many time periods. We inherit situations, including situations of injustice. In such a house, we do not address every crack in the foundation before ensuring that the walls are termite-free. We may not even refinish the floor before getting a new sofa. Burke's view would suggest that between 1776 and the Civil War no virtuous Americans could have considered any other aspect of the common good but the moral imperative to outlaw slavery. That position strikes me as too extreme.

Ultimately, it is implausible to hold that the common good requires focus upon only one issue at a time. By casting the discussion in these terms, Burke and others like him do not advance the actual discussion that citizens will sorely need to conduct. The question is not whether issues other than abortion are relevant to the common good; the question is whether the differences between the actual candidates on other relevant issues outweigh abortion, given what is necessary and possible to accomplish with respect to that issue and other issues. These are mixed questions of factual judgment and moral wisdom. The fact that they cannot be settled decisively does not mean that they cannot be discussed fruitfully.

COOPERATION WITH EVIL OR POLITICAL COORDINATION?

Pro-life groups might contend that regardless of whether electing pro-life politicians is sufficient to outlaw abortions, much less to reduce their number significantly, it is nonetheless a necessary step. Given the constitutionally protected status of abortion, the pro-life movement must convince a majority of voters not only to oppose abortion but also to make opposing it in a coordinated, disciplined fashion a top political priority. In my judgment, this is the underlying motive of most of the pro-life bishops and commentators who argue that it is a sin to vote for a pro-choice politician. Their actual goal is to mobilize an effective political movement to change an unjust legal framework, not to caution Catholic voters against potentially sinful cooperation with evil. This goal is, I think, clear in a passage from the full transcript of Archbishop Chaput's 2004 interview with the *New York Times*:

> [Archbishop]: . . . I think it is important for Catholics, whether they are Republicans or Democrats, to get over this compromising, "yes, but" and just give a very clear, collective "no!" A grand refusal to vote for anybody who is pro-choice, so that we have some political influence on this issue. You know, if Catholics voted on this issue as the central issue of our time, we would change things quite drastically, quite quickly, and if we don't do

it, it's our responsibility, and we participate somehow in the awful history of abortion in our country. So, I think we better just stop playing around with these words.

NYT: You said, "if Catholics started voting on this issue as the central issue of our time, we would change things quite rapidly and quite . . ."?

[Archbishop]: Radically![38]

This argument that voters must coordinate and prioritize the issue of abortion is clearly intelligible as a piece of pro-life political strategy. It is not, however, relevant to the purpose of the traditional matrix of cooperation with evil. The point of that matrix is negative; it aims to identify the actions that must be avoided in order to avoid sinning. It is not meant to provide the positive engine for a program of social reform. Still less is it meant to use the threat of sin and eternal damnation to promote the coordinated action necessary to overcome systemic injustice. It is a mistake for anyone, prelate or lay Catholic, to deploy the framework for cooperation with evil around the voting question in order to mobilize a pro-life political action movement.

Voting is an act that has its own integrity. As I argue in chapter 8, in casting their votes, citizens must focus on the entire common good as it will be advanced by the particular candidates in a particular election. Sometimes urgent issues—such as a catastrophic global economy—must be prioritized over fundamental issues, particularly if the urgent issues are more amenable to immediate political attention. Moreover, the common good is always the good of all, not merely the good of the most disadvantaged group. Voters exercise their stewardship for the entire community through their votes; they fulfill their particular obligations to their children, elderly family members, and fellow parishioners in part by casting their votes. To insist that voters in every election must cast their ballots with a lexically ordered primary regard to the issue of abortion is to fail to recognize the full moral and prudential dimensions of the act of voting.

Second, and more broadly, the question of whether and how to participate in a political movement designed to change an unjust law is a question that citizens must discern for themselves. To say that all citizens are morally obliged to prioritize the battle against abortion in their political decision making is to go too far. Analogously, people are not morally obliged to make the pro-life cause their only charity; they may give to disaster victims in Haiti and in New Orleans rather than to crisis pregnancy centers, and they may dedicate their political efforts to prison reform rather than pro-life politics.

Third, it must be remembered that the focus on electing pro-life politicians, particularly a pro-life president, is not primarily a matter of political morality; instead, it is a question of political strategy. The strategic goal of the pro-life movement is to remake the cast of Supreme Court justices in a way that will enable that court to overrule *Roe v. Wade*. But another strategy is equally conceivable (or equally inconceivable); *Roe* could also be overturned by constitutional amendment. Understandably enough, important segments of the pro-life movement judged that the indirect route of revamping the Supreme Court bench is more likely to succeed. Implementation of that approach, however, must respect the immense differences between voting for a single amendment versus voting for someone to make or execute an entire body of laws. In other words, the movement cannot rightly treat voting for president as the functional equivalent of voting for a referendum on abortion.

AN EMERGING PROBLEM IN MORAL THEOLOGY

The traditional category of cooperation with evil offers little assistance in addressing the question of voting for politicians who favor abortion rights; it also does not help us evaluate other questions, such as whether we should shop at big-box stores, where goods may be less expensive because they are made in sweatshops. Nor is it very useful in thinking through the issues involved in paying taxes that support an unjust war. Does that mean that these actions raise no moral problems? Absolutely not. Rather, it means we need to develop new ways of analyzing the involvement of individuals in systemic structures of complicity.

Of course, the idea of structural complicity is not new to Christian thought. As I argued earlier, the doctrine of original sin has long pointed to the common human plight of failing to live up to our obligations to God and one another. St. Augustine, Pope John Paul II, and liberation theologians have all examined how individuals can be caught up in social practices marred by entrenched sinfulness.

It seems to me, however, that individual involvement in structural wrongdoing has garnered more attention in the present era. Why? For one, residents of developed countries are enmeshed in increasingly complicated webs of production and consumption. We buy goods made on the far side of the globe. We ensure our safety not only by deploying US soldiers but also by forging alliances with other nations and private contractors. Our network of relations is increasingly pluralistic. Consequently, we do not share the same values with all members of our political community, and still less with those in our global economy. Thanks to the Internet, ordinary individuals know far more about these political and economic relationships than in the past; coordinating action, including boycotts and other protest campaigns, is also far easier than it used to be.

In short, individuals are not isolated agents. Nor are they totally immersed in their own families or churches or communities. They are networked agents. How does the "networked self" experience moral responsibility? Catholic moral theology has done a good job of analyzing the actions of individuals and small groups, on the one hand, and the social structures that contribute to just and unjust societies, on the other. There needs to be more reflection, however, on the intersection of these two realms: How should we think about the actions of individuals and small groups in relation to larger social structures? Can we say anything more helpful than "it is original sin" or "it is remote cooperation with evil," justified by "proportionate reason"? The fact that moral theology has long ago expanded beyond the context of the confessional and is now being integrated with Catholic social teaching means that we can move beyond the focus on the particular wrongful acts committed by particular individuals. Making progress on these questions will require more sophisticated theoretical treatment of three issues.

Aggregated Agency

As traditionally articulated, the category of remote material cooperation would include a citizen casting a ballot for a politician who supports unjust policies, a big-box store customer buying cheap goods made by slave labor, and a worker paying taxes that at least partially support an unjust war. Traditional moralists would also use the category of remote material cooperation to cover taxi drivers delivering drunk passengers from the airport to the Las Vegas strip and custodians maintaining heat for hospitals that provide morally unacceptable services. What sets the first three examples apart from the last two, however, is the pressing problem of aggregated agency that they raise.[39] Taken by themselves, my individual vote, my isolated purchase, and my paltry tax payment are largely inconsequential. But taken together, the actions of voters, consumers, and taxpayers have a significant effect on the practices they facilitate.

When should I think of myself primarily as a member of a class in evaluating my action, and when should I take into account my own individual needs and desires? This question is relevant for two distinct purposes. The first has to do with the development of my own character and the characters of others for whom I am responsible, such as family members.[40] What sort of obligation do

I have to inform myself about the way in which the activities of my daily life are enabled by broad patterns of collective wrongdoing? What sort of barrier should I set between myself and the large social evils of our time? How can we express solidarity with persons harmed by those evils? If we need to shop at a big-box store because of the prices or location, is there any countervailing action we can take to offset complicity, such as donating to an organization that combats child labor? If we vote for a pro-choice politician, can we find time to volunteer at a crisis pregnancy center?

The second purpose in distinguishing between individual and aggregate needs in analyzing actions is related to bringing about social reform by coordinated action. Once a social evil has been identified, how do we determine that it deserves to be addressed? Moreover, what means should be used to bring about change? In essence, the bishops who tried to forbid all Catholics from voting for any pro-choice politician were trying to organize a political boycott. A boycott is a legitimate method of agitating for social change, as demonstrated by Martin Luther King Jr.'s famous boycott of the segregated bus system in Montgomery, Alabama.[41] It is not always, however, an appropriate or successful method, as Dr. King found out a few years later in Albany, Georgia, when his broader and more diffuse protests not only failed to produce the changes he sought but also engendered frustration and violence.[42] When is a boycott a legitimate method to protest injustice, and when are its ancillary costs, including harm to innocent parties, too great?

The Roman Catholic tradition has long had just war theory to help discern when it is morally appropriate to take up arms. As our weapons become more and more destructive, the circumstances in which armed conflict will be an appropriate response to injustice become fewer and fewer. Moreover, the ordinary forms of addressing unjust situations will be forms of political organization and the tools of public protest, including civil disobedience, boycotts, and other forms of nonviolent resistance. Although they are nonviolent, they are not without either significant power or meaningful moral import, particularly in an era in which information—and protests—can travel like lightning over the Internet. The Catholic tradition needs to supplement its "just war theory" with a "just protest" theory to address these new circumstances.[43]

Currents of Action

How should we think about broad causal patterns and our place within them? Systemic injustices cannot be analyzed by looking solely at the actions of individuals. We are dealing with the actions and reactions of institutional agents, including nations, transnational regulatory bodies, and multinational corporations. Moreover, these various entities do not always act independently; each entity can respond to incentives and pressures created both within and outside the category to which it belongs. Corporations, for example, move production facilities abroad when they cannot continue to make a profit for their shareholders at home. The Catholic moral tradition has done a very good job of analyzing the practical reasoning and deliberations of individual moral agents. However, more work needs to be done with respect to the manner in which institutional agents can be said to "act." In particular, we need to consider how to evaluate the "wake" of the actions of corporate agents—the manner in which they shape the context for other agents, both corporate and individual, who plan their own actions. In sum, we need to think about how corporate agents affect the common good directly as well as indirectly by creating incentives for other agents to act.

The Inbreaking Kingdom of God

As Catholics, we know that the kingdom of God has already been inaugurated by Christ's death and resurrection; we also know that it will not be fully realized until the end of time. Until then, Christians need to hold two values in creative tension by honoring the insights advanced by two sorts of devout Catholics, whom I dub "prophets" and "pilgrims."[44] Prophets emphasize the importance of clear, unambiguous witness to the transformative power of the inbreaking kingdom of God. They believe that the purity of their witness to those values will be compromised if Catholics, and especially Catholic institutions, appear resigned to the great systemic evils of our time. Consequently, in evaluating questions of complicity, the prophets are likely to stress the need to maintain significant distance from the wrongful acts of others, particularly if significant portions of the population do not agree that those acts are wrongful—as in, for example, abortion or extramarital sex.

In contrast, pilgrims are acutely aware of just how far human society still remains from the kingdom of God and how difficult the journey continues to be. The consequences of sin and the sting of death are still all around us. The only way to ameliorate those consequences is by doing justice, loving mercy, and walking humbly with God. It is not enough to avoid sin; we have to love and serve our neighbors. Ameliorating injustice and practicing the corporal works of mercy often involve contact with, and sometimes cooperation with, wrongdoers. We cannot expect to avoid such contact until the end of time. Until then, the wheat and tares will grow together.

The different eschatological sensibilities of prophets and pilgrims account for their different judgments on issues such as whether it is permissible to provide condoms in developing countries to prevent HIV infection or whether Catholic hospitals may ensure their financial stability by affiliating with systems that perform sterilizations. In the best of circumstances, the tension between prophets and pilgrims can be creative, pressing us to think more deeply about both requirements for following Jesus Christ. But what we must guard against at all costs is allowing creative tension to become mutually assured destruction.[45]

NOTES

This chapter has its seeds in M. Cathleen Kaveny, "Catholics as Citizens," *America*, November 1, 2010, 13–16.

1. Meg G. Kinnard, "No Communion for Obama Supporters, Says South Carolina Priest," *HuffPost Politics*, November 13, 2008, www.huffingtonpost.com/2008/11/14/no-communion-for-obama-su_n_143804.html.
2. Wayne R. LaFave, *Criminal Law*, 4th ed. (St. Paul, MN: West Publishing, 2003), §§ 12.3, 13.3.
3. Dan B. Dobbs, *The Law of Torts* (St. Paul, MN: West Publishing, 2000), § 335.
4. See Victoria J. Barnett, *Bystanders: Conscience and Complicity during the Holocaust* (Westport, CT: Praeger, 1999); Christopher R. Browning, *Ordinary Men: Reserve Police Battalion 101 and the Final Solution in Poland* (New York: HarperCollins, 1992); and Robert Jay Lifton, *The Nazi Doctors: Medical Killing and the Psychology of Genocide* (New York: Basic Books, 2000).
5. For a historical account of the development of the theological doctrine, see Tatha Wiley, *Original Sin: Origins, Developments, Contemporary Meanings* (Mahwah, NJ: Paulist Press, 2002). For a broader cultural approach, see Alan Jacobs, *Original Sin: A Cultural History* (San Francisco: HarperOne Reprints: 2009).
6. *The New-England Primer: Improved for the More Easy Attaining of the True Reading of English, to Which Is Added the Assembly of Divines and Mr. Cotton's Catechism* (Boston: Edward Draper, 1777), http://ia600301.us.archive.org/20/items/newenglandprimer00west/newenglandprimer00west.pdf.
7. Richard Thompson, "Explaining the Link between Maternal History of Childhood Victimization and Child Risk of Maltreatment," *Journal of Trauma Practice* 5, no. 2 (2006): 57–72.
8. The story of Adam and Eve, of course, has had wide-ranging implications for Christian conceptions of the role of women. See, e.g., Elaine Pagels, *Adam, Eve and the Serpent* (New York: Vintage Books, 1989).
9. Reinhold Niebuhr, *Moral Man and Immoral Society: A Study in Ethics and Politics* (New York: Charles Scribner's Sons, 1932).
10. "Sin, in this Catholic view, is irreducibly personal. However influenced by external conditions and circumstances, the individual freedom and accountability at the heart of human dignity remain the source and object of sin proper. 'There is nothing so

personal and untransferable in each individual as merit for virtue or responsibility for sin.'" Christine Firer Hinze, "The Drama of Social Sin and the (Im)possibility of Solidarity: Reinhold Niebuhr and Modern Catholic Social Teaching," *Studies in Christian Ethics* 22 (2009): 444 (quoting Pope John Paul II, *Reconciliatio et paenitentia* [1984], para. 2).

11. Ibid., 445.

12. See John Mahoney, *The Making of Moral Theology* (Oxford: Clarendon Press, 1987). As he details, there were confessors' manuals before the Council of Trent. There were also other forms of penitential books.

13. The particularistic focus of the manualists' analysis, sometimes called "casuistry," has come in for heavy criticism over the years, most notably in Blaise Pascal's *Provincial Letters* (1656–57). I argue that reframing casuistry in the context of virtue theory can address some of the problems. See M. Cathleen Kaveny, "Retrieving and Reframing Catholic Casuistry," in *The Crisis of Authority in Catholic Modernity*, ed. Michael J. Lacey and Francis Oakley, 225–58 (New York: Oxford University Press, 2011).

14. See, e.g., Henry Davis, SJ, *Moral and Pastoral Theology*, vol. 1, *Human Acts, Sin, and Virtue* (New York: Sheed & Ward, 1958), 341; Edwin F. Healy, *Moral Guidance* (Chicago: Loyola University, 1942), 43; and Dominic M. Prümmer, OP, *Handbook of Moral Theology*, trans. Gerald W. Shelton (Cork: Mercier,1956), 103. By "sinful," the manualists here mean "objectively morally wrong." Obviously, addressing the subjective sinfulness of any act would require taking into account the state of knowledge and the freedom of the agent who has committed it.

15. In 1679 Pope Innocent XI answered "no." See Heinrich Denzinger and Adolf Schönmetzer, *Enchiridion symbolorum*, 36th ed. (Freiburg: Herder, 1976), para. 2151.

16. A helpful list of the cases frequently considered by the manualists can be found in James Keenan, SJ, "Prophylactics, Toleration, and Cooperation: Contemporary Problems and Traditional Principles," *International Philosophical Quarterly* 29 (1989): 206–20; and Anthony Fisher, OP, "Co-Operation in Evil," *Catholic Medical Quarterly* 44, no. 3 (1994), 15–22. In addition, Germain Grisez addresses numerous cooperation problems in *The Way of the Lord Jesus*, vol. 3, *Difficult Moral Questions* (Quincy, IL: Franciscan Press, 1997).

17. Helpful introductions to the traditional categories can be found in Keenan, "Prophylactics, Toleration, and Cooperation," and Fisher, "Co-Operation in Evil." I briefly summarize the categories in M. Cathleen Kaveny, "Appropriation of Evil: Cooperation's Mirror Image," *Theological Studies* 61 (2000): 280–313. Important proposals for revising these categories can be found in Germain Grisez's "Appendix 2" addressing cooperation with evil, in *Difficult Moral Questions*, 871–91, and Catholic Health Association (CHA), "Report on a Theological Dialogue on the Principle of Cooperation" (2007).

18. If a cooperator's external act overlaps virtually entirely with the external act of the wrongdoing primary agent, the case is one of immediate material cooperation; if there is some distance between the two, it is called mediate material cooperation. Precisely because it is so difficult to distinguish immediate material cooperation from actual primary wrongdoing, most moralists said that the former could only be justified in

cases of duress (e.g., a bank robber forces a teller at gunpoint to unlock the safe and take the money).

19. If the two acts are close, the situation involves proximate (mediate) material cooperation; if they are not so close, it is called remote (mediate) material cooperation. All else being equal, the closer the act of cooperation is to the wrongful act, the harder it is to justify.

20. If the wrongful act will take place without the cooperator's act, it is a case of free cooperation; if the cooperator's act is a "but-for" cause, it is a case of necessary cooperation. All else being equal, necessary cooperation is harder to justify than free cooperation.

21. The technical meaning of "giving scandal" is not merely being "shocking"; it means leading someone to commit a wrongful act. See *Catechism of the Catholic Church*, 2nd ed. (Washington, DC: United States Catholic Conference, 2000), para. 2284.

22. See, e.g., M. Cathleen Kaveny and James Keenan, SJ, "Ethical Issues in Health Care Restructuring," *Theological Studies* 56 (1995): 136–50.

23. See CHA, *Report on a Theological Dialogue*, and USCCB, *Ethical and Religious Directives for Catholic Health Care Services*, 5th ed. (Washington, DC: United States Conference of Catholic Bishops, 2009), part 6, "Forming New Partnerships with Health Care Organizations and Providers."

24. I leave aside here the difficult question of what counts as an act of the health care facility, which is a corporate agent. I assume it is an action of those persons that the facility assigns, controls, and directs in the course of their employment. A hospital could engage in immediate material cooperation with, say, an act of euthanasia if it permits such an act to be done by an independent physician to a patient in its facilities using its equipment and narcotics.

25. There may be exceptions in some cases, usually to avoid an immediate harm to third parties or a direct harm to the common good. Aquinas, for example, said that there was no need to return a deposit (usually an obligation in justice) to one who was going to use it to fund enemy supplies. Thomas Aquinas, *Summa theologica*, 3 vols., trans. Fathers of the English Dominican Province (New York: Benziger Bros., 1948), II-II, q. 57, art.2, rep. ob. 1.

26. For another take on the question, see John Finnis, "Just Votes for Unjust Laws (2004)," in *Philosophy of Law*, vol. 4 of his *Collected Essays* (Oxford: Oxford University Press, 2011), 436–66.

27. Augustine of Hippo, *City of God*, trans. Henry Scowcroft Bettenson (London: Penguin Classics, 2003), bk. 20.

28. David Kirkpatrick and Laurie Goodstein, "Group of Bishops Using Influence to Oppose Kerry," *New York Times*, October 12, 2004, A1. See also Archbishop Chaput's column, "How to Tell a Duck from a Fox: Thinking with the Church As We Look toward November," *Denver Catholic Register*, April 14, 2004, reprinted at Archdiocese of Denver's website, www.archden.org: "Candidates who claim to be 'Catholic' but who publicly ignore Catholic teaching about the sanctity of human life are offering a dishonest public witness. They may try to look Catholic and sound Catholic, but unless they act Catholic in their public service and political choices, they're really a very different kind of creature." See also another column, found at the Archdiocese's

website: "Let's Make a Deal: Catholic Conscience and Compromise," *Denver Catholic Register*, September 22, 2004: "Next month, October, is Respect Life month. It's a good time to reflect on the meaning of the Kennedy-Cuomo legacy. In brief, it's OK to be Catholic in public service as long as you're willing to jettison what's inconveniently 'Catholic.' That's not a compromise. That's a deal with the devil, and it has a balloon payment no nation, no public servant and no voter can afford. And real Catholics should vote accordingly." Chaput later expressed surprise that his statements were taken as an indication that he doubted the good faith of Catholics who voted for pro-choice candidates despite (not because of) their stance on abortion. See his interview with Melinda Henneberger, "Abortion Politics: An Interview with Archbishop Chaput," *Commonweal*, April 20, 2007, 7: "Do I think there are people in the last election who voted for a prochoice candidate and did so sincerely after reflection and prayer? Yes, I do. Did they do wrong? No, they followed their conscience. But that serious reflection and prayer, that's really important, and not just being swayed by party sympathies or that's the way you always vote. It has to be about the issues." In my view, there is a striking difference in both tone and content between his statements of 2004 and 2007.

29. Penny Starr, "Vatican Official Says Catholics Who Voted for Obama Cooperated with Evil," *CNSNews.com*, March 25, 2009, www.cnsnews.com/node/45629. Burke has repeatedly made such statements. See John Thavis, "Vote for Supporters of Abortion Never Justified, Vatican Official Says," Catholic News Service, October 29, 2010, www.catholicnews.com/data/stories/cns/1004453.htm.

30. "Vatican, US Bishops: On Catholics in Political Life," *Origins* 34 (2004): 133.

31. Archdiocese of Denver, "All the News That's Fit to Print . . . Sort Of," www.archden .org/images/nyt_transcript.pdf.

32. Archbishop Joseph F. Naumann and Bishop Robert W. Finn, "Our Moral Responsibility as Citizens," September 8, 2008, *The Catholic Key Blog*, http://catholickey.blogspot .com/2008/09/could-catholic-in-good-conscience-vote.html.

33. Chris M. Hebert, "The Earned Income Tax Credit and Abortion," *Social Science Research*, May 31, 2011, doi:10.1016/j.ssresearch.2011.05.003. As part of their annual reporting requirement, agencies in three states asked women why they were getting an abortion. Some 30–60 percent of the women indicated lack of economic support as one of the factors in their decision for abortion. Center for Health Statistics, "Induced Abortions in Minnesota January–December 2010: Report to the Legislature," July 2010, www.health.state.mn.us/divs/chs/abrpt/2010abrpt.pdf, table 17 (30 percent cited "economic" as a reason); Nebraska Department of Health and Human Services, "Nebraska 2009 Statistical Report of Abortions," Feb. 2010, http:// dhhs.ne.gov/publichealth/Abortion%20Reports/2009%20Statistical%20Report%20 of%20Abortions.pdf, table 4 (59.7 percent cited "socio-economic" as a reason); and South Dakota Department of Health, "Induced Abortions 2009," http://doh.sd.gov/ statistics/2009Vital/Abortion.pdf, table 73 (50 percent cited "can't afford a child" as a reason).

34. See Center for Reproductive Rights, *What if Roe Fell?* (2007), http://reproductiverights .org/sites/crr.civicactions.net/files/documents/Roe_PublicationPF4a.pdf.

35. Archbishop Raymond Burke, Keynote Address, National Catholic Prayer Breakfast,

LifeSiteNews.com, May 8, 2009, www.lifesitenews.com/news/archive/ldn/2009/may/09050819.

36. Ibid.

37. See, for example, the federal regulations "Protection of Human Subjects—Additional Protections for Pregnant Women, Human Fetuses and Neonates Involved in Research" codified at 45 CFR Part 46, Subpart B. In addition, some states absolutely prohibit experimentation on fetuses. See, for example, Ind. Code Ann. § 16-34-2-6 (West 2006) and Ariz. Rev. Stat. Ann. § 36-2302 (West 2009).

38. Archdiocese of Denver, "All the News That's Fit to Print . . . Sort Of."

39. I hope to explore these questions more fully in a forthcoming book on complicity. Helpful contributions on group agency include Christopher Kutz, *Complicity: Ethics and Law for a Collective Age* (Cambridge: Cambridge University Press, 2000); Albino Barrera, *Market Complicity and Christian Ethics* (Cambridge: Cambridge University Press, 2011); and Christian List and Philip Petit, *Group Agency: The Possibility, Design, and Status of Corporate Agents* (New York: Oxford University Press, 2011).

40. I have argued that the cooperation with evil matrix is best understood against the background of virtue theory. See Kaveny, "Appropriation of Evil."

41. Clayborne Carson, ed., *The Autobiography of Martin Luther King* (New York: Warner Books, 1998), chaps. 7–9.

42. Ibid., chap. 16.

43. For an extremely helpful ethical analysis of civil disobedience, see James F. Childress, *Civil Disobedience and Political Obligation* (New Haven: Yale University Press, 1971).

44. For an expanded account of how one's orientation toward the inbreaking kingdom of God can affect one's view of the permissibility of cooperation with evil, see M. Cathleen Kaveny, "Tax Lawyers, Prophets, and Pilgrims: A Response to Anthony Fisher," in *Cooperation, Complicity, and Conscience: Problems in Healthcare, Science, Law, and Public Policy*, ed. Helen Watt, 65–84 (London: Linacre Centre 2005). See also Anthony Fisher, "Cooperation with Evil: Understanding the Issues," in *Cooperation, Complicity, and Conscience: Problems in Healthcare, Science, Law, and Public Policy*, ed. Helen Watt, 27–64 (London: Linacre Centre 2005).

45. I discuss the tensions between "prophets" and "casuists" in M. Cathleen Kaveny, "Prophecy and Casuistry: Abortion, Torture, and Moral Discourse," *Villanova Law Review* 51, no. 3 (2006): 499–579.

Concluding Reflections

I N WRITING THIS BOOK, I was motivated not only by specific intellectual questions but also by more diffuse goals, concerns, and worries. As I bring this work to a close, I want to summarize the former and articulate the latter more explicitly. I want to situate, in other words, my reflections on law's pedagogical function in the broader context of law, religion, and politics in the contemporary United States.

LAW AS A MORAL TEACHER

The overarching purpose of the volume is to make a case for the way in which law can and should function as a moral teacher, even in a pluralistic representative democracy committed to individual liberty, such as the United States. Isidore of Seville, a seventh-century historian, proposed a compact definition of the criteria for good law that was then appropriated by Thomas Aquinas in the thirteenth century. According to Isidore, "Law shall be virtuous, just, possible to nature, according to the custom of the country, suitable to place and time, necessary, useful; clearly expressed, lest by its obscurity it lead to misunderstanding; framed for no private benefit, but for the common good."[1] An animating conviction of this volume is that Isidore's formal criteria for good law are just as useful to us today as they were in ancient times, despite the fact that we would doubtless not interpret the substance of each item on his list in the precise way he did.

These chapters are not intended to provide an exhaustive account of my broadly Thomistic theory of law or to defend that account against the whole possible range of objections emanating from secular and religious sources. Nor are these chapters meant to address each and every issue at the intersection of law and morality in a completely comprehensive manner. An entire volume could be dedicated to the role of law as a moral teacher with respect to each of the three issues I touch upon at some length: abortion, genetics, and euthanasia. Finally, I certainly do not intend to provide a complete analysis of the morality of voting, a topic that is only now beginning to receive the scholarly attention it deserves.

Rather, my aim in the book is to sketch a model for how it might be possible to think of law as a teacher of virtue in a pluralistic society, as well as to proffer some concrete examples for how such an approach would deal with important and contentious issues. Throughout the volume I emphasize the key virtues I think the law should teach—autonomy and solidarity—even as I try to work through the basic implications of those virtues for more particular questions of law and policy. I am not trying to formulate a one-size-fits-all view of the pedagogical function of the law, or to hide the values animating my own account. I do not take my account as beyond dispute by all reasonable persons, or by all persons of good will. I think that the effective exercise of the pedagogical function of the law in a pluralistic society must grapple with the fact that some citizens will conscientiously disagree with some aspects of the moral message being proposed, particularly on contentious issues.

The United States is a religiously and morally pluralistic society. Yet Americans nonetheless share a significant number of overlapping moral beliefs, as evidenced by the less contentious aspects of our legal norms. I find a deeply admirable moral vision of solidarity and autonomy in the Civil Rights Acts, the Americans with Disabilities Act, the Family and Medical Leave Act, and the Patient Protection and Affordable Care Act. Equally pervasive but more workaday moral norms animate tort and contract law, which have developed richly textured notions of how "reasonable" men and women ought to treat one another in their social dealings.

I do not mean to deny that our nation is divided on many issues, including not only abortion and euthanasia but also sexual morality, stem-cell research, the legalization of drugs, the death penalty, and torture. But I think that our disagreements may be ameliorated, if not abated, by putting the legal and moral dimensions of an issue in a broader frame. Is the activity under discussion actually performed by the state (torture), funded by it (stem-cell research), or merely permitted by it (abortion)? Does the regulatory scheme confer approval (same-sex marriage) or simply tolerance (decriminalization of drugs)? We can examine the costs and benefits of an actual practice, as opposed to resting content with advocating or opposing the legal principle allowing the practice. For example, polls show that many Americans support legal abortion but also think that more than one million abortions annually is "too high."[2] Other studies indicate that, while most Americans support the death penalty, they also are worried by the number of innocent people likely to be on death row.[3]

Breaking up issues into subissues, looking at law and practices, and considering the entire sweep of relevant law rather than merely the criminal law may uncover more commonalities in our views than the current political debates suggest. Too frequently the discussion assumes that our law offers a binary framework in which a particular type of action can be treated either as morally objectionable, criminally prohibited, and widely avoided, on the one hand, or as morally good, federally funded, and widely practiced, on the other. The relationship between law and morality in a pluralistic society is far more complicated than that dichotomous picture would suggest—and not merely because both sides have failed to muster the political power to implement their respective programs as fully as they would want to do.

BEYOND THE CULTURE WARS

In this book I explicitly defend a more nuanced account of the pedagogical function of law that I hope can provide both the reasons and the means to resist this dichotomous framework. In fact, resisting this dichotomy is crucial to an implicit aspiration of mine in writing the book: I would like to help move our discussion beyond the "culture wars" that have so influenced American debate over issues such as abortion and euthanasia for over fifteen years now.[4]

What are the "culture wars"? The term, in my view, reflects an unstable amalgam of secular and religious ideas and concerns. University of Virginia sociologist James Davidson Hunter first popularized the term in his book *Culture Wars: The Struggle to Define America.*[5] He argues that Americans have divided themselves into two warring camps, battling over issues such as abortion, drug use, church–state relations, sexual morality, and other hot-button issues. One group is socially conservative or traditionalist while the other is socially progressive. In Hunter's view, these polarized cultural outlooks are more fundamental than other divisions among Americans, including religious and geographical distinctions. In Hunter's use, then, the term "culture war" focuses particularly on the American political scene.

A few years later Pope John Paul II issued his encyclical *Evangelium vitae* (1995), which identifies a global battle between the "culture of life" and the "culture of death." The culture of life, in his view, values human life in all stages of dependency and opposes practices such as abortion, euthanasia, and contraception while the culture of death defends those practices as essential means to independence, equality, and freedom. The pope contends that the culture of death is marked by the hostility of the strong against the weak and dependent. Consequently, a culture of life not only legally opposes private killing but also provides generous social services and support to vulnerable persons and to those who care for them.

The pope's use of cultural analysis is not narrowly focused on America. Its academic home is not sociology but Catholic philosophy and theology. Not surprisingly, then, the ideological overlap between Hunter's categories and John Paul II's categories is far from complete. The American conservatives described by Hunter manifest a significant libertarian strain; it is hard to imagine, for example, John Paul II being an enthusiastic supporter of the right of private individuals to carry concealed weapons. Furthermore, building the pope's "culture of life," which includes a strong safety net for families and vulnerable individuals, likely involves far more government support and regulation than many of the conservatives described by Hunter would be willing to accept.

More significantly, however, Hunter and the pope do not mean the same thing by the term "culture wars." Hunter describes two ideological camps within society while Pope John Paul II uses the term "culture" to evoke the larger legal and social pressures exerting influence upon all persons within a given social context. To say that a particular individual has moved from "progressive" to "orthodox" is intelligible in Hunter's terms. To claim, however, that the individual has moved from "the culture of life" to the "culture of death" does not make quite as much sense in the pope's framework because John Paul II is deploying cultural analysis to describe the background social conditions in which individuals must make their decisions for or against abortion, euthanasia, or contraception.

Despite the significant differences, Hunter's categories and the pope's categories began to merge in the national discussions as the millennial presidential election approached. Republican strategists worked out how to bring Catholics into a coalition with American fiscal and social conservatives. In a televised debate, Republican presidential candidate George W. Bush used the term "culture of life" to highlight his differences from his opponent, Democratic candidate Al Gore, and to appeal to Catholic voters.[6] The rhetorical gerrymandering that the abortion issue has required of both political parties has been tracked by scholars of political rhetoric. Ann Gordon and Jerry L. Miller draw the following conclusion from their study of the first Bush–Gore debate: "Clearly Bush and Gore relied on different values to appeal to voters. Bush emphasized individualism, while Gore stressed equality. The most notable exception to these emphases was with respect to the abortion issue. Gore framed the issue of abortion in terms of individual freedom, while Bush turned to a morality frame. While there was a great deal of contrast in the values chosen, Bush and Gore were similar in the strategies they employed."[7]

George W. Bush repeatedly invoked the papal language of the "culture of life" in his speeches over the next years as a central theme of his Republican administration. Moreover, many of those who supported him, including prominent Catholic prelates, began to portray the Democratic Party—and those who cast their votes for Democratic politicians—as minions of the "culture of death."[8] While reaching its greatest intensity in 2004, the "culture wars" language has persisted beyond the Bush era, affecting the 2008 contest between John McCain and Barack Obama and making an appearance in some of the "Tea Party" rhetoric that became increasingly prominent in the 2010 elections and beyond.

In my judgment, the rhetoric and mind-set of the "culture wars" do not facilitate the kind of nuanced, respectful discussion that citizens in a pluralistic society need to have about the relationship of law and morality. To see one's fellow citizens as enemy combatants triggers an attitude that colors everything in terms of winning or losing a battle or the war. It can tempt politicians and activists to adopt an idealized political program in which full implementation is "victory" and any deviation involves some degree of "loss." It does not encourage us to frame the question in terms of what legal or political framework will best advance *our* common good—the common good of all of us, including those who disagree with us about what constitutes the common good.

The problems of American "culture war" language in general are exacerbated by its amalgamation with John Paul II's language of the "culture of life" and the "culture of death," for two reasons. First, I believe the pope's effort to situate individual choices for or against abortion and euthanasia within the broader current of social patterns, pressures, and opportunities is an enormous advance in Catholic moral theology; his attempt knits together personal decision making and social justice in a way that reflects the tradition's bedrock anthropological conviction that human beings are essentially social. At the same time, his analysis of broad trends that permeate a culture cannot be reduced without distortion to two distinct, opposing camps within it. Still less can it be shriveled to two political parties battling for control of the country. Neither the Democratic Party nor the Republican Party fulfills the positive social vision of *Evangelium vitae*. The Republicans express their commitment to outlaw abortion while the Democrats express their support of the social policies that will provide the positive help needed by vulnerable people, including the unborn, children, the disabled, and the elderly.

Pope John Paul II called both for the legal prohibition of abortion and euthanasia and for the provision of social support to those tempted to avail themselves of these practices. Importantly, he did not lexically order these moral imperatives. He did not say, in other words, that first we must work to outlaw abortion and only then turn to the question of social support. In fact, he seemed to contemplate that the two would go hand in hand.[9] In a representative democracy such as the United States, legal strictures against abortion and euthanasia are not likely to be enacted or retained unless the relevant social supports are in place. If push comes to shove, most people will not choose to deprive themselves of such legal options unless they know they can rely upon other forms of assistance. Perhaps this decision would not be made by martyrs, or by those of heroic courage. In my estimation, however, it would reflect the standard of ordinary virtue—and it is with that standard that the secular law must be concerned.

Second, while the labels "culture of life" and "culture of death" serve as useful tools in social analysis, they do not function as beneficially in actual encounters. The problems in using bellicose imagery for political engagement are substantial; those difficulties are raised to an entirely different level if some participants think of themselves as participating in a war against the minions of the "culture of death." If we configure people in such a fashion, how likely is it that we will engage them in a serious conversation, much less cooperate with them in any political or social endeavor? How can we see any good in them whatsoever? Thinking of our political and moral opponents in this way comes dangerously close to demonizing them. It undermines the basic respect we need to have for one another as fellow citizens if we treat them as deliberate destroyers of the basic values of the community. We can regard others as morally mistaken—indeed, deeply mistaken—without reducing them to moral monsters.

In my view, the "culture wars" model of political engagement is not conducive to the common good of this nation. Yet directly critiquing the paradigm runs the risk of being conscripted or lured into the battles themselves. A more fruitful strategy may be to set forth another, less militaristic model of promoting human dignity, autonomy, and solidarity in a pluralistic society. My implicit hope in writing these chapters is to sketch a view of law's moral pedagogy in a pluralistic society that could foster a culture of life without fueling the culture wars. My hope is that more Americans will try to be teachers rather than warriors.

NOTES

1. Thomas Aquinas, *Summa theologica*, 3 vols., trans. Fathers of the English Dominican Province (New York: Benziger Bros., 1948), II-II, q. 95, art. 3 (citing Isidore of Seville).

2. In a recent survey, 62 percent of respondents agreed that women had sufficient access to abortion. But after being informed that 41 percent of all viable pregnancies in New York City end in abortion, 64 percent of respondents said that number was "too high." John McLaughlin, "New York City Survey Results," Memo to Greg Pfundstein, *Chiaroscuro Foundation*, February 23, 2011, http://nyc41percent.com/Docs/NYC_Abortion_Memo_0223.pdf.

3. "In US, Two-Thirds Continue to Support Death Penalty," *Gallup*, October 13, 2009, www.gallup.com/poll/123638/in-u.s.-two-thirds-continue-support-death-penalty.aspx.

4. There have been other "culture wars" in the United States and elsewhere. In contemporary times, the term has been extended to cover a number of topics, including the battle between FOX News (conservative) and MSNBC (progressive). See Roger Chapman, ed., *Culture Wars: An Encyclopedia of Issues, Voices and Viewpoints* (Armonk, NY: M. E. Sharpe, 2009).

5. James Davidson Hunter, *Culture Wars: The Struggle to Define America* (New York: Basic Books, 1992).

6. See "October 3, 2000, Transcript: The First Gore-Bush Presidential Debates," *Commission on Presidential Debates*, www.debates.org/index.php?page=october-3-2000-transcript.

7. Ann Gordon and Jerry L. Miller, "Values and Persuasion during the First Bush-Gore Presidential Debate," *Political Communication* 21 (2004): 71–92, at 86–87.

8. For example, in 2008 Raymond Burke, formerly archbishop of St. Louis and currently Cardinal Prefect of the Supreme Tribunal of the Apostolic Signatura, accused the Democrats of becoming the "party of death." In this claim he was echoing the language of Republican activist Ramesh Ponnuru in his book, *The Party of Death: The Democrats, the Media, the Courts, and the Disregard for Human Life* (Washington, DC: Regnery Publishing, 2006). Archbishop Charles Chaput, formerly of Denver and now of Philadelphia, directed biting criticism not only toward Democratic presidential candidates but also toward groups that argued Catholics could support such candidates despite their position on abortion. In Chaput's view, they "have done a disservice to the Church, confused the natural priorities of Catholic social teaching, undermined the progress pro-lifers have made, and provided an excuse for some Catholics to abandon the abortion issue instead of fighting within their parties and at the ballot box to protect the unborn." Eric Gorski, "Archbishop Criticizes Obama, Catholic Allies," *USA Today*, October 19, 2008, www.usatoday.com/news/politics/2008-10-18-1132206159_x.htm. Although Chaput denied that his remarks were partisan, it did not go unnoticed that his interventions overwhelmingly favored Republicans. During election season, he rarely, if ever, pointed out the ways in which Republican candidates diverged from Catholic teaching. Moreover, he did not encourage anyone to probe the deeper questions about whether a Republican pro-life stance on abortion would actually make any practical difference.

9. See Pope John Paul II, *Evangelium vitae* (*The Gospel of Life*) (1995), para. 90.

Index

abortion: and age of women, 81; American public's opinion on, 217*n*50, 272, 277*n*2; assistance for women with crisis pregnancies as alternative to, 90–91; availability even when prohibited, 88; and Catholic health care organizations, 249–50, 267*n*24; characterization as medical method for dealing with pregnancy, 85, 88; "conscience clause" provisions allowing refusal to perform, 104; debate about, 5, 46, 73–74, 75–76; and economic crisis, 209; and "Faithful Citizenship," 195–97, 207–9; first-trimester, 89, 101–2, 208, 242*n*33; as fundamental right, 216–17*n*47; funding, 84, 103–4, 208, 217*nn*51–52; informed consent requirements for, 86; as intrinsic evil, 233–36; John Paul II's opposition to, 68*n*25, 89–90, 195, 215*n*33, 240*n*20, 276; late-term abortion ban, 88–89; as liberty interest, 216–17*n*47, 233, 242*n*34; partial-birth abortion, 102–3; and poverty, 81, 209, 217*n*53, 268*n*33; and prenatal testing, 120; protection for, 210, 233; realism of activists in opposing, 2–3, 88–89; restrictions on, 85, 99, 101–2, 217*n*51; state control over, 85–86, 216–17*n*47; in 2008 election, 208; as voting issue, 191, 195–97, 207–8, 244. *See also* Freedom of Choice Act (FOCA); pro-life movement; *Roe v. Wade* (1973)

Abortion and Divorce in Western Law (Glendon), 91

Abortion and the Politics of Motherhood (Luker), 73–74

abstaining from voting, 197, 198, 216*n*39, 253

Abu Ghraib, 77

accessory liability, 245

ADA. *See* Americans with Disabilities Act of 1990

Adam's original sin, 246, 261, 265*n*8

adultery, 225

aggregated agency, 262–63

A.G.R. v. D.R.H. & S.H. (2009), 69*n*42

Alan Guttmacher Institute, 94*n*26

alcoholism, harm from, 47

Allen, John, 233

Allen, Woody, 142, 144

Alzheimer's victims, caregivers for, 81

American law: and autonomy and solidarity, 18–19, 33, 37; challenges for, xi–xii, 3–6; and free speech, 59; and pro-life movement, 78–82; "reasonable person" standard in, 80. *See also* criminal law; lawmaking

Americans with Disabilities Act of 1990 (ADA), 34–38, 65; employment provisions, 35–36; enforcement

disabilities, persons with: as defined by
ADA, 34–35; EU provisions for, 43n73;
and philosophical anthropology, 79;
and the ugly law, 15–17, 37, 79; and
"vulnerable person" standard, 80. *See
also* Americans with Disabilities Act of
1990 (ADA)
discrimination: EU provisions for,
43n73; and genetic information, 119;
governmental response to, 38. *See also*
Americans with Disabilities Act of 1990
(ADA); Civil Rights Acts
divine grace, 239n13
divine punishment, 223–24, 238–39n13
DNA mapping. *See* Human Genome
Project (HGP)
Down syndrome, women involved in
maternal screening for, 117–18
drugs in medical treatment: and end-of-life
decision making, 147, 148, 152, 161n38;
"smart" drugs, 115
drug war, costs of, 55
dueling hypothetical, 64–66, 88
Due Process Clause, 167, 171, 174
Durandus of St. Pourçain, 237n3
Dutch practice of assisted suicide, 174–75,
184n31
duty to rescue, 78, 87
Dworkin, Ronald, 23, 173
dying. *See* end-of-life decision making

economic conditions: correlated with
frequency of abortions, 209; correlated
with frequency of suicides, 218n55
economic crisis of 2008, 10, 206–7
Eisenstadt v. Baird (1972), 68n38,
240n24
elderly, costs of care for, 150, 160n35
election guides. *See* "Forming Consciences
for Faithful Citizenship"; "Political
Responsibility"
elections: as collaborative project, 198–99.
See also voting

Emory University's interdisciplinary
initiative "Vulnerability and the Human
Condition," 93n19
employment: ADA provisions for, 35–36;
and FMLA, 83
Employment Division v. Smith (1990), 105
end-of-life decision making, 9, 141–62; art
of dying [well] (*ars moriendi*), 141–43,
158n3, 160n29; and Catholic framework,
143–47, 150, 152, 159n24, 171–72;
equal treatment of dying persons,
167–70, 172; foreseen-but-unintended
side effects, 147–48, 152; and *The Gift
of Peace* (Bernardin), 9, 144–46; good
death, described, 142; and intensive
care, 182n13; and law as a moral teacher,
167–68; liberty, protection of, 167, 172,
174; ordinary vs. extraordinary means,
143, 149–51, 156, 179; overcoming
suffering, 155–56, 157; place of death,
165–66, 182n10; rules and compelling
exceptions as legal guidance for, 169–70,
184n30; social policy influencing,
165–66; suffering in terms of autonomy
and solidarity, 151–55, 161n38; by third
parties and surrogate decision makers,
143, 165, 166; treatment decisions,
149–51. *See also* assisted suicide and
euthanasia; Bernardin, Joseph Cardinal
enforcement of laws: costs of, 2, 55;
effectiveness of laws determined by, 226.
See also law as police officer
equal treatment of dying persons, 167–70,
172
eternal law, 58
eternal life, 144
*Ethical and Religious Directives for
Catholic Health Care Facilities* (National
Conference of Catholic Bishops), 149–
50, 249
ethics of genetic information, 119
The Ethics of Voting (Brennan), 215–16n39
Etymologies (Isidore of Seville), xi